D1071633

Talking to children

LANGUAGE INPUT AND ACQUISITION

Talking to children

Language input and acquisition

Papers from a conference sponsored by the
Committee on Sociolinguistics of the Social Science
Research Council (USA)

Edited by

CATHERINE E. SNOW
Institute for General Linguistics, University of Amsterdam

CHARLES A. FERGUSON
Professor of Linguistics, Stanford University

CAMBRIDGE UNIVERSITY PRESS

Cambridge
London   New York   Melbourne

Published by the Syndics of the Cambridge University Press,
The Pitt Building, Trumpington Street, Cambridge CB2 1RP
Bentley House, 200 Euston Road, London NW1 2DB
32 East 57th Street, New York, NY 10022, USA
296 Beaconsfield Parade, Middle Park, Melbourne 3206, Australia

First published 1977

Printed in Great Britain at the
University Press, Cambridge

Library of Congress Cataloguing in Publication Data
Main entry under title:
Talking to children.
Bibliography: p.

1.   Children—Language—Congresses.   2.   Mother
and child—Congresses.   3.   Sociolinguistics—
Congresses.   4.   Languages—Psychology—Congresses.
I.   Snow, Catherine E.   II.   Ferguson, Charles
Albert, 1921-   III.   Social Science Research
Council (USA).   Committee on Sociolinguistics.

P118.T3   401'.9   76—11094
ISBN 0 521 21318 5

Contents

Preface

The interests of linguists, anthropologists and psychologists converge in many areas, and it often happens that they are working at the same time on the same problem with little or no contact. When they do get together to exchange views, research methods, findings and conclusions, the experience is almost invariably of value to members of all the disciplines. Such an interdisciplinary conference, entitled Language Input and Acquisition, was held 6–8 September 1974 at the American Academy of Arts and Sciences in Boston, Massachusetts, under the sponsorship of the Committee on Sociolinguistics of the Social Science Research Council of the USA.

The conference was organized in an attempt to bring together linguists who had been studying baby talk as a sociolinguistic phenomenon, psychologists who had been studying speech to children as a factor in language acquisition, and anthropologists who had been comparing mother–child interaction across several cultures. These three groups spent two and a half days presenting and discussing their most recent research findings. The discussion was enriched by the comments of the discussants, Susan Ervin-Tripp and Allen Grimshaw, presenting the points of view of the psychologist and sociologist, respectively.

The papers collected in this book grew out of that conference, though the book is not a direct reflection of what went on at the conference. Some papers given at the conference are not included in the book, either because they were progress reports on ongoing research which is not yet completed, or because they have been published elsewhere since the conference. Some of the papers in the book were written subsequent to the conference; these include the two discussion papers and Roger Brown's introduction. In addition, the papers by James Bynon, Toni Cross, Sara Harkness, Elissa Newport and Henry and Lila Gleitman, and Marilyn Shatz and Rochel Gelman include data analyses performed since September 1974. All the papers in the book benefited from the discussions held at the conference, and many were written or revised with the help of the excellent discussion notes taken by Sandra Weintraub during the conference.

The purpose of a book like this is not only to make available an interesting body of work on a single topic. It can also serve to increase awareness among its readers of the importance of phenomena like baby talk and other simplified registers, the nature of speech to young children and differences in styles of child care. Increased awareness on the part of linguists, psychologists and anthropologists that such phenomena constitute interesting areas of research, which are also relevant to the study of language acquisition, might lead to more attention being paid to the environment in which language acquisition occurs and to the social-interactional nature of what is acquired. One hopes thus to progress from a situation in which linguists, psychologists and anthropologists read one another's papers, to one in which they ask some of the same questions and occasionally provide one another with answers.

This book is much more a progress report than a summing-up. An informal questionnaire recently circulated among the 30 participants in the Boston conference elicited information about several ongoing projects concerned with how caretakers talk to children and why they talk the way they do. For example, Jean Berko Gleason reported recently to the Georgetown Roundtable that the speech of adult males ('fathers and other strangers') to children was quite similar to that of adult females, but that fathers' speech was less precisely attuned to their children's level than mothers' speech. Gleason and Sandra Weintraub also reported at the 1975 Stanford Child Language Forum on how parents teach children specific politeness formulas. Gleason is currently starting, together with Weintraub and Esther Greif, a project called Studies in the Acquisition of Communicative Competence, in which the speech of mothers and fathers to boys and girls will be collected, as well as information concerning what parents know about their children's linguistic and cognitive abilities.

Marilyn Shatz is engaged in several projects concerned with how interaction influences the child's induction of linguistic structure. For example, mothers' non-verbal behaviors and their attempts to repair misunderstandings are being analyzed as sources of information about language; the functions of mothers' questions and availability of cues about their meaning are also being studied. Elissa Newport is studying the effects of repetition on comprehension, besides continuing, with the Gleitmans, the kinds of analyses reported in their paper on both new and already collected material.

More extensive description of baby talk is being provided by the project headed by Ben Blount, in which 34 baby talk features have been identified on the basis of material from nine families. Jacqueline Sachs has been studying the emergence of the various features in the baby talk of one child between the ages of 20 and 60 months. This study follows on from the analysis Sachs & Devin (1976) made of baby talk produced by four children aged 3 ; 9 to 5 ; 5, published in the *Journal of Child Language*.

Charles Ferguson is continuing his work on simplified registers, comparing characteristics of baby talk and 'foreigner talk' and exploring the relation between such registers and the simplification of the 'broken language' of second language learners.

Patricia Broen is studying mothers' speech to retarded (Down's syndrome) children in an attempt to determine whether that speech is as appropriate as a basis for language acquisition as speech to normal children. Catherine Snow is analyzing the speech addressed to children and adults learning a second language in a natural situation, operating from the same hypothesis that impaired language acquisition might directly reflect inappropriate input.

Finally, Mathilda Holzman and her colleague Elise Masur as well as Catherine Snow are carrying out studies of social interaction and the nature of mothers' speech during the first year of life. Holzman is especially interested in the means by which non-verbal communication is established and how clues to the meaning of the mother's utterances are provided. Snow is interested in cross-cultural differences in the nature, style and frequency of social interaction, and in the language used by the mothers to structure the interactions.

This is, obviously, only a very incomplete list of ongoing research in the field of language input and acquisition, but it does give a sense of the depth and breadth of the current activity. The conference held in Boston in 1974 may have to some extent contributed to this activity; the appearance of this book may be hoped to reinforce it.

The editors wish to express their warm appreciation to David Jenness and the Social Science Research Council for their organization of the Boston conference, to the Grant Foundation for their funding of the conference, and to all participants in the conference, who contributed greatly to the final versions of the papers by their useful discussion. The preparation of this book was carried out while

Catherine Snow was a visiting scientist at the Unit for Research on the Medical Applications of Psychology, University of Cambridge, and Charles Ferguson a visiting fellow at the Department of Phonetics and Linguistics, School of Oriental and African Studies, University of London; we are grateful to both these institutions for providing the facilities and the propinquity which made the collaborative editing possible.

Amsterdam and Stanford   C.E. Snow
February, 1976   C.A. Ferguson

Introduction

ROGER BROWN[1]

*Department of Psychology, Harvard University,
33 Kirkland Street, Cambridge, Massachusetts 02138, USA*

Let us begin by offending all those good souls who deplore the increasing dehumanization of our lives. The human infant may, I put it to you, be represented, without significant remainder, as a conjunction of values of binary features. Something on the line of Fig. 1. Of course, I do not know just what features should be entered in Fig. 1 nor even that binary features make a better representation than a set of continuous dimensions, and so Fig. 1 is not to be taken seriously. Except insofar as it makes a general point that helps to place baby talk with reference to talk of other kinds.

$$\begin{bmatrix} + \text{ inspiring affection} \\ + \text{ inspiring tenderness} \\ + \text{ inspiring intimacy} \\ - \text{ verbal production} \\ - \text{ verbal comprehension} \\ - \text{ cognitive competence} \end{bmatrix}$$

Fig. 1. The human infant represented as a conjunction of values of binary features.

THE PLACE OF BABY TALK IN THE WORLD OF LANGUAGE

None of the features in Fig. 1 is specific to the human infant. They, all of them, apply also to other classes of human beings as well as to

1

some animals, and it is only the conjunction that is unique. If the features marked with the minus values are all switched to positive values and the positive features left as they stand, we transform the infant into an approximation of the adult lover — still inspiring affection, tenderness, and intimacy, but verbally and cognitively competent. If we let the negative values of Fig. 1 stand as they are and neutralize the positive values, then the human infant is transformed into a rough representation of the adult second-language learner; someone who is not highly proficient at language production or comprehension, but who inspires no special affection, tenderness, or intimacy. The same pattern, with a first language substituted for a second, will serve as an approximate representation of an adult retardate, conceivably someone afflicted with Down's Syndrome. If we do nothing to Fig. 1 but add the feature '—human' we have a representation that would roughly fit either Animal Pet or Household Plant, and the psychological nearness of these categories to the Human Infant has some truth in it.

In some such fashion, allowing ourselves to play fast and loose with features, we can easily represent many categories of persons, animals, plants and even inanimate objects as they are conceived by an unspecifiable but clearly large and familiar population. The only value of the featural form of representation is that it makes salient major differences and similarities among these categories. The categories all have also the property of eliciting speech from some or all persons; instances of human infant, adult lover, second-language learner, retardate, animal pet and household plant all sometimes function as addressees of speech. Talk to members of one of these categories — the human infant — is the focus of this volume, and the special features of this talk are called the baby talk (BT) register.

Grimshaw (this volume)[2] expresses some understandable puzzlement at the number of descriptive studies of BT which omit the most elementary of controls (though he must except so elegantly controlled a study as Garnica's). How can we know that some feature or other of talk addressed to babies is peculiar to such talk and not to be found with every sort of addressee? Oddly enough, it would seem that we can sometimes tell, and that no control is necessary. Simplification of consonant clusters, *Ammenton* or 'nursery pitch', the use of proper names or kin terms in place of pronouns, hypocoristic affixes, rising terminals on imperatives and so on can surely be tested against the investigator's intuition and reliably judged to be peculiar to the BT register.

Still, I think that Grimshaw is basically right, but that the problem of controls is neither simple nor primarily methodological in interest. Our intuition works, I would guess, by testing the hypothetical BT characteristic against the imagined speech of a Generalized Adult Other speaking to another of the same. Such adults will not say *pwetty* for *pretty* or *faw down* for *It fell down* or *Make pee-pee* for *Spend a penny* (British English). They will not use nursery tone or speak very slowly and with exceptional clarity. We know all these things for sure and could judge as confidently another 100 or so features of BT. Nor does this picture change if control data of an appropriate sort are actually collected, as they have been by Garnica, Snow and others. This is because the most accessible adult—adult control on adult—infant speech is casual conversation between normal native-speaking adults who are acquainted but not intimately so, quite often one mother to another or a mother to the investigator. That sort of speech seems to approximate very closely to what is to be expected from a generalized adult other, and the results are much the same whether it is imagined or transcribed. This minimal control does serve to show that the characteristics of BT are not also to be found in adult speech, at least not in adult speech of a certain kind, the speech between generalized others, the common coinage of linguistically competent adults who stand in no specific relation to one another.

But surely there would be something inconsistent in the student of BT supposing that anything like a single control could be ultimately sufficient. The mother—child dyad is not the only social relation in the world, and the human infant as we have indicated is only one of many major classes of addressee. In this volume, it is Ferguson, the senior scholar in the modern study of BT, who gives the greatest attention to what he calls the 'extended functions of the register'. BT itself, he sees as one of a set of simplified registers for use with people felt to be unable to understand normal adult speech. He even names another of these: the 'foreigner register'. Voegelin & Robinett (1954), we learn, found that, in the BT of an adult informant who was a teacher, pronunciation was clarified in much the same way as when that same informant was dictating Hidatsa in his field seminar. In English and in Marathi it is attested that BT is used to animals. Alexander Woolcott used BT in addressing his dice at backgammon. In the 1840 presidential election in the United States, Harrison's political opponents mocked him by speaking BT to him. Wills notes that the use of *let's* or *we'll* in place of the singular *I* or *you* is common not only in BT but also in politician talk. Rūķe-Draviņa tells us that Latvian BT may be used between lovers and to young domestic animals. Bynon enters the only contrary report. Berber BT, it seems, has no secondary uses; it is not spoken by lovers nor addressed to animals.

It begins to be difficult to reconcile all these reports with one another and with my own observations. Clearly, we have no more than a start on the detailed data that would serve to place BT in the world of language generally, but it is worthwhile describing a possible outcome if only in hope that the problem will interest investigators in the future. Ervin-Tripp, with her sharp eye for the missing piece in a puzzle, calls for studies of the co-occurrence of the many features of BT. I take her to mean co-occurrence in the speech of many mothers speaking English to many babies. How often when you have feature 'A', say high pitch, do you also have feature 'B', exceptional clarity of pronunciation, and are 'A' and 'B' more reliably linked with one another than either is with 'C', which is the use of the diminutive as in *doggie*? If this is the kind of analysis Ervin-Tripp has in mind, it is essentially a procedure for doing a componential analysis of BT. Surely, the 100+ features that constitute English BT are not all equally likely to be found in conjunction.

Ferguson has really made a kind of impressionistic componential analysis, not of English BT alone, but of BT generally. He does not present it as such, but rather as a system for classifying the different kinds of processes found in BT. These processes are of three major types: 'simplifying' (as in replacing difficult consonants with easy ones or eliminating inflections or replacing pronouns with proper names); 'clarifying' (as in speaking slowly, clearly and with many repetitions); and 'expressive' (as in the use of hypocoristic affixes, 'cute' euphemisms and 'nursery tone'). I suggest that these three processes would collapse into two 'components' in a co-occurrence analysis and that the features in question would cluster together not primarily because of the derivational processes involved, but rather because processes belonging to the same component spring from the same sentiment and are intended to accomplish the same sort of function. Simplifying processes derive possibly from a desire to communicate, to be understood, with, perhaps, some interest also in teaching the language to the child. Clarifying processes, so far as I can judge, have the same purposes behind them, so I suggest that there is but a single component of simplification—clarification which has as its motive the desire to be understood and, possibly, to teach. The 'expressive' processes look to me like a clear second component which has as its chief motive the expression of affection with the capturing of the addressee's attention as a secondary goal.

The suggestion until this point is that BT is created by the conjunction of two principal components: communication—clarification (hereafter COMM) and expressive—affective (hereafter AFF). Can we, on this assumption, make any sense of the relation of BT to the rest of a language? There seem to be two principal kinds of phenomenon to explain. One of these is the 'extended' use of BT as a register for addressing persons or things other than babies. If the observations in question are correct, and the two-component analysis is also correct, then we should find BT maintaining its two-component formula. What have we been told? That beloved animal pets and household plants and Alexander Woolcott's dice all are or were addressed in the BT register and that lovers use BT between themselves. In all of these cases, feelings of affection are reasonably assumed. But in none of these cases is it reasonable to assume that being understood or teaching language would play any part. Animals, plants and dice can never comprehend or speak whereas lovers can do so but need no instruction. The results seem then to contradict our assumptions at some point, for our assumptions must lead us to anticipate not the extension of two-dimensional BT in these cases, but rather of only one component of BT, the AFF component.

Yes, but can we be sure of the facts? All of them, after all, are anecdotal in nature. May it not be the case that the AFF features are more noticeable? They are, after all, the 'kitchy-koo' features that are the hallmark of BT, whereas slowed speech, clarified pronunciation, deleted inflections, repetitions, etc. are less distinctive. Perhaps Bynon, working in a careful deliberate way with an exotic language, has drawn a conclusion correct for all: BT is not extended to any other social relation, not to animals and not between lovers. If we understood BT to be the two-component register described, his statement may be entirely correct even for English. It may only be the AFF component that is extended to lovers, pets, and plants.

There is another quite different possibility. It may be that the BT register is so powerfully integral that both components, which in conjunction define the register, are organized together in the brain and invariably are extended as a unit even though only one of the two components makes any sense at all. I find that these questions are too fine-grained to be answered out of my experience of English. My intuition does not supply an answer, but, of course, empirical research could find the answer.

There is a second phenomenon to consider. Ferguson described BT as only one of a set of simplified registers for use with people felt to be unable to understand normal adult speech, and he even named one of these: the 'foreigner register'. The implication, if the two-component theory of BT is adopted, is that one-component extensions of the COMM factor do exist. Just above, we have spoken of the possibility of extending the other component alone, the AFF factor. In general then, the second question, already discussed in part, is the possibility of extending either of the two components alone, and the first question, already discussed, was the possibility of extending both components together or, since in conjunction they define BT, of extending BT.

I began this Introduction with some fanciful social categories described in featural terms. The features were not verbal features, but rather features in the conception of the persons in question. Looking back at them, we see that they divide neatly into features concerned with affection (affection-inspiring, tenderness-inspiring, intimacy-inspiring) and features concerned with communicative competence (verbal production, verbal comprehension and cognitive competence). Putting together the features for the conception of persons with the two-component analysis of BT, I suggest that: persons, animals and things whose primary characteristic is cognitive and linguistic incompetence will be addressed in a one-dimensional COMM register; and that persons, animals and things whose primary characteristic is the inspiration of affection will be addressed in a one-dimensional AFF register; and that persons combining cognitive and linguistic incompetence with the inspiration of affection and intimacy will be addressed in the two-dimensional COMM—AFF register which is, in fact, BT. That is the full hypothesis.

We have already considered two categories in which the inspiration of affection and intimacy is strong without there being any question of cognitive or verbal incompetence: lovers, on the one hand, and pets and plants on the other. The question as to whether the speech register is a one-dimensional AFF or a two-dimensional BT, I have already acknowledged to be beyond the resolving powers of my intuition. Let us then consider the contrasting cases of incompetence without special affection: the adult second-language learner and the adult retardate. In these cases, interestingly enough, my intuition comes through loud and clear. They will be addressed in the one-dimensional COMM register. Perhaps Ferguson thought the same since his 'foreigner register' suggests a COMM register. It is unthinkable that one would address an adult second-language learner with such diminutive forms as *doggie* and *kitty* or with such euphemisms as *tummy* or *make pee-pee*, or with 'nursery tone' and so on. It is unthinkable because it would be insulting. Between adults and infants, all else being equal, there is a status difference, and so to use the COMM—AFF register, which is BT, would be offensive. The same does not apply to pets, plants and dice because the status difference is evident from the start and of no concern to the lesser member. Between lovers, the possibilities are more complex. There could be a difference of social status, the BT register might be reciprocal or might be asymmetrical. No wonder my intuition was silent.

There is a more complex general set of possibilities than we have considered, and it must at least be acknowledged. Consider Ferguson's 'foreigner register' as an example. Very possibly he does not conceive of this as simply the COMM component of the BT register. It is very likely that the many features of BT proper change their co-occurrence relations when they are extended to other addressees. It is also very likely that quite new features are added and that some, found in BT, are dropped. In short, the relations between BT and other registers may be vastly more complicated than I have admitted.

With BT and its components, as with every sort of register, complex possibilities of mockery, irony, humor and the like arise when the register that would normally be used in a certain kind of relation is not used. We already have heard of the mocking use of BT to a presidential candidate. It is my impression that when an adult young woman in the status of mistress to an older man adopts full BT and, seeing her lover fall into a drunken stupor, says 'Ooh, Daddy, go s'eepy bye', this combination of a false kin term, a hypocoristic suffix, an all-purpose auxiliary and a reduced consonant cluster is, at best, 'kittenish'.

To sum up, I think that the BT register can be thought of as a complex clot in the linguistic blood stream. Many more than 100 features have come together around the human infant. I do not think this is the only standardized register in English or any other language. Why is it, however, that BT has reached a level of general consciousness beyond any other register I know of. The great importance of babies is obvious. The possibility that BT constitutes a superior set of what Cross calls 'language lessons' is tantalizing. But there is also the universality of infant status. With respect to any other speaker of the language, an infant, and indeed every infant, is less competent linguistically and cognitively, and is an object of some affection. As a result, BT can be widely useful; it is the way to talk to babies. Compare the lover who is only a lover to one other and for a limited time; the foreigner who is not a foreigner to everyone. Perhaps the hospitalized adult comes closer than any other human category to the

generalized status of the infant. I should not be surprised if 'sick-
room English' proved to be a rather stable register.

WHERE DOES BABY TALK COME FROM?

In one sense of the question the answer is obvious. BT comes from
the standard adult language. By reduction, clarification, overgeneralization, repetition and so on. There are only a very few attested examples of the utilization of sounds or morphemes not in the standard
language. Latvian offers such an exception; Rūķe-Draviņa reports
that a bilabial vibrant not present in adult speech is used in a few BT
words as are several diminutive suffixes. Several of the authors in this
volume write rules deriving BT forms from adult sources. Wills, for
example, writes the most complete and elegant description of deixis
in English BT that I have ever seen. Her rules employ the roles:
Sender, Receiver and Other. The rule: Receiver → *we* (*let's*), for example, describes such familiar sentence types as: 'Let's be gentle with
the pages, all right?' Ferguson, using 'AS' for adult speech, writes for
Japanese, the rule: AS[s] → BT[tš] which summarizes the replacement in BT of the polite suffix -*san* by the familiar, and affectionate
-*chan*. Bynon, writing about 100 BT words in the language of the
Berbers of Central Morocco, derives them all from adult sources by
such processes as 'mutation', 'deletion', 'gemination' and 'reduplication'. Deletion, the most important of these, simply drops the
initial and/or final segment(s). In only two cases is the internal segment dropped. In general, then, there is ample documentation for the
fact that BT forms can be derived in a lawful way from adult sources.
   The exact status of rules such as those reported is a puzzling
matter. Ferguson points out that they are synchronic rather than
diachronic rules. They are not like the rules of historical linguistics
showing how some Latin form, for instance, was replaced by or
'became' a similar form in Spanish. In fact, the derivational rules of
BT are plausible notations for mental processes. It is not inconceivable that the Japanese adult thinks -*san*, but then, noting his child
addressee, says -*chan*, making use of a completely general rule of
replacement. Nor is it inconceivable that an English-speaking adult
first thinks, 'You be gentle with the pages, all right?' and then sub-
stitutes *let's* for *you* by a general rule that has the effect of softening
the imperative.
   However, Ferguson goes on to add something, not usually noted,
which I believe is of great importance for the conception we form of

the psychological process by which adults generate BT. Consider the rules for generating BT *tummy* from AS *stomach.* With 'C' for consonant and 'V' for vowel, 'y' for the semi-vowel, they are as follows:

AS #CCV → BT#CV   In effect: *sto* → *tv*
AS VC# → BTV#   In effect: *ach* → *a*
AS CV# → BTC-*y*#   In effect: *a* → *y*
                In effect: *stomach* → *tummy*

As an alternative to this derivation one could, of course, write an entirely specific but trivial rule directly converting AS *stomach* into BT *tummy*. Ferguson's derivation is convincing because each of the single rules has other uses well-attested for the creation of BT. The first rule is a usual process of initial consonant cluster reduction, the second is for final consonant deletion, and the last replaces final vowels by the diminutive suffix -*y*. The use of three rules in conjunction, all of which have other uses in deriving BT from AS, is convincing as an *ad hoc* derivation never can be. Furthermore, it is general rather than specific, and so more than a trivial restatement of a known fact. However, the point I find so interesting is associated with this same generality.

The rules deriving *tummy* from *stomach* are general and, in principle, allow for the creation of a great many BT words. But, as it turns out, the rules are *not used* generally. English BT does not use *toppy* in place of *stopper* or *pinny* in place of *spinach*. And this is the case for most or all of the serious rules that can be written to derive BT from AS. This seems to be an argument against the view that such rules represent the psychological processes by which adults today create BT. My guess is in agreement with Ferguson's own interpretation: the rules may well have functioned once when the word *tummy* was created, but were not generalized to all possible cases then and are not used now at all.

It seems plausible to me that many BT forms have something in common with frozen metaphors in the adult language. When the expression 'hit the nail on the head' was first used to describe a proposal perfectly designed to meet a need or a statement ideally expressing a shared thought, I am sure the aptness of the concrete reference was alive and functioned as a psychological process. It probably was alive for quite a time but is so no longer, and a special effort would be required to bring the concrete origins to a speaker's attention. It may be just so with many BT forms; they were originally, perhaps, derived by rule from AS but by now are not psychologically related at all to their adult origins.

If BT forms were, originally at least, lawfully derived from AS, it is essential to ask what guided the formulation of the derivations. If, for example, there are many rules for the simplification of initial consonant clusters, it is necessary to ask what guided the conception of simplification. For whom are the reductions simpler than the AS originals? The answer, of course, is — for babies. How do we know? Not originally from any general principles of phonology, but from the fact that babies, themselves, created the simplified clusters. In attempted imitation of AS consonant clusters, babies produced systematic reductions which were then adopted by adults and became features of BT. To put it succinctly, the baby talk of adults seems to have originated in the talk of babies to adults (TB). That fact, when you ponder on it, is distinctly paradoxical.

Because not every aspect of BT is based on TB it is necessary to list a small sample of the very many features that are, so that the dimensions of the paradox may be appreciated. A sample is easily drawn from just the papers in this volume. Both Sachs and Garnica have shown that BT and TB alike use a higher fundamental pitch than talk between adults. Wills and others have shown that both BT and TB substitute proper names for pronouns in certain contexts. Cross has shown that, among the many features characteristic of both BT and TB, are imitation, repetition, low MLU, a low upper bound on length and low semantic complexity. Snow, in a review of seven major studies, verifies all of these similarities and many others. Snow has also shown that Dutch mothers, like the mothers representing eight other languages reviewed by Brown (1973), largely limit their first multi-morphemic utterances to the expression of just eight semantic relations. Snow adds that the mothers in her sample also make frequent use of Dutch equivalents of the wh- questions, *What is that?* and *Where* NP (*go*)*?* She wonders at their absence from Brown's (1973) report on Stage I. If I may be allowed to respond here, the forms were as frequent in Stage I English as in Stage I Dutch, but I deferred their discussion for a later stage (Stage III) when they could be related to the creation of every sort of wh- question.

Perhaps we have had enough examples to motivate us to take the paradox seriously. It is as follows. Babies already talk like babies, so what is the earthly use of parents doing the same? Surely it is a parent's job to teach the adult language. A kind of parallel paradox arises in connection with the linguistic relations between teachers who speak a culturally dominant dialect and pupils who know a minority dialect. In one Boston elementary school several years ago where most of the pupils were black, and the teachers white, the well-intentioned teachers proposed to begin the study of reading by using examples from the Black English dialect. The parents of the pupils gathered to protest the policy. The force of their argument was: 'They already know how to talk like black folks; what they need to learn is how to talk the white way.' Babies, by analogy, already know how to talk like babies. And there are even some parents, very education-oriented, who intend never to use BT since babies already know it. Every such parent that I know only succeeds in avoiding the few features of BT that everyone knows about, such as the diminutive, and unwittingly uses about 100 others. Fortunately for their children, perhaps.

WHY IS BABY TALK USED?

This is not the same question as: 'What does BT accomplish?' The present question has to do with the intentions of parents, not with their effects. Ferguson reports that some parents have been asked the question of intentions and that the most usual answer from American parents as well as from Berber and Comanche was: 'To teach the child to speak.' I, too, have been given that answer, and yet I presume to question whether it is exactly right.

My doubt begins with the observation that when adults, explicitly and beforehand, enter upon a language-teaching session, what they do is singularly unimpressive. The parents I know do not get much beyond the effort to elicit vocabulary using the quiz items: 'What is that? Come on, you know what that is. It's a ——.' Very unrewarding, as a rule.

Dr David Rigler of the Los Angeles Children's Hospital has, in a telephone conversation with me, described the efforts deliberately to teach language made by a great variety of persons: nurses, aides, patients, doctors, visitors, etc. All were directing their efforts at the same very special and sad person, Genie, a girl nearly 14 years old, who, because of a combination of terrible experiences, was prevented from hearing or using any speech and was mute when rescued and brought to the hospital. For several months, Genie received no 'official' language tuition, but everyone who encountered the young woman made an effort to teach her to speak. Without any suggestion from me, Dr Rigler said that their teaching efforts largely consisted of one or the other of two questions. Holding up two fingers, the would-be teacher asked: 'How many?' Or else the tutor pointed at some article of Genie's clothing and asked: 'What color?' Probably,

Dr Rigler has somewhat sharpened this amusing account, but, allowing for that, it does suggest the quite limited notions activated in the
amateur by an explicit intention to teach language. It should be compared with the richness of BT which even children, three to four
years old, know how to produce when addressing two-year-olds.

If BT is an effort to provide language lessons, it is certainly employed with some very unpromising pupils. By some reports, these
include pet animals and household plants. But then, as we have
noted, it may not really be BT but rather the AFF component that
is used in these cases.

What I think adults are chiefly trying to do, when they use BT
with children, is to communicate, to understand and to be understood, to keep two minds focussed on the same topic. In coming to
this view, I have been vastly influenced by the data Cross has presented in this volume. In an ingenious effort to determine whether or
not the speech of mothers is fine-tuned to the cognitive and linguistic
abilities of their young children, Cross has studied the speech of
mother and child (19–32 months in age) in 16 mother–child dyads.
She has measured just about everything you can measure in both.
Some variables appear, as we have already noted, in both BT and TB.
These include imitations, repetitions, high pitch and so on. She also
included features one finds only in adults, such as 'expansions'. The
point of central interest here is a special interpolation into the
mother's speech: a receptive ability test. This test consisted of 100
syntactically diverse sentences that the mother was asked to inter-
polate in small doses at natural junctures. Each sentence was such as
to call for some kind of overt evidence, verbal or not, of comprehension. And so for each child there is a 'receptiveness score' which
could, just as appropriately, be called a 'comprehension' score.

The receptiveness score can be, and was, correlated with every
assessed aspect of the mother's speech. These correlations could be,
and were, compared with the correlations between every other aspect
of the child's performance and every aspect of the mother's. The
result, of course, is only a correlational matrix and can be used to
support a variety of notions of cause and effect. However, Cross
favors one particular interpretation, and I agree with her. One can
see the matrix as evidence for the degree to which the mother's
speech is tuned to (or guided by) each of the aspects of the child's
performance.

The result that impresses me so strongly is that the receptiveness
score is, on the whole, more highly correlated with what the mother
does than is any other aspect of the child's performance. And many

of these correlations are really high. With expansions used by the mother, for instance, receptiveness correlates − 0.85. By Cross's and my interpretation, this means that the less comprehension the child showed, the more his mother used expansions. Expansions are, in my experience, intended as communication checks. In effect, the mother asks with her expansion: 'Is this what you mean by what you just said?' Expansions, of course, decrease with development. Another maternal possibility, reference to non-immediate events, definitely increases with development. The correlation of this variable with the receptiveness score is + 0.72.

Cross's matrix also includes an index of the 'comprehensibility' (or intelligibility) of the child's speech which is obtained by checking the number of child utterances that the mother and other adults cannot understand. It is the performance side of communication on the child's part and the passive side on the mother's. Unlike comprehension, there is a sizeable non-intellectual performance factor, and so I have always thought it a less pure index of communicative success. In Cross's data it generally correlates less highly with aspects of the mother's speech than does receptiveness (e.g. − 0.61 with expansions) but seems to be better than almost anything else.

Very many of Cross's correlations are high, and I think she is right to conclude that mothers' speech is fine-tuned to the child's psycholinguistic development. I also think she is right to conclude that communication is the most important single determinant of tuning, more important than grosser, less psychological, variables such as mean length of utterance (MLU) or age. It is true that Harkness found evidence that BT in the Kipsigis village of Kokwet, Kenya, was tuned to the child's MLU, but then so did Cross; the difference is that Cross had a 'receptiveness' score while Harkness did not. I do realize that Cross's data do not prove these things and that I am responding quite selectively and with partiality because her major results, as she chooses to interpret them, accord well with my own experience.

What else is there to suggest that the wish to communicate with someone of low communicative ability is the force behind BT? Several investigators (e.g. Lord, 1975) who have studied maternal speech to a child both before and after the child produced what the mother took to be a first word, have found that the speech is more complex and less like BT before the first word than it is afterwards. Bingham (1971) has somewhat refined this interesting result by showing that prelingual children (infants, literally) are addressed in a simplified register by mothers who judge that infants have the capacity to understand quite a bit, but not by mothers who set a lower estimate on the infant's capacity. Blount brings to our attention what may be a cultural difference. In Luo, it seems, when the child's first word is heard, the number and frequency of BT features decline, and it functions thereafter chiefly as an affectionate register in which adults console or placate the child. It may be that only the AFF component of BT acts in this way, for Blount, in general, agrees with us that the child's caretakers are chiefly concerned with his ability to communicate.

All of these results are interesting because, on the whole, they strongly suggest that BT is elicited by indications of some psycholinguistic ability rather than by something like age, but the results do not clearly distinguish between the intention to teach and the intention to communicate since comprehension ability and teachability are not really distinguished.

Garnica interviewed her subjects after she had collected data on their speech to their children and asked if they had realized that they changed their speech depending on whether the addressee was an adult or a two-year-old child. In her experimental circumstances, with one addressee (the investigator) followed directly by another (the child), most mothers were aware of certain differences (Garnica concentrated on six prosodic features). Asked why they changed register for the child, the most common response was that it helped them to communicate. One mother said:

> There are plenty of times I don't stop to think that he's two, and I'll just mumble something at him and don't really think about whether or not he can understand it. And that's when he's most likely not to respond at all.

I do not think that these reports on the intention that motivates BT conflict at all with Ferguson's report that parents asked in the abstract why they use BT are likely to say, 'To teach language.' The difference probably is in a report made immediately following register shifts, when an informant probably has good access to recent intentions, and a report on something not recently done but asked about in the abstract. In these circumstances, I should think an informant might credit himself or herself with a too pedagogical motive.

If we assume that the operative intention in BT is to communicate rather than to teach, how does that help to resolve the paradox (remember the paradox?) that BT is largely derived from TB. It does so most obviously in the fact that, if parents were really primarily

concerned with teaching the language, they ought to limit themselves
to forms more advanced than baby's own. If they are really exclusively concerned with communication, with keeping two minds on
target, they ought to restrict themselves to what baby knows, to BT
and nothing else. I do think parents are exclusively concerned with
communication. I do think they continuously monitor the child for
signs of distraction or incomprehension and when they see them,
promptly act (especially with the six prosodic features Garnica has
isolated) to correct the situation. But if this is strictly so, we have
only exchanged one paradox for another; because the fact is that
little children learn more than BT. Very soon, BT is for them, as for
adults, simply one register, among many available to them. How can
that happen if adults, wishing only to communicate, never go beyond
BT?

I do not intend to drag out this paradox as I have its predecessor.
It is effectively answered by a fragment of dialogue from Gleason's
paper.

> Mother: (Nods.) Book. Book.
> Child: (Grabs book.)
> Mother: See the book.

'See the book' is not BT and, in the example, the mother drops the
BT 'book' directly she sees any sign of comprehension in her child.
And that is always the case. Parents seek to communicate, I am sure,
but they are not content to communicate always the same limited
set of messages. A study of detailed mother–child interaction shows
that successful communication on one level is always the launching
platform for attempts at communication on a more adult level.

The statement that parents bent always and only on communication will move from BT in the direction of AS and guarantee the
child a richer model than BT is easily buttressed with other factors
having the same effect. Going back to Ferguson's discussion of the
reality as psychological processes of rules deriving BT from AS, we
recall that those rules, if they were once active, were not applied to
all possible cases. So even standard BT is not a simple rule-governed
register; it is replete with inconsistencies and irregularities which
guarantee continuous change. More importantly, the parent is like
the hypothetical one-time creator of BT forms in that he or she is not
consistent, not uniform. For all the reliability and statistical significance of the differences between BT and AS, no one has gone so far
as to propose that any mother always uses attested BT forms to her
children, and never any others. Rightly so, since such mothers do not

exist. They always lapse in and out of the register, even though the addressee remains the same two-year-old child. This mainly, I think, in pursuit of communication on ever higher levels, but also from simple fatigue or forgetfulness, as in the case of the mother quoted by Garnica.

Finally, of course, not all of BT is ultimately imitative of TB. What Ferguson calls the clarification processes and the affection expressing processes are not based on what the child left to himself would do. The clarification processes, for instance, are specifically designed to improve his performance. I think the best authenticated processes not invented by the child are the six prosodic features Garnica has isolated. The parent speaking to a two-year-old child (as opposed to either another adult or, usually, a five-year-old child)uses:

(1) a significantly higher fundamental frequency (about 267 Hz);
(2) a greater range of pitch;
(3) a rising terminal intonation, not just on questions but on imperatives;
(4) occasional whispering;
(5) longer duration in speaking such separable verbs as *push in*;
(6) two primary syllabic stresses on words calling for one.

All of these are clearly demonstrated features of BT, and it is doubtful that any of them were invented by babies. These six prosodic features give one the immediate impression that they *could* be profoundly valuable in laying bare structural features of the language, and we shall want to refer to them again in that connection. However, Garnica's interview data suggest that mothers use them, not with that tutorial goal in mind, but to control attention, improve intelligibility, mark utterances as directed at the child. Generally, in short, to guarantee communication.

I will close this section on 'Why is Baby Talk Used?' by calling attention to some very new ideas and data, too new to have been included in this volume but too important, in my view, not to be referred to. The work in question is largely that of Eleanor Rosch, Jeremy Anglin and Michael Posner. For various reasons I have been studying this work this year, and it seems to me that when all the pieces are put together (the psychologists involved have not worked in collaboration) we have nothing less than a new paradigm or model of linguistic reference and of concept formation. It is a model that is much more nearly right as well as more profound and more interesting than the model that has long dominated experimental psychology. The old model was really standard set theory and is more like a logical canon or ideal than it is like the human mental processes it purports to model. The new paradigm is often called 'fuzzy-set theory'. There is certainly no space here to describe in full either the model or the research results related to it, and for that I can only refer you to Anglin (1976), Rosch (1973), Rosch *et al.* (1976), Posner & Keele (1968), Brown (1976, and in preparation).

Several papers in the present volume (e.g. Ferguson's, Bynon's and especially Rūķe-Draviņa's) have included the use of a restricted lexicon among the features of the BT register, and that is the context in which the new work should be placed for it concerns, in part, the naming practices of adults. In the paper, 'How shall a thing be called?' (1958), Brown pointed out that every distinct referent has multiple equally correct names falling at different taxonomic levels. A *dime* is also *money* or a *coin*; a *cat* is also an *animal*; an *ant* is an *insect*; a *collie* is a *dog* and an *animal*, and so on. Brown argued in this early paper that for each referent it seemed that there was *one* name, of all the possible names, that seemed the *best* or 'truest' name.

This 'truest' name, the 'real' name, did not regularly fall at any one taxonomic level. So far as Brown could see, without benefit of data, the 'real' name of an object fell at the taxonomic level of its most 'usual utility'. That is, a referent dime is best named *dime* because, at that level, one instance of the category is equivalent for almost all purposes with every other instance of the category. To call a referent dime *money* would be to suggest its equivalence with everything properly called *money*, including nickels, quarters and dollars, and that is not the way our currency works. Rosch (Rosch *et al.*, 1976) has greatly deepened and enriched this idea, and she refers to the best name as the name at the 'basic object level'. The basic object level it has now been shown is the level of greatest physical distinctiveness as well as the level where the greatest variety of uses of the referent exists as well as the level of optimal imageability.

Anglin (1976) has collected extensive data on the practices of mothers naming pictures in a book for their own two-year-old children. For each picture, the language offers multiple appropriate names at different levels. However, mothers agreed almost perfectly on the particular names they chose for each picture, and these names were, furthermore, not consistently at any one taxonomic level. Thus, they said *dog*, not *collie*; but *ant*, not *insect*. They said *flower*, not *carnation*; but *pineapple*, not *fruit*. For the most part, they named at the basic object level, as independently determined for many of the words by Rosch *et al.* (1976).

Anglin (1976) also asked his mothers to name the same pictures for an adult and, for quite a few pictures, there was a difference. What was *money* for a child was *dime* for an adult; *carnation* for an adult, but *flower* for a child; *pigeon* for an adult, but *bird* for a child. In short, Anglin found considerable evidence for a BT register in linguistic reference, one name being given to a child and another to an adult. The most probable explanation is that divergences occurred just where there were divergences in what constituted the basic object level for an adult and what constituted that level for a child. For a child, all money is equivalent in that it is dirty and inedible, but not to be thrown away; an adult requires more differentiation in this domain. For a child all flowers are alike in that they may be sniffed, but are not to be picked. Once again, an adult needs more differentiation.

If parents generally name everything for a child at its basic object level, and especially at its basic object level for him, then the child's early lexicon should be made up almost entirely of such terms. Using familiar objects in nine different taxonomies, Rosch had identified, from behavioral evidence, terms at the basic object level as well as terms above that level (more abstract) and terms below that level (more concrete). Her group borrowed copies of all the protocols belonging to Stage I (Brown, 1973) for the child we have called Sarah. There are 31 half-hour protocols in that set. Rosch's group checked through all 31 lexicons for all terms falling at any level in their nine taxonomies. The results are clear: 67 different nouns at the basic object level and seven at any other level.

The last result I will describe is the most important. It was done by Rosch & Mervis (1976) and is a sorting task for children at various ages, but a sorting task unlike any other ever done. Because the youngest children were to be only three-year-olds, the sorting task was in the maximally simple form called the 'oddity problem'. Three toy objects are presented; in an average study they might be an apple, an orange, and a fish. The problem? To put together the two things that belong together and separate out the odd item. In the present example, of course, an apple and an orange are fruits, and a fish is not. Rosch & Mervis observe that, in this very representative task, the basis for sorting together is not at the basic object level but at a more superordinate level — fruit. And so it seems always to have been in sorting tasks with children, and in such tasks very young children typically sort in ways that are different from the adult way.

What other kind of oddity problem could one devise? Suppose we have apple No. 1 and apple No. 2 (both clearly apples, but quite unlike as two apples can be) and an orange. Now put together the ones that belong together. Absurd, too obvious to be worth doing. But notice that the two objects belong together on the basic object level; each would be named *apple* for a child, not *fruit*. Rosch & Mervis composed some problems of the usual type such that the basis for sorting is superordinate to the object level, and they obtained the usual type of result, odd sortings in the younger children with adult-type sortings increasing with age. Rosch & Mervis also composed some oddity triads of the kind they invented such that one would respond correctly by appealing only to the basic object level. Of course, such problems are very easy, and responses were 100 % correct for all children over three years old, and even the three-year-olds were correct 96 % of the time. So what have we learned?

Add one additional item of information. On six problems the children were asked to give the basis for their sorting, and the usual answer was the shared name: *apples* for the object level problem and *fruit* for the superordinate level problem. The results were strong and clear. As you would expect, the object level names were more often given than the superordinate names. However, in all cases, the ability to sort correctly was vastly superior to the ability to name correctly. But that means the children cannot have needed the names to support their sorting. They were putting together two animals, for instance, almost all the time, when they almost never supplied the word *animal*.

For me, this is a profoundly consequential result. I have long thought of the names that parents give children as major forces in category formation, the names teaching the child what things are to be treated as members of the same class. Instead, it now appears that children form their categories or classes at the basic object level on the basis of appearances and uses and not, primarily, upon the basis of names. The concept is then there beforehand, waiting for the word to come along that names it. There is semantic priority. Many people have though this might be the case (e.g. Macnamara, 1972), but I know of no prior evidence that so clearly establishes it.

The result interacts interestingly with our hypothesis that what parents are chiefly concerned to do with BT is to communicate. And how should they do so if not by talking about things the child is prepared to understand? If you do not speak to a very young child about what he knows and what interests him, he will, as Gleason points out, tune you out. The lead, it now appears, is not in the parents' hands as far as early content is concerned. It appears to lie in an interaction between the nature of young children and the nature of the physical world. Only now, perhaps, can we properly understand the amazing uniformities in what is named and what kinds of relations are talked about in Stage I speech. These uniformities, which are universal as far as they have been tested, appear to arise not from the predilections of parents, but from the nature of human children and the world they live in.

WHAT DOES BABY TALK ACCOMPLISH?

We all know the teacher who holds out a promise that the disjointed remarks of a semester will be integrated at the end of the course and then runs out of time. I carried over that practice to the present task, leaving for last the most difficult question which motivates all the others. I had rather hoped for a printers' strike.

By very good luck, Snow has shown herself more courageous and discussed this question with a greater mastery than I could bring to it. And so I have very little to add.

A number of authors in this volume have driven home the principal point. The by-now overwhelming evidence of BT (in Arabic, Berber, Cocopa, Comanche, English, French, Gilyak, Greek, Hidatsa, Japanese, Kannada, Kipsigis, Latvian, Luo, Maltese, Marathi, Romanian, Spanish) refutes overwhelmingly the rather off-hand assertions of Chomsky and his followers that the preschool child could not learn language from the complex but syntactically degenerate sample his parents provide without the aid of an elaborate innate component. But it has turned out that parental speech is well formed and finely tuned to the child's psycholinguistic capacity. The corollary would seem to be that there is less need for an elaborate innate component than there at first seemed to be.

The ubiquity of BT is great, but we still do not have the data empiricists require to call any particular set of features universal, and Ferguson, and everyone else, has been careful to say so. Nevertheless, the range of some features is universal as far as empiricism has gone. I think it might not be too soon to raise the question whether any child is known to have learned a first language without benefit of any of the characteristics of BT. The question occurred to me partly because I could think of a child of whom it might or might not be true: Genie, the terribly abused little girl who was almost entirely deprived of *any* speech until she was almost 14 years old. While Genie was mute when she was rescued and taken to the Los Angeles

Children's Hospital, she now speaks something that is very like a late Stage I English (Brown, 1973), together with some features beyond Stage I, but Genie's speech, generally, is a very long way from normal competence.

Genie, it appears, has, however, learned parts of English without benefit of BT or, indeed, any talk in her pre-adolescent years, the years Lenneberg (1967) considered to be the critical period for language acquisition. The question that interested me, which I could not find answered in print anywhere, was whether, when Genie was given speech instruction, any of the many standard features of BT was used. It seemed conceivable that they might not have been since Genie was nearly 14 years old. On the other hand, if the intention behind the multitudinous characteristics of BT is essentially to facilitate *communication* with someone not ordinarily competent verbally, then BT characteristics should have been automatically elicited from anyone who spoke to her and hoped to be understood.

Dr David Rigler and Dr Victoria Fromkin were both associated with the efforts to help Genie, and I deeply appreciate their willingness to answer, on the telephone, from memory, their impressions as to whether BT was used. In such circumstances, we obviously cannot hope for a detailed or final answer though such an answer can eventually be made from the records that exist.

Genie's father is reported to have had an intolerance for noise, and had believed Genie to be mentally retarded, with the result that she had been punished whenever she vocalized at all. Genie's mother was nearly blind and spoke only very softly, perhaps inaudibly, to the child. The mother came to believe that her husband would never help the child, and she eventually fled with Genie to the grandparents, and shortly after that Genie was admitted to the Los Angeles Children's Hospital.

Dr Rigler saw Genie in the early months, and I have already reported his observation concerning the language-teaching efforts of everyone who contacted Genie in this first period. It was, furthermore, his impression that they all simplified and slowed their speech. Dr Fromkin saw Genie after some months. I could not, of course, ask her about all the 100+ features of standard BT, but Dr Fromkin volunteered the observation that Genie seemed to ignore talk not addressed to her, talk between adults. Dr Fromkin thought it quite possible that the speech directed to Genie was even slower, more repetitious, more simplified and clarified than ordinary BT. Pending a more detailed study, it appears that Genie is not the exception we sought — a child learning a first language without benefit of BT. For the fact that her speech is still very far from normal, there are, of course, many possible explanations.

The discovery that speech to very young children is not a complex degenerate sample, but a sample fine-tuned to the child's psycholinguistic capacity, is certainly an advance over past views in the sense that it is true as they were not, but whether it is an advance in the sense of making the total acquisition problem simpler is not clear. Look at it this way. The older view posed the problem as: AS → CS (adult speech to child speech); the new view poses it as: AS → BT → CS (adult speech to baby talk to child speech). It may be easier to develop a theory deriving CS from BT than deriving it from AS, but notice that the new view includes a new problem: AS → BT.

In one sense we have already discussed, if not solved, the AS → BT problem, and that is the original derivational business of getting rules that mediate between the two. But we passed over another problem, a psychological process problem. How does the adult or, for that matter, the four-year-old child select features appropriate to use with a two-year-old? The paper by Shatz & Gelman offers the only data directly relevant to this problem and they worked, in fact, with four-year-olds talking to two-year-olds. Their findings do not encourage us to hope that the problem of the selection of the BT register will be an easy one. They worked with wh- complement constructions (e.g. *I know what time it is*) and with what they call 'that' predicate complements (e.g. *I think [that] this is mine*).

The problem, setting aside many other matters of interest, is that each syntactic form is coordinated, in the speech of these children, with distinct semantic intentions. This means that is it not clear how to answer the very first question one might ask about this process of moving into a BT register? Is the movement guided by semantics or by syntax?

Clearly, a vast amount of research remains to be done. Blount reminds us that the child does not learn only the structure of his native language, but also learns what Hymes (1962) calls the 'ethnography of speaking'. This is, I believe, equivalent to what Van der Geest calls the pragmatic function; in effect, learning how to communicate, to say felicitously what you mean to say. There is only one point on which I believe that I disagree with Blount and Van der Geest. They seem to me to believe that problems of syntactic structure and semantics are solved by children before pragmatic problems. By my observation that is sometimes true, but often not. For example, I have seen many children who know that the question, 'What color is that?' requires in response some one of eight or nine color terms (*blue*, *green*, *red*, etc.), and they always answer as the discourse role requires. But at referential random. Not being able to identify colors as yet, they just spin their color wheels and come up with a term of the right class. More mysteriously, I have known several children (including Adam) whose very courteous mothers almost always used elaborately indirect forms to guide their actions rather than simple imperatives. In Adam's case, it always was: 'Why don't you . . .' something or other. This was not, as Holzman (1972) has pointed out, intended as a question though it was so, syntactically. What has always amazed me about these pseudo questions is that Adam, long after he was answering genuine *Why* questions with 'Because', and some explanation or other, did not once apply this syntactic and semantic analysis to fake *Why* questions, but invariably treated them as orders — which is what they, pragmatically speaking, were.

There are, in the present collection, a few new attempts directly to answer some aspects of the question: 'What does baby talk accomplish?' Harkness, working in the village of Kokwet in Kenya with 20 very young children, has come up with a new strategy. Since her subjects interacted both with adults and with older children, but in individually varying degree, and since these two classes of potential tutor involved different speech styles as well as interaction styles, one might conceivably see how the effects of near peers compared with the effects of adult relatives. There are numerous points of incidental interest such as the fact that peer interaction was less verbal than interaction with parents. Causal relationships, however, proved as ultimately elusive as ever. Subjects who interacted more with adults did more talking and, in addition, had higher MLUs (corrected for age). This might mean that adult interaction results in more rapid psycholinguistic development (as indexed by MLU) than does peer interaction. But, alas, it could also mean that, with no difference of linguistic competence, subjects formed longer utterances for adults, responding at the upper end of their competence range, whereas with peer addressees they attempted less. MLU, it must be remembered, is not psycholinguistic competence but only an imperfect index, of no interest in its own right.

Van der Geest has probably written the most condensed and difficult paper in the book. He makes a direct assault on the language acquisition problem and says many things that I find reasonable and provocative but I remain uncertain how well-grounded in evidence he judges some of his conclusions to be. To begin with, Van der Geest relates his data to the paper by Brown & Hanlon (1970) on tag questions in which it was concluded that cumulative derivational complexity was the major determinant of acquisition order. One problem with cumulative derivational complexity (as noted also in Brown, 1973) is that it requires, in the first place, an explicit generative grammar for the constructions to be compared. Furthermore, even when such derivations exist, only a small number of closely related constructions can be compared. One can only deal, even in English, that most studied of languages, with small sets of partial orderings.

I gather from Van der Geest's conclusion, which is that semantics has priority over syntax in acquisition, that he sees his results as somehow contradictory to those of Brown & Hanlon (1970). But I cannot see how this can be the case. He deals with 43 linguistic variables and, while I am totally ignorant of the degree to which Dutch has been described in terms of a generative grammar, I am completely certain that there are not 43 constructions that can be ordered in terms of cumulative derivational complexity. Indeed, Van der Geest says as much in admitting that it is difficult to order by complexity many constructions, such as the prepositional object and the indirect object, etc. I, myself, doubt that hardly any of the 43 constructions in question can be ordered in the Brown & Hanlon manner. So let us forget about relevance to Brown & Hanlon and look at the study in independent terms.

The study involves eight Dutch mother—child dyads and 43 grammatical and semantic forms, such as subject, object, tense, modal, desiderative and so on. Sessions of interaction over time are coded and the session is noted in which each semantic feature and each syntactic feature reaches its peak frequency in mother and child. Of great interest is the statement that semantic features commonly reach their peaks first in children and later in mothers, whereas 'realization rules' meaning, I assume, syntactic forms, reach their peaks in mothers in earlier sessions than they do in children. This suggests to the author the interesting idea that a child sets the tolerable semantic—cognitive level of a session and that the mother later provides appropriate realization rules as the opportunity arises. Van der Geest also finds that the child responds to the mother's sentences when they are close to his own level of spontaneous speech, but not too simple.

Everything that I have reported above about mother—child interaction sounds plausible and important. But, for lack of a few definitions or because of inadequacies in my reading, I cannot decide whether Van der Geest has proved his case. For instance, I can find no place in which he explains how he determines the child's semantic—cognitive level, in the absence of adequate realization rules, but he must be able to do so to draw his conclusions. For complexity, itself, I can find a definition, but it does not ease my mind. The author writes: 'Structures which are well established are semantically and/or syntactically less complex for the child than those which are not.' If 'well established' means what it suggests, then it becomes a tautology to find that less complex structures (semantically or syntactically) precede more complex structures.

I regret this lack of comprehension very much as the paper is on the level of *interaction*, which is, I agree with Snow, the right level. I have never thought that the metaphors of the child swimming in a sea of BT made a very good condition for the study of acquisition.

Finally, there is one sentence in this book which, more than any other, must be taken to heart by all of us. Snow writes: 'The role of BT in language acquisition cannot be determined until we have the *correct* description of language.' True and terrible. For linguists do not, today, even have a consensus on the general form of a correct description. No language has been fully described in *any* form. No serious model of the psychological process of speaking exists. Are we, perhaps, a century premature? We do not like to think so.

We have no choice but to enter into the enterprise of linguistics, and linguists, if they think about it, have no choice but to pay attention to work in developmental psycholinguistics. The study of language is one, distributed between academic departments to accommodate the limitations of human intelligence but, ultimately, one subject. The sciences do not build like pyramids with the higher layers waiting for completion of the lower. They build like partial views of the Leviathan growing towards one another and a complete view.

Happily, the study of BT and of language acquisition need not wait upon the *completion* of the correct conception of language. One can, long before that, become convinced of the correctness of some aspect of the study of language: constituent segmentation; inflection; reference; the relation of wh- questions and wh- predicate complements to declaratives. I am convinced that all these are essentially correctly understood today; these and much besides, though form and notation may change. Garnica seems to me to set us all a good model in that she appears to be convinced of the reality of segmentation above the phonemic level and can see how the prosodic features of BT might facilitate the acquisition of segmentation. She has only to complete the study and show that children do acquire knowledge of segmentation with greater ease if the prosodic features of BT are used as they usually are. Nothing unethical is involved since not all children in ordinary life have equal opportunity to benefit from prosodic BT.

There is also something beyond a correct conception, I think. One wants to work on a non-obvious, non-trivial, feature of language. It is no trick to do obvious studies of acquisition. Vocabulary can be increased by direct tutelage, variety of picture books, or more trips outside the home. But who does not know that? We want to increase our knowledge, not confirm what is already banal. That is why we, in our field, must study linguistics and not content ourselves with a layman's view of language.

This review of the volume leaves me optimistic. All the papers together suggest a process of articulation so fine-grained and so nearly universal that it cannot be unimportant. Life for about two years after birth seems to me now only moderately less determinate than life before birth. BT and child response to it seem as close to embryology as to social interaction.

Though the articulation process is almost foolproof, it leaves me with an answer to a parental question for which I have never had an answer. The question, of course, is: 'How can a concerned mother facilitate her child's learning of language?' My answer, after studying this book, is as follows: 'Believe that your child can understand more than he or she can say, and seek, above all, to communicate. To understand and be understood. To keep your minds fixed on the same target. In doing that, you will, without thinking about it, make 100 or maybe 1000 alterations in your speech and action. Do not try to practice them as such. There is no set of rules of how to talk to a child that can even approach what you unconsciously know. If you concentrate on communicating, everything else will follow.'

This is a volume of very fine research papers. I have not presumed to retell the stories they, themselves, tell so well. My goal has been to extract the dialogue on major issues that is latent in the papers and is always difficult to bring forward on the occasion when the papers are first read.

NOTES

1.   Roger Brown's research is supported by a grant from the National Science Foundation, No. GSOC-7309150. A graduate student at Harvard University, Miss Bella DePaulo, who has a long-standing interest in the subject treated in this

volume, very kindly read all of the papers, and the author benefited from discussions with her about the issues involved.

2.   When referring, in this Introduction, to contributions appearing in this volume, I shall hereafter only name the scholar whose contribution it is, omitting the phrase 'this volume'. Contributions not appearing in this volume will be cited in the usual fashion, by author and reference.

Section I

Maternal speech styles

1 Mothers' speech research: from input to interaction

CATHERINE E. SNOW

Institute for General Linguistics, University of Amsterdam, Spuistraat 210, Amsterdam, The Netherlands

ISSUES IN MOTHERS' SPEECH RESEARCH

The first descriptions of mothers' speech to young children were undertaken in the late sixties in order to refute the prevailing view that language acquisition was largely innate and occurred almost independently of the language environment. The results of those mothers' speech studies may have contributed to the widespread abandonment of this hypothesis about language acquisition, but a general shift of emphasis from syntactic to semantic—cognitive aspects of language acquisition would probably have caused it to lose its central place as a tenet of research in any case. It is thus important to point out that even the very first mothers' speech studies, those most concerned with refuting the innatist view of the language input, were relevant to several other important issues, and contributed to the general acceptance of significant new ideas about language acquisition. I think it is valuable to identify these issues, and to touch upon the research findings relevant to them, precisely because they will shape the future of research in the field of language input. Very briefly, since I will return to them again and again in the course of this paper, I would like to mention three basic assumptions about language acquisition whose acceptance has been furthered by the results of mothers' speech research:

(1) Language acquisition is the result of a process of interaction between mother and child which begins early in infancy, to which the child makes as important a contribution as the mother, and

31

which is crucial to cognitive and emotional development as well as to language acquisition.

(2) Language acquisition is guided by and is the result of cognitive development.

(3) Producing simplified speech registers is one of the many communicative skills whose acquisition is as interesting as the acquisition of syntax or phonology.

The first task undertaken by mothers' speech researchers was simply to describe the characteristics of mothers' speech when they were talking to children learning language. This task was interpreted as one of describing the input in a way very similar to the way children's speech studies of the same period were describing output. The underlying theoretical notion was quite similar to the Language Acquisition Device paradigm — that the only interface between input and output occurred in the child's head. The early mothers' speech studies (and too many of the more recent ones as well) paid little or no attention to what the child was saying or doing. The notion that mothers' speech, like children's speech, occurs in conversations (see Lieven, 1976; Gleason, this volume; Newport, 1976), and that the need to communicate with one's conversational partner affects the structure of one's utterances, had not yet affected the way research into mothers' speech was carried out.

Description of the characteristics of the speech was primarily accomplished by seven papers which looked at mothers' speech in a general way, and by an additional five which concentrated on the description of particular features. These studies have been reviewed in detail by Farwell (1973) and Vorster (1975). The seven — Broen (1972),Drach (1969), Phillips (1970; 1973), Remick (1976), Sachs, Brown & Salerno (1976) and Snow (1972) — among them looked at 34 dependent variables, which can be roughly divided into measures of prosody, of grammatical complexity and of redundancy. In Table 1.1 I have listed these variables, noting which studies made use of which variables. Mean Length of Utterance (MLU) and a few others are notable for their ubiquity, but in general very few measures have really been intensively studied. It is thus encouraging to note that the five specialized descriptions concentrated on some of the points that are only lightly touched upon in the general descriptions, these being interrogatives (Holzman, 1972), pragmatic features and ellipsis (Holzman, 1974), repetition (Kobashigawa, 1969), discourse features and teaching devices (Moerk, 1972) and syntactic complexity (Pfuderer, 1969), respectively. Two of the

Table 1.1   *Dependent variables in mothers' speech studies. X indicates the variable has been tested experimentally. Y indicates the variable has been employed only descriptively*

	Broen, 1972	Drach, 1969	Phillips, 1970	1973	Remick, 1976	Sachs, et al., 1976	Snow, 1972
PROSODIC FEATURES							
Rate of speech	X	X	—	—	—	X	—
Ease of segmentation	X	Y	—	—	Y	—	—
Disfluencies	X	Y	—	—	—	—	—
Pitch	—	Y	—	—	X	Y	—
Pitch range	—	Y	—	—	X	—	—
COMPLEXITY FEATURES							
Amount of speech	—	—	—	—	X	—	X
MLU	—	X	X	X	—	—	X
Variance of MLU	—	X	—	—	—	—	—
Subject of utterance	—	—	—	—	X	—	—
Verb forms	—	—	X	X	—	—	—
Verb tense	—	—	—	—	X	X	—
Complex sentences	—	X	X	X	—	X	X
Modifiers	—	—	X	—	—	—	—
Preverb length	—	—	—	—	—	—	X
Utterance fragments	Y	—	—	—	—	—	X
Conjunction	—	X	—	—	—	—	—
Deletions	—	X	—	—	—	—	—
Adverbials	—	X	—	—	—	—	—
Imperatives	Y	X	—	—	—	—	X
Questions	Y	X	—	—	X	X	X
Declaratives	Y	X	—	—	—	X	—
Negatives	—	X	—	—	—	—	—
One-word utterances	Y	—	—	—	—	—	—
Adjectives	—	X	—	—	—	—	X
Possessives	—	X	—	—	—	—	—
Function words	—	—	X	X	—	—	—
Content words	—	—	X	X	—	—	—
Old English verbs	—	—	X	—	—	—	—
Weak verbs	—	—	X	—	—	—	—
REDUNDANCY							
Type—token ratio	X	X	X	X	X	—	—
Concreteness/nouns	—	—	X	X	—	—	—
Phrase repetition	—	—	—	—	—	—	X
Sentence repetition	—	—	—	—	—	—	X
Paraphrases	—	—	—	—	—	—	X

Table 1.2 Independent variables in mothers' speech studies

	Listener variables			Speaker variables		Other	Situation variables	
	Age	Sex	Linguistic ability	Age	Social class		Activity	Listener reaction
Anderson & Johnson, 1973	1½ years 3 years 5 years Peer Adult	—	—	8 years	—	—	Story-telling Block-stringing Free play	—
Bakker-Renes & Hoefnagel-Höhle, 1974	—	—	—	—	—	—	Eating Bathing Dressing Chatting Free play Reading	—
Gleason, 1973	Baby Peer Adult	—	—	4–5 years 7–8 years Adult	—	—	—	—
Bingham, 1971	—	—	High Medium Low	—	—	—	—	—
Broen, 1972	18–26 months 4–6 years Adult	—	—	—	—	—	Free play Story-telling	—
Cherry & Lewis, 1976	— —	Male Female	—	—	—	—	—	—

Table 1.2 (continued)

	Listener variables			Speaker variables			Situation variables	
	Age	Sex	Linguistic ability	Age	Social class	Other	Activity	Listener reaction
Phillips, 1973	8 months 18 months 28 months Adult	Male Female	—	—	—	—	—	—
Ringler et al., 1975	12 months 24 months	—	—	—	—	High contact Low contact	—	—
Sachs & Devin, 1976	Baby Peer Mother	—	—	2–5 years	—	—	—	Child Doll
Shatz & Gelman, 1973	2 years Peer Adult	—	—	4 years	—	—	—	—
Snow, 1972	27–40 months 9–12 years	—	—	—	—	Mother Non-mother	Easy Difficult	Absent Present
Snow et al., 1976	—	—	—	—	Academic Lower middle Working	—	Free play Story-telling	—

papers in this volume fit into this rubric of intensive description of a subsystem — Olga Garnica's description of prosodic features in mothers' speech and Dorothy Wills' study of the pronoun system specific to child-directed English. The broad outlines of mothers' speech to children — that it is simple and redundant, that it contains many questions, many imperatives, few past tenses, few co- or sub-ordinations, and few disfluencies, and that it is pitched higher and has an exaggerated intonation pattern — are quite well established. Filling in the rest of the details will be one of the research tasks of the next few years.

As soon as enough is known about a phenomenon like mothers' speech to identify it as a phenomenon, researchers, especially those of us who have survived formative experiences in departments of experimental psychology, want to test its strength. We want to know what situations make it disappear and what situations make it stronger. We want to know if everyone does it, if you become better at it with practice, whether you do it because you learn to, if men as well as women do it, if children do it, if all social classes do it. And so came the second wave of mothers' speech studies, which overlapped with the first in the sense that some of the central studies also incorporated experimental independent variables and that some of the second phase studies added to the basic description of mothers' speech. Table 1.2 gives an overview of the experimental studies and of the independent variables manipulated in each of them. Age of the addressee has, of course, been an independent variable of central importance, tested necessarily in the seven central studies in order to identify and define the phenomenon of mothers' speech. The general-ity of the phenomenon was a matter of interest to Phillips (1973) and to Cherry & Lewis (1976), who tested whether both boys and girls elicit mothers' speech, and to Snow (1972), who compared mothers to non-mothers as producers of mothers' speech. The effect of early mother–infant contact on the tendency of mothers to produce modified speech was studied by Ringler, Kennell, Jarvella, Navojosky & Klaus (1975).

Mothers' speech has been compared in different situations — in easy versus difficult tasks (Snow, 1972), in free play versus book-reading (Broen, 1972; Snow, Arlman-Rupp, Hassing, Jobse, Joosten & Vorster, 1976), and in playful versus caretaking situations (Bakker-Renes & Hoefnagel-Höhle, 1974). Task difficulty has little effect on mothers' speech, but kind of activity has a large effect. Bakker-Renes & Hoefnagel-Höhle compared six situations, of which three involved caretaking (dressing, bathing and eating) and three were unstructured and 'for fun' (playing, chatting after lunch and reading a book). They found that mothers' speech was more complex in free situations than in caretaking situations, and most complex in book-reading, as measured by length of utterance and length of paraphrase. Snow *et al.* (1976) also found that book-reading elicited more complex speech than free play. It might be that the need to communicate efficiently produces simpler speech in the caretaking situations, and that the extra situational support of pictures in the book-reading situation limits the possible topics sufficiently that the comments can be more elaborated than in less well-defined situations. These studies, which found that mothers' speech varied with situation, made it clear that mothers' speech could not be characterized as a single corpus, but must be seen as the product of specific interactions between mothers and their children. Mothers' speech varied in simplicity and redundancy, depending on the communicative demands of the situations in which it was used.

The idea that mothers' speech is a product of carefully adjusted interactional processes appears in Phillips' (1973) finding that true mothers' speech does not appear reliably until children are old enough to respond to adults' speech, and in Snow's finding that even an experienced mother is not capable of producing fully adequate mothers' speech if the child is not present to cue her. The child's role in shaping the interaction is discussed by Jean Berko Gleason (this volume). How the mother's beliefs and perceptions shape the interaction has been described by Bingham (1971), who found that prelingual children elicit simplified speech from adults who believe that the children are cognitively advanced and can understand a great deal, but not from adults who do not believe this. Thus, even prelinguistic infants can elicit the typical mothers' speech style from adults, if the adults are willing to treat the infant as a participant in the interaction. It has been suggested that adults' persistent attempts to carry on conversations with inadequate conversational partners may account for several of the striking features of the mothers' speech style, such as the redundancy and the high frequency of questions (Snow, 1977). The variable of how adults perceive and interpret the behavior of children becomes especially important when we realize that there are large (sub) cultural differences in both what is believed about and expected from children (see, for example, Blount, 1972*b*; Tulkin & Kagan, 1972). Specific social class comparisons of mothers' speech have been made as far as I know only twice (Holzman, 1974; Snow *et al.*, 1976). Holzman compared content, elliptical features and pragmatic force of utterances in the speech of two middle class and two lower class mothers. She found interesting individual differences but could not relate these to social class. Snow *et al.* found that academic and lower middle class mothers produced more expansions, fewer imperatives, more substantive deixis and fewer modal verbs than working class women. Whether these differences are in any way significant can only be decided after direct comparison of features of the input with speed and ease of language acquisition (see Cross, this volume; Newport, Gleitman & Gleitman, this volume).

The idea that mothers' speech is a sociolinguistic skill which children have to acquire along with all their other linguistic skills has been treated in four papers; Shatz & Gelman (1973), Sachs & Devin (1976), Andersen & Johnson (1973) and Gleason (1973). Children as young as three years can modify their speech for younger listeners and, even more surprisingly, seem to modify it in much the same way that adults do, by simplifying, repeating and using attention-getters. Marilyn Shatz and Rochel Gelman (this volume) suggest a mechanism which might explain how very young speakers can modify the linguistic complexity of their speech so effectively.

MOTHERS' SPEECH AND LANGUAGE ACQUISITION

The central theme of mothers' speech research, of course, one which was present implicitly if not explicitly in all the studies mentioned above, is the relevance of mothers' speech to language acquisition. The generality of mothers' speech, including young children's ability to produce it, had to be established in order to show that all language-learning children, even those raised by fathers or older siblings, have access to a simplified speech register. No one has to learn to talk from a confused, error-ridden garble of opaque structure. Many of the characteristics of mothers' speech have been seen as ways of making grammatical structure transparent, and others have been seen as attention-getters and probes as to the effectiveness of the communication. But experiments in which language acquisition is the dependent variable and quality of input the independent variable have unfortunately been rare, and those few that have been performed have not all led to the conclusion that the input greatly affects language acquisition. Perhaps the best-known attempt to find a direct relationship between input and language acquisition, Hess & Shipman's (1965) study, predated all the recognized mothers' speech studies, but was nonetheless clearly addressed to the same issues.

Hess & Shipman concluded that poor quality input, by which they meant input insufficiently adapted to the level of complexity the child could process, hindered language acquisition.

The only truly experimental manipulations of input have all been based on the observation that expansions occurred frequently in adults' speech to children (Brown & Bellugi, 1964). Expansions seem ideally designed to teach children about the structure of language, since they provide information about the correct realization of a specific structure at the time the child most wants to know it. The first two attempts to demonstrate that providing expansions speeded up language acquisition (Cazden, 1965; Feldman, 1971) were, however, unsuccessful. No positive effect of providing expansions to children was found. An experiment in which children received not only expansions of their incomplete utterances (syntactically correct and complete versions of telegraphic utterances which retain all the content words of the child utterance in their original order) but also recast versions of their complete sentences (repetition of the child's sentence in a new syntactic form) did demonstrate an effect on children's language ability after 22 20-minute sessions (Nelson, Carskaddon & Bonvillian, 1973), compared to an untreated control group. A second treatment group of children who received the same amount of interaction with an individual adult but no expansions or recast sentences were not significantly different from the expansion—recast sentence group (though their mean scores on all the measures of language ability were lower), suggesting that conversation with an interested adult may be more crucial to the acquisition of syntax than any particular techniques used by the adult. It may be that expansions are relevant to language acquisition only because parents who produce expansions during one stage of their children's linguistic growth provide relevant, responsive and interesting input at all stages of linguistic development. Children learn to talk by conversing with adults. The quality of the conversation which is carried on may be the crucial variable affecting language acquisition (see Cherry & Lewis, 1976; Cross, 1976, this volume; Harkness, this volume; Lieven, 1976).

The most recent published report of a comparison of input and output, Nelson's (1973) monograph, concluded that language acquisition is retarded if the linguistic input is of poor quality in the sense of not matching the child's cognitive organization. This finding indicates the importance of taking individual differences between children, and thus between appropriate styles for interacting with those children, into account when evaluating maternal speech (Lieven, 1976).

A SEMANTIC APPROACH

When trying to relate what mothers say to what children learn, it is crucial to operate with a 'correct' description of language acquisition. 'Correct' does not here mean immutably true, but does mean a description which can account for (*a*) the facts of children's speech production and (*b*) the facts of what children know about language. 'Correct' is used in the sense that pivot-open grammars have convincingly been shown not to be correct (Bloom, 1971; Bowerman, 1973; Brown, 1973; Van der Geest, 1974*a*), since, even if they do describe the output correctly for at least some children, they do not in any sense describe what children know about language, how children's linguistic knowledge is internally organized. A reasonable study of input factors in language acquisition relies on and must wait for a reasonable description of language acquisition. It has been remarked that psycholinguistics is always five years behind linguistics in its theoretical assumptions. I would suggest that mothers' speech research is another five years behind child speech research, and thus, considering the advances linguistics can make in 10 years, hopelessly out of date linguistically.

The mothers' speech studies discussed above were largely conceived of, planned and carried out between 1967 and 1973, and they show the influence of the child language studies of 1962–68 in their concentration on syntactic description (as can be seen from Table 1.1). The problems faced by children in learning to talk were seen as syntactic — establishing word order, learning about agreement, distinguishing subjects from objects and the like. But as semantic rumblings began to be heard in linguistics, these were picked up by developmental psycholinguists. Generative semanticists and case grammarians pointed out that syntactic representations have less than perfect correlation with semantic representations; for example, the syntactic constellation Subject–Verb–Object can represent Instrument–Action–Patient or Dative–Action–Agent in simple active sentences as easily as Agent–Action–Patient. This is an aspect of language that children have to learn just as much as they have to learn to invert subject and verb to form questions. So developmental psycholinguists began describing child language in different terms, not as 'phrase structure rules plus a few transformations' but as a 'subset of the possible semantic relations'. The overwhelming preponderance of animate nouns in subject position in child sentences became more important than Subject–Verb word order. Information from context and situation became crucial in studying child speech because what children meant was more important than what classes of words they combined or what they deleted.

It has been about five years now since the semantic revolution in child speech, so perhaps it is time to try some semantic analysis of maternal speech. Semantic aspects of mothers' speech have not been entirely ignored until now. Juliet Phillips (1970) pointed out that the most striking characteristic of mothers' speech was its here-and-nowness, its everydayness. Mothers' speech is effectively limited to discussions of what the child can see and hear, what he has just experienced or is just about to experience, what he might possibly want to know about the current situation, as is well-documented in many of the interaction sequences quoted by Moerk (1972). That this is so, of course, is an important piece of evidence in favor of a semantic primacy theory of language acquisition. Mothers make very predictable comments about very predictable topics, which is precisely what must happen if Macnamara (1972) is correct in his suggestion that children are able to learn to talk because they can work out the meaning of the sentences they hear independent of the sentences themselves.

How can we characterize the semantics of mothers' speech more explicitly? An obvious place to start would seem to be the semantic characterizations which have been offered for child speech. These have mostly been based on some sort of case grammar, though they have not necessarily been completely consistent with any of the specific case grammars offered for adult speech. I have chosen to apply the semantic characterization used by Brown (1973) for several reasons — it is pleasantly eclectic, it seemed relatively easy to use and and, most importantly, it accounted for about 70 % of the multi-morpheme utterance types produced by children in Stage I, i.e. it would seem to reflect children's linguistic knowledge fairly well. Brown found that eight 'prevalent semantic relations' are sufficient to represent most of the children's two-term utterances: Agent—action, action—object, action—locative, agent—object, possessor—possessed, entity—locative, demonstrative—entity, and entity—attribute. Children's three-term utterances consisted of any three of the four terms agent, action, object and locative, and four-term utterances consisted of precisely these four terms. Notable for their absence from these prevalent semantic relations are such functions as instrumental (The *key* opened the door), dative (John gave *Mary* the book) (within Fillmore's (1968) case grammar, possessor is in the dative case, but this seems to be too abstract a classification for child language, see Bowerman, 1973), complement (John sang a *song*), and experiencer (*Mary* saw a cat).

How far can we get by applying these same semantic relations to mothers' speech? I have done a Brown-type analysis on 13 samples of about 200 mother utterances each, and the results of that very preliminary and in many ways imperfect analysis suggest that the prevalent semantic relations provide a very adequate description of the content of mothers' speech.

The samples which I analyzed were collected from nine Dutch-speaking mothers while they were playing and reading a book with their 23- to 35-month old daughters (see Snow *et al.*, 1976, for data collection procedure). The mothers of two of the children, Jolanda and Sabine, were tested twice more at two- to four-month intervals, producing 13 samples in all.

What are the practical considerations associated with scoring maternal utterances using Brown's system? Brown's system was designed for two- to five-word long child utterances which consisted primarily of uninflected content words. The mothers' speech samples consisted of utterances up to 20 words in length, averaging three to six words, which in almost every case contained all the required inflections, prepositions, articles and other grammatical morphemes. Thus, in classifying the child utterances of Stage I the semantic relations were in principle exhaustive. They described everything the children had to know in order to produce those utterances. In classifying the maternal utterances, the semantic relations describe only the kernel, the propositional meaning, and fail to capture any of the grammatical knowledge which allowed the mothers to produce correct, complete sentences. But this is not a crucial difference for our purposes. We are not trying to describe maternal competence, we are trying to describe output limitations in their language use. Classifying the semantic relations expressed may enable us to do that.

Precisely because Brown was interested in describing competence, he based his data analysis on utterance types. Because I am more interested in classifying a body of utterances, one of whose primary characteristics is repetitiveness, I have classified utterance tokens.

Brown did not include in his classification one sentence type which figures centrally in maternal speech, the wh- question. It is not entirely clear to me why wh- questions were excluded from the analysis. In general, Brown ignored the modality part of the child sentences, scoring, for example, 'doggie chair' as entity—locative whether it was said with normal, declarative inflection or with a rising inflection which would indicate a yes—no question. Why, then, not score 'where doggie' as entity—locative as well? *Where* is an element which questions locative by saying, in effect, fill locative in here, and as such seems to me to qualify as a locative as much as the element which it questions would. Following this line of reasoning I have scored *where* as locative in questions like 'Where is the doggie?' and *who* as agent in questions like 'Who is riding the bike?' One very frequent question in maternal speech is 'What is that?' (*Wat is dat?* in Dutch) and its minor variants. Because these occur in numbers sufficiently large to greatly influence the results, I have scored these separately but, still following the reasoning above, as demonstrative —entity—question. The other very common maternal question, *Wat doet NP?*, is ambiguous between the readings 'What is NP doing?' and 'What does NP do?', and thus could be scored only by taking the expected answer into account. In most cases it was scored as agent—action, the minimal specification for a correct response being action (e.g. *eating* or *reading*). Sometimes, however, the verb *doen* was used not as a dummy verb but as a lexical verb, and the question required specification of the NP *wat*, e.g. in animal-noise sequences like '*Wat doet de koe?*' '*Boe*' (How does the cow go? Moo). In this case I scored the question as agent—action—complement, taking *wat* as representing the unspecified complement.

Many features of adult speech fall outside the representation in semantic relations. Tense, time adverbials, manner adverbials, modal verbs, imperatives, negation — these aspects of sentences all fall into the modality component and, since the semantic relations are meant to represent only the proposition, I have ignored them. This means then that the sentences:

> *Zet jij de boot op het water neer* (You put the boat on the water).
> *Wil je de boot op het water neerzetten?* (Do you want to put the boat on the water?)
> *Ik heb de boot op het water neergezet* (I put the boat on the water, past tense).
> *Ik ga de boot niet op het water neerzetten* (I'm not going to put the boat on the water).

all are scored identically, as agent—action—object—locative.

What, then, are the results? First we must subtract from the approximately 200 utterances per sample those that express no relations, those that consist of only one term (see Table 1.3). These accounted for an average of about 30 % of the mothers' utterances, a large number of which (36 %) were instances of nomination. Actions and demonstratives used alone were fairly common (30 %

Table 1.3   One-term utterances in the speech of mothers to two-year-old children. Scores in the first five categories represent percentages of one-term utterances

	Jolanda I	Brigitte	Jolanda II	Sabine I	Marion	Liesje	Sabine II	Saskia	Sabine III	Barbara	Bibi	Monique	Jolanda III	Average
Nomination/entity	70.9	11.8	33.7	49.1	14.3	29.6	27.4	37.6	40.0	37.8	23.8	45.8	44.7	35.9
Action	7.1	33.8	16.3	18.7	11.9	9.9	35.3	10.6	16.0	29.7	4.8	12.5	2.1	16.1
Demonstrative	7.1	5.9	10.9	5.7	2.4	5.6	0.0	11.8	18.0	5.4	2.4	4.2	8.5	6.8
Case functions	7.1	10.3	18.5	20.7	25.0	29.6	11.8	17.6	12.0	10.8	40.5	20.8	27.7	19.4
Unanalyzable	7.9	38.2	20.6	5.7	46.4	25.3	25.5	22.3	14.0	16.2	28.6	16.7	17.0	21.9
% of utterances containing only one term	57.7	34.9	45.3	25.1	41.2	32.4	24.3	40.9	24.5	16.4	18.3	12.8	23.3	30.6

Table 1.4 *Multiterm utterances in the speech of mothers to two-year-old children. All scores represent percentages of multiterm utterances*

	Jolanda I	Brigitte	Jolanda II	Sabine I	Marion	Liesje	Sabine II	Saskia	Sabine III	Barbara	Bibi	Monique	Jolanda III	Average
TWO-TERM														
Agent–action	11.8	19.7	1.8	15.8	16.7	17.6	10.1	10.6	12.3	6.9	10.2	9.8	4.5	11.4
Action–object	2.2	7.1	0.0	0.6	0.8	2.0	3.1	0.0	4.5	9.6	1.1	0.6	4.5	2.8
Action–locative	1.1	6.3	0.0	0.6	2.5	1.4	2.5	1.6	3.2	0.0	0.0	0.6	1.3	1.6
Entity–locative	14.0	7.1	11.7	3.2	14.2	7.6	13.8	11.4	11.7	1.6	15.5	5.5	16.8	11.1
Possessor–possessed	2.2	6.3	1.8	5.1	5.8	1.4	0.0	4.1	3.9	3.7	7.5	6.7	2.6	3.9
Entity–attribute	22.6	6.3	9.0	8.2	11.7	15.5	9.4	6.5	10.4	9.0	19.3	17.1	12.3	12.1
Demonstrative–entity	14.0	3.9	22.5	13.3	9.2	10.1	16.4	16.3	7.8	19.9	12.3	9.8	12.3	12.8
Prevalent semantic relations	67.7	56.7	46.8	46.8	60.8	55.4	55.3	50.4	53.9	50.0	65.8	50.0	54.2	54.9
Demonstrative–entity–question	16.1	19.7	18.0	19.0	1.7	14.9	10.1	9.8	9.1	9.6	0.5	2.3	6.5	10.6
Total prevalent semantic relations	83.9	76.4	64.9	65.8	62.5	70.3	65.4	60.2	63.0	59.6	66.3	52.4	60.6	65.5
Other semantic relations	3.2	4.7	2.7	4.4	1.7	2.0	1.3	1.6	1.3	2.1	2.1	4.3	2.6	2.6
THREE-TERM														
Agent–action–object	0.0	0.8	4.5	0.6	6.7	6.1	1.9	4.9	5.8	11.7	1.6	6.7	1.9	4.1
Agent–action–locative	0.0	5.5	1.8	1.3	5.8	3.4	1.9	9.8	1.3	1.6	2.7	3.7	1.9	3.1
Agent–object–locative	0.0	0.0	1.8	0.0	0.0	0.0	0.0	0.0	0.6	0.0	0.0	0.0	0.0	0.2
Action–object–locative	1.1	2.4	0.9	2.5	5.8	0.0	1.3	0.0	0.6	4.3	0.0	0.0	3.2	1.7
Prevalent semantic relations	1.1	7.6	9.0	4.4	18.3	9.5	5.0	14.6	8.4	17.6	4.3	10.4	7.1	9.0
Other semantic relations	0.0	1.6	0.0	10.1	0.8	2.7	1.9	5.7	3.2	9.6	4.8	7.3	2.6	3.9
FOUR-TERM														
Agent–action–object–locative	2.2	0.0	0.0	0.0	2.5	1.4	1.3	1.6	1.9	0.0	1.6	2.4	1.9	1.3
Other semantic relations	0.0	0.0	0.0	1.3	0.0	1.4	4.4	0.8	3.9	5.3	3.7	0.0	2.6	1.8
ALL MULTITERM														
Unanalyzable	9.7	9.4	23.4	13.9	14.2	12.8	20.8	15.4	18.2	5.9	17.1	23.2	22.6	15.9
Total prevalent semantic relations	87.2	84.1	73.9	70.3	83.3	81.2	71.8	76.4	73.3	77.2	72.2	65.2	69.8	76.3

and 6 %), and 11 % of the single term utterances could be assigned case functions on the basis of context. Sixteen percent were unanalyzed, either because the cases they represented had not been included in the scoring possibilities (e.g. vocative, experiencer) or because they were not susceptible to case analysis.

Of the approximately 70 % of utterances that consisted of more than one term, 66 % contained exclusively the prevalent semantic relations identified by Brown, and another 10 % consisted of variants of 'What is that?', i.e. demonstrative—entity—question (see Table 1.4). Brown found that about 70 % of children's utterances were accounted for by the prevalent semantic relations, and argues that these relations express precisely the kinds of ideas to be expected of a child in the sensori-motor stage. It would seem that mothers of sensori-motor children limit their sentences to expressions of these same ideas. This is perhaps not surprising; after all, mothers know pretty well what their children will and will not be able to understand, and they certainly want to produce comprehensible utterances. It would be enlightening to analyze samples of adult—adult speech for the presence of the prevalent semantic relations. It may be that, at least in certain contexts, much adult—adult speech is also limited to discussions of agents, actions, objects, locatives, possessives and the attributes of entities. However, discussion of thoughts, feelings and attitudes is also an important aspect of conversation with adults (see Shatz & Gelman, this volume) which seems to be largely missing from talk to two-year-olds.

Of the remaining multiterm utterances, 15 % were unanalyzed. These included utterances for which experiencer would have been necessary among the semantic relations, some metalinguistic utterances, utterances in which *kunnen* (can) or *mogen* (may) or other non-actions were used as the main verb, sentences expressing comparisons or purposives, and other utterances for which the semantic relations simply were not clear to me.

About 6 % of the utterances contained a complement, dative or instrumental. The three-term utterances can be described with the rule

$$(\text{agent}) \ \text{action} \left(\begin{Bmatrix} \text{complement} \\ \text{object} \end{Bmatrix} \right) \left(\begin{Bmatrix} \text{dative} \\ \text{instrumental} \end{Bmatrix} \right) (\text{locative})$$

plus an output limitation of maximally three terms, and the four-term utterances can be described by the same rule with a four-term output limitation. No utterances of more than four major terms were produced.

The subjects in Tables 1.3 and 1.4 are arranged according to MLU of the mother, with the lowest on the left. It would have been preferable to arrange them according to MLU of the child, but I simply had insufficient information about the children to be able to do that. I will have to assume that the MLUs of the children increase with those of the mothers, an assumption supported by the fact that the MLUs increased with time in the two mothers who were tested longitudinally. Judging from the transcripts of the children's utterances and from their longest utterances, I would judge that only Jolanda I and Brigitte are still in Stage I, and that some of the later children are probably in Stage IV. It is perhaps surprising that mothers' utterances are largely limited to the prevalent semantic relations of Stage I even after their children are beyond Stage I. Is there any evidence in these data for a shift from the prevalent to the other semantic relations at some point on our continuum of mother–child pairs? If we estimate this roughly, simply by dividing the mothers into a group with MLUs below 4.0 and a group with MLUs above 4.0 (between Sabine II and Saskia), only one striking difference between the groups appears. The mothers with shorter MLUs produce almost three times as many demonstrative–entity–questions as the other mothers (14.2 % versus 5.4 % of all multiterm utterances). The only other difference is that mothers with longer MLUs produce more multiterm utterances (77.3 % versus 62.7 % of all utterances). It might seem self-evident that longer utterances are more likely to be multiterm, but, after all, there are many ways mothers can lengthen their utterances besides adding semantic relations to them.

INPUT AND OUTPUT

The purpose of this exercise in semantic analysis was not simply to show in yet another way how simple mothers' speech to children is. The point is that the semantic content of mothers' speech is largely limited to constructions the child has already mastered, and it is this semantic limitation which produces the grammatical simplicity. The semantic content, unlike the grammar, of mothers' speech is limited to what the child can already produce himself. A further point is that the interpretation of the rather conflicting results of the (too few) studies correlating input with output which have appeared to date depends crucially on recognizing differences between the semantics and the syntax of input and output. Brown (1973) has shown very convincingly that order of acquisition of grammatical

words and inflections is determined by their grammatical and semantic complexity, not by the frequency with which they are encountered in the input. Brown & Hanlon (1970) presented a similar argument for the order of acquisition of grammatical structures such as
negation, questions, etc. Yet such features of child language as the
order of subject (S), verb (V) and object (O) are quite clearly determined by frequency in adult language, so that if S—O—V is the highly
dominant order in the mother's speech the child will adopt S—O—V
(Klein, 1974), and if several possible orders are encountered in the
mother's speech the child will use all of them in the same order of
dominance as the mother (Bowerman, 1973).What is the difference
between rules for word order and rules for inflections? If we assume,
with Macnamara (1972), that children start to learn language with a
store of cognitive abilities which determine what they say, the difference must be that a choice of order for S, O and V is a minor
matter of mechanism for expressing ideas the child already has, while
the acquisition of inflection in Stage II reflects the need to learn the
meaning of the inflections as well as their syntactic or phonological
realizations. Frequency of a structure in the linguistic input, even
specific teaching of and practising with the structure, can have an
effect on language acquisition only after the child has independently
developed the cognitive basis which allows him to use that structure.
At that point, the frequency and saliency of the structure in the
input language can have a crucial effect on its acquisition. The child
whose cognitive development has just brought him to a distinction
between, for example, past and present, will be hindered in his
language acquisition if he can at that point find no unambiguous
past tenses in his mother's speech. If his mother is responding at all
adequately to this fictitious child, it is of course highly unlikely that
he would find no past tenses. He himself, by referring to past events,
creates the situation in which his mother can produce past tenses, e.g.

Child: See grampa.
Mother: And what did grampa give you when you saw him?

or

Child: Breakfast.
Mother: You've had your breakfast already.

   This description of the language acquisition of a fictitious child is
not entirely imaginary. It is based partly on my own experiences as
an adult language learner in a more-or-less natural situation, and on
my observations of and discussions with other adult second-language

learners. Making progress in learning a second language seems to be a three-step process: in the first stage you are doing something completely wrong without knowing it, in the second stage you know you are doing it wrong but do not know how to do it right, and in the third stage you have worked out how to do it right and it all seems very simple. The second of these adult-stages is analogous to the child-stage of having a concept but not being able to realize it syntactically. The transition to the third stage can, in my experience, be the result of a trivial event — being corrected, or happening to hear the problematical construction used a couple of times in succession — or of relatively long exposure. I have no doubt that children's discovery of syntactic devices is a similarly irregular process, except of course that they have the advantages of more intimate interactions with native speakers and less input of a confusing nature.

Some experimental evidence supporting this account is also available. Ton van der Geest has reported that, in a longitudinal study of eight mother—child pairs, frequency peaks for semantic features, i.e. aspects of the paraphrase or 'rich interpretation' of utterances, occur earlier for children than for their mothers, whereas frequency peaks for features actually realized in the utterances occur earlier for the mothers (Van der Geest, Snow & Drewes, 1973). Children use certain semantic features frequently before their mothers do, perhaps indicating thereby to the mother that she can now also use those semantic features in her speech.

This view of language acquisition implies that the simplicity and redundancy of mothers' speech are the effects of very specified adjustments to the child, cued by what he says and tries to say as much as by his attentiveness and comprehension. The consistent simplicity and redundancy may primarily serve the purpose of minimizing confusion and helping to consolidate gains in language acquisition. The big steps forward in language acquisition, the insights concerning how to apply some rule or produce some structure, may occur as the result of interactions and sequences such as those described by Moerk (1972) and Snow *et al.* (1976). Accordingly, investigators of the role of input in language acquisition may want to shift their emphasis from descriptions of large samples of mothers' speech to characterizations of what can be and is learned from specific interactions.

2 The adaptive significance of linguistic input to prelinguistic infants

JACQUELINE SACHS

Department of Speech, U-85 University of Connecticut, Storrs, CT 06268, USA.

In research on linguistic input to children, the focus has been on mothers' speech to children who are already beginning to use language themselves. The characteristics that have been observed, such as simplicity and repetition, probably reflect the mother's belief that the child is ready to understand some of her speech and learn from it. Phillips (1973) found that speech to 18- and 28-month-old children was structurally simple, but that speech to 8-month-old babies was not. It was, in fact, quite complex structurally, but differed from adults' speech to adults in other ways. Although most papers on input report the existence of 'special' characteristics in speech to prelinguistic babies, there has been almost complete neglect of this area. Not only do we have very little descriptive work, but also there has been even less discussion of the possible significance of the type of input that young babies receive.

I believe that speech to prelinguistic babies deserves serious consideration along with the syntactic, semantic and phonological modifications of input that have been studied. Specifically, in this paper I will argue that the characteristics we find in adults' speech to infants have adaptive significance for the development of the infant's communication with its social world. The way adults talk to prelinguistic children is not simply a culturally-transmitted, functionless ritual. Rather, this type of speech has many of the earmarks of a species-typical pattern whose evolution has been determined by the sensory capacities of infants and by the infant's requirements for the development of normal communication with its social world.

What sort of evidence could one use to argue for a species-typical

51

pattern? First, such a behavior pattern should be universal cross-culturally. Second, if universality can be established, then one can look for reasons for the particular features of the behavior. It could not be accidental that adults everywhere modify their speech in just the same way. I will present evidence that there is a 'tuning' of the adults' productions to the infants' sensitivity. And third, species-typical behaviors often show accelerated ontogenies. That is, the behavior appears relatively early with respect to the other capacities at that time. I will present evidence that the same characteristics used in adults' speech to infants are characteristics that are controlled early by children when they begin to use language themselves.

The argument will be organized around several characteristics of adults' speech to young infants. These are (1) higher pitch, (2) special intonation patterns, (3) rhythmic and temporal patterning and (4) use of particular sounds. For each of these characteristics, three types of data will be discussed:

(1) Evidence that the characteristic is present in adults' speech to prelinguistic infants, including cross-cultural evidence where available.

(2) Evidence for a special perceptual sensitivity in the infant to the features used in the adults' speech.

(3) Evidence for early control of those features in the infants' own productions.

HIGHER PITCH

Adults' productions

Almost every researcher who has described speech addressed to babies and young children has mentioned that adults seem to use overall a higher pitch, and these studies include a wide variety of languages. Such reports are found, for example, in Ferguson (1964) for Arabic, Spanish and English, in Kelkar (1964) for Marathi, in Rūķe-Draviņa (this volume) for Latvian and in Drach (1969) and Sachs, Brown & Salerno (1976) for English. Studies of the speech of English-speaking mothers have substantiated these impressions with objective measures of pitch. Remick (1971) measured the fundamental frequencies in adults' speech to young children (between 16 and 30 months) and found that the average fundamental frequency correlates highly with the age of the child being spoken to, with younger children hearing higher pitched vocalizations. Garnica (1974) found that the average fundamental frequency of adults' speech to two-year-old children was higher than that to adults. The frequency range, especially at the high end, was greatly expanded, with many frequencies in the 400–600 Hz range. It seems that we can safely assume that prelinguistic babies are spoken to with higher pitched voices.

Infants' perceptual sensitivity

A number of studies have shown that young infants not only can discriminate differences in frequency, but that they respond selectively to certain frequency ranges. Using a habituation paradigm and measuring heart-rate responses, Stratton & Connolly (1973) demonstrated that three- to five-day-old infants could discriminate pitch, intensity and temporal differences in tones. The frequencies involved in the pitch discrimination were 500 and 2000 Hz. Kearsley (1973) measured infants' responses to tones which varied in frequency (and a number of other dimensions). The responses reflected either orientation toward the stimulus (eye opening and heart deceleration) or a defensive reaction (eye closing, heart acceleration and head turning). Optimal orienting responses were found to tones of 500 and 2000 Hz. The other frequencies tested, 250 and 1000 Hz, did not produce orienting responses. Unfortunately, no experiment as yet has tested infants' responses to frequencies other than those mentioned above, but the results at least suggest that 500 Hz is a frequency that infants favor perceptually. Frequencies close to this would be what they would hear in adults' speech to them, whereas much of the speech of adult to adult that they might overhear would be in a lower, less perceptually salient, range.

Infants' productions

An experiment by Webster, Steinhardt & Senter (1972) showed, as did the experiments just described, that infants are sensitive to the frequency range they typically hear, but, furthermore, that their own vocalizations change as a result of stimulation with sounds of different pitches. They stimulated seven-month-old infants with recordings of vowels spoken by a woman. The fundamental frequency of the stimuli were high (500–600 Hz) or low (150–250 Hz). The number of infant vocalizations, the average fundamental frequency of these vocalizations and the average duration of a vocalization were measured during a high pitch and low pitch period for each infant. During the high pitch stimulation, the infants vocalized less and their average fundamental frequency changed significantly from a baseline of 335 Hz to 360 Hz. The results indicate that the infants perceived the difference between the two frequency levels they were exposed to, and demonstrate that the productions were influenced by the characteristics of the stimuli. These findings support an observation reported by Lieberman (1967). He measured the frequency of the vocalizations of two infants while they were in different situations. For both children, the fundamental frequency of the vocalizations moved toward that of the parent in the interaction. Conflicting data, however, have been reported by Delack (1974), who has measured the fundamental frequency when alone, when with an adult, and when vocalizing to an object (e.g. a toy). The infants did not change the fundamental frequency in these situations. Delack does conclude, however, from the patterns of the fundamental frequency within utterances, that infants gain control of their pitch levels during the first year of life.

Studying somewhat older children, Weeks (1971) found that the use of high pitch was quite frequent, especially when the children were using baby talk (BT) style. The earliest example of use of high pitch that she found in her data was at one year seven months, used in combination with exaggerated intonation for a BT style. In my data (unpublished) on speech to dolls, the first example of high pitch that I found was at two years three months, and again it was used with BT intonation. The children studied in Sachs & Devin (1976) quite consistently used higher pitch to babies, to baby dolls, and when role-playing that they were babies.

SPECIAL INTONATION PATTERNS

Adults' productions

As well as higher pitch, special intonations have been reported for a large variety of languages whose BT has been studied (e.g. Ferguson, 1964; Kelkar, 1964; Drachman, 1973). Kelkar, in describing Marathi BT, refers to 'colorful' intonations, and others have claimed that they seem 'exaggerated', but little systematic work has been done as yet describing the intonational features. We do not know, for example, whether the intonation patterns in BT are very similar across cultures, or whether they are simply in each case different from the adult patterns. Even if the patterns vary across cultures, they may all have in common some characteristics that are the relevant functional features for the child's perception. For example, they may always expand the frequency range used by the adults.

Infants' perceptual sensitivity

In the literature of child language studies, there are numerous claims that children respond to intonation patterns before they understand other aspects of language. For example, Schafer (1922) reported that a child of nine months looked at the clock after hearing *Wo ist die Tick-tock?*, but made the same response if the intonation pattern was maintained with other words substituted. Lewis (1936) cited similar examples of responses which might be taken to indicate language comprehension, but actually showed that the child could differentiate a certain intonation pattern. Although such examples seem correct to many people who have studied young children, there has been little systematic investigation of the child's responses to intonation in the prelinguistic period. One experimental study (Kaplan, 1969), using a habituation paradigm, showed that eight-month-old infants could discriminate between falling and rising intonation contours. Data about preferences, when only intonation is varied, are not available, but a study by Friedlander (1968) bears on the question. Friedlander tested infants' preferences for auditory stimuli by allowing them to control which of the available input channels they would listen to. The testing device, called the Playtest apparatus, consists of a lever that the child can push. This lever then switches on one of the messages. Infants chose to listen to nursery songs three to four times as long as they listened to other kinds of verbal recordings. Unfortunately, in this study we do not know which of the many features of the nursery songs held the children's interest, but I have placed this study in the 'intonation' section because it seems likely that this aspect may have played a role. Another study that may be relevant is one by Lewis & Freedle (1973), who found that 12-week-old infants vocalized more when the mother vocalized to them than when she vocalized to an adult in the room. Again, the basis for the discrimination has not been deter-mined, but the difference in intonation may be involved.

Infants' productions

Although there is a limited amount of evidence, it is quite commonly accepted that the child uses prosodic aspects of language at an early point in language development. Most children produce complex strings of babbled sounds with 'sentence-like' intonation contours before they begin to say single words. This phenomenon is often referred to as 'jargon babbling'. One intriguing characteristic of jargon babbling is that it sounds at a distance as if the child were really talking, though of course no words are distinguishable. This has led some researchers to suggest that the child has actually learned the general intonation contours of his language before he learns any other aspect. However, it has not yet been demonstrated that the child has picked up the intonation patterns of a particular language at this early stage. There is the danger of interpreting any sort of variation in pitch and stress as a sign that the child is somehow controlling these variations.

It is possible that the child, in producing long strings of babbled sounds, simply generates enough variability in the prosodic features so that the babbling will sometimes sound like the input language. In that case, the child would not be credited with controlling intonation patterns at all. Rather, the patterns are a result of the adult's perceptions. On the other hand, the child could use particular patterns differently in different situations. These patterns might not signal differences in meaning. For example, some children produce jargon babbling only in specific situations. One child I observed used this style of babbling only when she talked into the telephone (with no one at the other end). My daughter, at about 14 months, jargon babbled when she looked at books, and would occasionally insert one of the few words she knew into the strings of nonsense syllables. This behavior seemed to mimic adult reading. Delack (1974) has also found that children's babbling is different when the child is alone as compared with babbling with an adult.

It would be especially useful to determine whether children use intonation to signal differences in meaning before using other aspects of language. Just as young children often invent words to communicate ideas, they might also invent prosodic features to communicate their intentions. A number of investigators have argued that children actually learn some of the intonation patterns of the input language in the first year of life. Tonkova-Yampol'skaya (1968) presented evidence to show that intonation matches the adult pattern for such diverse functions as commands, narrations, indicating discomfort, and requests. However, the behavioral evidence for whether the child actually 'meant' these functions is very weak. Von Raffler-Engel (1973) claimed that her son used humming with 'sentence intonation' before he used words. For example, humming with a

rising pitch would have been used when he pointed at some things
he wanted and 'asked if he could have them' (*ibid.*, p. 11). When
the child learned his first word, according to von Raffler-Engel, he
applied different intonation contours to signal meanings before learning other sounds to signal contrasts. He used the word *màmà* to call
for his mother, and *mamá* to call for his father. Eventually the /p/
sound appeared and the word *mamá* changed to *papá*. 'Here, the first
phoneto—phonemic difference was not in the articulation but in the
intonation. The melodic factors, then, appeared before the articulatory ones' (*ibid.*, p. 10). Similar data have been described by Peters
(1974). Again, the difficulty in interpreting these claims is that no
independent behavioral evidence for interpreting the child's meaning
is specified. Some recent research involves detailed recording of the
child's behavior and analysis in terms of the non-linguistic context,
and such research may provide more convincing evidence of the
child's control of intonation. For example, Dore (1973) claimed that
one-year-old children used words with appropriate intonation
contours. Falling contours were used for labelling, rising contours
for requesting, and abrupt rising—falling contours for calling.

After the child begins to use language, his use of intonation
remains striking. Weir (1962) studied the pre-sleep monologues of
her child, and found that he invented various substitution patterns,
some of which contrasted intonation patterns. Also, when a child
imitates adult words or sentences, the intonation is typically retained.
In studying a mother's speech to her child, Kobashigawa (1969)
found that a new word was often presented in a question frame (e.g.
Can you say doggie?). When the child imitated the new word, he
would do so with the rising intonation that was on the last word.
Since the word intonation would then be incorrect, the mother
would say the new word once more in isolation with the appropriate
falling intonation contour, and the child would imitate it again. My
data on young children speaking to dolls (Sachs & Devin, 1976, and
other unpublished data) also indicate an early control of appropriate
intonation in a BT situation. In a tape of a child at two years one
month there are examples of distinctive intonation patterns for
several different speech functions. These include scolding speech
(*Lie down! I told you! I told you, Georgie!*), nurturant speech
(*That's right. Want a pillow? Good baby.*), and instructional speech
(*Look at the flower. OK? Look at the flower, yep. Petal. That's right.
This is a petal. And it's green. Pink. Brown.*).

RHYTHM AND TEMPORAL PATTERNING

Adults' productions

All cultures seem to have certain songs, rhymes, games and language routines that are used for interacting with babies. Moerk (1972) has suggested that this is a universal characteristic of language use and has described some typical interaction patterns for English-speaking mothers and babies. The routines generally have definite rhythmic structure, rhymes and sound duplications.

Infants' perceptual sensitivity

Although every culture uses rhythmic patterns, there has as yet been little research on the perceptual consequences. An intriguing recent experiment may be relevant, however. Condon & Sanders (1974) played tapes of adults' speech to newborn infants and filmed the body movements of the infants while they were listening to the tapes. Using a frame-by-frame analysis, they found that as early as the first day of life the neonates' movements were in synchrony with the voices. To rule out the possibility of a spurious correlation, they also analyzed the infants' movements against another voice-track, and found no correlation. These results suggest that the infants were responding to the temporal patterns in the speech the adults used to them.

Infants' productions

Children use rhythmic structure early in their own productions. There are many reports in the literature of children making up sound pattern routines. Again, the most thorough documentation of this behavior is in Weir's study of pre-sleep monologues.

USE OF CERTAIN SOUNDS

Adults' productions

I have noticed that when adults 'babble' to young babies to gain and hold their attention, they use an unusually large proportion of initial stop consonants, especially the voiced forms. For example, the adult might say *ba ba ba*, with a particular intonation contour. BT lexical items also tend to have a concentration of stop sounds, perhaps for the same reasons, but that is actually in a period that is later than the one under consideration here.

Infants' perceptual sensitivity

A growing body of research has demonstrated that the stop consonants occupy a special place among speech sounds (see Liberman, Cooper, Shankweiler & Studdert-Kennedy, 1967). It might be expected that these sounds would be perceptually salient for infants, and, in fact, several recent studies have shown that infants can discriminate the consonants /b/, /p/, /d/, /t/ and /g/ (Moffitt, 1971; Morse, 1972; Trehub & Rabinovitch, 1972). Furthermore, Eimas, Siqueland, Juscyk & Vigorito (1971) demonstrated that the boundary between /b/ and /p/ on the voice onset time continuum is at the same point for six-week-old infants as it is for adult speakers of English. Small differences in voice onset time were not discriminated unless the small difference occurred at the boundary between the two consonants. These results suggest that the categories of input leading to the perception of the stop consonants are not dependent upon experience with the language. Most recently, Eimas & Corbit (1973) and Eimas, Cooper & Corbit (1973) have argued, on the basis of selective adaptation of aspects of the sounds, that 'feature detectors' are involved in the processing of these sounds. The use of the term 'feature detector' is appropriate for a perceptual mechanism that is specially tuned to certain features of the organism's sensory input.

Infants' productions

In babbling, the infant typically uses [b] and [g] by the eighth month, and [d] by the ninth (Pierce, 1974). Unlike the perceptions, the production of the contrasts (phonemic) among the various stop sounds must be acquired gradually (e.g. Port & Preston, 1972). However, the earliest phonemic contrasts made by children seem almost always to involve a vowel-stop consonant contrast.

THE FUNCTION OF EARLY LINGUISTIC INPUT

If there is a perceptual sensitivity in infants to the various characteristics that we find in early input, then this input may function in a special way in (1) gaining and holding the infant's attention, (2) establishing the affectional bond between the infant and the caregiver and (3) allowing the earliest communication between them to take place. I would not suggest that the type of linguistic inter-action that we typically find between infant and caregiver is necessary for normal development, because I have no evidence about develop-ment when such interactions do not take place. It may well be that visual and tactile interactions play as much or more of a role than auditory interactions, or that increased input in another modality is substituted when auditory input is not present. The development of deaf children or hearing children of deaf parents would be one place to look for evidence about this question. I am suggesting ways that the linguistic input of the caregiver may function in the typical case.

Initially, the caregiver's vocalizations may function to gain and keep the infant's attention. If the adult uses the pitch, intonation patterns and so on that most capture the infant's attention, the infant will become quiet, face the speaker, and establish eye-contact. A number of recent studies have shown that eye-contact is very important for the establishment of a bond between infant and care-giver. The parents of congenitally blind infants often experience difficulty for this reason (Fraiberg, 1974). Some autistic children avert their eyes and turn their heads away from the face to face position as early as the second week of life (Stern, 1971). In contrast, the normal pattern of eye-contact is very subtle and rich. Jaffe, Stern & Perry (1973) have found that 'gaze-coupling' between mothers and their three-month-old infants very much resembles conversational turn-taking in adults. Some mothers also established play-routines with their looking behavior, alternately fixating on the infant's face and then playfully turning away. (During these sessions, the mother was vocalizing to her infant, but the pattern of the vocal-izations was not studied.)

There is also evidence that the early linguistic input influences the child's vocalizations. Lewis & Freedle (1973) investigated the effect of maternal vocalization on a number of infant behaviors at 12 weeks of age. If the mother vocalized to the infant, the behavior with the highest probability of occurrence within a 10-second period was an infant vocalization, followed by an infant smile. Looking at some-what older children (9—18 months), Clarke-Stewart (1973) found that the amount of verbal stimulation that a mother gave directly to her child was highly correlated with measures of the child's linguistic competence. The amount of maternal speech that was not directed to the child did not correlate with language development. This result would suggest that overall quantity of verbal stimulation is not important for development, but that the quantity of direct mother-to-child input is. Special intonation, pitch and so on may be cues to the child as to which speech is addressed to him, so that he may be able to 'tune out' (or never tune in) other vocalizations that he hears.

In the infant's productions, the first aspects of language that he controls are the very ones that are prominent in the speech of the caregiver to him. This may allow the child to enter into a 'dialogue' very early with his caregiver, long before he has words or sentences. By looking at these mutual 'babblings', we may be able to trace communicative interactions back long before the onset of speech and see the roots of language in the 'prelinguistic' period.

In summary, I have suggested that there is adaptive significance in the characteristics we find in adults' speech to prelinguistic infants. These characteristics match the perceptual sensitivities of the infants. A little later, the infants' earliest productions use these same characteristics, allowing for the first vocal communication between the infant and the caregiver.

3 Some prosodic and paralinguistic features of speech to young children

OLGA K. GARNICA

*Department of Linguistics, Ohio State University,
Columbus, Ohio 43210, USA*

It is now often claimed that speech addressed to children and speech addressed to adults differ in systematic and identifiable ways. This view represents a reversal of the direction taken by Chomsky (1967) and others (e.g. McNeill, 1970) who held the view that adult speech was mostly ungrammatical, replete with false starts, hesitations and slips of the tongue regardless of the addressee. This was supported to a certain degree empirically by Bever, Fodor & Weksel (1965) who made calculations of grammatical and ungrammatical sentences in several speech samples.

This view had a strong influence on the theory of language development that was proposed. If the verbal input to the child is fragmented, confusing, and to a great degree unsystematic, then acquisition probably occurs independently of the linguistic environment. The input to the child must play a minimal role in the acquisition of language. Some verbal input is necessary, of course. This was clear from cases of children totally deprived of the opportunity to hear language. But input was relegated to a secondary role. Much of language acquisition was attributed to the child's innate capacities. The reasoning was that, if what the child hears or overhears is not of a form that reveals the underlying systematicity of language, then some other mechanism must be available to the child in order for him to be able to abstract rules and gain knowledge about this systematicity.

Not all persons held this view. One of the strongest opponents was Labov (1970). He pointed out

> The ungrammaticality of everyday speech appears to be a myth
> with no basis in actual fact. In the various grammatical studies
> that we have conducted, the great majority of utterances —
> about 75 % — are well formed sentences by any criterion. When
> rules of ellipsis are applied and certain universal editing rules to
> take care of stammering and false starts, the proportion of truly
> ungrammatical and ill-formed sentences falls to less than two
> percent.   (*ibid.*, p. 42)

Although Labov makes no specific reference to speech directed to
children, others had noted that the language heard by children is
likewise neither phonologically nor grammatically deviant (Brown &
Bellugi, 1964; Waterson, 1971).

What are the consequences of this alternative view of the role of
the verbal environment for a theory of language development? One
possible consequence is that greater emphasis is placed on the
mother—child verbal interaction and the contribution of this experience to the child's learning of language (Macnamara, 1972; Snow,
1972, this volume). A direct result of this is that the importance of
the innate mechanisms is de-emphasized. Another consequence is
that the child's role becomes more important since the child can be
seen as a more active participant in the language-learning process.

There are two questions relating to the verbal input to the child
and his language development. First, what are the linguistic characteristics of speech addressed to the child? This is a purely descriptive
question but necessarily preliminary to the second question: what
features of the verbal environment are critical for learning language?
Certainly, the latter question is more relevant to a theory of language
development and, more broadly, to the problem of cognitive development. Its answer, however, depends significantly on the answer
to the first question.

Studies of speech directed to young children have considered
phonological and lexical features (summary in Ferguson, 1964; see
also Ferguson, this volume) and syntactic, semantic and redundancy
features (reviewed in Snow, this volume). All these features suggest
that the child is the recipient of language which is highly reduced in
structure but with a dramatic increase in redundancy.

One aspect of the language used to address children which has
received little syntactic consideration is prosodic features, i.e.
'features whose arrangement in contrastive patterns in the time
dimension is not restricted to single segments' (Lehiste, 1970: p. 3).
These features include pitch, stress and quantity. Some acoustic

correlates are duration, fundamental frequency (F_0) and intensity. When these features are used to mark lexical and grammatical differences they are referred to as prosodic. When they are used to indicate emotional and attitudinal aspects of communication the term 'paralinguistic' is often applied.

A number of observations on the prosodic and paralinguistic use of these features are available. Ferguson (1964) notes that even the casual observer may notice that adult speech to young children is characterized by higher overall pitch and a preference for certain intonational contours. Gleason (1973) also mentions a rise in the fundamental frequency of the voice when addressing the young child. This feature is again noted in Sachs, Brown & Salerno (1976) in their study of speech to a two-year-old. They also note an increase in pitch change within a sentence and more instances of emphatic stress. Furthermore, they notice that in speech to the child the majority of sentences which they classified as interrogatives were, by their word order, simple declaratives with a rising intonation. Only a small portion of the 'interrogative' sentences contained question words or had inverted word order. Sachs *et al.* suggest that rising sentential intonation may signal something other than 'question' in speech to the child, and that the rising intonation may be a special kind of pitch change.

These same characteristics are mentioned by Grewel (1959) who astutely added a number of other features to the list on the basis of his own casual observations of adult speech to children. He notes a higher overall pitch and, in simple sentences, a rising intonation at the end of the sentence. He observes, further, that longer sentences are divided up in sections with each section having its own completed rising or falling contour. Frequent successive repetitions of the same contour are also noted. Speech to the young child is slower in tempo with obvious (prolonged) pauses between words, word groups, and particularly between sentences.

Grewel makes some further comments which, though suggestive, are ambiguously stated and difficult to interpret. He asserts that 'the dynamic accent in speaking to babies is strikingly diminished as compared to speaking to adults' and also that 'when a dynamic accent is used, it is as it were compensated by a prolongation of the stressed word' (Grewel, 1959: p. 196). As an example of the latter he offers the sentence: 'No, that we ca . . . n't do!' The term 'dynamic accent' is not defined and could be interpreted as meaning any of several different things. From the example above, it seems at least likely that Grewel is using the term to mean emphatic stress. In any case, the prolonged duration of stressed words also seems to be a probable characteristic of speech directed to the child.

Remick (1971) reports the only empirical evidence on prosodic feature characteristics. She studied the speech of 10 mothers to their children (ages 1; 4 to 2; 5). She calculated both median fundamental frequency and frequency range from narrow band spectrograms for a subsample of sentences from each subject. The spectrographic analysis was run on 14 to 17 utterances per subject from each of two distinct speech situations: (1) speech directed to an adult and (2) speech directed to the child addressee. Her finding was that only the mothers of the youngest children used a higher median fundamental frequency and a greater frequency range when addressing the child. The speech of mothers whose children had begun to acquire language showed 'a dramatic restriction in both median and range' (Remick, 1971; p. 32).

Several methodological inadequacies in this study led us to question the data on fundamental frequency and range as well as the conclusions drawn from them. Some of these inadequacies are acknowledged by the investigator. First, since the recordings were made in the subjects' home, the quality of the recordings was in all likelihood poor. The choice of sentences for spectrographic analysis was thus biased toward those with a more favorable signal to noise ratio. The investigator reports that only a limited number of readings could be obtained even from the measurable sentences. Second, in reporting the findings Remick gives no account of the procedure used for making measurements. This leaves open the question of how certain decisions were made, decisions that could have profoundly affected the values obtained. Third, there was no attempt to match sentences measured from each of the two situations in terms of their composition. A number of investigations (e.g. House & Fairbanks, 1953; Lehiste & Peterson, 1961) have shown that vowels have intrinsic pitch, i.e. there is a connection between vowel quality and the relative height of the average fundamental frequency associated with it: higher vowels have higher fundamental frequency. In any attempt, therefore, to compare the fundamental frequency in two or more situations or even across subjects within a single situation, it is necessary to obtain measurements on the same verbal material. If the phonetic composition of the samples varies greatly, the differences observed may only reflect a difference in the composition of the two samples. Finally, no statistical tests were run on the frequency data. Thus it is not clear that the observed differences between speech to the child and speech to the adult were significant.

One final observation about prosodic features in speech to young children is that the use of such characteristics seems to diminish or disappear in most contexts by the time the child addressee is four to five years of age. This has been noted in the case of higher fundamental frequency (Grewel, 1959; Gleason, 1973). The situation for the other characteristics is as yet unknown.

The purpose of the present study is to specify the prosodic and paralinguistic features of speech directed to young children in a more precise and detailed manner by testing two hypotheses:

Hypothesis I: The use of prosodic and paralinguistic features in adult speech directed to young children differs systematically from the presence and distribution of these features in adult—adult speech.

Hypothesis II: Differences in the present use of these features vary as a function of the relative age of the child addressee. Generally, the older the child, the closer the usage pattern of these features will approach the pattern in adult—adult speech.

These hypotheses are tested under experimental conditions where the speech context remains constant and the addressee is varied.

METHOD

SUBJECTS

The subjects were 24 women college graduates residing in a predominantly white, upper middle class university community. Twelve of the women had a child in the 1;10—2;6 age range (mean age — 2;3) (group C1). The other 12 women had a child in the 5;1—5;7 range (mean age — 5;4) (group C2). There were an equal number of male and female children in each age group. The subjects were native speakers of American English with minimal or no knowledge of a foreign language and had lived in California for at least one year. Their speech was devoid of any discernible speech disfluency.

TESTING SESSIONS AND RECORDING

Each adult took part in two testing sessions, and performed three verbal tasks in each session. In the first session the subject directed her speech to another adult (adult listener session). The adult listener in all cases was the investigator. In the second the subject directed her speech to her own child (child listener session). Because it was highly desirable to obtain speech samples of both types of listeners without revealing the purpose of the study, the sessions were only ordered in this one way. All subjects accepted the request for the adult—adult session before the adult—child session for the purpose of familiarizing them with the materials.

All testing sessions took place in an acoustically treated room. They were recorded in their entirety on a Revox A77 tape recorder with a Sony ECM-16 microphone attached to a lavaliere holder. The tape recorder was calibrated to a flat frequency response of ± 2 dB over the range of 50—10 000 Hz. The calibration was checked at regular intervals during the study and was found to be reliable.

VERBAL TASKS

The subjects performed three tasks in each testing session: (1) a picture task, in which the subject told a story about the persons and events depicted in each of a series of pictures; (2) a story reading task, in which the subject read a short descriptive passage; (3) a puzzle task, in which the subject gave a series of instructions on how to solve a puzzle.

The order in which the tasks were performed by each adult was different in each testing session. The adults in each group (C1 and C2) were randomly assigned to one of the ordering sequences in the adult—listener session.

Picture task. Five colored pictures depicting situations thought to be of interest to children were chosen from several magazines. The pictures showed a boy eating a hamburger, some boys dressed up as Indians sitting around a campfire, a family on a picnic, a family doing household chores, and a little girl and her mother baking. Each picture was mounted on a 9″ x 11″ (22.9 cm x 27.9 cm) piece of colored cardboard. A short declarative sentence related to the events depicted in the picture appeared below each photograph when it was presented to the subject. The sentences were (1) They are both hungry. (2) It is cold. (3) They are glad that it didn't rain. (4) Everybody is doing his chores. (5) Next time the girl will do it herself. The subjects were asked to make up a short story to go along with each picture. They were told to incorporate the exact wording of the sentence accompanying the picture into their story.

Puzzle task. In the puzzle task the subjects were asked to give verbal instructions to the listener on how to solve a puzzle. The puzzle was a small wooden object in the shape of a barrel. Solving the puzzle involved taking the barrel apart by pushing and removing certain color coded pieces in a specified order. The subjects were told that the barrel could be taken apart and were given the necessary instructions. They gave these instructions to the addressee so that he/she could disassemble the puzzle. The instructions were (1) Push in the green square. (2) Take out the piece. (3) Push in the red piece. (4) Take out the piece. (5) Push in the blue piece. (6) Take out the orange piece. (7) Take out the purple piece. (8) Take out the brown piece. The five-year-old children, by and large, had no problem identifying the correct pieces and following the instructions. Some of the two-year-olds, however, either did not recognize some of the color terms used in the instructions or confused them. In these cases the mother was instructed that she could assist the child only *after* each instruction was presented as it appears in (1)–(8) above.

Story reading task. A short passage about rainbows accompanied by a picture depicting a rainbow and other items mentioned in the passage (sun, raindrops, etc.) was presented to the subject. The passage was the first paragraph of the Rainbow Passage (Fairbanks, 1940):

> When the sunlight strikes raindrops in the air, they act like a prism and form a rainbow. The rainbow is a division of white light into many beautiful colors. These take the shape of a long round arch with its path high above, and its two ends apparently beyond the horizon. There is, according to legend, a boiling pot of gold at one end. People look, but no one ever finds it. When a man looks for something beyond his reach, his friends say he is looking for the pot of gold at the end of the rainbow.

The subject's task was to read the passage out loud. In the adult listener session the subject simply read the passage out loud in the presence of the investigator. In the adult–child session the subject read the passage to the child. The Rainbow Passage was chosen for several reasons. First, the subject matter was thought to be of interest to children even though some of the sentences were quite complex and, second, Horii (1972) has shown that there is a high correlation (+ 0.98) between average fundamental frequency measurements for the second sentence and all other sentences in the passage. Thus, it is possible to measure a small sample (one utterance per subject) and generalize these measurements for the entire passage.

INTERVIEWS

An interview was conducted with each subject upon completion of the verbal tasks in the child listener session. The purpose of the interview was to determine whether the subjects in the study were aware that they modified their speech when addressing their children, especially whether they noticed any prosodic modifications. If they were aware of such changes, what kinds of modifications did they notice?

The questions included in the interview focussed on eliciting from the adults information on their knowledge of the adjustments they made in their speech when addressing young children and the types of techniques they used in maintaining verbal interaction with the child. The rather broad (imprecise) term 'same sort of voice' was used in an attempt to elicit comments from the subjects on the prosodic aspects of their speech. The probes were also structured to steer the subjects' responses in this direction.

After the interview was completed, the subjects were informed of the actual purpose of the study and of the general hypotheses and predictions advanced by the investigator. They were encouraged to pose questions regarding any aspect of the study. All the subjects concurred that they had not been aware that their own speech rather than the child's behavior was the primary focus of the study.

SELECTION AND MEASUREMENT OF UTTERANCES

A total speech sample of 30—40 minutes was obtained for each subject (both sessions combined). A subsample of these utterances was chosen for perceptual and acoustic analysis. The utterances selected for analysis were the sentences provided in the picture task (five sentences), the instruction sentences from the puzzle task (eight sentences), and the second sentence from the reading task (one sentence). This yielded a sample of 14 sentences from each of 48 testing sessions. A total of 672 sentences were analyzed. These particular sentences were selected in order to make inter-session and inter-subject comparisons on samples in which the lexical items were the same. With lexical content held constant, the analysis could focus on the properties that were of interest in the study.

The utterances selected for analysis were dubbed from the original recordings using a duplicate Revox A77 tape recorder. The total set of utterances was then processed on the Pitch Extractor in the

Phonetics Laboratory at the University of California at Berkeley. This Pitch Extractor produces a display indicating the fundamental frequency of the voiced portions of utterances (Krones, n.d.). The machine was optimally calibrated for the utterances produced by each subject in each testing session. Calibration tones were used to record the frequencies represented on the displays for each new calibration. The displays were produced at what was judged to be an optimum rate — 100 mm/sec. The displays produced for each subject were inspected for instances where the frequency was outside the maximum or minimum of the optimal frequency range. Utterances in which this had occurred were processed again with a new calibration.

The utterances selected for analysis were transcribed by the investigator. The total transcription consisted of a broad phonetic transcription of the segmental portion of each utterance in International Phonetic Alphabet notation, and a transcription of the accentual pattern. Four levels of stress were marked: Stress 1 (primary stress), Stress 2 (secondary stress), Stress 3 (tertiary stress) and Stress 4 (unstressed).

Measurements of fundamental frequency and duration were made for each syllable nucleus in each utterance. The following information was recorded: (*a*) the fundamental frequency at the beginning, peak, and end point of the syllable nucleus; (*b*) the location of the peak within the syllable nucleus; (*c*) the duration of the syllable nucleus; and (*d*) the intensity at the peak of the syllable nucleus.

Clear plastic templates were constructed from the calibration sheets for measuring fundamental frequency. A separate template was used for each calibration. The template was superimposed on the fundamental frequency display for each syllable nucleus and the frequency of the beginning, peak and endpoint was determined. Measurement error was estimated at ±5 Hz. In most cases the syllable nucleus corresponded to a separate syllable in the utterance. However, in certain cases the boundaries between two syllables were not well enough defined on the frequency display and the two syllables were considered, for measurement purposes, as a single syllable nucleus. For example, this was the case for the words *in the* in some speakers' renditions of the sentence 'Push in the [ɪn ə] green square.'

Occasionally the endpoint of the last syllable nucleus in an utterance was impossible to measure because the subject's voice exceeded the limitations of instrumentation at the lower values. It was expected that such instances of unmeasurable phonation would arise. The frequency with which this occurred varied with the subject and type of session. In no case did this occur in more than 5 % of the sentences in any one session. When it did occur, the lowest observed frequency value for that subject was assigned.

Duration was measured from the beginning point to the endpoint of each syllable nucleus. A transparent metric ruler was used. The location of the frequency peak in the syllable nucleus was also recorded.

The intensity curves for each utterance were recorded directly below the frequency display. Intensity was not calibrated to an absolute scale. The values for intensity corresponding to the peak of a syllable nucleus were therefore recorded in millimeters. This made it possible to compare the intensity at the peak of one syllable nucleus with the intensity at the peak of another syllable nucleus.

Intra-observer reliability was obtained for measurements of fundamental frequency and duration. A 10 % sample of sentences was chosen randomly for remeasurement. Remeasurement of duration yielded values identical to the initial measurement. No statistical analysis to determine reliability was therefore performed. Remeasurement of fundamental frequency did yield slightly different results. The correlation between the initial fundamental frequency measurement and the remeasurement values was + 0.97. The intra-observer reliability was considered acceptable.

RESULTS

FUNDAMENTAL FREQUENCY

The average fundamental frequency was computed for each subject for each session from the speech samples that were measured. The mean fundamental frequency by session and age of listener is shown in Table 3.1. The mean fundamental frequency for the C1 group was 197.6 Hz in the adult listener sessions and for the C2 group it was 202.8 Hz. These figures are within the expected range of values for female speakers (Linke, 1953; Peterson & Barney, 1952; Snidecor, 1951). The variations from speaker to speaker result primarily from differences in the size of the vocal folds. The difference between the means for C1 and C2 subjects in speaking to an adult was not significant ($t = 0.75; p > 0.05$).

The mean fundamental frequencies for the C1 and C2 subjects in the child listener sessions were 267.3 Hz and 206.4 Hz, respectively. For the C2 subjects, where the listener was a five-year-old, the

Table 3.1 *Comparison of fundamental frequency and frequency range data for C1 and C2 subjects*

	C1 subjects ($N = 12$)		C2 subjects ($N = 12$)	
	Adult listener	Child listener	Adult listener	Child listener
Mean fundamental frequency (Hz)	197.6	267.3	202.8	206.4
Mean fundamental frequency (st)	43.2	48.4	43.6	43.9
Mean total frequency range (st)	10.5	19.2	10.9	12.6

Hz = hertz.
st = semitones above the zero frequency level of 16.35 Hz.

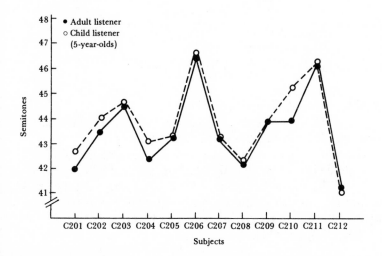

Fig. 3.1. Mean fundamental frequency level for C2 subjects by type of listener.

frequency level in speech to the child was not very different from the level in speech to the adult. The difference between these two means is not significant ($t = 2.0; p > 0.05$). The small differences between the two types of sessions is evident in the graphic representation in Fig. 3.1. For only one C2 subject (C210) was the difference between speech to the adult and speech to the child more than one semitone (1.4 sts).

The difference between the means for the child listener and adult listener conditions for the C1 subjects is quite large — 197.6 Hz

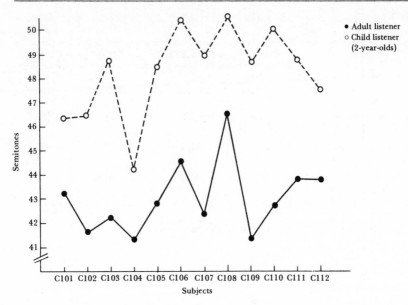

Fig. 3.2. Mean fundamental frequency level for C1 subjects by type of listener.

versus 267.3 Hz. This difference is highly significant ($t = 11.55$; $p < 0.01$). For all C1 subjects, the fundamental frequency level in speech to the child was considerably higher than in speech to the adult. The differences between the two types of sessions ranged from 3.0 sts to 7.4 sts. It is evident that the subjects used a higher pitched voice when speaking to the two-year-olds only (see Fig. 3.2). No such effect was found in speech to the five-year-olds. The interaction effect for subject group and type of listener is highly significant ($F(1,22) = 108.97, p < 0.001$).

FREQUENCY RANGE

The frequency range for each subject was determined for each session separately. The range was defined by the lowest and highest frequency produced in the session. The ranges represent the lowest and highest frequencies actually employed by the subjects in their speech during the session. The ranges for the C1 and C2 subjects in the adult listener sessions extend from 75 to 80 Hz at the low end to 160 and 185 Hz at the high end. These figures represent a span of approximately a half to one octave (Figs. 3.3 and 3.4). This range

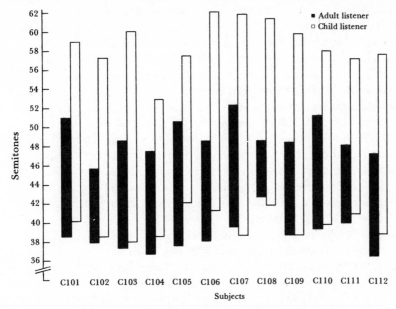

Fig. 3.3. Frequency range for C1 subjects by type of listener.

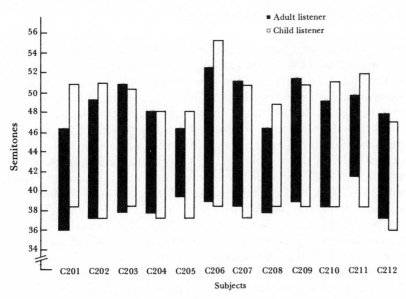

Fig. 3.4. Frequency range for C2 subjects by type of listener.

span corresponds well to findings for female speakers by other investigators (e.g. Linke, 1953). The mean ranges for the C1 and C2 subjects in the adult listener sessions are quite similar — 10.5 and 10.9 sts. This difference was not significant ($t = 0.61; p > 0.05$).

The frequency ranges of the C1 and C2 subjects in the child listener sessions were greater than those in the adult listener sessions. The smallest and largest spans were 200 and 425 Hz among the C1 subjects and 125 and 250 Hz among the C2 subjects. For a number of C1 subjects, the ranges approach a two-octave span. The differences between the frequency ranges used to adult listener versus child listener for the C1 subjects was highly significant ($t = 9.48$; $p < 0.01$). This difference in the range in speech addressed to an adult listener versus a child listener was also significant for the C2 subjects ($t = 3.376; p < 0.01$).

In speech to the two-year-old listeners the low end of the frequency range is about the same as it is in the adult listener sessions. The range is expanded greatly at the higher frequency end. The effect is similar in speech to the five-year-olds, but the increase in the span is not as large. However, the range frequencies for C205 and C211 show another pattern. Here the range in the child listener session is extended at both the lower and higher end.

SENTENCE FINAL PITCH TERMINALS

The sentences sampled from the picture task were declarative and imperative and therefore we would expect these sentences to have a falling final pitch terminal. All the sentences were produced with a falling terminal by the subjects in the adult listener sessions. This was not the case, however, in the child listener sessions. A prominent feature in speech to the two-year-olds (C1 subjects, child listener session) was a rising final pitch terminal in the puzzle task sentences and occasionally in the picture task sentences. Of the sentences spoken by the C1 subjects, 25 % ended with a rising terminal. All but one subject (C108) used the rising terminal in at least one sentence during these two tasks. This result was significant (Fischer sign test, $B = 11, p < 0.01$). Furthermore, most of the sentences with rising pitch terminals (85 %) were produced in the puzzle task and were therefore all sentences in the imperative form.

A rising pitch terminal was also present in speech to the five-year-olds but was much less common. Nine percent of the sentences spoken by the C2 subjects in the child listener sessions ended with a rising terminal. Seven out of the twelve C2 subjects used the rising terminal in at least one sentence in the two tasks but no subject used it more than twice. This is not statistically significant (Fischer sign test, $B = 7, p > 0.10$). Here again most of the sentences with rising terminals were produced in the puzzle task. Thus, we find that when the two-year-old child is the addressee some of the sentences are produced with a rising terminal, even though they are in the form of statements and, surprisingly, imperatives. Ordinarily, in adult speech the rising terminal is restricted to questions. The rising terminal was used only occasionally in speech to the five-year-olds.

USE OF WHISPERING

An unexpected finding was the preponderance of whispering used by the C1 subjects in the child listener session. Whispering never occurred for either C1 or C2 subjects in the adult listener sessions. Only two C2 subjects (C206 and C208) used whispering in the child listener session, and then each used it in only one of the sampled sentences. However, nine out of the twelve C1 subjects used whispering in at least one sentence when speaking to the two-year-olds. The number of sentences (out of 13) in which whispering was used by each subject was: one sentence (C106, C112), two sentences (C105, C110, C111), three sentences (C101, C102, C109) and four sentences (C107). In only one case was the entire sentence whispered. Most often the last half of the sentence contained the whispered syllables. A check of the complete transcripts of the child listener session for the C1 subjects revealed that the use of whispering was not restricted to the subsample chosen for acoustic and perceptual analysis but was evident throughout the entire session; in some cases, the use of whispering was more extensive in the unanalyzed portions of speech. In the case of the three C1 subjects that did not use whispering in the sentences analyzed, all of them made at least some use of whispering at other points in the child listener session. Of the C2 subjects, only the two subjects mentioned above made any use of whispering in the child listener session. The use of whispering by and large seems to be restricted to speech to two-year-olds.

DURATION

Two content words from each of six sentences in the puzzle task

Table 3.2   *Mean average duration (in sec) of content words in sentences from Puzzle Task*

	C1 subjects		C2 subjects	
	Adult listener	Child listener	Adult listener	Child listener
Verbs (push in/take out)	210.97	248.89	223.06	228.72
Color words (green/red/blue/ orange/purple/brown)	214.16	277.67	216.86	263.26

were chosen for the comparison of average duration of syllables between the adult listener and child listener sessions. The six sentences contain both a verb (push in/take out) and a color term (green/ red/blue/orange/purple/brown). The average duration of the syllable nucleus (in msec) was computed for each subject by session. Verbs and color terms were tabulated separately and are shown in Table 3.2.

In computing the average durations for the verbs, the two word sequence (e.g. *push in*) was considered as one and the durations were added together. In the case of *purple*, the only color term pronounced with two syllables, the two syllables were also considered as one item. The color term *orange* was always pronounced as one syllable, e.g. [arnd3].

The results for the verbs and color terms will be discussed separately. For the verbs, the difference between the means for the C1 and C2 subjects in the adult listener session was fairly small (210.97 and 223.06, respectively). This difference was not significant (Wilcoxon rank sum test, $W^* = 0.87, p > 0.05$). However, for 10 out of 12 C1 subjects the average duration of the verbs was higher in the child listener session than in the adult listener session. Only six of the C2 subjects showed a similar difference. The difference between the durations in the adult listener and child listener session for the C1 subjects was significant (Wilcoxon signed rank test, $T^* = 2.30$, $p < 0.05$). However, for all the subjects there was an increase in average duration of color terms in the child listener session. The difference between the means for the two sessions for both C1 and C2 subjects reflects this fact (C1 subjects — 214.16 versus 277.67/C2 subjects —216.86 versus 263.26). Both are significant (Wilcoxon signed rank test, $T^* = 3.45, p < 0.001$).

One factor which has not yet been considered in this analysis is the perception of differences in duration. It is not the case that a one-millisecond difference between two stimuli will be perceived and this should be considered in interpreting the results. In fact, the just noticeable difference (j.n.d.) for duration increases as the duration of the standard stimuli increases. There are several studies on the perception of durations but they do not seem to agree on the size of the j.n.d. for different duration values (Stott, 1935; Henry, 1948; Ruhm *et al.*, 1966). However, if we approximate conservatively from the available information (i.e. that 30 msec is the j.n.d. for durations of 150–200 msec, 35–40 msec for durations of 200–250 msec and 45 msec for durations of 250–300 msec), we should have enough information to correct for the potential effect of the perceptual factor in evaluating differences in duration between the adult listener and child listener sessions. For C1 subjects we find that the difference between average duration values for the adult listener and child listener sessions are larger than the perceptual threshold. This is the case in all instances for the verbs. For the color terms, this is the case for all subjects except C104 and C106. Taking the perception factor into consideration therefore does not change the results for the C1 subjects. The original results also hold for the C2 subjects. For verbs, the difference between the adult listener and child listener sessions is not significant. Taking the perceptual factor into consideration reduces the number of changes from adult listener to child listener to one subject (C212). For color terms, the perceptual factor likewise does not alter the results since only two subjects (C201 and C209) are affected. Thus, we find that the duration of verbs and color terms is significantly longer in sentences spoken to the two-year-olds. Only the duration of the color terms is longer in sentences spoken to the five-year-old children.

DISTRIBUTION OF PRIMARY STRESS

One result of the perceptual analysis was the finding that primary stress placement was different in speech directed to the child listener than to the adult. The difference observed was the appearance of two primary stressed syllables in a sentence which ordinarily in adult–adult communication would contain only one primary stress. The sentences in which this phenomenon occurred were the six sentences of the form 'Push in ——' and 'Take out ——' in the puzzle task.

There were only scattered instances of use of double primary stress in speech directed to the adult listener. Five out of 144 sentences sampled fall into this category, amounting to approximately 3 % of the sentences directed to the adult listener in the puzzle task. Only three of the C1 subjects (C101, C105, C112) and two of the C2 subjects (C202, C207) showed use of double primary stress. This stress distribution appeared in only one sentence for each of the subjects. The situation is somewhat the same in speech directed to five-year olds. Only one C2 subject (C202) used double primary stress in the child listener session.

On the other hand, 10 of the C1 subjects used double primary stress in at least one sentence (Fischer Sign test, $B = 10, p < 0.01$). Of these, three subjects used double primary stress in each of three sentences from the puzzle task, two subjects in two sentences each, and five subjects in one sentence each. This represents a total of 18 out of 72 sentences or about 25 % of the puzzle task sentences directed to the two-year-old child listener. Only two C1 subjects (C103, C109) did not exhibit this characteristic in their speech.

It seems evident, therefore, that the assignment of more than one primary stress to the short and simple sentences of the puzzle task occurs primarily in sentences directed to the two-year-old. Only scattered instances occur in speech directed to the adult listener and the five-year-old.

SUMMARY OF RESULTS

Six major analyses were performed on samples of speech directed to adult listeners and to child listeners. Speech to the two-year-olds differed on the six analyses from speech to the adult listeners. Only some of these differences were found between speech directed to the five-year-old child listener and the adult listener.

The results indicate that

(*a*) The average fundamental pitch of the speaker's voice is higher to the two-year-old than to the five-year-old.

(*b*) The frequency range of the speaker's voice is greater to the two-year-old and to the five-year-old in comparison with the speech range to the adult listener. The expansion occurs at the high end of the range.

(*c*) Speech to the two-year-old contains instances of rising sentence final pitch terminals in sentences where the grammatical form would normally dictate a falling pitch, e.g. imperatives. This feature is absent from speech directed to the adult listener and to the five-year-old.

(*d*) Whispered parts of sentences appear in speech directed to the two-year-olds. This characteristic is absent from speech directed to the adult listener and to the five-year-old.

(*e*) The duration of certain content words is prolonged in speech to the child listener as compared to that to the adult listener. In the puzzle task sentences, the verbs and the color terms had longer durations in speech to the two-year-olds than to the adults. Only the duration of the color terms were so affected in speech to the five-year-old.

(*f*) Speech directed to the two-year-old contains many cases of more than one instance of primary stress assigned within a sentence unit. This feature is absent in speech directed to the five-year-old and to the adult listener.

DISCUSSION

It has been shown that some prosodic and paralinguistic aspects of speech directed to young children systematically distinguish it from speech directed to an adult. The question that arises is what functions these particular features serve. Of what potential use is this 'special' speech to the child learning language? I suggest that the various features can serve at least two functions — an analytic function and a social function. Features which serve an analytic function are thought to assist the child's analysis of linguistic materials. The prosodic features of speech are a primary means by which a speaker organizes units above the level of phonological segments into groups. Thus, cues at this level may assist the child in delimiting sentences, words and other constituents.

Knowing specific linguistic rules, however, is not enough to communicate effectively. The child must know, among other things, the rules for how to engage in a verbal exchange with another person. And, in order to interact with a child, it is necessary to gain the child's attention for conversation. Getting the initial attention of your interlocutor in a conversation is a primary prerequisite to beginning a communicative exchange. Keeping the attention of your interlocutor is necessary for the maintenance of communication. It is hypothesized that some of the features discussed above have a social function, i.e. to initiate and maintain communication between adult and child (and likewise between an older child and a young child).

Prosodic and paralinguistic features can cue the child to pay attention and listen to the speech of the person attempting to communicate with him. Other verbal means used include frequent repetitions of the child's name. The features which serve a social function complement these features and assist the child's analytic endeavor, since a child must attend to a particular set of speech in order to utilize whatever analytic cues are provided.

As the findings of this study are considered in terms of these two functions, it becomes apparent that some features may play a dual role, i.e. simultaneously serve a social and an analytic function. Other features seem to serve predominantly one function or the other.

SOCIAL FUNCTION

The higher pitched voice used by the subjects in this study to the two-year-olds can be viewed as serving primarily a social function. The higher pitch is unique to this function. It may in fact be the most salient characteristic that serves to mark and thus set apart speech directed to young children. Even the most casual observer seems to notice it. An utterance spoken with a higher pitched voice marks that message as intended for the child listener. The message may in other respects be 'tailored' to the language abilities of the child. A message so marked prosodically is foregrounded against the background of adult—adult communication.

The question arises as to whether the higher pitch level is in some way more salient to the child. This question is discussed in detail by Sachs (this volume). At present one can only speculate on whether this factor plays a role. In any event, it is at least plausible that a higher pitch level serves a social function by regulating communication with the child. It attracts the child's attention to verbal material directed to him.

The expanded pitch range observed in the speech of the adult subjects to both groups of child listeners (two-year-olds and five-year-olds) also has a similar function. The extension of the range was primarily in the upward direction. The presence of high pitch peaks in utterances intended for the child listener may be salient cues that mark particular sections of a speaker's speech and therefore make them stand out. The finding of higher pitch in speech to the child listener should be considered with the understanding that such speech is not characterized by high levels of pitch in every syllable nucleus. It is rather the case that the peaks which appear in a

sentence unit are in many cases exaggerated in comparison with
speech to adults.

The use of whispering also may also be considered as an example
of the social function. Whispering, in fact, is very closely allied with
the extension of the range capabilities of speech. Whereas the range
is expanded at the higher end by the presence of higher syllable
peaks, an extension at the lower end of the range may result in the
voice eventually going into whisper. There is ample evidence from
languages using tone that when a speaker produces an exaggerated
rendition of a low tone, a whisper may result. In Serbo-Croatian, for
example, Ivić & Lehiste (1969) observed that the voices of speakers
who exaggerated the low-to-high tone at the end of an utterance,
went into whisper on the low tone portion of the utterance. In some
African languages when there is a lowering of tone at the end of
questions, whisper often appears (Will Leben, personal communication). Thus it seems that the expansion of range in the baby talk
register occurs at both the high and the low end of the voice range.
Both the high pitched syllable and the whispered syllable stand out
and perhaps have attention getting properties.

Finally, the preponderance of rising sentence final terminals in
speech to the child listener may serve a social function — to regulate
conversation between adult and child. The predominance of rising
terminals may cue the child as to when he is expected to respond,
since the question is the grammatical form most often associated
with a rising terminal, and questions normally demand an answer.
Also, it has been noted that sustained or rising pitch in place of
terminal falls is generally used to indicate 'unfinished business'
(Bolinger, 1964).

It is not uncommon to observe an adult asking a child listener a
question and then answering the question if the child does not respond immediately to complete the exchange. The completeness of
the question/answer sequence in terms of a communication unit is
best seen if one thinks of the question forming the first half of a contour (ending with a rising pitch terminal) and the answer continuing
the contour and ending with a falling pitch terminal which signals
completion of the contour and simultaneously the completion of the
exchange. The presence of many rising pitch terminals may serve,
then, not only to regulate the conversation between adult and child
but also to keep the child's attention. One must pay attention in a
conversation in order to know when it is one's turn to speak.

ANALYTIC FUNCTION

Some of the characteristics observed in this study seem to serve an analytic function. One feature which plays a dual role is the preponderance of rising pitch terminals. These may be used to cue the child to the location of sentence boundaries. The fact that a high pitch is attained at the end of the sentence (the boundary) is significant because the high pitch would tend to accentuate the termination of the sentence by the speaker. Furthermore, the rising pitch terminals were associated with sentences which by grammatical form were imperatives and not interrogatives. It is unlikely that the adults were using the imperatives as questions since the context of the sentences was the administration of instructions for a task. Making the imperatives into questions would indicate that the speaker was unsure of the instructions. This never occurred even in the adult—adult sessions when the subject was completely unfamiliar with the task and the instructions she was to administer. It is more likely that the rising pitch terminals on sentences of the imperative form functioned as a signal both to regulate the verbal exchange (social function) and to mark the sentence boundary (analytic function).

The longer durations of certain words (one or both content words in the sentences studied) can also be seen as potentially serving an analytic function. Duration is an important correlate of stress, although there is no direct, one-to-one relationship between the duration of a syllable and the degree of stress it carries. For the following discussion, the situation will be somewhat simplified by disregarding the other factors involved.

In speech to the five-year-olds the durations of the color terms were significantly greater than those directed to the adult listener. The extension of duration in color terms can be viewed as a way to supplement the function of contrastive stress on the unit. By prolonging the duration of the syllable nucleus of *red* in *Push in the red piece* the speaker implies with greater force the propositions 'not the yellow piece, not the blue piece'.

In speech to the two-year-olds, the duration of both the color terms and the verbs was greater than to the adult listener, indicating both emphatic stress on the verbs and contrastive stress on the color terms. This may be a device used by the adult to indicate to the child the 'key' words in the sentence. These were the only words the child needed to understand in order to carry out the command correctly. For example, in the case of the first sentence *Push in the green square*, the listener had only to attend and understand the words *push* and *green* to correctly complete the demanded action. The word *square* is redundant here since there were no other green pieces.

The longer durations of verbs and color terms to the two-year-olds no doubt contributed greatly to the perception of two primary stresses in many sentences directed to them. When two primary stresses were transcribed, they were marked as falling on the verb and color term of the sentence. Aside from the above mentioned function (to indicate key words), two primary stresses may serve to divide up a sentence perceptually into smaller units. The adult thereby segments the sentence into pieces he/she thinks are of adequate size for the child to process easily. The same sentence which, when directed to the adult, would normally contain only one primary stress, would be divided into multiple units for the child. Furthermore, it is interesting that the chunks that sentences such as *Push in the green square* are divided into are the major constituents of the sentence. By this division, the adult may be providing the child with important information about constituent structure. A look at more sentences with different structures is necessary. An initial inspection of all the sentences contained in the Rainbow Passage, as read to the child listener, confirms the hypothesis. In reading to the child listener (to the two-year-olds in particular) the longer sentences are divided up prosodically (here with respect to stress only) into smaller units. These smaller units are in most cases the major constituents of the sentence.

Finally, the longer durations of the color terms and verbs and the extra primary stress may function to teach the child how to systematically mark emphasis in his own speech. This is undoubtedly secondary to the direct communicative benefit of these features, but it is something that must be learned at some point since languages differ in the ways in which they express emphasis.

EFFECT OF AGE OF CHILD LISTENER

As evidenced by the various prosodic differences found between speech to the two-year-olds and to the five-year-olds, some of the devices which are commonly used to the first group have disappeared or are greatly diminished in the speech to the second group (Table 3.3). The prosodic features that serve primarily a social function disappear earlier from the speech of the adults than those serving an analytic one. These include higher fundamental pitch, the use of whispering and the use of rising final terminals in sentences of

Table 3.3   *Presence and absence of some prosodic characteristics in adult speech by function and age of child listener*

	Function(s)	Age of child listener	
		Two-year-olds	Five-year-olds
Higher fundamental pitch	Primarily social	Yes	No
Expanded frequency range	Primarily social	Yes	Yes
Use of whispering	Primarily social	Yes	No
Rising sentence final pitch terminals	Social/Analytic	Yes	No
Longer durations	Primarily analytic		
of verbs		Yes	No
of color terms		Yes	Yes
Use of two primary stresses per sentence unit	Primarily analytic	Yes	No

imperative form. By the time most children reach the age of four or five, their attention span has improved greatly, leading the way to the use of more subtle attention-getting and attention-holding devices on the part of the speaker. Furthermore, by this age most of the children have learned the rudimentary rules of conversational exchange and some have already become masters of more sophisticated conversational skills such as verbal manipulation of hearer actions.

One feature which does seem to remain is an expanded frequency range, indicating that some instances of high pitch do appear in utterances directed to the five-year-olds. Not all of the mothers' speech directed to the five-year-olds exhibited this characteristic. Those that did are in the minority, and these subjects' speech exhibited high pitch peaks in only some utterances. The reasons for these differences between individuals is difficult to determine. My observations indicate that the occasional use of higher pitch to the five-year-old has little to do with the child's verbal abilities. Instead, it seems to be determined primarily by how interested the child is in the task at hand. When the five-year-old child is distracted from the task, some mothers will use higher pitch as a device to bring the child back to the task.

By the time the child is five years old, many of the features which are hypothesized to contribute to the child's analytic endeavor have also either disappeared or are greatly reduced in frequency. The emphatic stress on the verbs in the puzzle task sentences and the use of two primary stresses per sentence are among these. Since the five-year-old is producing, and therefore presumably fully comprehends, sentences of the type in the puzzle task it is no longer even potentially useful to cue the child to the 'key' words (the verb) as was necessary earlier. Also, the utterance need not be divided up into such small units as before. The speakers, however, still feel it necessary to modify their speech by prolonging the duration of the color terms in the puzzle task.

SPEAKER INTERVIEWS

Interviews were conducted with the mothers who participated in the study. Some statements made by the respondents are of potential value not only to the interpretation of the experimental results of the study but also to the clarification of certain broader issues that are at the moment vague.

Most of the subjects noticed differences in their speech as a function of the type of listener (child versus adult).

The kinds of changes that the C1 subjects noted were a higher pitch of voice, an expanded range, less volume in voice and slower speech. The C1 subjects admitted using these features during almost all verbal interactions with the two-year-olds, but reported using them most when trying to get the child's attention or during a one-to-one interaction with the child. They believed that they used the features in their speech because it got them results, i.e. it helped make their communication with the child more effective. Several subjects noted that when they failed to use these features, their communication was not understood by the child. As one subject put it,

> There are plenty of times I don't stop to think that he's two and I'll just mumble something at him or make some kind of demand on him and don't really think about whether or not he can understand it. And that's when he's most likely not to respond at all. (C106)

All the subjects felt that using the features (higher pitch, etc.) got them results in communicating with the child and admitted using them in their speech.

All the C2 subjects, however, were more qualified and they specified the particular situation which would trigger these modifications in their speech to their five-year-old. All the C2 subjects who observed differences emphasized that the changes in speech to the

five-year-old were not present at all times. Rather, the changes occurred in particular situations. The most common situations mentioned were (*a*) when the child was in a certain state — tired, emotion-
ally upset; (*b*) when the adult had to restate a request or command,
etc. after failure to convey the message adequately; and (*c*) when the
adult was presenting new information to the child, which might be
difficult to understand or carry out.

Although all the subjects interviewed had something slightly different to say about the devices they used to get a child's attention,
they all agreed that changing one's voice so that it would maximally
contrast with the ongoing level of speech was the most effective
means.

> Often I find I have to do something clever to get a young child's
> attention. And it's more effective to do something completely
> ridiculous or out of the ordinary. Anything that departs from
> the ordinary or expected. That gets their attention best. (C202)

The devices mentioned ranged from raising the pitch of the voice,
talking louder and wide variation in pitch on one end to speaking
softer, slower and using whispering. The latter approach was associated with a particular style of dealing with the situation.

> It's the background I've had. My mother did that to me too. If
> she really wanted to get my attention she always whispered. I
> remember that my sister and I always sat up and took notice. I
> find it works with my children also.   (C205)

These persons were in the minority. Most mothers chose the first
approach.

It seems then, in general, that foregrounding the speech directed to
the child by using devices that produce contrast was what the
mothers found through experience to be most effective with young
children. This would uphold the interpretation suggested above that
some of the prosodic features serve a social function, i.e. to attract
and hold the child's attention.

4 Some interactional aspects of language acquisition

TON VAN DER GEEST

Institute for General Linguistics, University of Amsterdam, The Netherlands

In this paper I want to deal with two aspects of mother–child interaction:

(1) semantic and syntactic aspects of mothers' and children's conversations with one another, and their relevance to language acquisition;

(2) certain syntactic and pragmatic errors in child language that can be explained from the adult model sentences.

These two aspects will be discussed in the perspective of whether language is acquired on the basis of innate language-specific prerequisites or on the basis of general (interactive) learning strategies.

SEMANTIC AND SYNTACTIC ASPECTS OF MOTHER–CHILD INTERACTION

The relation of semantic and syntactic aspects of mothers' and children's speech to one another was investigated in a study undertaken in response to the problem put by Brown & Hanlon (1970). Brown & Hanlon concluded from their analysis of children's speech that derivational complexity of utterance types determined their order of acquisition, not the frequency of the utterance types in the input speech. However, since it was felt that a too restricted sample of linguistic structures had been analyzed by Brown & Hanlon, and that their analysis of the input speech was too casual, the speech of eight Dutch children and their mothers in an interactive setting was

89

investigated (Van der Geest, Snow & Drewes, 1973). The collection of data started immediately after the first two-word sentences appeared. Once a month for six months 100 child utterances (types) and all utterances spoken to the child by the mother during each session were recorded.

All the aspects of the child's grammar, both semantic (or functional: Slobin 1973a) and syntactic, in the earliest stages after the emergence of the two-word sentence were analyzed. Fuller information about the scoring system can be found in Van der Geest, Gerstel, Appel & Tervoort (1973). It consisted of an exhaustive inventory of semantic elements (e.g. subject, object, present tense, past tense, modal, desiderative, assertive, locative, temporal, definite, indefinite, etc.) and an analysis of whether each semantic element was correctly or incorrectly realized and correctly or incorrectly omitted in the utterance as produced. Utterances were, furthermore, classified as spontaneous or non-spontaneous and in terms of whether they were responded to or not. Spontaneous utterances were defined as those which opened a new topic of conversation; one might therefore expect them to be semantically simpler and syntactically less elliptical than non-spontaneous utterances. Utterances were classed as responded to if they were followed by an utterance from the conversational partner which continued the same conversational topic.

The statistical analysis was limited to the 43 linguistic variables which occurred in sufficient frequency for all mother—child pairs. They were distributed as shown in Table 4.1.

Table 4.1   *Distribution of linguistic variables*

	Spontaneous	Non-spontaneous	Totals
Semantic assessment	14	15	29
Realization assessment	7	7	14
Totals	21	22	43

The data were analyzed in four different ways; fortunately, the picture one gets from all the various analyses is almost identical, so for purposes of clarity only one will be presented here. The number of sessions by which the peak frequency of each variable in the mother's and the child's speech differed was counted. Each mother—child pair received a plus score of that many months if the mother's

Table 4.2   *Data analysis of mother–child speech (for explanation see the text)*

Child speech	Maternal speech				Totals
	Spontaneous		Non-spontaneous		
	Reacted to	Not reacted to	Reacted to	Not reacted to	
Semantic assessment					
Spontaneous	− 8	− 7	− 9	+ 6	− 18
Non-spontaneous	− 3	− 5	+ 4	− 5	− 9
Realization assessment					
Spontaneous	+ 4	+ 19	+ 14	+ 16	+ 53
Non-spontaneous	+ 1	+ 13	+ 5	+ 14	+ 33
Totals	− 6	+ 20	+ 14	+ 31	+ 59

peak preceded. Thus if, for example, the mother's peak frequency for use of indefinite articles occurred in the second session, and the child's in the fourth, then that mother–child pair received a score of + 2 for that variable. Table 4.2 presents the resulting data, totalled over the eight mother–child pairs and the 43 variables.

Semantics versus realization

The most interesting result from these data is the large difference between semantics and realization. The semantic aspects of the child's speech appear to be more advanced than the mother's speech, whereas in terms of syntactic realization the mother's speech is more advanced (− 27 versus + 86). The difference is significant (Wilcoxon signed rank test, $p < 0.02$).

This suggests that in mother–child interaction the child somehow determines how complex the daily conversation with him may be in semantic cognitive terms, and that the mother takes the opportunity to provide the child with the correct realization rules to cover the semantics of the conversation. For example, the child indicates to the mother that she can talk with him about the future or the past, about permission, ability, necessity, motion and direction, possession, etc., and the mother then takes these opportunities to teach the child the rules of language necessary for expressing these contents correctly.

Spontaneous versus non-spontaneous utterances of the child

When we compare the spontaneous and non-spontaneous utterances of the child, we find that the horizontal column totals for spontaneous utterances are higher (+ 35 versus + 24). This implies that the non-spontaneous utterances of the child are closer than the spontaneous ones to the level of the mother's speech. This suggests then that the occurrence of conversation between mother and child positively influences both the grammatical and the semantic complexity of the child's speech. Children's utterances which continue a conversational topic are more similar to adult speech than those which initiate a conversation.

Spontaneous versus non-spontaneous utterances

The vertical column totals (columns 1 and 2 versus 3 and 4) demonstrate that there is a strong tendency for the spontaneous maternal utterances to be less advanced over the level of the children's utterances in both semantics and in realization than non-spontaneous maternal utterances. This tendency suggests that the mother makes a rather simple start in the conversation with her child, and produces sentences which are more complex (both semantically and syntactically) thereafter.

There are some indications (see Van der Geest *et al.*, 1973) that the absence or presence of certain structures relates to the semantic complexity and perhaps therefore to syntactic complexity of these structures (see also Brown & Hanlon, 1970). Although this relation could not be established for all variables (it is not always clear how, for example, it can be determined whether an indirect object construction is simpler or more complex than a prepositional object, whereas the indirect object in this sense cannot be compared to declarative at all), I will assume with respect to the following discussion that structures which are well established are semantically and/or syntactically less complex for the child than those which are not.

Thus it seems that a conversation between mother and child starts at a low level of both semantic and syntactic complexity, and that after contact has been made both types of complexity tend to increase. This can be explained from the fact that in the first sentence of a discourse the topics of the conversation must be introduced and identified. Such a sentence contains, therefore, only new information and must be relatively simple. After the introduction of the conversational topic(s), the common contextual knowledge and therefore the complexity of the sentences increases.

Maternal sentences which are adequately responded to versus those which are not (adequately) responded to

From the vertical column totals (+ 8 versus + 51) it appears that maternal sentences which the child reacts to are generally less advanced both semantically and syntactically than those to which the child does not react. This suggests that

(1) the initial maternal sentence must be relatively simple if the child is to react (linguistically or not) (column 1 versus 2);

(2) non-spontaneous maternal sentences are apparently in many cases too complex for the child to react to (column 3 versus 4);

(3) initial maternal sentences must be close to the child's level in order for them to make contact with the child.

Maternal sentences and semantic complexity

From all the analyses one gets the impression that the variables '+ or − spontaneous' and '+ or − reaction' are more relevant for the realization than for the semantics of the maternal sentences. Although the score differences in the semantic assessment are less remarkable than those in the realization, they generally reflect the tendencies already discussed. There is just one irregularity in the semantic assessment which can be seen in all the four analyses; a maternal sentence which a child does not react to is semantically much less complex than (*a*) the non-spontaneous child sentence, and − more interestingly − than (*b*) the maternal sentence to which the child reacts. Furthermore, it appears that these maternal sentences are much more complex than the child's spontaneous sentences. The mothers evidently have to manoeuvre the semantic complexity of their sentences between the Scylla of too simple and the Charybdis of too complex in comparison with the child's non-spontaneous sentences.

The semantic complexity of the spontaneous sentences from the mother, to which the child does not react, is unexpectedly lower than the semantic complexity of the child's non-spontaneous sentences. This can only be explained by assuming that a decrease of semantic complexity in the mother's sentence corresponds with non-reaction on the part of the child and, furthermore, that the child's linguistic reactions are semantically more complex than those utterances of the mother to which he does not react. Sentences with too low semantic complexity are presumably not attractive enough for the child to want to continue the conversation.

Some general conclusions

The findings suggest that there is a subtle interplay in mother–child conversation by which the partners can influence each other's interactive role. Furthermore, it is clear that the frequencies with which the mother models various syntactic structures determine the order in which their children acquire syntactic rules. These frequencies, however, are largely determined by the child's semantic cues. Derivational (or syntactic) complexity does not apparently predict the order of acquisition as well as modelling frequencies, as it appears that syntactic complexity is derived from semantic complexity. This suggests that the child's syntactic development derives from two sources: his own growing cognitive semantic abilities and his mother's provision of syntactic information about how to express his progressively more complex ideas. The child's semantic development does not seem to depend upon modelling in the child's linguistic environment. The semantic structures occurring in the mother–child conversations were used initially not by the adult but by the child. This finding strongly supports the position of semantic primacy; it holds not only that semantic maturation comes to prevail over syntactic maturation but also that the former is a necessary prerequisite for the development of the latter, at least in the initial stages of language acquisition (Van der Geest, 1974b). Initial semantic development can be described as a natural progression with simpler semantic features being mastered before the more complex ones (see Van der Geest et al., unpublished; Bruner, 1975).

SYSTEMATIC ERRORS IN CHILD SPEECH

Systematic errors in child language are of primary importance in deciding whether language is acquired on the basis of an innate linguistic theory or by means of certain general learning procedures. In my thesis (Van der Geest, 1975c) I argued that there is no reason a priori to accept that the four possible error types, omission, redundancy, substitution and inversion result from mere linguistic reasoning. Furthermore, in Van der Geest (1975a, b) it is argued that word order differences can all be traced back to the typical learning strategy of semantic cognitive overgeneralization of regularities observed in the data base and, furthermore, that some syntactic structures (such as actives and passives, and comparatives and superlatives) are incorrectly used by children in free variation for a time since they do not at that particular developmental stage realize the underlying cognitive

differences (e.g. exclusion versus inclusion in comparative and superlative, respectively). These errors, therefore, are caused by non-
linguistic but cognitive semantic peculiarities of child development.

In this paper I would like to discuss in more detail a set of errors
produced by my older son Mark in several stages of his development,
most of which I have since noticed in the utterances of other children of the same age. All the errors reflect not so much a violation of
a linguistic rule as lack of pragmatic knowledge about how to use
language in certain concrete situations. Furthermore, a systematic relation will be demonstrated between the correct sentence the adult
could use in a certain situation to produce a given effect and the in-
felicitous utterance the child produces to attain the same effect.

Incorrect application of intonation

Initially Mark relied heavily upon intonational contours. They seemed
to indicate to him whether or not the adult was addressing him. A
speaker could, by using the exaggerated intonation patterns typical
in communication with children when speaking to an adult, cause
Mark to attend to him for a while. During this same period Mark produced the following sorts of deviant utterances:

(1) *Mee?* (literally: 'with ?'; Are you going with me?) (Age 1;6)

Mark used the question intonation in cases where it was evident from
bodily behavior that an imperative was meant. This phenomenon occurs regularly in almost all children's speech (see also Leopold,
1939–49; Ingram, 1971*b*). Adult sentences to Mark in the same situation had the same question intonation. The wrong intonation pattern was also used in the following observations:

(2) *Steenbok ?/Marmot ?/ Gems ?/Vlinder ?* (Ibex ?/Guinea pig ?/
    Chamois ?/Butterfly ?)

Mark produced these utterances while looking at a particular book in
which on every two-page-spread was a picture of an animal. Because
we thought these words were too difficult for him to produce, we
normally asked him whether or not a particular name belonged to
the picture he was looking at. It is likely that for this very reason
these particular pictures were always referred to by Mark with the
question intonation. A last type of sentence in which the use of intonation was different from the adult's system occurred in permission asking sentences. Some examples are

(3) *Aardbei ?* (Strawberry ?) (Age 1;9)
(4) *Kaas hebben ?* (literally: Cheese have ?) (Age 2;1)

with the meaning of 'can I have an *x*'. This reading is blocked in the adult system. If the adult does not use an auxiliary at the verbal level, he has to rely upon the imperative intonation, e.g. *Your passports, please!*, meaning something like 'May I have your passports, please!?'. Utterances (3) and (4) spoken by an adult could only be understood as 'Do you want to have an *x*'. However, the ultimate effect of the adult (3) and (4) spoken to the child, and of the child sentences (3) and (4), is the same: the child will ultimately have the strawberry or cheese. Thus to Mark the meaning of (3), whether it is spoken by the child to the adult or vice versa, is apparently something like

(3.*a*) Is it true that Mark will have a strawberry?

Systematic pragmatic deviation at the verbal level

At a later age we find the pragmatic aspects dealt with above explicated at the verbal level, for example

(5.*a*) *Doe ik dat even ?* (Am I just doing this ?)
(6.*a*) *Ik ga even kijken, he ?* (I am just having a look, aren't I ?)
(7.*a*) *Ik moet zitten!* (I have to sit down!)
(8.*a*) *Ik krijg niks meer!* (I don't get anything else!)
(9.*a*) *Goed vasthouden!* (Hold on well)

These utterances had the following meanings:

(5.*b*) *Mag ik dat even doen ?* (Can I just do this ?)
(6.*b*) *Mag ik even gaan kijken ?* (May I just have a look ?)
(7.*b*) *Ik wil zitten* (I want to sit down)
(8.*b*) *Ik wil niks meer hebben* (I don't want to have anything else)
(9.*b*) *Ik houd het goed vast* (I'll hold on to it well)

In these utterances the following pragmatic oppositions are ignored:

(5.*c*) Information versus permission question
(6.*c*) Tag versus permission question
(7.*c*) Necessity versus desiderative
(8.*c*) Assertion versus desiderative
(9.*c*) Imperative versus promise/assertion

Utterances (5)–(9) can also be explained from the adult model utterances, if we accept the hypothesis that the child literally adopts the adult's utterance in a specific situation, while neglecting the functional pragmatic roles in communication. With respect to (5.*a*) one should note that an adult asking a favor can say:

(5.*d*) *Doe jij dat even ?* (Literally: Will you just do this ?)

The same can be said for (6):

(6.*d*) *Ga je even kijken ?* (Are you going to have a look ?)

The adult model sentences for (7.*a*) and (8.*a*) are:

(7.*d*) *Jij moet gaan zitten* (You have to sit down)
(8.*d*) *Jij krijgt niks meer* (You don't get anything more)

and for (9.*a*) it is:

(9.*d*) *Hou het goed vast/vasthouden* (Hold on well) (Imperative/in-
  finitive form)

The child (*a*) utterances are similar to the adult (*d*) utterances in the sense that they all serve the same ultimate effect: viz. Mark will do something (5 and 6), he will sit down (7), he will not eat anything more (8) and he will hold onto the bannisters well (9).

In these sentences Mark literally adopted the adult model sentence insofar as the functional pragmatic aspect of the sentence was concerned, while changing the pronouns so that it was clear who was the actor, the goal, etc. In these cases Mark also neglected the communicative roles, in the sense that he failed to differentiate between the speaker or the addressee who desired the ultimate effect represented in the propositional structure.

Mark also used certain everyday expressions of common politeness in the appropriate fixed situations but disregarding that these expressions are all role-specific. Consider, for example,

(10) *Asjeblief/dank je wel* (please/thank you) (Age: 2;6)

Asjeblief ('please') is used in Dutch when the speaker offers something to the addressee. The addressee is expected to say in that situation after acceptance *dank je wel* ('Thank you'). During a short period when Mark was 30 months old, he interchanged the two expressions systematically. This interchange again suggests that Mark disregarded the communicative roles. Mark used *dank je wel* when offering something to an adult, who said *dank je wel* to him after acceptance. This expression was for Mark just an empty phrase accompanying a transfer in any direction in which he was involved. From these observations it is clear that Mark had at that time already started to internalize the rules of the social system. However, what he failed to explore at every new occasion was the role specificity of such expressions as (10); in other words he failed to recognize that his own role was different from that of the adults speaking to him given a fixed situation.

Systematic errors with respect to reference

The deviations to be discussed also represent violations of role-specific behavior. They differ, however, from the earlier observations in the sense that they all consider the lexicon in its relation to situational differences between speaker and hearer.

Initially, in the adult—child interaction, the personal and possessive pronouns are avoided by the adult. Instead of these pronouns such nouns as *papa* ('daddy') and *mama* ('mommy') and names are used to refer to people and animals (see Wills, this volume). This avoidance of pronouns by adults in their communications addressed to children in the earliest stages of their language development illustrates how adults adapt their language use to the child's rather limited linguistic abilities in order to be understood.

After Mark was first confronted with the personal and possessive pronouns he made some systematic errors relevant to our present discussion. Around age 2;2 he could be expected to say such things as

(11) *Jij doet dat* (You do that); meaning: 'I do that.'
(12) *Is dat van jou ?* (Is that yours ?); meaning: 'Is that mine ?'
(13) *Ik moet dat maken, jij kan dat niet.* (I must repair this; you can-
    not repair it); meaning: 'You must repair this, I cannot repair it.'
(14) *Is dit jouw melk ?* (Is this your milk); meaning: 'Is this my milk ?'

The explanation for this peculiar phenomenon is quite simple. In the adults' speech addressed to Mark *jij/jouw/jou* (you/your/you) refer-red always to Mark. This generalization is copied in (11)—(14). *Ik/mij/mijn* (I/me/my) on the contrary always referred to someone other than Mark, viz. the adult partner of the conversation. This generalization is copied in (13). Mark once again adapted to the adult model too literally, disregarding the textual function of the personal and possessive pronouns with respect to their reference to speaker and addressee in the sense that *I* becomes *you* when the speaker becomes the addressee.

Mark's usage of the locative adverbs *hier/daar* (here/there) showed a similar mistake. Although the exact applicabilities of these adverbs in their opposition are difficult to determine, it is at any rate obvious that if one wishes to refer to his own position, the usage of *here* is mandatory. Until age 2;6 Mark always, however, used *daar* (there) when referring to his own position. For example, once answering the question *Mark waar ben je ?* (Mark, where are you ?) he said:

(15) *Ik ben daar, in de slaapkamer* (I am there, in the bedroom)

This phenomenon can once again be explained from Mark's too literal adaptation of the model sentence. The adult speaker would of course use the word *daar* (there) to refer to the position of the addressee (in this case: Mark).

Similarly, Mark often ignored contextual conditions in using time adverbs. For example,

(16) *Heeft het buurmeisje vanavond opgepast ?* (Did the girl next
     door baby-sit this evening ?)

spoken by Mark the morning after the day he was told that the girl next door would take care of him that evening. In this case he overlooked that *this* of *this evening* refers to the day in which (16) is produced.

A last illustrative example occurred when Mark was almost 33 months old. The situation was as follows: Mark was on the first floor, mommy was on the ground floor and daddy (that's me) was on the second floor. Mark wanted to go upstairs, but mommy thought that too dangerous:

mommy: (17) *Mark hou je goud vast aan de leuning en kom naar
             beneden* (Mark, hold onto the banisters well and come
             downstairs)
Mark: (18) *Ik hou me goed vast aan de leuning en kom naar boven*
             (I hold onto the banisters well and come upstairs)

In this case Mark adopted the adult sentence almost literally. The correct adult utterance in this case must be

(18.a) *Ik hou me goed vast aan de leuning en ga naar boven* (I hold
       onto the banisters well and *go* upstairs)

In this case Mark disregarded the fact that the appropriate use of *come* as opposite to *go* implies that certain conditions with respect to the direction into which the motion takes place are met. The appropriate use of *come* in promise sentences implies that the motion takes place into the direction of the addressee (18.a).

Conclusions

The paraphrases of (1) and (2) are not adequate in the light of their interpretation within context and situation. The bodily behavior accompanying (1) contrasted with the question intonation. The fact that Mark never failed to name the pictures in the book correctly means that even a question intonation arising from uncertainty must be doubted in the production of (2). For both cases then, the intonation was misleading. This was, however, not the case for all utterances produced at this time: most of the time Mark used the correct intonation patterns. The alternative explanation for the use of the special intonation in (1) and (2) is that the parents used this intonation in the same situations. An adult, for example, might well say to a child *Ga je mee?* even in cases when the child's answer *Nee* will not be accepted or expected. But in that case the adult's bodily behavior may not contrast with the question intonation. In (2) a normal presupposition of the question, viz. that the speaker does not know the answer, is violated, as occurs normally in a teaching situation. In both cases (1) and (2) the child apparently failed to notice the subtle functions of language use in this early period. The adult's utterance *Ga je mee?* and *Is dat een steenbok?* were apparently understood as an imperative and as assertive respectively.

In (3) and (4) the principle of sentence realization, based as it is on stress preference, may cause the understressed words *mag/ik/een* and *hebben* (may/I/a/ and have) not to be realized. Although this would explain these two utterances it seems more likely that they, like the other examples, result from the child's general tendency to use the literal maternal sentence, given a certain situation.

The example utterances indicate that the child initially regarded an adult model utterance that is quite specific for certain fixed situations as directly available for him to be used in the same situation. This interpretation suggests that the child at this stage was not aware that speaker and hearer play different roles in communication, and, therefore that he was not completely aware of his own individuality in communication. The utterances (5)—(9) and an analysis of the errors they include (Table 4.3) illustrate this more explicitly.

In all these utterances either the speaker—hearer roles, the grammatical communicative function (such as assertive, imperative and the like) or some pragmatic element like the desiderative auxiliary is inadequately realized. Although all the utterances were grammatically completely correct, the conversational postulates, determined by the sentence qualifier (see Van der Geest, 1974*b*; Seuren, 1969) and the qualifier, are violated. We could say that the child has not yet

Table 4.3   *Error analysis of observations (5)–(9)*

Observation	Sentence qualifier		Qualifier
	Role	Function	
(5)	+	+	−
(6)	+	+	−
(7)	+	+	−
(8)	+	+	−
(9)	+	−	−

mastered the pragmatic system of language use, but such a statement explains only that the sentences used are incorrect. What must be explained are the regularities in the errors under discussion. The following points are of interest for this explanation:

(1) these errors are used in fixed situations;

(2) at the propositional level (the state of affairs) the roles are well indicated;

(3) at the pragmatic level the role references are not consistently indicated;

(4) the result of both the appropriate and the incorrect speech act is the same;

(5) the adult model sentences covering the fixed situations are well formed.

In other words, the propositional structure is correctly dealt with and at the pragmatic level the resultative function is validly accounted for. The way in which the result is arrived at as it has to be expressed by the sentence qualifier, and the qualifier, is either disregarded or literally adopted from the adult model. The child at this level of his development is aware of and could express the state of affairs that he intended to produce by speaking. Furthermore, these observations support the hypothesis of semantic primacy as worked out, for example, by Macnamara (1972): what the child still has to learn after having mastered the appropriate expression of cognitive semantic structures is how to use them in communication. That Mark during this stage fell back on the adult's communicative role points to the fact that he was only beginning to acquire knowledge of conversational structures.

As far as the primacy of semantics over syntax is concerned the problem looks more complicated. Although Slobin's (1973a) statement that new forms express old functions and that new functions are first expressed by old forms (old functions apparently in the meaning of the appropriate and already implicitly understood and expressed function), there are some observations (see Van der Geest, 1975 *a*, *b*; and Systematic errors in child speech, above) that illustrate that the opposite may also occur, for example

(19) *Eerst moet ik eraf gesprongen worden en dan moet jij eraf gesprongen worden* (Mark, 3;2)
(literally: First I have to be jumped off and then you have to be jumped off)
(meaning: First I have to jump off and then you have to jump off)

and:

(20) *Ik wil optillen* (Joost, 3;1)
(literally: I want to lift)
(meaning: I want to be lifted)

In the first observation the passive was used without underlying adequate passive meaning; the actor remained the grammatical subject: in the second utterance the active was used without underlying adequate active meaning; the logical object became the grammatical subject. (It should be admitted that Mark's parents often deliberately used the passive voice to him around the age of 3;0.) Such contrasting observations in different children may lead to the hypothesis that children may take different routes to adult mastery of more complicated structures like passives, superlatives, etc.

Psychologically Mark's literal adaptation to his model is more difficult to explain within current developmental theories. It is common sense, of course, that the child is developing from an almost totally dependent creature, perhaps not aware of his own individuality, to a person fully aware of his individuality and uniqueness. How and along what lines such a development takes place is not quite clear, let alone how this development influences language acquisition.

Piaget's (1951) theory may cast light on this developmental process. Initially the child's imitation is characterized as occurring without the child being aware that he is imitating. Rather, it is as if the child tends to repeat the act believing it to be his own. This characterization suggests that the child does not differentiate between his model and his 'self' as yet. The final development occurring at the sixth stage of the sensori-motor period is, according to Piaget, 'deferred imitation' (i.e. a covert imitation), meaning that the imitation does not necessarily take place directly after the model act. Semantic primacy would suggest that the child initially does not distinguish between the specific roles in communication, because he is not sufficiently aware of his own individuality. What he is learning is a standard repertoire of structural frames derived from his model, covering the state of affairs that he wishes to be established. The standard repertoire can be characterized as a set of deferred imitations in the sense that the literal model frames are applied. Semantically, however, the present observations can be characterized by Piaget's term 'representative imitation'. In this type of imitation reproductive imagination (i.e. the mental activity by which the role of the adult in the past can be reproduced by the child in such a way that he plays the adult role) is presupposed. Within such a framework the systematic errors discussed above can be accounted for, as can be illustrated with (6):

(6.*a*) *Ik ga even kijken, he ?*
    (I am just having a look, aren't I ?)
    deferred imitation: NP$_{(agent)}$ *ga even kijken, he ?*
    representative imagination: QU(estion) PERM(ission) NP$_{(agent)}$
    ga even kijken
    productive rule: *jij* ⇒ *ik*

If we accept this view of language acquisition, then it is clear that the adult's role in the child's emergence of the communicative system is not insignificant; not only does the adult offer the model sentences, but also the child 'imitates' the adult, in other words accepts the adult as his model. Furthermore, because the role system we are dealing with could only be learned from conversations among adults, it is apparently the adult speech directed to the child himself that serves as the actual data base for him to learn his language from.

DISCUSSION

The preceding suggests that the child's semantic cognitive development may play an overall important role in his acquisition of language. From the first study it seems that the child's semantic development determines what kinds of syntactic structures occur in the data base; semantic development thereby determines what kinds of structures a child will use one or two months later. From the second study it is clear that systematic errors in the child's speech, which can all be related to the adult model, can be accounted for by the presence or absence of certain (semantic or pragmatic) knowledge.

    It is clear that both studies cover only a small number of the problems involved in the establishment of an explanatory model of language learning. Such an explanatory model must be set up as a dynamic device (or system) in order to be capable of accounting for all kinds of changes in the child's communicative system. Explanatory adequacy can therefore be attained only by measuring a system's prognostic capacity. This measurement can be achieved by comparison of the successive child grammars in terms of the dynamic device (see Fig. 4.1; for the rest of the proposed tentative model see the text further on.)

Most models developed so far start with a notion of innateness and (probably therefore) all fail in prognostic capactiy. Changes in the child's language system are generally referred to as changes in the child's language acquisition theory: from word-dictionary to sentence-dictionary, from a structuralistic pivot-open grammar to an immediate constituent grammar somehow covering the basic grammatical relations and incorporating the technical notion of semi-grammaticalness, etc., and then to a transformational grammar, and from a topic-comment grammar to a transformational grammar (McNeill, 1966b, 1970; Gruber, 1967; Menyuk, 1969). It is not made sufficiently clear why such theoretical changes are mandatory on the basis of the data, nor how children could arrive at such changes in their theories. Even if a consistent theory is applied in formulating child grammars in different developmental stages, it appears that successive grammars are difficult to relate to each other (Bloom, 1970).

It seems reasonable to assume that a valid dynamic device should be able to deal appropriately with at least the following three topics (see also Fig. 4.1):

(a) The nature of the data base. This can be exemplified by the child's learning of morphology. In the initial stages of language acquisition the child uses only the infinitive verb form even when a third person singular past gerund meaning is intended (Brown, 1973). In the next relevant stage the child seems to have mastered the correct strong and irregular verb forms, e.g. *was/had/gave/eaten*, etc. At a later age the child uses the regular verb forms correctly, although he may generalize them to the strong and irregular verbs: *gived/bringed*, etc. After that period the child starts to use both the irregular and strong forms again. In this stage new mistakes can occur initially, for example

(21) *zingen, zong, gezongen*/sing, sang, sung.
     brengen, *brong, *gebrongen/bring, *brang, *brung
     (correct forms: *brengen, bracht, gebracht*/bring, brought,
     brought)

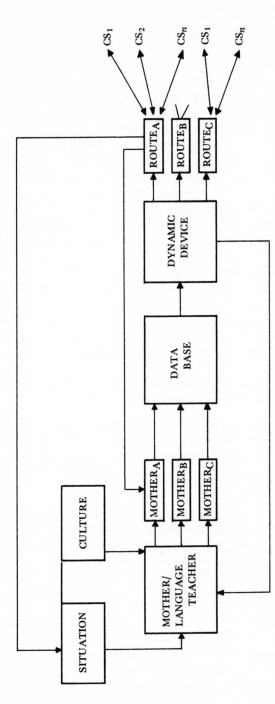

Fig. 4.1. Successive child grammars (or communicative systems (CS)) from the perspective of explanatory adequacy.

If we accept that the irregular verbs are most frequently used in speech, and especially in early mother–child conversation in which initially very simple content is communicated, then the above mistakes can easily be explained from changes in the data base: initially the child is almost exclusively confronted with a small number of verbs which are generally irregular, and the child has to memorize their forms as individual lexical items. Thereafter — as the child indicates that his range of possible conversational topics has expanded (see the first section above) — a larger number of regular verbs will occur in the data base. The mother, even if she were aware of these changes in her speech to the child, cannot control such a change, as she will not produce ungrammatical forms.

(b) The relevant characteristics of the adult 'language teacher'. Some of these characteristics are the adult strategies used in the interaction with the language-learning child (e.g. correction, expansion, modelling, repetition and the interaction continuing strategy, see the first section), the intelligent provision of data to the child (from simple to more complex, see the first section), culturally and sub-culturally determined simplifying strategies, and some personality features relevant to the interaction with a specific language learner and therefore to the child's language development (see also Nelson, 1973).

An example of one of the culturally-determined kinds of simplification occurring in mothers' speech to children is the familiar form

(22) *Mama* (= *ik*) *zal de auto wel even maken* (Mommy (= I) will repair the car).
(23) *Mark* (= *jij*) *mag het doen* (Mark (= you) may do it)

It is clear that at a certain stage such simplifications make mother–child conversations easier. But they lead to the child also using constructions in which pronouns are avoided. Furthermore, it is even doubtful whether such a strategy is advantageous in the long term, as it seems that children always provided with the correct adult usage of pronouns do not show such ungrammaticalities as

(24) You (I) may do this
(25) I (= mommy = you) must repair this

(c) Relevant characteristics of the language learner. Some of the characteristics of the language learner which may affect the course of acquisition are the child's language-learning principles (e.g. generalization, analogy, imitation, etc.), his interactive strategies (e.g. reaction versus non-reaction, see above), and certain personality characteristics relevant to the interaction with specific language teachers (see also Nelson, 1973).

As far as the child's personality is concerned, the dynamic device should account for the different routes children may take to language maturity. As the observations (19) and (20) may suggest, Mark and Joost developed the passive structures along different lines. Mark built up his repertoire through the process of (deferred) imitation and reproductive imagination (see above) notwithstanding the fact that his semantic and pragmatic systems were not yet adequate to the speech he was producing. This did not only hold for the pragmatic deviations dealt with in the second section and for the passive construction, but also for his use of the superlative structure and the comparative structure and such intersentential relations as causal, consecutive, etc. Joost, on the contrary, developed his communicative and semantic and cognitive abilities more rapidly than his syntactic ability, as indicated by his expression of passive meaning in an active sentence (10). This difference between Mark and Joost might also correspond to Nelson's distinction 'expressive' versus 'referential' as it appears that Mark and Joost differ on this dimension as well. It will be evident that different attitudes to the possibilities of language usage (see also in connection with the first section) may lead to different routes in language development.

5 Mother, I'd rather do it myself: some effects and non-effects of maternal speech style[1]

ELISSA L. NEWPORT

Department of Psychology, University of California, San Diego,
La Jolla, California 92093, USA

HENRY GLEITMAN

Department of Psychology, University of Pennsylvania, Philadelphia,
Pennsylvania 19174, USA

LILA R. GLEITMAN

Graduate School of Education, University of Pennsylvania,
Philadelphia, Pennsylvania 19174, USA

How is natural language learned? A major problem in accounting for this feat, approximated by even the dullest child but not even the brightest chimpanzee, arises from the contrast between the input and the final product: speech forms and their privileges of occurrence in a language are so varied that any heard sample will support countless generalizations about the items, structures and meanings that are to be acquired. How could one get the right data for constructing all and only English, if one were learning English; Basque, if one were learning Basque?

Some theorists have approached this dilemma strictly in terms of the interaction of this heard speech with language-specific mental structures in the child learner. They stress that the child has rich and specific hypotheses for evaluating incoming linguistic data; i.e. he will entertain only certain candidate generalizations among those that are logically possible, owing to innate language-learning predispositions, and hence he will construct only certain grammars from a wide variety of sample inputs (see, for discussion, Chomsky, 1965; McNeill, 1966a; Fodor, Bever, & Garrett, 1974). Probably no one will contest at least a weak version of this position: to account for why human children but not house-cats acquire language it is necessary to look to species-specific and perhaps task-specific ways of responding to linguistic input.

But some recent investigators concentrate on another issue, one that is also indisputably relevant in accounting for language learning: they study the communicative settings in which the child acquires his language competence. This broader focus has led, for example, to studies of gestural and postural interactions between mothers and preverbal infants as precursors and possibly organizers of the speech-acquisition process to follow (Bruner, 1974/5). And in particular, this broader focus on the communicative environment has led to more explicit studies of the child's strictly linguistic environment — the utterances he hears (see Snow, this volume, for a review of this literature). A claim that has been made, on the basis of such studies, is that the child is not at first confronted with all the complexity and variety of natural language. It is asserted, on the contrary, that mothers introduce forms and meanings to the learning child in a principled way, thus narrowing the candidate generalizations about language structure the learner is in a position to hit upon (Levelt, 1975). If this assertion is correct, it might bear on the kinds of procedures the child must be supposed to bring to the language-learning situation.

In the discussion here, we will accept and hopefully clarify both these kinds of claim: to some extent, the child is biased to organize incoming linguistic data in specified ways; and to some extent, the mother preorganizes these data, essentially by speaking in certain ways and in certain communicative settings. Moreover, we argue in favor of a further mechanism supporting language acquisition: the child has means for restricting, as well as organizing, the flow of incoming linguistic data; he filters out some kinds of input and selectively listens for others. This is a sense of 'preprogramming' for language acquisition that has not been widely considered (but see Shipley, Smith & Gleitman, 1969; Slobin, 1973a; Ervin-Tripp, 1973, for discussion of this possibility).

The investigation reported here focuses on maternal speech style and the influence this exerts on the course and rate of language acquisition. The interest in maternal speech, widespread in recent years, arises on very clear grounds. Part of the argument that language learning must be guided by rich and restrictive hypotheses about universal grammar turns on a consideration of naturally-occurring adult speech. Putatively, this forms the child's data for constructing his language. But ordinary speech is a haphazard, disorganized sample of sentences in the language. Also, this sample is partly degenerate (containing false starts, mumbles and ungrammatical sentences) and is only loosely tied to referents and situations the child observer could perceive, or likely conceive from context (telephone conversations about repairing the lawn mower, talk about zebras that goes on when out of the zoo). If these are the environmental circumstances, and if language acquisition is nonetheless successful for all within narrowly circumscribed time limits (and it is, in gross outline, despite some individual differences in vocabulary and overall fluency), then the learners must have been strongly predisposed to construct only certain outcomes. That is, this argument is to the effect that children construct the same language knowledge under widely varying environmental influences — the claim is that the environment need not be narrowly specified, nor does the input need to be ordered in any principled way.

This conclusion can be brought into some question if it can be shown that naturally-occurring adult speech does not constitute the child's linguistic ambience, his effective environment. For example, it has been suggested that the child may listen primarily to high-pitched speech, to speech accompanied by pointing, eye-contact and other gestures, to speech which begins by calling his name and to speech which contains some familiar words. That is, he may attend selectively when he has reason to suppose that he is being addressed, and such speech may have special properties good for language learning. But of course this comes down to claiming that the child has certain internal predispositions that aid language acquisition — in this variant, a kind of filter on input.

The view that language learning is heavily influenced by forces from outside the child rather than by dispositions inside him is best made if it can be shown that there is a language teacher who, purposely or not, presents data to the child in an orderly way. The prime candidate is the mother. In its strongest form, this claim is that the child can construct language knowledge only from a very carefully circumscribed kind of data, presented to the child selectively in correspondence with his language growth. Hence the best beginning argument in favor of an acquisition process that demands highly specific kinds of environmental support would be the finding that maternal speech is not just adult speech.

Many recent investigations do reveal that mothers' speech differs from speech among adults (e.g. Drach, 1969; Pfuderer, 1969; Phillips, 1970; Remick, 1971; Broen, 1972; Snow, 1972; Sachs, Brown & Salerno, 1976; Newport, 1976; Snow, this volume). Similar effects are apparently found for any speaker addressing a very young child (Shatz & Gelman, 1973; Sachs & Devin, 1976). This stylistic variant of everyday speech is systematic enough to deserve its own name; we have called it 'Motherese'.

In the first sections of this report, we will take a close look at the taxonomy of Motherese and its adjustment to the child's stage of language learning. The data for this inquiry were collected in the context of natural conversation among mothers, their children and one of us (ELN). We simply chatted with the mothers and children, and then compared the mothers' speech to the experimenter with their speech to the children. We also computed correlations between language measures of the children and the maternal speech, simple correlations which presumably reflect adjustments of maternal speech style to listener sophistication. These procedures allow us to raise some questions in principle about how Motherese might affect specifics of language learning. Our conclusions are more modest than those of some writers on this topic. We find that Motherese is hard to characterize as a simplified teaching language on the basis of its structure and content. To the contrary, some of our findings retrieve the intuitions of every grandmother-in-the-street: the properties of Motherese derive largely from the fact that the mother wants her child to do as he is told right now, and very little from the fact that she wants him to become a fluent speaker in future. Whatever influences Motherese exerts on language growth have to operate within these intentional constraints. It would not be surprising, therefore, if certain differences between Motherese and adult talk, no matter how striking and uniform, are inconsequential for the child's linguistic development.

In later sections of this report, we ask more directly to what degree and in what respects Motherese influences language learning. Notice that the finding that Motherese exists cannot by itself show that it influences language growth, or even that this special style is necessary to acquisition — despite frequent interpretations to this effect that have appeared in the literature. After all, Motherese is as likely an effect on the mother by the child as an effect on the child by the mother. To approach these problems of cause and effect, we held a second interview with our mother—child pairs six months following the first one. We now were in a position to compute a language growth score for each child for this time interval, and to compare this against the mother's speech style at the first interview. But some ticklish questions of interpretation would arise if these comparisons were made in terms of simple correlations between mother's usage and child's language growth.

To understand the problem here, suppose we were able to discover certain speech forms that could rightly be called Basic Motherese. And suppose we found that some mothers of our subject children use these forms more than other mothers. Suppose, finally, that the children of precisely those mothers who used Basic Motherese most consistently were the children who showed the greatest language growth during the six-month interval. Can we now assume that the use of Basic Motherese was responsible for this accelerated growth? No, on many grounds. One cause for skepticism is that Basic Motherese may be used more when the child is least sophisticated linguistically, but also the child may grow the fastest the less his linguistic sophistication, i.e. the more he has left to learn. Then the conclusions from these hypothetical findings could only be (*a*) a mother speaks to a linguistically unsophisticated speaker–hearer in Basic Motherese; and (*b*) a linguistically unsophisticated speaker–hearer moves very quickly, over time, toward increased linguistic sophistication – language growth curves decelerate. It would not follow that (*c*) Basic Motherese is what caused this burst of new language knowledge in the unsophisticated party. For many reasons of this sort, any assessment of the influence of maternal speech on child language growth requires analyses more complex than simple correlations.

Our approach to disentangling cause and effect in interpreting our findings derived from the convenient fact that not all our mother subjects were the same, even when differences among them due to differences among their offspring are left aside. Beyond the adjustment of mothers each to her own child's abilities (revealed in the initial correlational analysis) there remained some variance in maternal speech styles which appeared to be attributable only to individual differences among the mothers. It is this residual variance that constitutes differences in the linguistic environments of our child subjects, independent of environmental differences due simply to differences in the children themselves. In addition, not all our child subjects' growth rates were the same, even when differences among them due to differences in their age and absolute levels of achievement are left aside. It is this residual variance in growth rates that constitutes individual difference in the speed of learning, independent of whether the child is a beginner or more advanced at the initial interview. Accordingly, we equated statistically for differences in Motherese and differences in child growth rate due to children's differing ages and language knowledge by simultaneously partialling out effects of both these factors. The effect of this procedure is to equalize all subjects on these dimensions — it is now 'as though' all subjects had been identical in age and language skill at the first interview, for such differences as existed have been erased. Now, correlations between the mothers' usage at interview 1 and language growth differences among these equalized children can tell us something about how the mother influences the child. Our discussion of how Motherese contributes to language learning is therefore based on such a second-order correlational analysis (see 'Procedure' for other details).

The conclusions from this analysis are again modest, partly because limitations on both sample size and procedure preclude strong claims, and partly because one cannot be certain of cause–effect relationships from correlational analyses, no matter how complex. But the pattern of the findings does support some suggestions about how Motherese influences learning. Summarizing these findings: individual differences among mothers in communicative styles seem to influence language learning in complex ways. An interaction between the child's listening biases and the mother's presentation of aspects of syntactic structure predicts the rate at which the child learns certain language-specific constructions. But at the same time many general properties of emerging language competence seem to be insensitive to characteristics of the maternal speech environment.

PROCEDURE

METHOD

Fifteen mothers and their young daughters were visited in two two-hour sessions held six months apart. At the first recording, the children fell into three age groups (12—15 months, 18—21 months and 24—27 months). All of the families were middle class. The mothers were initially told that we were interested in their children's language learning, and that conversation should simply be 'natural'. After the second interview, we told the mothers that their own speech had been part of the investigation, and asked them whether we had their approval to use the recorded data. All agreed. The entire sessions were transcribed by the experimenter and a research assistant. The analysis of Motherese was carried out on a sample segment of the first interview (approximately 100 utterances from each mother to her child and 50 utterances from mother to experimenter). Analysis of the effects of individual mothers' styles was first carried out on the same sample (as reported in Newport, Gleitman & Gleitman, 1975) and then cross-validated on the entire transcripts, as well as on even—odd page split-halves of the transcripts.

CODING

The mothers' utterances

Maternal utterances were separated into those addressed to the experimenter and those addressed to the child. A set of utterances for each listener type was coded for well-formedness, sentence length, structural complexity (indexed, for preliminary purposes, as number of sentence-nodes (S-nodes) per utterance and derivational length), psycholinguistic complexity (explicitness with which the surface form preserves the underlying structure; see Bever, 1970), sentence type (declarative, imperative, etc.), intelligibility, frequency of self-repetition and imitation of the child, deixis (the use of linguistic variables to make reference, e.g. '*This* is the apple'), and expansion (the case in which the mother repeats what the child has said, but corrects his 'telegraphic' version into well-formed adult English; see Brown, 1973). Table 5.1 provides example maternal sentences and their coding assignments.

The children's utterances

Child speech was coded for syntactic complexity, estimated through mean length of utterance (MLU), mean noun-phrase frequency and length, mean verb-phrase frequency and length, inflection of noun-phrases (plural marking), and auxiliary structure (modals and tense marking) for both the first session and the succeeding one six months later. Table 5.2 shows example child utterances and their coding assignments. In addition, total vocabulary size at each session was estimated. Finally, 'growth scores' were obtained for each of the children by computing the difference between the first and second interviews on each of these measures.

Table 5.1 *Manner of scoring for measures of mothers' speech*

Measure	Manner of scoring	Example
Well-formedness		
Grammatical utterance	% of all utterances which are complete, colloquially acceptable sentences	*What do you wanna eat?*
Sentence fragment	% of all utterances which consist only of isolated constituents or phrases	*The apple.* *Under the table.*
Interjection	% of all utterances which are one of the following: yes, no, uh-huh, uh-uh, right, okay, etc., spoken in isolation	*Okay.*
Ungrammatical	% of all utterances which are ill-formed even in colloquial speech	*The boy Susan didn't do it.*
Unanalyzable	% of all utterances which were either incomplete and broken off in mid-stream or were either partially or wholly unintelligible	*He said that he. . .*
Sentence complexity		
MLU	Mean number of words/utterance	*That's a big dog* = 5
S-modes/utterance	Mean number of underlying sentences/ utterance	*I think that's a big dog* = 2
Sentence type		
Declarative	% of grammatical utterances	*You can sing a song.*
Yes–no question	% of grammatical utterances	*Can you sing a song?*

Table 5.1 (*continued*)

Measure	Manner of scoring	Example
Imperative	% of grammatical utterances	*Sing a song.*
Wh- question	% of grammatical utterances	*What can you sing?*
Deixis	% of grammatical utterances	*That's a dog.*
Discourse features		
Expansion	% of all utterances which repeat, in whole or in part, utterances of the *child* and in addition add extra morphemes	C: Boy dog. M: *Yes, that's the boy's dog.*
Repetition	% of all utterances which repeat, in whole or in part, previous *maternal* utterances (i.e. self-repetition)	M: That's a dog. *That's a big dog.*

Table 5.2 *Manner of scoring for measures of children's speech*

Measure	Manner of scoring	Example
		The boy can hit balls.
MLU	Mean number morphemes/utterance	6
Noun-phrases/utterance	Mean number noun-phrases/utterance	2 *boy, balls*
Words/noun-phrase	Mean number words/noun-phrase	*Boy* = 1, *balls* = 1, mean = 1.0
Noun inflections/noun-phrase	Mean number noun inflections/noun-phrase (plurals)	*Boy* = 0, *balls* = 1, mean = .5
Verbs/utterance	Mean number main verbs/utterance	1 *hit*
Auxiliaries/verb	Mean number auxiliary words/verb	1 *can*
Inflections/verb	Mean number verb inflections/verb (past tense, past participle)	0
Vocabulary size	Total number word types (as opposed to tokens) produced during the interview	5

ANALYSIS

A description of Motherese

Selected samples of the mothers' speech from interview 1 were subjected first to an overall descriptive taxonomy, according to the proportions of utterances that fell into the various coding categories. In addition, the data were analyzed for the adjustment of maternal speech to gross listener differences (by considering differences to adult listeners versus child listeners) and also to finer distinctions of the age, syntactic usage and vocabulary size of the child listeners (by noting the simple correlations between mothers' speech features and child measures at interview 1). These analyses of the speech from interview 1 form the basis for describing Motherese and its 'tuning' to the child's current stage of language sophistication. Results of this analysis were reported in detail in Newport (1976) and are summarized in 'The nature of Motherese' below.

Effects of Motherese on the child's language growth

The next, and in some sense the primary, task was to ask whether individual differences in mothers' speech predicted the child's language growth. For reasons stated in the introductory remarks, this task calls for more than a simple correlational analysis between various features of the mother's speech during the first observation (e.g. the mean length of her child-directed utterances) and changes in the child's linguistic output over the six-month span (e.g. the increase in the mean length of the child's utterances). In fact, we obtained many such correlations. The trouble is that these correlations may not reflect an effect of the mother upon the child's language growth at all. Instead, they may be spurious by-products of several other factors. The child's language growth was assessed by a difference score, but the children differed in their starting ages and levels. The initial analysis (see above) revealed that to some extent mothers adjusted their speech to such factors. Since this is so, the correlations between indices of mothers' speech and children's growth rates may reflect the joint operation of (a) the adjustment of the mothers to their child's age and initial linguistic level, and (b) the fact that the amount of the child's improvement over a given time span depends upon his age and base line at the beginning of the interval (this must be so since the language acquisition curves are not linear). We therefore equated starting levels statistically by simultaneously partialling out both the child's age during the first interview and his level on any given linguistic measurement at that time. The resulting partial correlations ($r_{xy \cdot ab}$) are our primary means for assessing how individual differences in maternal speech styles effect accelerated or delayed growth of the child listeners.

Cross-validation

Leaving aside the inherent difficulties of assessing cause and effect from correlational studies, the procedure just described has another problem: the partial correlations obtained were those statistically 'significant' effects that derived from comparing a very large number of variables (child and mother measures) against each other. Under the circumstances, some of the significant correlations would be expected by chance alone. It was obviously necessary to cross-validate these results. As a first procedure, we analyzed the entire transcripts (including the segments that formed the basis for the initial analysis), now looking only at those maternal variables that seemed to be relevant to early stages of language growth on the basis of the earlier results. These included the significant effects from the initial analysis as well as certain variables first found not to yield an effect, but theoretically likely candidates for affecting growth. The partial correlations with child measures were again computed on these data. In a second procedure, we conducted the same analyses on two halves of the protocols separately, on an even—odd page, split-half basis. With minor exceptions, which will be noted, the results of these procedures reproduced those of the original analysis. It should be noted, however, that these procedures are not enough. A further cross-validation, now underway, involves a replication of the entire procedure using new subjects. Since this step is incomplete, the conclusions presented here must be considered tentative.

CHARACTERISTICS OF THE CHILD POPULATION

The subject children, ranging from 12 to 27 months at the first interview, varied quite a bit in their speech. Some children spoke solely in one-word utterances, while others used many multi-word utterances (MLU ranged from 1.00 to 3.46 with a mean at 1.65; the mean upper bound on sentence length was 4.67). The mean number of noun-phrases per utterance ranged from 0.80 to 1.47 (mean = 1.02). The mean number of morphemes per noun-phrase ranged from 1.00 to 1.46 with a mean at 1.17. Mean verbs per utterance ranged from zero to 0.65 (mean = 0.23) and the mean morphemes in the verb structure (when present) ranged from 1.00 to 1.75 (mean = 1.17). The number of different words used during the whole interview ranged from 3 to 210, with a mean at 84. Almost all of these measures intercorrelated significantly (not surprising, since few of them are independent of each other), and MLU was the single measure that intercorrelated most highly with all the others (again, not mystifying, since it is independent of none of the others). Overall then, there was a reasonable range of primitive speech to compare against mothers' speech.

THE NATURE OF MOTHERESE

THE SYNTACTIC PATTERN OF MATERNAL SPEECH

Like other investigators, we found that the speech of mothers to young children looks at first glance 'simpler' than speech to adults. For one thing, it is short (mean MLU was 4.24, while the mean MLU to the experimenter was 11.94, $p < 0.001$). Further, Motherese is highly intelligible: only four in every hundred utterances to the child were impossible to transcribe because of mumbles and slurs. (The percentage of unanalyzable adult-directed speech was 9%, again a highly significant difference between the corpora types.) And finally, the speech of mothers to children is unswervingly well formed. Only one utterance out of 1500 spoken to the children was a disfluency. Differences between the adult-directed and child-directed corpora are on this dimension again highly significant ($p < 0.001$). Yet it should be noted that the difference in proportions here is absolutely small and unimpressive: contrary to some expectations, disfluencies (true garble) in the adult-directed corpora were only 5% of all utterances. The majority of utterances to both listener types were *bona fide* grammatical sentences (60% of those to the children, 58% of those to the adults). The rest were well-formed isolated phrases (e.g. 'the ball' and 'under the table', as naming utterances and answers to queries) and stock phrases and interjections (e.g. 'Ooops!', 'OK' and 'Thank you'). In summary: adult–adult utterances are enormously longer than those to little children; a higher level of intelligibility is maintained for the children, probably (although we did not measure this) as a consequence of slower speech rate with resulting diminution of junctural deformations at morpheme boundaries; and finally, there are fewer disfluencies in child-directed speech.

A preliminary guess from this quick brush with the facts might be that Motherese is a simplified teaching language, designed to inculcate

the forms of English by presenting easy examples to little minds. But
if this is so, there are a number of perplexing characteristics of
Motherese. To understand these, we have to be more specific about
what could be meant by a 'simple style' of speech.

Suppose one were teaching a foreign language and wished to write
a systematic supporting curriculum. A good simple principle might
be to present canonical sentences of the new language first. For
English, these would surely be the simple active declarative sentences,
with Subject—Verb—Object ordering of the grammatical relations.
But Motherese is not simple on this principle. It is more complex
than ordinary talk among adults. While only 30 % of mother-to-child
utterances are declaratives, a whopping 87 % of adult-directed utterances are declaratives. Furthermore, 28 % of clauses in the Motherese
utterances are undeformed, i.e. involve no optional movement or
deletion transformations. But fully 45 % of clauses in the adult-directed utterances are undeformed. Put anotherway, length of derivational history would be longer for the Motherese utterances. Admittedly,
the attempt to identify 'psychological complexity' with derivational
length has a checkered history in psycholinguistic research. We are
not putting it forward as a 'good' measure. (See Brown & Hanlon,
1970, for an alternative measure of 'cumulative complexity' that is
rather more natural.) The attempt here is to give some explicit statement of what might be meant by the frequent claim that Motherese
represents a syntactic simplification of everyday speech. One candidate is derivational length. We consider further candidates below —
all will fail to predict in any detail the characteristics of Motherese.

Consider a second principle for the foreign-language curriculum:
even if you don't want to begin teaching with simple active declaratives, at least introduce one new construction at a time rather than all
mixed together. But on this principle Motherese is again more complicated than normal speech. There is a wider range of sentence types
and more inconsistency to children than to the experimenter. For
example, questions and imperatives are almost non-existent in the
adult-directed corpus, thus narrowing the range of types, but 18 % of
the Motherese utterances are imperatives and 44 % are questions of
various kinds. In what sense, then, is Motherese a simple form of
English? Only in one sense described earlier: the sentences to children are shorter because they go one proposition at a time. Embed-
dings and conjunctions are rare in the Motherese corpora.

Overall then, 'syntactic simplicity' is a pretty messy way to characterize Motherese. Only one finding fits in with such an interpretation:
the number of S-nodes in maternal speech (its propositional

complexity) is low. We do not deny that this could be a crucial and real simplification, despite the fact that others (use of canonical sentences, construction of sentence type) go by the board when we look at the taxonomy of Motherese. But we will show somewhat later that even the finding of low propositional complexity is probably better interpreted in terms of a gross bias toward brevity in maternal speech rather than in terms of a metric of syntactic simplicity. Then we can hardly agree with such writers as Levelt (1975) who asserts that Motherese has been shown to present the child with a syntactically limited subset of sentences in the language; and that 'from the purely syntactic view the urge for strongly nativist assumptions has been diminished by these findings'. On the contrary, nativist assumptions are left intact by a close look at Motherese — they neither gain nor lose plausibility. The point is that demonstrating that speech to children is different from other speech does not show that it is better for the language learner. Most investigators have jumped from the finding of a difference, here replicated, to the conclusion that Motherese is somehow simple for inducing the grammar. But the finding that Motherese has properties of its own does not show that these give acquisitional support. Notice, at any rate, that the view of Motherese as a syntactically simple corpus merely transfers a very strong claim about the child (that, owing to restrictive and rich hypotheses, he can deduce the grammar from haphazard primary data) to a very strong claim about his mother (that she has some effective notion of what constitutes syntactic simplicity so that in principle she can choose utterances on this basis).

It remains to be said that, as a third principle, our curriculum designer would surely move from the simple to the complicated as his pupils progressed. A related claim, then, is that maternal speech — if it is a teaching language — will grow syntactically more complex in a fine-tuned correspondence with the child's growing linguistic sophistication. Our findings are not consistent with this view. The proportion of canonical declaratives *increases* ($r = 0.51$) with the MLU of the children. The sentence range *narrows*, e.g. imperatives decrease ($r = -0.58$). Though the mothers' MLU and propositional complexity (number of S-nodes per utterance) do increase with the children's MLU, the correlations within this range of sophistication come nowhere near statistical significance ($r = 0.22$ with maternal S-nodes per utterance and $r = 0.40$ with maternal MLU).

Although there are gross differences in the complexity of speech to adults versus speech to young children (and these are confounded with sheer length of utterance), there is no compelling evidence in our data that mothers tune their syntactic complexity to the growing language competence of their children through this crucial age of syntax acquisition, the period from one to two and a half years. We will show, eventually, that maternal syntax likely does have some impact on syntax acquisition — but these effects are subtler and more restricted than has sometimes been claimed.

A FUNCTIONAL DESCRIPTION OF MATERNAL SPEECH

It appears that Motherese is not a syntax-teaching language. But if not, what accounts for its special properties? Along with some other investigators (see Shatz & Gelman, this volume), we believe this language style arises primarily in response to the pressures of communicating with a cognitively and linguistically naive child in the here-and-now, not from the exigencies of the language classroom. There are at least three factors that seem to produce this style: (*a*) only a few topics are of mutual interest to mothers and infants. If even this minimal meeting of minds is to be served by language, then (*b*) strains on the attention and processing capacities of the child have to be minimized, and (*c*) some special discourse features marking points of misunderstanding will have to be employed.

Topical constraints

Mothers want their children to drink their juice and clean up the playroom, so these are the things that are talked about. Children, in their turn, are almost always galvanized into action by such speech as they attend to and comprehend, even on those rare occasions when an action response was not the intent of the speaker.[2] On these grounds, the topic of Motherese is, by and large, a set of instructions to the child to act upon (or at least gaze upon) some objects (see also Shatz & Gelman, this volume; Gelman & Shatz, 1976). This singularity of intent does not require the mother to mind her syntax and, in fact, broadens the range of likely sentence types.

Let us first consider whether this claim can in principle be correct: can the same intent be expressed by differing sentence types? The sentences below, despite radical difference in form, can all be interpreted as directions to perform an action, though, to be sure, the direction is sometimes indirect and 'polite'. (For discussion of the conversational meaning of speech acts in approximately this sense and the 'indirect directive' see Searle, 1969, 1975.)

(1) Put the block in there! (imperative)
(2) Where does the block go? (wh- question)
(3) Doesn't the block go in there? (yes—no question)
(4) Oh, the poor block fell on the floor! (declarative)

Leaving aside the formalism by which the meaningful relationships among these sentences can be explicated (a matter on which we take no stand), it is clear that the common language allows interpretation of all of them as directions to perform the same act (getting the blocks in there). But (2) and (3) can also be interpreted as requests for information, and (4) can be interpreted as a mere commentary on the current state of affairs. 'Rich interpretation' of the context of our Motherese utterances (cf. Bloom, 1970) suggests that they are almost uniformly action-directives, whatever the form. Considering the problems of determining the mothers' true motives, we will not try to support this claim with a close quantitative analysis.[3] Instead, we will argue by inference from the distribution of sentence types.

Imperatives and questions are the most common syntactic devices for requesting action from a listener. Sixty-two percent of utterances to the children took these forms (18 % imperatives, 15 % wh-questions, 21 % yes—no questions and 8 % deictic questions). Only 11 % of utterances to the experimenter were of these forms (2 % imperatives, 1 % wh- questions and 8 % yes—no questions), a highly significant difference ($p < 0.001$ for each measure). The mother can hardly exchange information with her young child, and so only 30 % of her utterances to him took the usual declarative, commentary form. In contrast, 87 % of her utterances to the experimenter were declarative. Summarizing, the Motherese utterances are unified by an underlying intent to direct the child's action, and this intent results in a scatter of linguistic types.

The adjustment of Motherese to the child's maturity supports the same interpretation. Features of maternal speech related to conversational meaning correlate with a wide variety of measures of the child listeners, including age, vocabulary size and syntactic sophistication. For example, *negative* correlations between the proportion of maternal utterances which were imperative and child variables range from −0.35 (with child's mean number of noun-phrases per utterance) to −0.72 ($p < 0.01$, with child's mean number of verbs per utterance and vocabulary size). Positive correlations between maternal utterances which were declarative range from 0.33 (with child's mean number of noun-phrases per utterance) to 0.69 ($p < 0.01$, with child's mean number of morphemes per noun-phrase). That is, these maternal speech features are apparently adjusted in detail to characteristics of the listener. Action-directives *decrease* and declarative comments *increase* as the child develops.

Processing constraints

The constraint on maternal conversational intent does seem to determine some aspects of her speech style. If the mother wants the child to eat with his spoon or dance for Aunt Fanny, she will have to put her requests in some form the child is likely to understand. Quite correctly, she seems to view her child listener as limited in attention span and processing capacity. She speaks slowly and clearly and keeps her utterances short. The advantages in comprehensibility here for a wandering and inadequately informed young mind are fairly obvious. The same perceived situational needs account naturally for the fact that Motherese is always well formed. An English-speaking mother surely is biased toward the belief that well-formed English is easier to deal with than garbled English — it is, for her, whether it is for the child or not. We are claiming, then, that three special characteristics of Motherese (brevity, well-formedness and intelligibility) arise for the purpose of here-and-now communication with a limited and inattentive listener, and cannot be described in terms of a language-instruction motive; this begins to suggest that they may not serve a language-learning purpose (a matter on which we argue more directly below).

Processing variables are not tied to language stage

A communicative interpretation of the three maternal variables under consideration here is supported by a look at how they are adjusted to particulars of the child listener. If they were effects of the mother's view to the future (helping the child learn English), or if they were to support learning whatever the mother's motive, then they ought to be tuned to the child's language sophistication. They are not. There are no significant correlations between the mother's tendency to speak grammatically, intelligibly, or briefly, and language characteristics of the particular child listener. Mother's MLU rises with the listener's age ($r = 0.53, p < 0.05$) but is uncorrelated with his verbal sophistication. The mother's grammaticality and intelligibility are uncorrelated even with child age and vary only across listener class (child versus adult). It is likely, then, that the mother adjusts in these regards rather grossly, in response to changing cognitive characteristics of the child that are only loosely tied to language.

Since this is so, it is hard to see how these adjustments could be of value to a learner conceived as requiring explicit, closely graded data presentation (syntax whose complexity is 'systematically expanded' as the child learns, as some claim). Similarly, if the three variables under consideration here were relevant to language acquisition in any direct way, those mothers who modulated them most effectively ought to have children who acquired English most quickly. Anticipating the study of this issue, reported below, none of these variables has any consequence for language growth rate, so far as we can see.

Processing simplicity, not syntactic simplicity

We believe that certain aspects of maternal speech styles are in the direction of easing the child's comprehension by reducing the attentional and processing tasks that are demanded. In particular, we believe that the constraint on length in Motherese utterances (the low MLU) is a constraint on processing complexity, not a constraint on syntactic complexity. A problem in making this interpretation is posed by the fact that surface length in morphemes and grammatical complexity (however this is defined) are pretty well confounded in English. A long utterance will generally also be propositionally complex, i.e. will contain many S-nodes. Thus analysis in either of these terms yields a highly significant effect of listener type. The issues here can be partly disentangled by looking at some cases where the two hypotheses yield different predictions.

Deletions. Deletion of underlying elements from a spoken sentence would seem to contribute to syntactic complexity on a number of definitions (it lengthens the derivational history; it increases the disparity between deep and surface structures). It is plausible that deletion increases processing complexity as well by leaving inexplicit some semantic elements; but deletion presumably contributes to processing simplicity too, by keeping the utterance short. Motherese is highly deleted compared to adult-directed speech. For instance, *do-you* deletion ('Wanna go out?' as opposed to 'Do you wanna go out?') is common in Motherese (6 % of all utterances) and non-existent in adult-directed questions. Similarly, isolated phrases such as 'on the table' occurred considerably more often to the children (17 %) than to the adults (9 %, $p < 0.05$). And of course, as reported earlier, the high proportion of subjectless imperatives is another demonstration that brevity has priority over syntactic simplicity or semantic explicitness in maternal speech.

Movement transformations. The fact reported earlier that Motherese contains many questions (which move a deep structure element from canonical position, e.g. the auxiliary moves leftward in '*Can* you eat?'), assures a longer derivational history for aspects of the Motherese corpora on this dimension. It would appear that any definition of syntactic complexity will rate declaratives (relatively rare in Motherese) as 'simpler' than questions (relatively common in Motherese). Furthermore, mothers show no tendency to use the syntactically simpler 'I put out the cat' (no particle movement) in preference to 'I put the cat out' (the version arising from the particle-movement transformation) to their children. In fact, the latter version is the more frequent in both corpus types. This form has been argued to be the simpler on processing grounds, for it keeps together the Subject—Verb—Object units on which real-time comprehension strategies are apparently based (Bever, 1970). Similar facts hold for other transformations, such as dative movement (Newport, 1976).

On balance then, processing simplicity seems the more natural description of these findings. Only because issues of processing and issues of syntax very often predict the same biases in the corpus is there an apparent effect in Motherese of direct reduction of syntactic complexity. This conclusion is bolstered by the finding that special syntactic properties of Motherese are not adjusted to the child's learning. If the view is that the small number of S-nodes in maternal utterances is a syntactic effect (rather than, as we have argued, an artifact of a processing effect), it is still not tuned to the individual learner well enough so that it could plausibly affect learning: the number of S-nodes per maternal utterance fails to correlate with any particulars of the child listeners — their age ($r = 0.28$) or their syntactic sophistication (r ranges between 0.02 and 0.27 on the various child measures) — but differs only grossly across age class (child versus adult listener).

To concretize the position we have taken, consider the following sentences:

(5) Where do you think the block goes?
(6) The block goes there.
(7) Want a block?

Utterances of these three types are typical of the Motherese corpora. The distribution of these types yields the overriding effect of action directives, the major but smaller effect of processing constraints, and, perhaps, the smaller yet effect of syntactic simplification. All three of these utterances are action directives; (6) and (7) are short and thus presumably easy to process, while (5) is not; both (5) and (7) are syntactically complex, (5) because it disguises by sequential re-ordering the grammatical relations that represent its underlying structure and (7) because it deletes constituents which are obligatory in well-formed English. Thus the mother's speech is best described in terms of conversational meanings (the topic of directing action) and adjustments to processing limitations (keep it short and sweet). The fine tuning between mother and developing child is in terms of these same issues, thus supporting the distinction between formal and functional adjustments in Motherese. It seems that the child learns the language in the absence of graded lessons in syntax.

Discourse features of Motherese

At last we arrive at three properties of maternal speech that might serve a teaching function: deixis, expansion and repetition. A *deictic* utterance, for our purposes, is one which names a referent by means of a variable whose identification depends on the speakers and their situations (*'There* is a ball', *'Here'*s your giraffe', *'That'*s your nose'). What *that* refers to depends on what is around and focussed on at the moment. Sixteen percent of the Motherese utterances involve deixis, compared to only 2 % of the adult-directed utterances ($p < 0.001$).[4] *Expansion* (Brown, 1973) is the case where the mother provides an adult version (e.g. 'Yes, the book is on the table') in response to the child's foreshortened or distorted attempt (e.g. 'Book table'). Six percent of the Motherese utterances are expansions, and obviously no adult-directed utterances are expansions. *Repetitions* are the case where the mother follows her own utterance (e.g. 'Go find the duck') with one or more exact or partial renditions of the same content ('Yes, go find it — the duck — go get the duck!'). Twenty-three percent of the mothers' utterances involve some repetition of this sort.

Plausibly, deictic usage might help build vocabulary, expansions might help build syntax and repetition might influence both to the extent that it could allow rehearsal or comparison among forms. Like the topical constraints discussed earlier, these discourse features are adjusted to a wide variety of measures of the child subjects. For example, deixis is positively correlated with the child's estimated vocabulary ($r = 0.62, p < 0.05$); exact imitation with expansion is positively correlated with the child's vocabulary ($r = 0.79, p < 0.01$) and partial imitation with expansion is positively correlated with every measure of child sophistication (ranging from $r = 0.52, p < 0.05$ with vocabulary to $r = 0.88, p < 0.001$ with MLU). Maternal self-repetition is *negatively* correlated with the child's age ($r = -0.55$,

$p < 0.05$) and to many measures of his linguistic sophistication (for example, $r = -0.68$, $p < 0.01$ with mean verbs per child utterance, and $r = -0.69$, $p < 0.01$ with his vocabulary). But these adjustments of maternal discourse features to aspects of the child listener do not yet allow us to distinguish between cause and effect (are they influences of the mother on the child or influences of the child on the mother?), or between teaching function and communication function. We therefore turn now to the second-order correlational analysis, whose outcomes may enable us to unravel some of these issues.

RELATIONS BETWEEN MATERNAL SPEECH STYLES AND LANGUAGE ACQUISITION

The previous analysis has established that some of the syntactic properties of Motherese grow out of the fact that she wants to make conversation with her young child rather than teach him generative grammar. We now report a more direct correlational study of the ways maternal speech styles may influence language growth. After all, despite the fact that the mother may merely want Johnnie to pick up his blocks or drink his juice, she nevertheless speaks in special ways to him to maximize her chances. That is, the result of the mother's mundane intents is a corpus restricted in topic, utterance length and certain syntactic features dependent on length limits. It is possible that these effects of mothers' transactions with children influence acquisition, regardless of the mother's motivation or the fineness with which the adjustments are made. We have so far only shown that mothers do not consistently simplify syntax. This merely disposes of the most obvious hypothesis (presentation of a 'miniature language' sample) about how the mother could train her child to talk.

We now examine correlations between individual differences in mothers' speech (i.e. the residual variance in maternal speech measures after partialling out that variance attributable to adjustments to the child's age *and* level of linguistic achievement at the first interview) and child growth rate (i.e. child language scores at interview 2 minus interview 1, with the same partialling procedure). Thus, as described in the section on Procedure, these partial correlations represent the relation between maternal speech and child growth, partialling out the effects of the child listener on the maternal speaker, which were reported above. These partial correlations are thus thought to reflect the effects of maternal speech styles on the child's progress with the language.

We will show that certain highly limited aspects of the mother's speech do have an effect on correspondingly limited aspects of the child's learning. Many other identifiable special properties of Motherese have no discernible effect on the child's language growth. The maternal environment seems to exert its influence on the child only with respect to language-specific structures (surface morphology and syntactic elements that vary over the languages of the world), and even then only through the filter of the child's selective attention to portions of the speech stream (roughly, utterance-initial positions, and items whose referents are clear). Thus learning does respond to narrowly specified features of the environment. But at the same time, this learning is contingent on what the children are disposed to notice in that environment, on their strategies of listening and the hypotheses they are prepared to entertain. We discuss separately below (1) those aspects of the child's learning that show effects of different mothers' styles and (2) those aspects of maternal speech that are effective and ineffective in predicting (producing?) varying rates of learning.

ENVIRONMENTALLY SENSITIVE AND INSENSITIVE ASPECTS OF LANGUAGE LEARNING

Major patterns of the double-partial correlations are shown in Table 5.3. (Please refer to Tables 5.1 and 5.2 for an explanation of the coding decisions involved in the measures tabulated here. A large number of slightly different breakdowns of these data were made, and are available from the authors; these yield similar correlational outcomes to the measures reported here.) To organize these outcomes, we discuss here the aspects of child language growth that are evidently sensitive to the mothers' speech styles (the columns of Table 5.3). The two left-hand columns pertain to the child's growth in nominal inflection (mainly, e.g., adding the *s* to *rat* and the *z* to *rag* to mark plurality) and in verb-auxiliary paradigms (the appearance of modals such as *can*, *will* and *do*; and progressive and perfective elements as in 'I *am* eating', 'I *have* eaten'). These inflectional and paradigmatic forms are specifics of the surface structure of English sentences; they are handled in rather different ways in other languages. The two rightmost columns pertain to the substantive and verbal notions that are becoming manifest in the children's utterances: the number of true verbs per utterance, and the number of noun-phrases per utterance. These are indices of the language features that carry the main

Table 5.3 *Double-partial correlations between maternal speech and child language growth, partialling out initial child age*[a]

Measures of maternal speech	Measures of child growth				
	Grammatical functors		Length	Propositional content	
	Auxiliaries/ verb-phrase	Inflections/ noun-phrase	Morphemes/ utterance (MLU)	Verbs/ utterance	Noun-phrases/ utterance
Declarative	0.25	0.01	0.10	0.16	0.02
Yes—no question	0.88***	−0.05	0.50√	0.35	0.16
Imperative	−0.55*	−0.52√	−0.38	−0.29	0.19
Wh- question	−0.36	−0.07	−0.29	−0.02	−0.24
Interjection	0.53√	0.22	0.42	−0.08	0.11
Deixis	−0.09	0.58*	0.13	−0.12	−0.08
Expansion	0.51√	0.14	0.23	0.03	−0.16
Repetition	−0.58*	−0.51√	−0.50√	−0.05	−0.27
Mean length of utterance	0.34	0.10	0.14	0.38	0.22
S-nodes/utterance	0.21	−0.05	0.37	0.05	0.31

√ $p < 0.08$ * $p < 0.05$ *** $p < 0.001$

[a] Slightly different values for these correlations have been reported previously (Newport et al., 1975). Previous correlations were performed on samples of the interviews. The present correlations were performed on the entirety of the interviews: see p. 120 for the details of this cross-validation procedure.

semantic burden of the child's message. They are what he is talking *about*. So far as we know, there is little or nothing unique in what can be talked about in English, in contrast to other languages. Plausibly, then, these latter measures are indices of the child's exploitation of universal aspects of language structure and content.

Column three shows the child's growth in MLU (mean number of morphemes per utterance). This is a composite measure, reflecting the contribution both of language-specific paradigmatic devices (e.g. tense and plural markers contribute to MLU) and language-general devices (e.g. obviously each verb in the utterance contributes to MLU). Thus inspection of Table 5.3 reveals that growth of child MLU grossly correlates with a measure of maternal speech just when a specific child measure (e.g. growth in auxiliary structure) correlates with a measure of maternal speech. Even so, none of the correlations with child MLU quite reaches statistical significance. Thus useful discussion turns on the more narrowly defined measures (columns one and two; columns four and five). We take it that the child MLU growth measure has no import independent of the various measures that contribute to it.[5]

As Table 5.3 shows, certain language-specific aspects of the child's speech seem to be influenced rather dramatically in their rate of growth by aspects of the mother's usage. The growth in mean number of elements in the child's verbal auxiliary yields a partial correlation with the mother's tendency to ask yes—no questions ($r = 0.88$, $p < 0.001$) and to expand ($r = 0.51, p < 0.08$), and a negative partial correlation with the mother's tendency to use imperatives ($r = -0.55, p < 0.05$). The child's growth rate for noun inflection also yields a partial correlation with the mother's tendency to employ deixis ($r = 0.58, p < 0.05$) and a near-significant negative partial correlation with the proportion of maternal imperatives ($r = -0.52$, $p < 0.08$).

In contrast, the measures of child language growth that we take to be indices of universal aspects of language structure and content are, so far as we can see in this limited study, insensitive to individual differences in maternal speech styles. The child's growth in the use of complex sentences (indexed as the number of noun-phrases and number of verb-phrases per utterance in Table 5.3) is unaffected by the aspects of Motherese examined here. None of these partial correlations comes anywhere near a probable non-chance effect. These phenomena of language use seem to be dependent on cognitive and linguistic maturity. While they are functions of the child's age, they are not related to specifiable features of the maternal environment.

These effects and non-effects of the environment on child language growth accord with many reports in the literature. Most centrally, there appears to be an early set of propositions, and some uniform surface-structure devices (mainly, word-order) for expressing the arguments of these propositions, among children learning a wide variety of languages (Slobin, 1968; Bloom, 1970; McNeill, 1966a; Brown, 1973; Edwards, 1973; Newport & Ashbrook, 1976). The same propositions and word-order devices seem to be used even by deaf children deprived of explicit linguistic models (Goldin-Meadow, 1975; Feldman, Goldin-Meadow & Gleitman, 1976). It is not surprising, then, that differences among mothers in speech style do not affect the child's growth along these dimensions. The obtained environment-dependent result for the growth of noun-phrase inflection and, particularly, auxiliary structure, again accords with related findings in the literature. For example Nelson and his colleagues (Nelson, Carskaddon & Bonvillian, 1973; Nelson, 1975) have reported selected effects on auxiliary growth (e.g. future and conditional tenses, negative questions) in a paradigm where expansions and recast sentences are specifically provided to the child learner.

Further support for the coherence of these findings comes from a source outside the usual domain of language acquisition studies, from a look at the evolution of languages of the world. Many linguistic studies reveal a changeable role of elements of the auxiliary structure in language design. Particularly relevant in this regard are pidgin languages (roughly, communication systems used for limited purposes between linguistic communities who speak different languages) and creoles (roughly, evolved pidgins, at the point when these come to be used in broad social settings and, in particular, acquire native speakers who do not know the parent languages). The study of pidgins and their creolization has generated much interest within linguistics in recent years (Labov, 1971b; Sankoff & Laberge, 1973). Apparently, pidgin languages are characterized by a sharp simplification of grammatical features. They use optional morphological devices to express time and aspect, and word-order devices almost exclusively to mark the grammatical relations (Slobin, 1975a). Elaborated auxiliary structure and inflectional devices appear rapidly during the process of creolization; evidently the rate of growth of such features during creolization vastly exceeds the rate of language change in an evolved language, even though in both cases the linguistic community is essentially monolingual at this point.

The relevance of such facts to issues in language acquisition has been discussed in a very important recent paper by Slobin (1975a):

various historically unrelated pidgins simplify grammatical features in similar ways, and these suggestively resemble the simplifications of early child syntax — the same inflectional devices and elaborated auxiliary structure are missing. A plausible inference from these facts is that there are universal principles of linguistic simplification that appear under specifiable conditions. Among these conditions may be the use of a language in restricted social settings and by non-native speakers (both conditions applying to pidgins) and the use of language by an immature novice (the condition applying to young children). If this account is essentially correct, then the inflectional and paradigmatic devices of mature English speech are not universal properties of human communication systems but, rather, are special language features that appear in certain environments and conditions of use. Then it is easier to understand why these features of syntax emerge developmentally in response to closely-specified environmental conditions (stateable maternal speech properties) more than do the universal language design features (which seem to emerge under diffuse environmental conditions).

Summarizing, many measures of child language growth are insensitive to differences in the speech styles of our subject mothers. Of course it is possible to suppose that these non-correlations reflect sameness among these mothers on dimensions relevant to the acquisition process. However, as we shall describe below, these mothers do vary along dimensions that have presumptive relevance to acquisition. For example, mothers do vary in their child-directed MLU, but this variance does not affect growth in the child's MLU as indexed by the partial correlations ($r = 0.14$). We conclude, then, that a broad range of language skills develops under diffuse environmental conditions. These skills are, so far as we can see, just those that reflect universal properties of human communication systems. In contrast, certain structures that are uniquely rendered in the surface forms of English (elements of the auxiliary, the inflection of noun-phrases) are sensitive to delicate variations in mothers' style. In short, to the extent that Urdu and Tagalog and English are alike, differences among mothers do not yield differing growth rates in our subjects (accounting for the lack of correlations in columns four and five of Table 5.3); but where learning 'from the outside' must logically be the primary factor — where the language has special individual properties — maternal speech styles evidently do affect the rate of that learning (yielding the many significant correlations of columns one and two of Table 5.3).

EFFECTIVE AND INEFFECTIVE ASPECTS OF MATERNAL SPEECH STYLE

We have described the aspects of the child's language that are closely influenced by the external model, as suggested by the effects in the columns of Table 5.3. We ask here what features of that model (which differences in input by mothers) have these selective effects. To do so, we return to Table 5.3, now considering the rows, which represent the various properties of Motherese. Here we simply state the findings. We reserve more general discussion for later when the findings for both child-effects and mother-effects are in.

Table 5.3 suggests that many properties of Motherese have no effect on language growth at all, not surprisingly, for it is already clear that Motherese is predominantly shaped for the local needs of communication. Thus the mother's MLU does not correlate with child growth rates (correlations range between 0.10 and 0.38). Her tendency to use the canonical declarative form is similarly ineffective (correlations between 0.01 and 0.25), as is the mean number of S-nodes in her sentences (her propositional complexity; correlations range between − 0.05 and 0.37). In sum, whether mothers speak in long sentences or short ones, restricted or wide-ranging sentence types, complex sentences or simpler ones − none of these plausible candidates for a teaching style have a discernible effect on the child's language growth during the six-month interval we investigated. To this extent, the picture that comes out of these results is one of a semi-autonomous unfolding of language capabilities in the child, rather than a fine sensitivity to specific syntactic features of the input model.

We acknowledge that these major non-effects have to be interpreted cautiously in light of the limitations of the procedure. First, since all of our subject mothers − and perhaps all mothers everywhere − speak Motherese, non-effects found here can only be said to exist within a narrow range of differences among mothers. Perhaps maternal simplifications are essential for normal acquisition but once some threshold of speech modulation is reached, further differences among mothers beyond this are not relevant; if this is the situation, our procedures could not discern this. Second, sheer frequency of differing usage across mothers may not be the correct variable to examine for growth effects. Third, the sample mothers (15 white middle class Americans) and the situation (four hours of conversation with a visiting psychologist) may give so unrepresentative a range of maternal speech styles that real and powerful effects of environmental difference are not visible. However, if these non-effects of syntactic style are attributable to faulty or insufficient observation, we should expect to find no correlations at all between mothers and their children, or only accidental and incoherent ones. But as Table 5.3 shows, there are clear partial correlations between the child's growth and restricted syntax and discourse features of Motherese. We turn now to closer inspection of these findings.

The pattern of correlations between maternal speech and the growth of surface syntactic patterning in child speech reveals complex effects of how often mothers produce certain constructions, in conjunction with the particular fashion in which they are presented. For example, the growth of the verbal auxiliary in the child is uncorrelated with the absolute frequency of auxiliaries produced by the mother ($r = 0.31$) but is correlated with her tendency to use auxiliaries in first utterance-position (as in yes–no questions, e.g. '*Can* you kiss your elbow?', $r = 0.88, p < 0.001$). But the mother's use of auxiliaries in utterance-medial positions (as in wh- questions, e.g. '*Where can* you sit?') is uncorrelated ($r = -0.36$) with the child's auxiliary learning, and the mother's use of positive imperatives – which have no auxiliary – correlates negatively ($r = -0.55, p < 0.05$) with the child's auxiliary learning.

Related findings concern the effects of discourse features of Motherese. The use of deixis (e.g. '*Those* are apples') correlates significantly with growth in noun-phrase inflections. The use of expansions yields a near-significant correlation with auxiliary growth ($r = 0.51, p < 0.08$). On a slightly different scoring (see footnote 5) partial-plus expansions show a much stronger relation to auxiliary growth ($r = 0.75, p < 0.01$). Self-repetition by the mother yields a negative partial correlation with both these child growth measures ($r = -0.51, p < 0.08$ with noun-phrase inflection, and $r = -0.58$, $p < 0.05$ with auxiliary structure). How can we explain these selective effects of Motherese on selected aspects of language learning? We try now to organize the findings in terms of the mechanics that may be at work in the child to produce them.

IDEAL MOTHERESE: SOME HYPOTHESES

The basic position for which we will now argue is that the child is biased to listen selectively to utterance-initial items and to items presented in referentially obvious situations: the child acts as a filter through which the linguistic environment exerts its influence (Shipley *et al.*, 1969; Ervin-Tripp, 1973; Slobin, 1973*a*).

The frequency and types of mother's utterances, then, influence growth only to the extent that they pass through this filter, i.e. when they occur under presentation conditions to which the child selectively attends. Particulars of mothers' style thus interact with the child's processing biases for language, producing differential rates of acquisition; specifically, the mother helps by talking when the child's eye (either the mind's eye or the face's eye) is one the word or construction referred to.

Maternal syntax and the processing bias

It has been demonstrated elsewhere (Shipley *et al.*, 1969) that children have their own ways of biasing their linguistic input. They pay special attention to the beginnings of utterances. If the beginning of an utterance is excessively unfamiliar, the child is unlikely to attend to the rest of this utterance. (Of course this bias must be imperfect, else the child would never learn anything he didn't know already.) If children are listening specially to sentence beginnings, it would appear likely that they would learn certain things faster if these were spotlighted in first position with some frequency.

A finding consistent with this hypothesis is that the growth of the verbal auxiliary is strongly correlated with the mother's tendency to use this in first position. In English, the auxiliary is so 'fronted' in certain kinds of questions (*'Can* you sing?') and in negative imperatives (*'Don*'t sing'). But in declarative sentences, the auxiliary either appears medially ('You *can* sing') or does not appear at all ('You sang'). In wh- questions ('What *can* you sing?') the auxiliary is again medial, and in the positive imperative ('Sing!') it does not occur. As we have seen, growth of the verbal auxiliary is positively correlated with yes—no questions (utterance-initial auxiliary), negatively correlated with positive imperatives (auxiliary absent), and uncorrelated with declaratives and wh- questions (medial auxiliary). This pattern of results suggests that aspects of the linguistic environment exert their influence on the child through his pre-set bias to focus on certain aspects of incoming utterances, properties of their beginnings.

Summarizing Table 5.3 thus far: (1) only language-specific aspects of the child's growth are influenced by narrowly-prescribed features of the linguistic input, and hence the significant effects are all in columns one and two, none in columns four and five; and (2) only those characteristics of maternal syntax that fit the child's listening biases for learning these yield significant effects. These are the yes—no questions, which support the processing bias (listening to beginnings).

Declarative sentences which present auxiliaries medially have no such effect and finally, auxiliary-absent imperatives do not provide the appropriate data and hence are negatively correlated with the child's growth rate.

Learning effects of the maternal discourse features

We now discuss the remaining effects in the rows of Table 5.3, which relate to discourse features of maternal speech style, primarily deixis and expansion. In earlier discussion (see 'The nature of Motherese') we asserted that these discourse features — and in fact much of the form and content of Motherese — can be described on the supposition that mother and child are mutually engaged in an attempt to communicate about the here-and-now, trying to get the local situation managed at the moment, rather than trying to make a frontal attack on the language acquisition problem. Bruner (1974/5) has recently presented and reviewed evidence that a similar communicative intent accounts quite naturally for interactions between mothers and even preverbal children: such postural–gestural interactions can be conceived as attempts by the communicative partners to single out and mutually focus attention on given objects and actions. Some relevant devices here are following the partner's line of regard, picking up and shaking the target object, etc. While, as Bruner points out, these activities do not explain how the child learns to refer or learns which linguistic or gestural entities refer to which objects and actions in the world, they do suggest that much preverbal communication is devoted to the infant and adult mutually 'indicating and differentiating the very limited set of objects with which they traffic'.

The same kind of intent — singling out and identifying the local referents in a communication situation — accounts quite naturally for aspects of speech from mother to infant. For example, Collis (1975) has shown that mothers tend to vocalize about an object primarily when their young child is looking at it (see also Bruner, 1974/5 for discussion). Surely this is a convenient tack to take in communicating successfully with a novice; but this same tack must surely be salutary to long-term language acquisition for it will help the child discover the conventional labels for identifiable referents. That mothers and young speaking children continue to engage in responsive looking, pointing and naming is a fact often cited in discussions of semantic development (Clark, 1974). The same intent to make mutually comprehensible reference seems to account naturally for why the mothers we have studied use linguistic deixis extensively

(16 % of all mother-to-child utterances involve deixis). Notice that the use of linguistic deixis — just like pointing the finger — demands as a condition of appropriate use that the listener already be looking at the object being referred to or that the speaker make an accompanying gesture — such as pointing, or looking himself, which conventionally has the effect of moving the listener's gaze toward that object. Then when such an expression appears in our corpora, we can be quite confident that the child listener had its referent directly in view — it would be an odd mother indeed who would say 'That's a ball' when she saw her child looking at a rhinoceros.[6]

Then since children must somehow use properties of visible referents as clues to the meaning of words, we might hypothesize that those of our subject mothers who use deixis proportionally most often are making this *referent-matching strategy* the more consistently available to their children, with possible effects on learning: they are providing a verbal label just when the child's eye is on its referent. The children of such mothers might be expected to acquire aspects of nominal expressions most rapidly. We did find a partial correlation between growth in surface structural aspects of the child's noun-phrases and the frequency of maternal deixis (inflections per noun-phrase are correlated with deixis, $r = 0.58$, $p < 0.05$, see Table 5.3). This finding suggests that the more the mother produces lexical items that are explicitly coincident with their referents, the more easily the child analyzes the constructions into which these items enter. But, rather surprisingly, we did not find a stable partial correlation between maternal deixis and the learning of the lexical items themselves (correlation between deixis and child vocabulary growth, $r = -0.15$). While a significant correlation was found in the initial analysis of transcript segments, it did not survive the cross-validation procedures. This non-effect may simply reflect the roughness of our procedure for estimating vocabulary size. Or it may be a true finding: this is one among many instances that we have reported where variations among mothers yield correlations with surface features of child syntax (here, inflection) but not with content variables.

Certain further findings can similarly be accounted for on the view that referent-matching plays an important role in the acquisition of surface syntax. Recall that mothers use affirmative imperatives in different proportions: children whose mothers use these the most often acquire auxiliary elements slowest. We argued earlier that this is because affirmative imperatives lack the auxiliary. But it is also so that affirmative imperatives are poor constructions from which to learn the language from the point of view of reference-making. They rarely map clearly onto the non-linguistic context: one says 'Throw me the ball' just when it is not being thrown and often when it isn't even in hand. Appropriately, then, the more frequently the mother produces imperatives, the more slowly the child grows not only in auxiliary structure but also in noun-phrase inflection (see Table 5.3).[7]

Another issue that we believe is related to the same strategy has to do with the mother's tendency to expand (imitate with addition or correction) the child's utterances. Is there an analogy to reference-matching here? The question is whether one can use a construction (e.g. an auxiliary) just when the child's attention is fixed on the mapping of that construction to its meaning. How can this be done? Neither syntactic forms nor the relations among them are visible in the world. But suppose that the mother often understands from the non-linguistic context some relation that the child is trying to express in the terms of his primitive syntax (see Bloom, 1970, for discussion of this 'rich interpretation' of the context of speech). Suppose, for example, the child utters the ambiguous sentence 'No eat!' under the following different circumstances: as he pushes away his food; as his sister greedily eats up his candy; or as a dog threatens to bite him. (These examples are broadly adapted from an incident in Maurice Sendak's (1967) linguistically and philosophically deep children's tale, *Higglety, Pigglety, Pop*) The obvious English interpretation might be 'I won't eat that rotten porridge!', 'Don't you eat my chocolates!' and 'Don't eat me up!'

Despite limited knowledge of English, the child's saying 'No eat!' in one of these contexts reveals — though not errorlessly — that such-and-such a notion, correctly expressed in English in such-and-such a way, is at that moment directly in the child's consciousness, in his mind's eye. If at that instant the mother provides an appropriate English form ('No, Shirley won't eat your chocolates, Harvey . . .') she effectively produces a construction when the child's attention is fixed on the notion that construction refers to in the language. This might ease the problem of mapping between conceptual relations and their syntactic reflexes in English (Cazden, 1965; Brown, Cazden, & Bellugi, 1968; Brown, 1973). And, as Table 5.3 shows, the more frequently the mother produces these expansions, the more quickly her child learns the surface forms of the verbal auxiliary.[8]

For completeness, it is fair to add that a great many hypotheses of other sorts might accommodate some of these findings. For example, maybe mothers who are polite and request action from their children, rather than commanding it, establish better human relations with their offspring. But wouldn't it be odd to suppose that, as a courtesy, the children return the favor by producing complicated verbal auxiliaries for their proud mothers? At any rate, a number of such hypotheses have been reviewed, and none seems to us to account for these data overall as well as the one just described. But much more extensive work along these lines, which we now have underway, is necessary to solidify this general approach.

The pseudo-effect of repetition on language growth

Earlier we reported many simple negative correlations between the child's age and linguistic stage and the mother's tendency to repeat herself. Such correlations, found in many previous studies, are often interpreted as suggesting that repetition aids language learning, either by providing drill (many exemplars, allowing rehearsal and efficient storage) or perhaps by allowing the child to compare a set of forms that keep meaning relatively constant (as in the typical repetition sequence 'Go get the duck — the duck — yes, get it — that's right — get the duck'). On this interpretation, as the child gets older and comes to know more of the language, the need for such drill diminishes, explaining the negative correlations. But notice that to account for the tremendous repetitiveness of mothers (23 % of all utterances involved some repetition) and for the simple correlations between maternal repetitions and child language sophistication, it is not necessary to invoke a teaching motive or function. It is sufficient to conclude that the younger and more linguistically naive the listener, the less likely he is to attend to, comprehend and obey the mother's initial utterance — so she repeats it. On this latter interpretation, repetition could hardly function to aid acquisition: if the child did not attend to the first rendition, then the second rendition would not be, for him, a repetition of just-previously stored information. (In fact, Newport (1976) showed that the child's tendency to respond to an utterance was unrelated to the serial position of that utterance in a repetition sequence, suggesting that its 'repeatedness' is irrelevant.)

To determine whether repetitions *influence* language growth, it is necessary to look at the partial correlations between maternal repetitions and child growth scores. Table 5.3 shows that maternal self-repetitions are negatively correlated with the child's growth rate both in auxiliary structure ($r = -0.58, p < 0.05$) and noun inflection ($r = -0.51, p < 0.08$). So at first glance there does seem to be an effect of repetition on language learning, but it is a puzzling effect indeed: if repetitions served the child's learning purposes, the double-partial correlations should have been positive. Since these correlations are negative, to hold onto the claim that repetition is relevant to language learning, one would have to conclude that it *delays* acquisition, either by narrowing the child's data base or, perhaps, by boring him to tears.

Luckily no such procrustean arguments are necessary. It turns out that the apparent effect of repetition is a simple consequence of the fact that the mothers' repetitive utterances consist preponderantly of syntactic types that are themselves negatively correlated with language growth. Specifically, since mothers are most often repeating instructions to act, a substantial number of repetitions are imperatives. This is hardly surprising on a communicative, rather than didactic, interpretation of maternal speech: when polite requests are disregarded, peremptory commands are likely to follow. We have argued above that imperatives, by virtue of their surface forms and their non-transparent referents, are poor exemplars for language learners. In fact, if imperative repetitions are excluded from the analysis of repetitions, the significant correlations between repetition and language growth disappear (e.g. $r = -0.27$ with growth in auxiliary structure); but if we remove the repetitive imperatives from the analysis of imperatives, the partial correlation between imperatives and growth scores remains ($r = -0.60, p < 0.05$). In short, the apparent effect of repetition on language learning is an artifact of the individual sentence types of which the repetitions are composed. Despite the initial plausibility, then, of the idea that re-presentation of forms might aid the language learner, there is no such effect in our data.[9]

A NOTE ON REINFORCEMENT

By what means does the mother have the effects she has on language growth? Generally, we have talked of the mother as an exemplar or model of language: what she says and when she says it matters to the child's learning, on some dimensions. But perhaps the mother can help further, essentially by red-pencilling the child's errors. Expansion is at least indirectly such a case, for here the mother provides the child with a 'corrected' model. There is another effect in our data which seems to be interpretable as a kind of feedback or reinforcement effect: the frequency with which the mother says 'Yes' or 'Mm-hmm' or even 'No' in response to the child's utterances correlates positively with the growth of vocabulary ($r = 0.58, p < 0.05$), with the growth of verb inflections ($r = 0.61, p < 0.05$) and with the growth of auxiliaries ($r = 0.53, p < 0.08$).[10] (This coding category is listed as *interjections* in Table 5.3) At first glance, this finding for interjections seems at variance with the report by Brown & Hanlon (1970) that mothers reinforce their children in terms of the truth value of their utterances, rather than in terms of syntactic niceties in these utterances. But there really is no paradox here. Our finding is not that mothers say 'mm-hmm' more often to well-formed sentences than to garbles — only that some mothers say 'mm-hmm' more than others, and that this influences the rate of language growth. It is plausible that mothers tend to respond with 'mm-hmms' more often when they understand what the child said (i.e. when he speaks in an English-like way) than when they do not. Such responses from mothers may constitute confirmatory evidence for a child trying to build some hypotheses about how to speak English effectively, so an 'mm-hmming' mother may be of use to the language learner.

But the question at issue here is whether such 'reinforcement', if that is what it is, can be an explanatory concept in describing the course and process of language acquisition. We have reported that many features of the child's language environment have no discernible effect on how his language grows; and many features of the child's speech grow in indifference to some variability in the environment. Very specific, very limited, structures in the child relate quite narrowly to aspects of the surround, and this relation is in turn mediated by pre-set strategies of listening and learning. This hardly denies that a little encouragement may be helpful. Surely, it is helpful. But no concept as broad and undifferentiated as encouragement (selective reinforcement) can get at exactly what is encourageable and in what ways: on how language is learned. Even if it could be shown that one was reinforced always and only for speaking grammatically, this would not explain — without begging the question — how it happens that generalization is always from old grammatical sentences to new grammatical sentences.

In answer to this more interesting question, we have considered some possible learning strategies in the child (e.g. listen to familiar beginnings; listen in the presence of identifiable referents). This does not commit us to the claim that language learning would take place without a cooperating mother (that you could learn English by watching television) or if that mother comprehended and applauded every garble the child uttered. We accept on the basis of our findings — as well as sanity — that a supportive and relevant environment will aid the language learner, but this does not suggest how language is learned.

SUMMARY AND SOME CONCLUSIONS

Our studies of mothers' speech have some curious implications for theories of language acquisition. It has often been assumed that mothers speak to their children in the distorted and complex ways of adult speech. Given this assumption, it follows that the function relating acquisition and environment is loose — leading to the further assumption that the child must be richly and specifically pre-programmed for language acquisition. Once investigators noticed that the first assumption was partly false (that Motherese differs systematically from speech to adults), they made an unwarranted assumption in their turn. They took for granted that Motherese is a well-designed 'teaching language', tailored for the specific purpose of language acquisition. Indeed this may be so, for all we know, but not on the assumption that this learning corpus is a constructionally simple one. Motherese is syntactically complex on most obvious definitions. Whatever constructional simplifications occur in Motherese seem to arise for interactional reasons — as constraints on the kinds of things one talks about to children and gross constraints on psychological complexity in the ways one talks to them. Moreover, whatever syntactic simplifications occur are not finely tuned to the child's developing language skills. Recent language-acquisition proposals hypothesize that the language environment of the child becomes successively more complex in correspondence with the child's growing language skills, and thus may be at all times appropriate for an environmentally-dependent acquisition process. For example, Levelt (1975) writes 'the child is presented with grammatical strings from a miniature language, which is systematically expanded as the child's competence grows'. Our findings suggest instead that many features of the mother's speech change in accordance with the child's age, not his competence with constructional features of the language.

Thus the fact that mother's speech is different from adult-directed speech can give only small comfort to those who suppose the child's language learning to depend on very specific or finely modulated environmental support. However, any theory which requires only rough appropriateness of the environment to the needs of acquisition is consistent with these results. We have suggested in outline a position of this kind in which (1) the acquisition of universal aspects of language design proceeds in indifference to the details of varying individual environments, at least within the range of some gross syntactic simplifications (which would appear to occur necessarily in any world where mothers wish to communicate with their children), and (2) individual differences in the linguistic environment, exemplified by the mother, exert their effects only on the acquisition of language-specific aspects of surface structure, and even then only through the listening biases of the child. We have suggested a processing-bias hypothesis and a referent-matching hypothesis as components of such a theory: to the extent that a mother makes syntax perspicuous for the child, underlining constructions by placing them in salient positions in surface structure, or by providing exemplars at the moment the child's attention is drawn to their referents (in the world or in the mind), the child acquires the appropriate formal devices more quickly.

Finally, it seems of some importance to fit these findings into the context of recent discussions of the acquisition of semantics and cognitive development. There has been a rather strong reaction in the developmental psycholinguistic literature against the bias of some linguists — Chomsky of course is the one most often cited — to concentrate attention on the acquisition of syntax rather than semantics, and to leave aside possibly related phenomena of cognitive development. Whether this is a fair construal of the acquisition problem for language by linguists is an exegetical matter, which we side-step. But clearly Chomsky (1965), Fodor (1966) and others have been perceived to take a strictly syntactic line when worrying about acquisition. This perception has provoked controversy. For example, Ervin-Tripp (1971) writes 'It is tragic to cut off from the domain of research the large field of cognitive relations which are found in early sentences . . . by assuming *a priori* that there are no problems in their acquisition.' Our findings suggest that these two kinds of concerns may be relevant to different and separable aspects of language growth: the conditions for the acquisition of cognitive—semantic relations (measured here only by the average number of nouns and verbs per utterance) and those for the acquisition of grammatical functions which elaborate those relations (here, auxiliary structure and noun inflections) seem different. We have nothing to say about how the child learns or develops with regard to the semantics of natural language. But we can say that, however this is done, it is accomplished with less close reliance on environmental linguistic support than is the acquisition of some properties of surface syntax. It is in this latter dimension that we find dramatic effects of an environmentally-dependent acquisition process — 'learning' in the traditional psychological sense of that word.

We have acknowledged in this discussion that our data collection and coding procedures were quite limited, and that the range of subjects and situations we investigated was rather narrow. But insofar as these studies fit in with and contribute to prior investigations of language and its learning, the thrust of the findings is this: the child is biased to acquire information about his language in terms of narrowly prescribed processing strategies and preconceptions about the world that language could represent. Working within these biases and presuppositions, the mother has little latitude to teach her child about the nature of language; but she can at least improve his English.

NOTES

1.   In order to be able to use pronouns in this report, we have adopted the convention of calling mothers 'she' and children 'he'. This convention is violated only when we speak of our child subjects individually, for all of them were girls. We wish to thank Heidi Feldman, John Jonides, Dan Osherson, Marilyn Shatz and our mothers, for their valuable contributions to our thinking about maternal speech styles, and for significant help in interpreting the experiments reported here. Thanks are also due to Herb Clark for a very helpful discussion of this work. The research was carried out with the support of NIH grant No. 23505, the William T. Carter Foundation, the Spencer Foundation, Academic Senate Research Grants from the University of California at San Diego and US Public Health Service Grant MH-15828 to the Center for Human Information Processing. Suzanne Hale and Dianne Simpson are thanked for meticulous work in coding and analysis.

2.   The discussion here centers on the mothers. Claims about the bias of children to respond by action to speech come from a variety of sources. As one simple demonstration, Shipley *et al.* (1969) showed that children of the ages under investigation here are as likely to throw a ball given that they touch it, when you say 'Ball!' as when you say 'Throw me the ball!' or even if, by experimental disingenuity, you say 'Gor ronta ball!' Balls are 'to throw'. Similarly, Shatz (1975) showed that young children tend overwhelmingly to respond to questions as action directives rather than as requests for information: although easy to 'set' for the action interpretation, they are hard to set for the information interpretation.

3.   Analysis of free speech along this dimension has been carried out by Shatz, (1975), Shatz & Gelman (this volume), and Gelman & Shatz (1976). Our data-collection procedures did not allow analysis in these terms. For one thing, we did not videotape the sessions, so our inferences would be based on the restricted information from the sound recordings. In any case, Bloom's method requires a measure of painstaking observation and coding that we prefer to admire from afar.

4.   One might well wonder how deixis is used in adult—adult speech. It is rare, but there are some reasonable show-and-tell contexts (e.g. 'This is our old dining-room suite; the expensive new chairs are out being cleaned'). In the experimental sessions, adult-directed deixis occurred only when the mother tried to identify for the experimenter some fuzzy speech-acts by the child, e.g., after the child said 'Mffwk', the mother said to the experimenter, 'That was "milk"'.

5.   A correlation of 0.55 on these analyses is significant at the 0.05 level. We

treat correlations above 0.50 ($p < 0.08$) as probably reflecting non-chance effects, and report them in the text. We do so for two reasons. First, as Table 5.3 shows, there is a major difference between language-specific and language-general ('universal') correlational outcomes. The language-general content variables never yield a whiff of significance (the largest r in the last two columns is 0.38, a number that is surely to be interpreted as a chance perturbation). In contrast, a number of the surface-syntax variables in the first two columns yield significant correlations. Near-significant misses (r in the low 50s, p between 0.06 and 0.08) also all fall in these columns, suggesting that they ought to be treated as more than chance differences from zero. Further, as Tables 5.1 and 5.2 show, we had to group and analyze our data in terms of a coding procedure that involved making some arguable decisions. For example, how to define 'expansion'? Clearly, if the mother says everything the child says and adds some more, that must be an expansion, on everyone's definition. But what if she says part of what the child says and then adds something new? For example, the child says 'Book table', and the mother responds '*On* the table'. Is this 'partial-plus' imitation functionally equivalent to a full expansion? We could hardly be sure, and so we analyzed the data in more than one way. 'Partial-plus' expansions, looked at alone, in fact yield a double-partial correlation of 0.75 ($p < 0.01$) with child's auxiliary growth. Since this is so, and since this measure could well be the right one, it seemed unrealistic to dismiss the result for a closely related measure (all expansions, see Table 5.3) just when it missed the 0.05 level of statistical significance by two or three decimal points. Anyhow, that has been our decision, over all measures. We nevertheless acknowledge that there is difficulty in evaluating the weaker obtained correlations. Cross-validations of these findings, now underway, will obviously help resolve these questions.

6.   We have reported 16% deixis in Motherese. The proportion, over mothers, is really much larger than this if we include such locutions as 'See the baby?', 'Look at that spot on your dress', etc. But the variety of expressions — and hence the coding problems — which can have deictic interpretation is enormous. We settled for claiming deixis only when the usual demonstratives (*here, this, there*, etc.) occurred appropriately in the utterance. Thus we have estimated deixis in Motherese very conservatively.

7.   The original analysis, on transcript segments, examined negative imperatives separately from affirmative imperatives. This separate analysis of the two types of imperatives has not yet been completed on the entire transcripts and is therefore not reported in the text. Note, however, that negative imperatives differ from their affirmative counterparts in two relevant ways. First, they do have a sentence-initial auxiliary, though it is always the same one (*don't*). Second, while affirmative imperatives rarely map clearly onto the non-linguistic context, negative imperatives almost always do. That is, one says 'Eat your peas' when they are not being eaten and 'Don't eat your peas' when they are. Appropriately, then, the frequency of negative imperatives in mothers' speech in the segment analyses did not predict the delayed growth in either noun or auxiliary structure that the frequency of affirmative imperatives did.

8.   The relations between expansion and language growth have been studied before (see, e.g. Cazden, 1965; Feldman, 1971) and generally the results have been negative. But Cazden studied effects of a visiting experimenter performing expansions with the child over a series of sessions. It may be over-optimistic to suppose that these sometime interactions could substitute for the mother's

prevailing speech style. Where mothers' spontaneous expansions have been directly observed, and where measures of the child's growth in relation to this were
selective, a relationship is discernible. Keith Nelson (1973, and personal communication) has collected data on both experimentally controlled and naturally
occurring expansions. He has found results like those reported here: the more
frequent the predicate expansions, the more rapidly children acquire auxiliary
structure.

9.   It is necessary to add here that a similar argument might be suggested to account for the apparent effect of *expansions* on language growth. But in this case,
analysis of expansions in terms of their syntactic features does not mitigate the
double-partial correlations: most expansions are declarative sentences; expansions
yield a partial correlation with language growth; but declarative sentences yield
no such partial correlation (see Table 5.3).

10.   The effects reported here did not appear in the original analysis of transcript segments. Perhaps, since this effect is one that does not 'go through' our
first cross-validation procedure (segment analysis compared to whole-transcript
analysis), it ought to be ignored until such time as it reappears under further
cross-validation. It is our own bias to hold this issue in abeyance, awaiting further work. Yet the concept of reinforcement has at least a surface persuasiveness
and a long theoretical history in the psychological discussion of language learning. It therefore seems unreasonable to suppress a finding which on the face of it
might be an effect of reinforcement, as that notion is generally conceived. We
acknowledge in the discussion that follows that such an effect probably exists —
but that it accounts for language learning only if the issues of 'what is reinforced'
and 'what is a reinforcer' are begged.

6 Mothers' speech adjustments: the contributions of selected child listener variables[1]

TONI G. CROSS

Department of Psychology, University of Melbourne, Parkville, Victoria, Australia 3052

Until quite recently, explanations of the problems posed by the existence of individual differences in rate of language acquisition have had a low priority in the study of child language. The primary concern of most researchers during the last decades has been to identify common denominators across children, and to demonstrate the existence of universals in child language — endeavours which have met with a remarkable degree of success. At the two- to three-word stage most, if not all, children appear to be attempting to express a common set of semantic relations, the emergence of which appears to be conditional upon their pre-existing levels of cognitive development (Brown, 1973; Slobin, 1973a; Wells, 1974). Thus while much research energy has been devoted to describing and defining the cognitive and linguistic equipment children bring in common to this task, much less has been directed towards examining the role of external factors in facilitating, retarding or possibly even shaping the course of acquisition.

Historically, this emphasis on the child's contribution also has its roots in early theories of language acquisition which assumed that the input to the child was the kind of speech adults use in normal conversations. Such an input would be extremely unfavourable to the task of learning the complex rule system relating meanings to the expressions the child hears. Adult speech is complex in syntax, semantics and vocabulary and is often rapid, disfluent and subject to unpredictable disruptions. But, as children nevertheless acquire language with surprising ease and efficiency, they were credited with

an intricate innate capacity to do so. In the absence of an appropriately structured input, it was necessary to hypothesize a highly structured child mind (Chomsky, 1965; McNeill, 1966b, 1970).

Although recently there has been a much greater emphasis on the
primacy of the cognitive equipment that the child brings to the task
of acquisition (Slobin, 1973a; Wells, 1974), we have not immediately
seen any significant change in the tendency to impute a relatively
minor role to factors external to the child. Despite the fact that the
problem of the role of the child's experiences is a central one in cognitive psychology, there has been little systematic re-evaluation of
the role of input factors in current theories of language acquisition.

However, recent studies of the speech actually addressed to children have reopened the question of the importance of the input to
the acquisition process. It seems that most, if not all, young children
have access to a highly specialized speech register (Ferguson, this volume) that is sensitive to their communicative immaturity (see Snow,
this volume, for a review of speech addressed to children). In adapting to their children's cognitive and communicative immaturity,
mothers are providing young language-learning children with a data
base that may be highly appropriate to their linguistic needs.

Support for this position has come from the results of a few studies
which have directly compared the speech of mothers to children of
different ages and levels of linguistic sophistication (among others,
Broen, 1972; Snow, 1972; Phillips, 1973; Cross, 1975). These results
have suggested that the register is flexible and sensitive to variations
in the listener. More-mature children hear maternal utterances that
are longer, more complex and more disfluent than less-mature children. They are also provided with fewer expansions and repetitions.
It is the possibility that mothers may adapt quite sensitively to even
smaller increments in their children's maturity and that they may
vary in their abilities to do this, that has prompted a re-evaluation of
the relative importance of the input to the acquisition process. If indeed the organization of the child's input, particularly at the syntactic level, can be shown to predict the child's linguistic growth, then
one may impute a less detailed structure to the child's innate cognitive and linguistic equipment and a more facilitative role to the nature
and quality of his linguistic experiences. Studies of mothers' speech
may thus provide insights into the complex interactions between the
child's capacities, his linguistic input, and the process of acquisition.

However, it has yet to be definitely established that any aspect of
mothers' speech is sufficiently adapted to the child's requirements to
warrant such a shift in emphasis. We know that mothers' speech is

sensitive to wide differences in listener sophistication, and that some mothers vary the level of expansions and repetitions closely in tune with small increments in children's linguistic maturity (Cross, 1975; Newport, 1976). But from what we know about the speed of language acquisition, this may not be sensitive enough. The speed with which children complete the acquisition course indicates that they make large gains over very small time periods. Brown (1973) has reported that Eve, the youngest of his subjects, showed considerable gains in utterance length at every two-week visit. To be appropriate to the child's requirements, it is clear that maternal speech adjustments must be made quite finely and continuously over the course of development. However, we do not yet know whether the register is adjustable to this degree.

Newport (1976; see also Newport, Gleitman & Gleitman, this volume) has suggested that if mothers' speech is to play a significant role in linguistic acquisition, it is at the syntactic level that sensitivity to child level should be most evident. She argues that an explanation of the child's rapid progress, in terms of an appropriately structured input rather than an appropriately structured mind, presupposes that mothers' speech presents a programme for learning that is always a step ahead of the child in linguistic complexity. Thus it must be adjusted, not grossly to global aspects of the child such as his cognitive sophistication, status, physical size or babyishness, but specifically to his linguistic competence or, more precisely, to the level of sophistication to which he will next move.

This brings us to the most recent characterization of the child's linguistic input and its importance in the acquisition process. Newport has reported that the syntactic complexity of mothers' speech to two-year olds is not tuned to differences in linguistic level (Newport, 1976). In fact, she found that it is not well tuned even to the children's ages; and she concludes that although mothers' speech may be in the 'right ball-park of complexity', it is not sufficiently suited to the child's linguistic requirements at any level of analysis to avoid 'the attribution of a fairly extensive prior structure to the language learner himself'.

HYPOTHESES

Each of these views of the relevance of the input to the process of language acquisition makes a prediction about the degree of correlation one should find between the child's linguistic sophistication and the structure of his input which can be tested in a correlational analysis of the relationships between features of mothers' speech and measures of their children's linguistic levels. This paper presents such an analysis.

(a) *The indifferent hypothesis.* The view held by Chomsky (1965), and others, that the input is unfavourable to the child's tasks, suggests that we will not find any clear pattern of correlation between the child's linguistic level and his mother's speech adjustments.

(b) *The fine-tuning hypothesis.* The position, referred to explicitly by Pfuderer (1969), Cross (1975), Newport *et al.* (1975) and Snow (this volume), among others, that the input is closely tailored to the child's linguistic requirements, predicts a high degree of correlation between mothers' speech features and child ability at all descriptive levels but particularly at the syntactic level.

(c) *The multi-factor hypothesis.* This view is put forward by Newport (1976), who argues that as mothers' speech is shaped by a multiplicity of purposes, it is not perfectly tuned at any level. Her conclusions predict that at any level of description there will be an uneven range of low to moderate correlations, but that at the level of syntactic complexity there will be only low correlations with the child's linguistic level.

METHOD

SUBJECTS

The subjects were 16 middle-class, English-speaking mother and child dyads, selected from a pool of mother—child subjects participating in an ongoing study of the role of input factors in language acquisition.

The children were six boys and ten girls between the ages of 19 and 32 months, who were selected because they showed signs of rapid language acquisition. All had obtained scores beyond the norms for children six months older on the Developmental Sentence Analysis (Lee, 1974), the Peabody Picture Vocabulary Test and on a test of receptive syntax developed for this project. All developmental histories indicated that they had surpassed the appropriate speech milestones during the preceding 12 months and they had satisfied the project's speech therapists that their speech was intelligible and fluent. These selection procedures yielded a sample of rapidly developing children whose mean utterance lengths ranged from 1.49 to 3.44.

The mothers were selected because they also had four- to six-year-old children at school or kindergarten whose teachers assessed them as being well in advance of their age norms in language use and comprehension. If the input does indeed play an important role in acquisition, it was assumed that mothers with two rapidly developing children would be providing optimally appropriate linguistic inputs and thus were an ideal sample to observe the kinds of interactions which promote acquisition. Each mother had a graduate degree or equivalent and each husband was engaged in an academic or professional occupation. All the mothers were solely responsible for the care of their children at home, the father and older children spending large parts of the week-day away from home. Therefore the mother was the primary source of linguistic input to the child.

THE SPEECH DATA

The speech data were audio and video recordings[2] of spontaneous conversations between the subject-child and the mother, taken in the child's usual playroom at home. There was at least one hour of tape for each dyad as well as detailed supplementary notes, containing contextual and phonetic information recorded on the spot by either the investigator or her assistant. The recordings were made on a stereo cassette recorder, and each mother and child used Sony miniature lavaliere microphones attached to long leads to permit freedom of movement.

The transcripts were prepared independently by three experienced transcribers, two of whom had been present at most of the recording sessions. Each transcriber had access to the video and audio recordings, as well as the phonetic and contextual notes. The final form of the transcripts for each dyad contained a completely faithful version of their utterances (including phonetic notation) and, where necessary (i.e. for telegraphic child utterances and incomplete adult utterances), a paraphrase or gloss of the transcriber's interpretation of the meaning of each utterance. Each record was checked for accuracy against the original tapes and notes at least four times and contained, for the mother's speech, a record of disfluencies, revisions, hesitations and pauses, as well as intonation information for all run-on sequences, questions, imperatives and incomplete sentences. Unintelligible or ambiguous utterances were marked using a simple notation system indicating the transcriber's degree of certainty about the gloss.

PROCEDURE

The procedure involved at least three home recordings and testing sessions and, occasionally, a fourth visit to complete testing. To reduce the contaminating effect of the observation procedures, the mothers were not informed that their contributions to the conversation would be examined.[3] They were asked to play with the child using a small set of miniature household toys and some flexible dolls representing members of a family and to respond as naturally as possible to ensure that the child was relaxed and spontaneous. Recording was commenced only after the mother and child appeared to be relaxed and involved in the play situation, and the speech data taken from a point approximately 15 minutes after the commencement of each recording.

THE LISTENER VARIABLES

Four measures of the children's spontaneous speech, one measure of their receptive ability, and their ages, were the listener variables selected for this study. Each was included on the grounds that it may represent an aspect of the child to which the mothers were sensitive.

(1) *The children's mean utterance lengths (MLU)*. This was included as a measure of the child's average utterance complexity. Each child's MLU was calculated using precisely the same method as Brown (1973) recommends (i.e. including all repetitions, 'yes', 'no' and similar single-word responses to questions and counting as one morpheme all concatenatives such as 'wanna', 'gonna', etc.). However, it has been argued elsewhere that this measure may underestimate the child's productive capacities (Cross, 1975). In short, it takes no account of the child's ability to use ellipsis in a discourse-appropriate way, and in fact penalizes the child who has learnt to systematically delete redundant sentence constitutents. In scoring all 'yes' and 'no' type responses to questions, it reflects the mother's tendency to use interrogatives as a speech elicitation device, thus artifactually depressing the scores of children who respond appropriately.[4] However, MLU was included in case mothers have a sense of their children's usual or average productive capacity and adjust their speech to this variable. It also permitted comparison of the stages of development represented in the present sample with others in the literature.

(2) *The children's maximum utterance lengths*. This measure was included to overcome the problem discussed for MLU. It was intended

to measure the child's spontaneous speech at moments when he was operating near the upper limits of his capacity. As many observers have noted, children who have an average utterance length of only one or two morphemes are frequently capable of surprisingly long utterances, especially when they seem highly motivated to communicate with others. To measure the child's performance at this extended level of production, we simply averaged the length of his 50 longest utterances in a sample of 500 utterances.

(3) *The children's receptive abilities.* A test of the child's ability to process and decode sentences was also included. It was reasoned that signs from the child indicating which utterances he could understand and which he could not were probably the most compelling source of feedback for the mother in adjusting her speech appropriately to his level. Using the mother to administer most of the test in small doses throughout the observation sessions, we assessed each child for his ability to give verbal and non-verbal evidence of comprehending the meaning of 100 syntactically different sentences. These were selected from a larger sample of 260 items which had been administered to 70 children between two and six years of age. The test, in final form, contained the 100 items which best discriminated between each age level.[5]

(4) *Child comprehensibility.* If mothers are more sensitive to their children's expressive than their receptive abilities, then they may be influenced more by the child's overall communicative proficiency (i.e. the ability to get a message across clearly) than by his purely linguistic sophistication. Success in getting the message across may depend as much on the child's non-linguistic as linguistic skills (e.g. in the use of context, intonation, gesture and facial expression). The child's proficiency in getting his message across was measured by counting the number of utterances that were obviously unclear, either to the child's mother (i.e. where she requested a repetition or stated that she had not understood him), or to any transcriber (i.e. were marked in the transcript as being of uncertain meaning or for which there was substantial disagreement between transcribers). The percentage of incomprehensible utterances was subtracted from the total number of utterances to give a 'comprehensibility' score. This measure correlated significantly with age, MLU, receptive ability and the extended production measure.

(5) *The child's conversational vocabulary.* Each child's type—token ratio was calculated for the first and last 100 words in each transcript. The child's expressive vocabulary was included in this analysis because Newport (1976) has reported that several categories of mothers'

speech were adjusted to the child's vocabulary rather than linguistic complexity.

(6) *The children's ages.* Each child's age was expressed in the number of weeks since his birthdate.

THE MOTHERS' SPEECH PARAMETERS

Sixty-two features of mothers' speech were selected for this analysis, based largely on the findings of previous documentations of mothers' speech. In most cases the operational definitions in the literature have been adhered to. Where changes in definition have been made these are indicated in the Appendix (p. 183—8).

CODING

Samples of 300 sequential utterances were taken from each mother's speech corpus. The coding was undertaken by the investigator alone, after a series of reliability checks and subsequent redefining of features had established that it could be used with inter-coder reliability indices of at least 0.68.

The following is a brief list of the main categories of features. The Appendix contains a more detailed breakdown for each category.

Discourse features

Semantic relationships between child and mother's utterances

Each maternal utterance was first classified by the extent to which it expressed or incorporated one of the child's preceding semantic intentions or was a maternal repetition.

(*a*) *Semantically related to child utterance.* Utterances that were imitations (exact or partial), expansions (complete, incomplete, transformed or elaborated), and semantic extensions of the child's preceding topic or predicate (using either the child's noun-phrase or a pronoun substitute).

(*b*) *Semantically unrelated to child utterance.* All utterances that were semantically new to the discourse, and those that were also semantically isolated in the discourse (i.e. were not repeated, elaborated or extended).

(*c*) *Maternal self-repetitions.* Sequential repetitions (exact, partial, transformed and paraphrases) as well as non-sequential repetitions, stock expressions and self-answers.

(*d*) *Synergistic sequences.* Utterances and utterance sequences which combined the criteria for the semantically related category and the maternal self-repetition category.

Referential characteristics

Utterances that referred to the immediate context (i.e. to the child's or the mother's activities or to persons and objects in the recording situation), as well as those that referred to non-immediate events (i.e. events, people or objects that were removed from the child's perceptions).

Conversational style

The volume of mothers' output over short time periods, the ratio of mother to child utterances, and the proportion of mothers' utterances per conversational turn.

Syntactic features

(*a*) *The syntactic complexity of mothers' speech.* The mother's MLU, the difference between the child's and the mother's MLU, the proportions of long, single-word and multi-propositional utterances, and their preverbal complexity.

(*b*) *The syntactic integrity of mothers' speech.* The proportions of disfluent, unintelligible and run-on sentences, as well as the percentages of complete and incomplete sentences.

(*c*) *Surface sentence types.* Proportions of questions (wh- questions and several categories of yes—no questions), imperatives (affirmative and negative), declaratives and deictic statements, as well as full noun-phrases and pronouns.

RESULTS

The simple product—moment correlations between each mother's speech parameter and the child listener variables are set out under the main category headings in Table 6.1, 6.2 and 6.3. It is clear that within the restricted stage of development represented by the children, mothers' speech is quite well tuned to variation in both their listener's

Table 6.1 *The mean percentages of mothers' discourse parameters and simple correlations with child listener variables*

Mothers' speech parameters[b]	Child listener variables[a]						
	Mean percentages	Receptive scores	Longest utterances	MLU (100 utterances)	Comprehensibility	Type–token ratio	Age (in weeks)
Semantically related							
Imitations	2.8	21	27	29	10	− 20	20
Expansions (incomplete)	5.8	− 74**	− 66**	− 62*	− 67**	− 58*	− 57*
Expansions (complete)	6.2	− 85**	− 70**	− 64**	− 61*	− 67**	− 65**
Elaborated expansions	3.0	− 69**	− 73**	− 59*	− 68***	− 66**	− 56*
Transformed expansions	2.8	− 46	− 49*	− 39	− 36	− 23	− 08
Total expansions/imitations	20.5	− 77***	− 68**	− 61*	− 62*	− 65**	− 65**
Extensions (child's NP)	12.0	− 26	− 20	− 17	− 22	− 41	− 22
Extensions (pronouns)	22.0	49*	45	37	22	35	44
Extensions (predicate)	0.6	01	00	06	00	− 04	− 02
Total semantic extensions	34.7	43	44	37	18	21	03
Expansions + extensions	55.1	− 22	− 13	− 13	− 33	− 30	− 04
Expansions + NP extensions	32.8	− 66**	− 58*	− 51*	− 55*	− 63**	− 58*
Semantically unrelated							
Semantically new utterances	15.9	39	27	24	42	35	44
Novel, isolated utterances	5.0	70**	56*	53*	58*	36	72**
Maternal repetitions							
Paraphrases	4.0	− 60*	− 59*	− 56*	− 41	− 25	− 14
Transformed repetitions	7.3	− 13	− 08	− 12	− 28	− 51*	− 35
Exact repetitions	1.3	− 54*	− 51*	− 38	− 41	− 58*	− 03
Partial repetitions	7.2	− 82**	− 79**	− 72**	− 53*	− 37	− 77**
Total sequential repetitions	19.9	− 75***	− 72**	− 66**	− 64**	− 22	− 66**
Non-sequential repetitions	9.4	− 62**	− 59*	− 47	− 52*	− 36	− 39
Total repetitions	28.2	− 81**	− 77**	− 67***	− 69***		− 63**

Table 6.1 (*continued*)

Mothers' speech parameters[b]	Child listener variables[a]						
	Mean percentages	Receptive scores	Longest utterances	MLU (100 utterances)	Comprehensibility	Type–token ratio	Age (in weeks)
Synergistic sequences							
Expansions × Repetitions	6.4	−78**	−71**	−59*	−77**	−51*	−77**
Extensions × Repetitions	14.0	−63**	−56*	−61*	−70**	−35	−67**
Other							
Self answers	2.9	07	07	−01	28	20	17
Stock expressions	2.5	−56*	−49	−40	−69*	−44	−46
Yes–no replies	10.6	33	22	31	26	15	17

* $p < 0.05$ ** $p < 0.01$.
[a] See Method for description of child listener variables.
[b] See the Appendix for definitions of mothers' speech parameters.

Table 6.2   Means of mothers' speech parameters coded for referential quality and conversational style and simple correlations with child listener variables

Mothers' parameters[b]	Child listener variables[a]						
	Means	Receptive scores	Longest utterances	MLU (100 utterances)	Comprehensibility	Type–token ratio	Age (in weeks)
A. Referential field							
Immediate references	72.9%	− 32	− 36	− 25	− 17	− 22	− 06
Child events	48.4%	− 54*	− 50*	− 44	− 67**	− 34	− 31
Mother events	15.5%	14	04	08	27	− 07	21
Child + mother events	63.3%	− 37	− 38	− 33	− 46	− 20	− 51*
Persons/objects present	9.0%	34	30	34	58*	31	28
Non-immediate events	13.2%	72**	62*	57*	39	44	60*
B. Conversation style							
Words/minute	74.9	− 12	− 20	− 03	39	41	36
Mother–child utterances	1.32	− 02	− 01	− 09	34	31	− 06
Mother utterances/turns	1.75	26	26	22	22	44	35

*$p < 0.05$ **$p < 0.01$.
[a] See Method for description of child listener variables.
[b] See the Appendix for definitions of mothers' speech parameters.

age and language maturity. However, there is considerable unevenness across the main feature categories, both in degree of tuning and in the aspects of the child to which the adjustments are made.

Most discourse features (Table 6.1), i.e. expansions, self-repetitions and stock phrases, are highly negatively correlated with all measures of the child's language skill but particularly with the child's receptive ability. Semantically new and isolated utterances on the other hand increase significantly with both age and receptive ability.

At the referential level (Table 6.2) the mother's references to her child's activity decrease with linguistic ability, while those to other persons in the immediate situation increase with child comprehensibility. However, utterances referring to non-immediate events are very positively related to the language measures, particularly the receptive test. In contrast, the conversational measures (Table 6.2) show no sign of close tuning to any listener variables.

The syntactic features (Table 6.3) present a very uneven picture. All measures of maternal utterance length are significantly related to child language maturity, especially receptive ability. Long utterances increase with child sophistication while one-word utterances decrease with vocabulary. Multi-propositional utterances increase with comprehensibility and receptive control, but preverb complexity increases only with age. The syntactic integrity measures are less tuned to all measures but some are positively related to age, while within the sentence types only questions are significantly associated with (i.e. decline with) child growth. The incidence of pronouns moderately increases with comprehensibility and receptive ability.

DISCUSSION

Of the 62 parameters of maternal speech examined in this study, 35 were significantly correlated with one or several of the listener variables. Of these parameters 15 were most closely associated with the children's receptive abilities, seven with child comprehensibility, seven with age, three with the child's conversational vocabulary, two with extended production, and one with MLU. If we recall that the children, on average, varied by less than two morphemes in their MLU scores, and by only 12 months in age range, this is evidence of a well-tailored input and entails a firm rejection of the 'indifferent' hypothesis. In general, the input to rapidly developing children is graded quite continuously in tune with their linguistic and communicative abilities.

Table 6.3 *Means of mothers' syntactic parameters and simple correlations with child listener variables*

Mothers' speech parameters[b]	Child listener variables[a]						
	Means	Receptive scores	Longest utterances	MLU (100 utterances)	Comprehensibility	Type–token ratio	Age (in weeks)
Syntactic complexity							
Mean length of utterance	4.8	75**	67**	56*	47	38	51*
Percentage of long utterances	8.7%	66***	61*	49*	49*	17	46
Difference child—mother MLU	2.6	−50*	−62*	−73**	−14	−17	−28
Single-word utterances	6.2%	−46	−33	−25	−35	−63**	−19
Propositions/utterances	1.03	55*	43	30	63**	33	36
Preverb complexity	1.63	33	16	04	09	15	55*
Syntactic integrity							
Disfluent utterances	3.3%	56*	44	35	34	33	64**
Unintelligible utterances	2.0%	24	07	03	−04	27	50*
Run-on sentences	9.8%	42	24	35	27	44	49*
Abbreviated utterances	18.0%	−40	−28	−23	−34	−44	−27
Complete sentences	61.0%	−11	−18	21	−10	20	06
Sentence types							
Questions	33.4%	−36	−42	−43	−32	−04	−52*
Wh- questions	15.4%	−42	−43	−49*	−46	−28	−50*
'Where is the NP?'	2.3%	−24	−20	−18	−32	09	−34
'What's that?'	5.3%	−57*	−58*	−52*	−63**	01	−43
Yes—No questions	18.2%	−08	−13	−11	00	−29	−19
Auxiliary-fronted questions	7.7%	12	05	03	07	21	06
Tag questions	5.6%	04	02	−04	−01	−30	02
Rising-intonation questions	5.0%	−20	−23	−17	−08	−46	−24
Imperatives	7.4%	−01	−01	11	35	10	01

Table 6.3 (*continued*)

Mothers' speech parameters[b]	Child listener variables[a]						
	Means	Receptive scores	Longest utterances	MLU (100 utterances)	Comprehen-sibility	Type–token ratio	Age (in weeks)
Negative imperatives	0.3%	01	00	08	−12	39	−27
Affirmative (subject included)	1.8%	−17	−17	−11	23	15	−28
(subject deleted)	5.9%	16	08	−22	36	08	−10
Declaratives	27.4%	−21	−10	05	23	36	22
Deictic statements	6.2%	14	18	17	−11	14	15
Other							
Noun-phrases/utterances	0.65	−37	−36	−40	−33	−45	−08
Pronouns/utterances	0.72	49*	35	23	51*	39	42

*$p < 0.05$ **$p < 0.01$
[a] See Method for description of child listener variables.
[b] See the Appendix for definitions of mothers' speech parameters.

DISCOURSE ADJUSTMENTS

The best evidence that the input may play an important facilitative role in these children's acquisition processes is provided by the finding that, in general, the mothers' discourse adjustments were most closely associated with measures of the children's psycholinguistic, linguistic and communicative abilities (i.e. receptive control, maximum output, mean utterance length and comprehensibility). Correlations with age exceeded those with language measures only twice in 26 discourse parameters. Of the 18 significant parameters, the child's receptive control is the best predictor of mothers' discourse adjustments on 11 occasions, his extended production, comprehensibility and vocabulary twice each, and the child's age once.

Most of the discourse adjustments examined in this study have been argued to provide the child with informal language lessons as to the formal means to express a communicative intention. Briefly, expansions and elaborations of the child's own communicative intention should directly help him to see what is lacking in his realization (Cazden, 1965; Brown, Cazden & Bellugi, 1968; McNeill, 1970). Semantic extensions, as they incorporate the child's previously expressed topic and therefore usually refer to his ongoing activities, have been argued to play a similar role (Cross, 1975, 1976). Maternal redundancy provides the child with extra opportunities to process and comprehend the original utterance, often clearly displaying the internal structure of the mother's expression (Broen, 1972; Snow, 1972). It stands to reason that any combinations of these devices, as found in the synergistic sequences in Table 6.1, should enhance the facilitating effect of each in isolation. If, as the negative correlations indicate, these tutorial opportunities are provided in much larger quantities to children whose comprehension is least mature, then it seems sensible to reject the notion that the input is unfavourable to the child's acquisition process.

Some explanation for maternal discourse adjustments

Few researchers in the area of mothers' speech would argue that the provision of language lessons to the language-learning child is the primary motivation for mothers' speech adjustments. Rather, they appear to be the incidental outcome of trying to converse with a listener capable of expressing and receiving meaning in verbal form, but with very undeveloped linguistic skills. The common finding for the discourse adjustments studied here is the mother's sensitivity to the child's receptive abilities and his extended production capacity. This combination accounted for the highest correlations on most of the parameters in Table 6.1. Correlations with the child's MLU, on the other hand, consistently failed to reach the same levels. Thus it seems that the mothers are sensitive to abilities or capacities which may underlie the majority of the child's utterances. The measures that most strongly predict their adjustments suggest that we should attribute to them an ability to monitor the child's psycholinguistic abilities rather than the characteristic linguistic level of his spontaneous speech.

(1) *Maternal self-repetitions.* The least difficult set of correlations to explain are those found between maternal self-repetitions and the children's receptive abilities. Of the seven repetition categories, five were most highly correlated with this child variable. Several observers have suggested that redundancy in mothers' speech is a response to the child's inability to process the original utterance (Kobashigawa, 1969; Snow, 1972; Cross, 1975). The majority of the originals of repetitions tend to be imperatives and questions — functions which require an overt response from the child (Cross, 1975). Cross has reported that the majority of maternal repetitions immediately follow the child's failure to respond or some sign that the child has misinterpreted the original utterance, and has suggested that these cues are directly responsible for the incidence of maternal utterances that are repeated, reduced or elaborated in sequence. The receptive test provided a measure of the child's ability to decode linguistic material, so it is not surprising that the mothers' repetition rates were sensitive to this measure. As the children improved in this ability, many more of the mother's utterances were presumably attended to and appropriately interpreted by the child, decreasing the need to repeat them.

(2) *Semantic relation to child's utterances.* The proportions of all expansion responses were also more closely (and negatively) associated with the child's receptive control and longest utterances than with MLU. Cross (1975) has suggested that in providing such checks on the child's communicative intention, mothers are responding to the telegraphicness of each utterance. The actual length of the child's utterance is not as relevant a determinant of the occurrence of an expansion as the number of extra morphemes required to form an adult version of the child's intention. This would explain why MLU predicted the expansion categories less well than did either the receptive scores or the extended production measure. It seems to be the lingu-

istic immaturity and the resulting communicative imprecision of child utterances, not their length, that influences the mother to provide expansions (Cross, 1975). As the child's utterances become less telegraphic and linguistically more complex, the mother's need to check or confirm his communicative intention by expanding or elaborating it is reduced, thus explaining the strong negative correlation with measures of the child's expressive and receptive abilities.[6]

A similar pattern of correlations was retained when those semantic extensions which explicitly incorporated the child's topic noun-phrase and all the expansion responses were combined. This combination accounted for 33% of all maternal utterances. The strong negative correlations here indicate that the mothers were somehow constrained to adhere to child-initiated topics, even to use the child's own words, by the immaturity of his psycholinguistic skills. As the children became more sophisticated, there was an increase in the mothers' tendency to introduce new topics into the ongoing discourse (i.e. semantically unrelated utterances). However, many of these were short stereotyped phrases like 'That's a good girl' or 'What happened?' which were often repeated throughout the discourse and were probably not intended as conversational initiatives. When we extracted these as well as utterances that were sequentially repeated, we were left with a very small proportion of utterances (5%) that were semantically unique to the ongoing discourse (novel, isolated utterances). The incidence of these was highly negatively correlated with the child's age and receptive abilities, reflecting clearly the declining proportion of maternal utterances that were semantically tied to the child's previous utterances.

(3) *Mothers' references.* This pattern is again closely echoed in Table 6.2 where the child's receptive ability and longest utterances also best predict the degree of contextual and temporal displacement of her utterances. The proportion of utterances that were unrelated to the child-initiated topics, and those that were unrelated to the immediate situational context are both inversely related to the child's psycholinguistic ability and age. There was a considerable degree of overlap between utterances that were semantically contingent on the child's preceding utterances and those that referred to the child's or mother's ongoing activities (child events and mother events, Table 6.2). As the child almost always talked about what he was doing, his mother's expansions, elaborations and extensions referred to these ongoing events.

The facilitative role of maternal discourse adjustments

The coincidence of immediate referentiality and semantic contingency may have considerable importance in accounting for the rapid rate at which these children were acquiring language. Of mothers' utterances, 55 % were incorporated exactly, or referred to their children's previously expressed topics. Based on Snow's evidence (this volume) we can estimate that the majority of these utterances will encode only the semantic relations that the child himself has mastered — a finding which she argues allows the child to concentrate on acquiring the linguistic aspects of the expressions he hears. In addition, Table 6.2 shows that 72 % of maternal utterances encoded either the child's or the mother's ongoing activities or referred to persons or objects present in the room. Thus, the vast majority of the expressions the child hears encode events that are perceptually, cognitively and semantically available and salient to the child. If we add the ingredient that the least mature children received significantly larger proportions of most of these categories, we can begin to understand why these children were acquiring language so rapidly.

Wells (1974) has argued that children will learn linguistic structure by experiencing it as adults encode situations and events which they already understand. The ideal situation would be 'a shared activity with an adult in which the adult gave linguistic expression to just those meanings in the situation which the child was capable of intending and to which he was at that particular moment paying attention' (*ibid.*, p. 267). The major proportion of these mothers' expressions seem to be 'ideal' in Wells' sense.

Furthermore, the remainder of mothers' speech seems to contain very few utterances that would create any acquisition problem for children at this stage of development. From the child's viewpoint (with the clear exception of the small number of semantically unique utterances) most of the utterances excluded from the above categories should present very little that is new to the child in the way of linguistic information. Three percent are exact imitations of the child's utterances, over 6 % are the simplest of all utterances — one-word utterances (Table 6.3). A further 10 % are simply 'yes', 'no', 'good', 'fine', 'OK' responses to the child's utterances. Nearly 8 % are simple stock phrases like 'Good girl', 'What's up?', 'That's fine', 'Never mind', or 'What's that?' questions (and variants) which the child frequently uses himself. Of course, these categories overlap to some degree; but a perusal of four transcripts for the youngest children showed that

42 % of all utterances coded as semantically non-contingent could be placed in one of these categories. Strictly speaking, such utterances cannot be said to comprise the input to the child's future acquisition process. Beyond this, we know that many 'new' utterances are repeated and therefore give the child a second or third chance to process much new information. Viewed from this perspective, the input to these children looks to be far from unfavourable or irrelevant to their ease of acquistion.

However, there was another category of discourse features that may play a very powerful role in acquisition. The repetition category tends to overlap to some extent with the semantically contingent and non-contingent categories. Table 6.1 presents under the heading *Synergistic sequences* the 20 % of maternal utterances that were cross-classified as both expansions (or extensions) and self repetitions.

Essentially there are two interactions situations which give rise to these coincidences. The first occurs when an expansion, extension or imitation of the child's preceding utterance is repeated, reduced or elaborated in one of the succeeding maternal utterances; the second when a maternal utterance is imitated by the child, and then the mother expands or extends that imitation. While the first interaction probably has the effect of driving home the linguistic information contained in the original expansion, the second would seem to be the more powerful. Here, the child having imitated all or part of the mother's original utterance then immediately receives feedback about his attempt. Slobin (1973b) has argued that the child may often imitate constructions in adult speech that are just beyond his capacity to assimilate and that this may be an external indication of his efforts to accommodate his linguistic system to the new material in the utterance, i.e. may indicate that the child is actively attempting to comprehend it. If this is so, then this type of expansion may be very well timed indeed and suggests an especially powerful way that maternal discourse adjustments may assist the child in the acquisition process. Once again, Table 6.1 shows that the least linguistically-mature children received the highest proportions. It can be argued that they are in the child's input in the largest proportions just when they may have the most relevance to his acquisition task.

One final set of potentially facilitative discourse features remains to be discussed. Table 6.2 contains some very general measures of the overall characteristics of the mothers' conversational style — the sheer amount of speech she directed towards the child (words per minute), the balance in output between the partners (proportion of mother–child utterances) and a measure which attempted to characterize the density of the conversational structure (the number of maternal utterances per conversational turn). Quite clearly, these features failed to show the sensitivity to listener variables noted for other discourse features. However, the data in the column headed 'Means' bears on the facilitative role of these adjustments. It shows that the mothers' contributions to the conversation were not much greater than the children's, and that there was a very regular conversation structure which provided the child with just under two utterances per turn.

At least two beneficial effects to the child's acquisition process may follow from this patterning. Firstly, the provision of less than two maternal utterances between conversational turns may enhance the perceptual salience to the child of the linguistic information contained in any single utterance. If several utterances were fired at him in rapid succession before he was provided with his turn, then presumably the processing of the original utterance would be interfered with as a function of the number of utterances in the turn. Secondly, the approximately one-to-one ratio between child and mother utterances indicates that the child is being given ample opportunity to practise the skills that he is acquiring. It also means that, as 55 % of mother's utterances were semantically related to his own, there is a better than even chance any new utterance he attempts will be immediately followed by one from his mother that contains some relevant feedback about his own expression.

Some conclusions about mothers' discourse adjustments

In general, it appears that at the discourse level of description, mothers' speech is more finely tuned to the child's linguistic, psycholinguistic and communicative abilities than to age. It has been argued that the discourse adjustments found to be most sensitive to child level in this study are precisely those that provide the child with ideal opportunities to learn the structure of his language. Thus, we can reject the hypothesis that the input to the child is unfavourable to his acquisition task — at least in the case of children acquiring language rapidly. For these children, the input has many features that are suited to their linguistic requirements. In addition, this analysis has shown that many of these adjustments are most finely tuned to the child's psycholinguistic abilities, particularly to his receptive control. If children acquire the form of language through the process of comprehension, then the mothers of rapidly developing children seem to make it easy for them to do so.

MOTHERS' SYNTACTIC ADJUSTMENTS

Having concluded that the general thrust of the evidence entails a rejection of the position that the child's input is indifferent to his acquisition process, we can now ask if it is programmed at the syntactic level to provide the child with precisely the linguistic information he needs to take his next steps in linguistic acquisition. To support a fine-tuning hypothesis, we require clear evidence that mothers' syntax is slightly ahead of the child's in complexity and is therefore better correlated with measures of the child's linguistic and psycholinguistic abilities than with age or vocabulary. A pattern indicating differential sensitivity of maternal features to various aspects of the children's growth would support the third hypothesis, the multifactor theory.

The complexity measures

The first two measures in Table 6.2, the mothers' MLU and the percentage of utterances that were longer than six morphemes (i.e. longer than average), clearly support a fine-tuning position. Not only does the overall length of mothers' utterances increase closely in tune with the children's receptive capacity, extended production and children's MLUs, but also these correlations are higher than for comprehensibility, vocabulary and age. Mothers' utterances become longer as their children become linguistically and psycholinguistically more sophisticated. However, we also need to know whether their utterance lengths are, on average, only a small step ahead of their children's.

This was indeed the case. Their MLUs (4.8) were on average less than three morphemes longer than their children's (2.2) and less than half a morpheme longer than the children's longest utterances (4.4). There was also a consistent and significant tendency for this discrepancy to converge in tune with increases in the child's utterance length – indicating, presumably, a very regular 'catching up' effect as the child drew closer to his mother's level of linguistic maturity.[7] And again, it is clear that the mothers are more sensitive to the children's underlying abilities than to the average length of their utterances.

However, this pattern is not present for any other syntactic parameter. It is not even clearly present for the rest of the complexity measures. Single-word utterances (excluding yes—no and like responses) decreased significantly only with child vocabulary, propositional complexity increased significantly with child comprehensibility and less so with receptive ability; and preverb complexity (the number of morphemes before the main verb) increased only with age. Although all these correlations are appropriate in direction, they do not support the hypothesis that maternal syntactic complexity is consistently and finely tuned to either the child's linguistic or psycholinguistic abilities. In fact, when viewed against the correlations for length of mothers' utterances they suggest that mothers are adjusting different aspects of their speech to different aspects of their listeners, producing a pattern that is more consistent with a multi-factor account than with the fine-tuning hypothesis.

The syntactic versus semantic complexity of mothers' speech

The correlations for utterance length echo the pattern found for many of the discourse adjustments. This gives the impression that utterance length is measuring something a little different from measures of the syntactic density of the utterance (i.e. their preverb and propositional complexity). The proportion of multi-propositional utterances is simply too small to satisfactorily account for the overall increase in length. Overall only 3 % contained more than one underlying proposition. The overwhelming majority were simple sentences, or less. Newport (1976) claims that maternal utterance length is increased primarily by the replacement of constituents that were previously deleted in the mothers' speech. But this does not seem to be the case for this sample. The proportion of deleted (abbreviated) utterances (Table 6.3) does not decrease significantly with any of the child measures, whereas the proportion of long utterances clearly increases.

A more likely explanation is that the mothers' utterances increase in length because they are simply increasing the amount of semantic information that they are trying to communicate to the child. Snow (this volume) has shown that mothers with longer MLUs produce more multiterm utterances at the semantic level than mothers with shorter MLUs. If, as she reports, most of their utterances express precisely the same semantic categories and relations that underly their children's expressions, then they will lengthen directly as a result of being tuned to the child's semantic growth in the ways she suggests. On this view MLU would reflect the semantic complexity of mothers' speech and only indirectly measure increases in its syntactic complexity.

In view of the earlier findings of the present study, this is not a surprising conclusion. The majority of utterances in this sample have been coded as incorporating all or part of preceding child utterances. In this respect, these mothers are attentive and very responsive to the child's semantic intentions. They seem to know what meanings the child is capable of intending and, judging by their ability to tune in to his receptive level, what meanings he can comprehend. Thus their fine adjustments in utterance length in tune with their children's abilities can be viewed as the direct result of efforts to match their children's semantic rather than syntactic levels. The few morphemes difference between the mothers' MLU and the children's may reflect their superior syntactic sophistication (i.e. in supplying grammatical morphemes that the child does not yet use); or, in view of the closeness of the mothers' MLUs and the children's longest utterances, may indicate once again that they are tuned to their children's maximum capacity rather than their usual expressive levels. The observation that both mothers' MLU and their proportions of long utterances are more closely correlated with receptive ability and maximum utterance length than with the children's MLUs would seem to support the latter conclusion.

Making a distinction between the semantic and syntactic complexity of maternal utterances may explain why we observed only lower correlations and less consistent tuning to child maturity for all other syntactic features in Table 6.3. These measures are more independent of semantic complexity than length of utterance. In the case of propositional complexity, the amount of semantic information the mother intends to communicate need not dictate the option of using either two separate simple utterances or a single complex one. In most instances it is possible to encode the propositions underlying complex utterances in two (or more) separate sentences. In the case of preverb complexity, mothers can (and frequently do) use deletion operations which reduce sentence-initial density without substantially changing the intention or function of the utterance. They can delete auxiliaries, and pronoun subjects (i.e. in yes—no questions), using intonation to carry the functional information. They can also omit articles, relying on context to supply this information. However, it is quite clear from Table 6.3 that they do not adjust these operations precisely and uniformly to the child's linguistic or psycholinguistic maturity. Where syntactic options are not automatically dictated by the semantic complexity of the mother's intention, we find a reduction in the fineness and consistency of the adjustments. Mothers seem to be less able to monitor either their own or their children's syntactic levels than other aspects of the communication situation. The purely syntactic features of the register are less sensitive than other levels of description (Cross, 1976).

This finding provides some support for Newport's (1976) observation that, in her sample, maternal syntactic complexity was not at all tuned to the children's MLU and its subcomponents. However, the present study, selecting as it did mothers of children exhibiting rapid rates of acquisition, found more sensitivity to overall growth than Newport found for her less selected sample. This suggests that mothers may differ in the extent to which they can monitor and respond to their children's abilities and, at the same time, control their own complexity levels. It may be that the higher degree of syntactic tuning in the input in the present sample was a factor in their linguistic acceleration.

The syntactic integrity measures

In the area of syntactic integrity in the input (i.e. the well-formedness of mothers' speech) the picture as presented in Table 6.3 is somewhat confusing. The relatively small proportions of disfluent, unintelligible and run-together sentences in the input indicate that the children are exposed to relatively clean, well-organized corpora. Only 15 % of all maternal utterances could be characterized as noisy, unanalyzable or confusing, and these tend to be only moderately negatively correlated with age and much less with the children's abilities. The youngest children were receiving even lower proportions of all three sources of confusion. One may explain this finding by hypothesizing that faulty utterances, because they are rare in mothers' speech (Broen, 1972; Newport, 1976), may represent the occasions when the mother slips back into a more adult speech style — particularly at the articulation level. The moderate correlations with age indicate that such lapses increase gradually as the child grows older. With age must come increased exposure to the individual speech styles of an ever-widening circle of conversational partners and, presumably, a concomitant improvement in the child's tolerance of noise in his input, and this may develop independently of strictly linguistic skills. His improving tolerance may influence his mother to slowly return to what, for her, is probably a more natural and relaxed speech style. However, as they are tuned primarily to the child's age and not to his linguistic abilities, they too support a multi-factor theory of maternal speech adjustments.

It might have been possible to sum up the findings for syntactic integrity by claiming that younger children are exposed to a generally cleaner, less confusing data base than older children, had it not been for the finding that 18 % of maternal utterances were grammatically incomplete (i.e. abbreviated utterances, Table 6.3) and that these were slightly more prevalent in the inputs of the least mature children. Newport (1976), noting a similar result, argues that this direction 'is inappropriate to notions of fine adjustment to listener competence'. She contends that large proportions of incomplete or deleted sentences in the child's input may be counter-productive for the acquisition of syntax, both in making the deep structure of the sentence less obvious to the child and by consistently failing to provide him with all the data he needs to construct complete sentences.

However, in our texts the incidence of abbreviated sentences was not restricted to any particular construction or to any of the sentence types coded (see also Brown, 1973: pp. 239—41). Thus the suggestion that some kinds of sentences are almost always incompletely realized in mothers' speech, while others are not, may be unwarranted. Furthermore, like Newport, we found that over 60 % of the mothers' utterances were fully realized, grammatically complete sentences whereas abbreviated utterances accounted for only 18 % (Newport's figure for sentence fragments is a very close 17 %). As the great majority of utterances the child hears are fully realized sentences, it is difficult to concede the point that the child is being systematically deprived of the structures he will need to produce a full range of sentence types.

The yes—no question is often singled out as an example of such systematic deletion. There is a well-documented tendency for mothers to delete the first auxiliary and/or subject pronoun of this sentence type. Table 6.3 sets out the mean percentages of the full and deleted (rising-intonation) versions. Of all instances of this question form, approximately 40 % were realized in full in the mothers' speech, 30 % as complete tag questions (i.e. the inverted auxiliary and subject pronoun were placed at the end of the sentence), and only 23 % as the deleted rising-intonation form. Thus children in this sample were exposed to more than twice as many complete as incomplete yes—no questions. This does not appear to represent linguistic deprivation in Newport's sense.

However, this does not completely overcome Newport's objection that a sizeable proportion of the child's input contains utterances which are not complete examples of the language the child is acquiring. Although children are exposed to over 60 % complete, well-formed utterances in their primary input, 18 % have at least one obligatory constituent deleted in realization. Whether such utterances are ill-formed by usual adult standards is by no means clear. Our transcripts of relaxed conversations between mothers, fathers and older siblings of these children contained 12 % of utterances that could be classified as abbreviated or incomplete in the same ways we observed in the present conversations, whereas the mothers' speech to the investigator (who was a relative stranger) contained only 7 %. Thus it may be that the presence or absence of abbreviated utterances may reflect stylistic variations that adults adopt in response to familiarity with their conversational partners and to the relative informality of the conversation situation. Maternal abbreviations, therefore, may not so much represent ill-formed sentences as simply stylistic options in informal conversational English, which the child will eventually have to learn to use and to relate to the formality of the speech occasion. This reasoning casts doubt on the assumption that the abbreviated forms of sentences are not part of the language that the child has to learn.

Whatever the explanation for the presence of abbreviated utterances in mother–child speech, it is clear that the coexistence of both abbreviated and fully realized versions of most sentence types must restrict the degree to which the level of complexity will be tuned to child level. This may be particularly the case for preverb complexity as many deletions of obligatory morphemes occur prior to the main verb. The examples of yes–no questions and imperatives which occur in both the full form and in the preverbally deleted form show that the input can contain several levels of preverbal complexity for the same sentence type. An examination of the sentence types in mothers' utterances will perhaps make this point clearer.

The distribution of sentence types

Table 6.3 also presents the correlational data for the major surface sentence types. About a third were questions, almost a third declaratives, 6 % statement deixis, and 7 % imperatives. The rest were either too fragmented or too disrupted to code reliably, or were yes–no responses to child questions.

Newport has argued that because mothers' speech is fairly evenly distributed across major sentence types, it may be thought of as being structurally and psycholinguistically complex for the child. She refers to the quite large proportions of wh- questions, yes–no questions and imperatives which, when fully realized, tend to obscure the canonical form of the English sentence. In these forms, surface constituents are either moved or deleted, thus making the deep structure less obvious, which, as she points out, is not the case with the simple declaratives and deictic statements. If the complexity of mothers' syntax is appropriately tuned to the child's level, then this argument predicts a decrease in the least complex sentence types (i.e. declaratives and deictic statements) and an increase in wh-, yes—no questions and imperatives as the children's psycholinguistic abilities advance. Instead, we found no evidence at all that this was the case. In fact, for questions, there was a tendency, reaching statistical significance with increase in age, for the reverse to be true. All questions moderately decreased with our measures of maturity, and wh- questions decreased significantly with both age and MLU. Full yes—no questions and imperatives showed no sensitivity to listener maturity, although the rising-intonation questions decreased almost significantly with vocabulary. Declaratives and deictic statements were quite insensitive to child maturity.

Undoubtedly, the proportions of sentence types in mothers' speech are dictated by functional considerations. Mothers are concerned to question the child to obtain feedback as to his state and wishes; they issue imperatives to direct and control his activities, use deixis to label and draw his attention to items in his environment, and declaratives to comment on his activities and interpret the events around him. Thus considerations of function will override considerations of the syntactic complexity of each sentence type and will contribute to the relative insensitivity of maternal syntactic adjustments.

The psycholinguistic complexity of mothers' speech

However, within sentence types, syntactic insensitivity seems to be produced primarily by the coexistence of multiple levels of realization for each sentence type. This is particularly clear in the case of yes—no questions. As mentioned previously, mothers realize this sentence type in at least three forms: in full form with auxiliary fronting, as tagged declaratives, or as rising-intonation questions. I will argue that the order of these subtypes in Table 6.3 may represent the relative psycholinguistic complexity of each form for the child. Slobin (1973a) has suggested the full yes—no questions may be quite difficult for the child to process and therefore to acquire. Any deformation of an utterance from the underlying structure of the sentence may place a strain on the child's simple interpretation strategies at this stage. The fronting of the auxiliary in the complete version may impede interpretation by defying one of the child's operating principles, i.e. 'avoid interruption or rearrangement of linguistic units' (Slobin, 1973a: p. 199). The rising-intonation form which deletes the fronted auxiliary seems better suited to this strategy. Brown (1973) has shown that this question form first appears in child speech, in Stage 1, in non-inverted form with rising-intonation contour. The full inverted form does not appear until well into Stage 3 or later. Precisely because of its similarity to the child's own early form, the rising-intonation question may be more easily processed and thus more learnable than the fully realized version. The tagged form (which, in this sample, usually carried an affirmative rather than a negative tag) may be intermediate in psycholinguistic complexity. It usually presents the utterance in the same form as the rising-intonation question but attaches the inverted auxiliary and subject pronoun at the end (e.g. 'You put that in there, did you?'). This may be a more salient and helpful position from the child's viewpoint. The child may process the intonation of the utterance relatively easily but immediately afterwards have his attention drawn to the syntactic devices for marking the interrogative function. Thus the coexistence of several levels of realization in the yes—no question type may represent several levels of psycholinguistic complexity for the child.

A somewhat similar case can be made for the wh- questions. Table 6.3 shows that about 50 % of the mothers' wh- forms consisted of 'What's that?' and 'Where is (the) NP?' sentence types. Brown has reported that these too are developmentally primitive forms in child speech, emerging in Stage 1, whereas more complicated wh- forms do not appear until Stage 3. As with the yes—no forms, mothers use both the developmentally early forms as well as forms which appear later in child speech (e.g. 'What is that thing called?' or 'Where did you put the NP?'). Imperatives, too, can be found in several forms ranging from simple one-word utterances like 'Look!', or 'Don't', to more elaborated forms like 'Look at this thing' or 'Don't put it in your mouth!'. And in more than 20 % of imperatives, mothers actually replaced the usually deleted subject, thus making more explicit the underlying structure. Viewed in this way, the problems posed to the language learner by large proportions of somewhat complex sentence types may have been somewhat overstated.

We now have a more complete answer to the observations that although the length of maternal utterances is well tuned to child level, the purely syntactic character is not. Where particular speech functions can be expressed at several levels of realization without significant alteration in semantic content, mothers do not consistently choose a single level. For this reason the syntax of mothers, even to rapidly developing children, is not uniformly pitched just a step ahead of the child in either linguistic or psycholinguistic complexity. Some utterances are pitched at the child's level, some even below this, and others are considerably in advance of what the children themselves can say. Undoubtedly it approximates the child's level in many ways; most utterances are well formed, short and grow longer as the child matures; multi-propositional sentences are rare, preverb complexity is low, and both increase with child growth. However, there is evidence across descriptive levels that mothers are sensitive to different aspects of the child's growth, suggesting a multi-factor account of some of the sensitivity patterns observed. The fine-tuning hypothesis, on the other hand, although providing an appropriate description of the discourse and semantic adjustments of mothers' speech, is not well supported by the data at the syntactic level.

An alternative view of the role of syntactic adjustments

Both the fine-tuning and multi-factor hypotheses assume that the child will be facilitated in acquisition only by an input that is structured at a level of complexity just a small step ahead of his current abilities. However, it is not clear that the provision of such an input will assist the child to discover how to relate his primitive structures to the more complex structure his mother is using. If we assume that he has no specialized faculty for syntax learning — as we should if we wish to assign a major role to his input — we have still to explain how he can process utterances that are, however slightly, beyond the reach of his current psycholinguistic capacity. As the child must be able to process the input before he can learn from it, an input uniformly structured a little in advance of his capacity will contain few advantages over one that is as much out of reach as normal adult speech.

What should we look for in mothers' speech beyond the fact that it is better formed and simpler than adult speech? Wells (1974) has suggested that we should look for conversational interactions between the mother and child which permit him to simultaneously entertain the meaning of an utterance and hear an appropriate adult expression of it. However, the child will not be advanced in these situations if the adult expressions are either too complex for the child to comprehend or already within his control. Thus the level of psycholinguistic complexity *is* a crucial factor. What the child may require is at least

two levels of complexity when he verbally interacts with adults in
Wells' ideal situation: one level pitched very close to his own so that
he can process it and comprehend the meaning, and the other slightly
in advance of his own syntactic abilities. The child should then be
able to comprehend the meaning and also see the relationship between his characteristic mode of expressing it and the more sophisticated version.

All the expansion responses and, presumably, many semantic extensions will fit this pattern, with the added advantage in the case of
expansions at least, that the semantic intention and the first level of
complexity are controlled by the child[8]. For the least mature
children this will account for more than 60 % of the utterances they
hear and much of what remains has been argued here to consist of
material that should already be within the child's control.

However, as Tables 6.1 and 6.3 show, there were also many utterances that were semantically new to the discourse (and were not
stock expressions) and many that were considerably longer than the
mother's average utterance length. Presumably among these there
would be utterances that were both semantically and syntactically
beyond the child's capacity. But as many as 50 % in both categories,
for the youngest children's samples, were either sequentially repeated
(in whole or part) or paraphrased by the mothers. If, as Cross (1975)
suggests, the large majority of repetitions are cued in by the child's
failure to comprehend the original, then many of these repetition
sequences may be instrumental in forcing the child to accommodate
to new semantic elements and relations as well as to more complex
linguistic devices. They combine the provision of semantically new
and linguistically complex utterances, which the child has failed to
comprehend, with subsequent maternal adjustment in expression to
achieve a better fit with the child's processing capacities. What often
results is the serial presentation of utterances which encode the same
semantic intention but vary in the level of realization – or, as has
been argued here, in psycholinguistic complexity.

At least 43 % of the repetition sequences directed to the four
youngest children in the sample contained at least two levels of complexity, i.e. one fully realized sentence and at least one abbreviated
version somewhere in the sequence which used the same content
words. A further 18 % contained a word change as well. Further,
many of them became *synergistic*, when the child interposed a partial
or exact imitation, suggesting that he was actively engaged in attempting to comprehend the meaning. If mothers are successful in penetrat-
ing the child's comprehension by manipulating psycholinguistic

complexity in this way, then we have an interaction that can potentially assist him to acquire both new semantic intentions and more complex linguistic expressions. This gives us yet another potentially facilitative interaction to add to the large list discussed in the discourse section of this paper.

CONCLUSIONS

Of course, we do not know whether this or any other interaction isolated in this analysis does actually advance the child's comprehension and, for this reason, most of the preceding discussion is purely speculative. But this was not the question which was addressed in the introduction. I would argue that we have come to a decision about the more limited question of whether the input to rapidly developing children is potentially organized to facilitate their acquisition processes, and that the answer is affirmative. At the discourse level of description most of it is. The deep concern of mothers to comprehend their children and to be comprehended by them results in an input that contains many interaction sequences that may quite powerfully assist the child in his acquisition — too many to list again. Most, if not all, of these interactions may have contributed to the ease with which their children were progressing through the course of acquisition.

On the more specific questions of whether mothers' syntactic adjustments can be said to programme this course, or whether they are adjusted to too many listener variables to do this well enough, the data are inconclusive. Some features are tailored to child capacity, others are not. While the child's receptive ability accounts for much of the variance with maternal utterance length, age predicts well-formedness. But the rest present no clear or consistent patterns. All we can do is suggest that we have been asking the wrong questions. It may have been better to ask how much of the input can be described in terms of learning situations in which specific linguistic acquisitions may take place. The answer to this question may tell us how better to balance the child's and mother's contribution to the acquisition process.

NOTES

1.   The author wishes to thank Pat Wiltshire, Katie Kirby, Joseph Kolega and John Fisher for their tireless attention to detail in the collection and preparation of the speech transcripts; Alex Wearing for his helpful advice during the preparation of this paper; and the sixteen families who so graciously provided the data for this study.

This research was supported in part by a grant from the Advisory Committee on Child Care Research, Australian Department of Education. The analyses for the paper were undertaken while the author was a guest in the Department of Communicative Disorders, Northwestern University, Evanston, Illinois, USA (1974–75).
2.   Full video-recordings were available for 12 of the dyads. For four others there were at least 30 minutes of video and a full hour of audio recordings supplemented by detailed on-the-spot notes.
3.   At the end of the data collection phase of the project, the purpose of the study was explained, and permission to use the mothers' contributions obtained.
4.   It was also noted that there was often a considerable variation in an individual child's MLU score over different sets of 100 utterances. This difference was sometimes as great as 1.5 morphemes between the first and last 100 utterances in the sample. In general, MLU was reduced in response to increasing familiarity with the recording situation and toys.
5.   See Cross (1975) for a brief description of items included in this test.
6.   Cf. Newport (1976) who reports significant positive correlations between mothers' expansion rates and measures of child utterance complexity. It seems likely that over a wider slice of development expansions may show a curvilinear relation to child utterances, increasing with utterance complexity until the three-word stage, and then decreasing as the child produces more complex utterances. (See Cross, 1975, for a discussion of the stage-relatedness of expansions.)
7.   This effect was not observed when the mothers' MLUs were calculated over the first 100 utterances (cf. Cross, 1975). For 300 sequential utterances mothers' average MLU decreased from 5.1 to 4.8 morphemes.
8.   Semantic extensions are included here because, as Cazden (1972) has argued, there is only a minimal distinction between extensions and expansions. As the majority of maternal extensions in the present study were also coded as 'referentially immediate', the meaning was presumably very clear to the child. In this respect and in incorporating part, at least, of the child's preceding utterance, they resemble expansions.

APPENDIX: DEFINITIONS OF MOTHERS' SPEECH PARAMETERS

DISCOURSE FEATURES

Semantically related to child utterance[1]

Imitation[2]

Any maternal utterance that repeated exactly, or in part, one of the child's preceding[3] utterances.

Expansions (Cazden, 1965)

Complete: An expansion of any preceding child utterances that formed a grammatically complete sentence.
    Incomplete: An expansion that did not form a complete sentence.
    Elaborated: A complete expansion that also contained additional lexical items.
    Transformed: A complete expansion that altered the sentence type (or function) of the relevant child utterance.

Semantic extensions (Cazden, 1972)

Noun-phrase extension: An extension of a preceding child utterance which incorporated exactly the child's topic noun phrase.

Pronoun extension: An extension as above, but which incorporated the child's topic (implicit or explicit) by using pronominalization.

Predicate extension: An extension of any lexical item in a preceding child utterance which was not included in the child's topic phrase.

Semantically unrelated to child utterance

Semantically new utterance

Any utterance that was not included in any of the above categories, with the exception of single word 'yes', 'no' or like replies to child questions (see Yes—no replies below).

Novel isolated utterance

Any utterance in the above category that was not a stock expression (see below) and was not repeated sequentially (see below).

Maternal self-repetitions (Snow, 1972; Broen, 1972)

Paraphrase (Snow, 1972)

An utterance which altered any lexical item contained in the original, but which was restricted to reiterating the sense of any preceding maternal utterance and was not a partial repetition (see below).

Exact repetition (Snow, 1972)

An exact sequential repetition of any preceding maternal utterance.

Partial repetition (Snow, 1972)

An utterance which repeated any phrase (or phrases) of a preceding maternal utterance, but was not an exact repetition.

Transformed repetition

A sequential repetition of any preceding maternal utterance that altered the sentence type (or function) of the original maternal utterance.

Non-sequential repetition

An exact but non-sequential repetition of any maternal utterance already coded in the speech sample.

Other discourse parameters

Stock expression

Any utterance in an individual mothers' speech sample that had previously been coded as a 'Non-Sequential Repetition' in at least two other mothers' speech samples. (See 'Routine-Like Utterances' in Cross, 1975.)

Yes—no reply

Any single-word response which expressed either affirmation or negation of a preceding child utterance.

Self-answer

Any maternal utterance which supplied an answer to the immediately preceding maternal question.

REFERENTIAL FEATURES

Immediate utterance (original to this project)

Child controlled events

Any maternal utterance that referred to any activity that the child either had just completed or was currently engaged in, or to any object that the child was manipulating or holding just prior to or at the same time the utterance was produced[4].

Mother-controlled events

As above, except that the activity or object was related to the mother's ongoing manipulations.

Persons or objects present

Any maternal utterance that referred to any person or object that was present in the immediate recording situation (i.e. in the room in which the recording was taking place).

Non-immediate utterance

Any maternal utterance that referred to events, persons or objects spatially and temporally removed from the recording situation.

CONVERSATIONAL STYLE

Words per minute (Broen, 1972)

The mean number of words per minute spoken by the mother in a 10-minute period, selected at a point between 10 and 16 minutes into the first recording session.

Proportion of mother—child utterances

The number of mother's utterances spoken during the time the child spoke his first 300 sequential utterances, expressed as a proportion of the child's utterances.

Proportion of mother utterances per turn

The number of mothers' utterances delivered during the first 100 conversational turns expressed as the proportion of utterances per turn.

SYNTACTIC FEATURES

Syntactic complexity

Mean length of utterance

This was calculated as Brown (1973) recommends for children, for the first 300 utterances in each mother's speech sample.

Long utterances

The percentage of utterances in 300 sequential utterances that were longer than six morphemes.

Difference between child and mother's MLU

The difference was calculated between the MLU of the first 100 utterances in each child's speech sample and the mother's MLU (as defined above).

Single-word utterance (Broen, 1972)

Any utterance that consisted of only a single word, including inflections. Yes—no replies were excluded.

Propositional complexity (Newport, 1976)

All multi-propositional utterances were calculated as Newport suggests (i.e. the number of S-nodes per utterance), with the exception that run-on sentences, which were distinguished by intonation contour, were excluded. The first 100 utterances in each sequence were used for this calculation. Expressed as a proportion of one utterance.

Preverb complexity (Snow, 1972)

The number of morphemes placed before the main verb in any clause, for 200 sequential utterances. Expressed as a proportion of utterances.

Syntactic integrity

Disfluent utterances (Broen, 1972)

The percentage of utterances that contained within-utterance revisions, hesitations, word repetitions or long pauses.

Unintelligible utterances (Newport, 1975)

The percentage of utterances that were classified partly or wholly as unintelligible by one transcriber.

Run-on sentences

The percentage of sentences that were *not* distinguished from the following sentence by a discernible pause, but which were coded as sentences on the basis of final intonation contour and grammaticality.

Abbreviated utterances

The percentage of utterances that contained at least one non-discourse deletion (as judged by two adult speakers) in comparison with the paraphrase provided in the transcript.

Complete sentences

The percentage of utterances that were judged to be complete, fluent and grammatical sentences.

Surface sentence types[5]

Questions: All questions were included if they were coded as one of the following sentence types:
   Wh- questions. (Including all 'What's that?', 'What is it?' and 'Where is [it] the NP?' questions.)
   Yes—No questions. (Including all auxiliary-fronted, tagged and rising-intonation questions.)
   Imperatives. (a) affirmative (with or without subjects)
               (b) negative (with 'don't').
   Declaratives. (Either simple or multi-propositional).
   Deictic statements. (Having the form 'That/this is [not] a NP').

Other syntactic parameters

Noun-phrases

The number of full noun phrases in the first 100 utterances, expressed as a proportion of utterances.

Pronouns

The number of pronouns of any kind in the first 100 maternal utterances, expressed as a proportion of utterances.

NOTES

1.   An utterance generally was defined by intonation contour and, except in the case of run-on sentences, by the presence of a discernible pause between it and the surrounding utterances in the text.
2.   Unless otherwise specified in the Appendix, all utterance categories in Tables 6.1, 6.2 and 6.3 are given as the average percentage of 300 sequential maternal utterances for the whole sample.
3.   By the word 'preceding' is meant within the current and immediately preceding conversational turn. 'Turn' is defined as one or more utterances bounded by a long pause or by the utterance of another speaker (see Cross, 1975).
4.   To qualify for this and the following categories, the 'immediate' event was required to take place during the preceding or current conversational turn.
5.   All percentages of each sentence type and subtype were calculated for the incidence in the first and last 100 utterances in the speech sample.

7 Beyond syntax: the influence of conversational constraints on speech modifications

MARILYN SHATZ[1]

Department of Psychology, University of Pennsylvania, Philadelphia, Pennsylvania 19174, USA and The Graduate Center, City University of New York, 33 West 42nd Street, New York 10036, USA

ROCHEL GELMAN

Department of Psychology, University of Pennsylvania, Philadelphia, Pennsylvania 19174, USA

It is by now a well-documented fact that the language addressed to very young children is different from adult-directed speech. Utterances spoken to young children are generally short, simple, well-formed and well articulated (e.g. Brown & Bellugi, 1964; Phillips, 1970; Broen, 1972; Snow, 1972). Even four-year-olds direct shorter, simpler utterances to two-year-olds than they do to adults or peers (Shatz & Gelman, 1973; Sachs & Devin, 1976). In this paper we question whether these speech modifications are produced in order to facilitate young listeners' acquisition of syntax. Even if one were to grant mothers such language teaching tactics, one would hardly expect four-year-olds to be little linguists who produce at will a special syntax that is tailored to the needs of language learners. Our position is a more plausible one: a speaker's understanding of the context-sensitive constraints operating on conversational interaction governs his or her speech adjustments. The ways in which these constraints influence the speaker's output depend on the specific communicative demands of a given situation as well as the cognitive–social status of the given participants in an interaction.

We introduce the notion of conversational constraints in order to

189

deal with the kind of child-directed speech that cannot be explained on the basis of syntactic simplification alone: the occurrences of complex constructions in speech addressed to young children. To illustrate the problem, we consider some data on four-year-old speech collected for an earlier study (Shatz & Gelman, 1973).

As reported in Shatz & Gelman (1973), we observed four-year-olds talking to two-year-olds and adults in two different situations. In the toy-task situation, the children were told specifically to talk about a particular toy to each of their separate listeners. Likewise, in the unstructured situation, children played with each of the listeners separately; but, this time there were no constraints on talking about or demonstrating particular toys. In both situations, the mean length of utterance, as measured in words, was shorter to two-year-olds than to adults. In both situations, this reduction in utterance length was accomplished to a large extent by decreasing the use of coordinate and subordinate conjunctions (and their attendant compound and complex utterances).

While the speech for two-year-olds tended to be syntactically simple, one cannot postulate that four-year-olds follow a general rule barring syntactically complex utterances to young children. For some of the utterances directed to two-year-olds were syntactically complex. For example, when four-year-olds talked to two-year-olds about the workings of a toy, they did use 'wh' predicate complement constructions as in (1)

(1) I'll show you how it moves.

Still, in the same conversational setting, they did *not* use similar complement constructions introduced by 'that' as in (2)

(2) I think (that) this is a cat.

One could account for these observations by postulating a more specific syntactically-based rule, i.e. 'Do not use "that" predicate complement constructions with two-year-olds'. However, the data across situations are inconsistent with such a rule. When we change the situation in which four-year-olds talk to two-year-olds, we do find them using 'that' predicate complements. In particular, when four-year-olds are not expected to explain a toy to a two-year-old and instead are left to talk about whatever they wish, utterances like (3) appear in their speech.

(3) I think we'll get washed.

The change from the toy-task to the unstructured setting has no

Table 7.1 *Frequencies of 'that' and 'wh' predicate complement constructions in long utterances produced by four-year-olds to two different-aged listeners in two situations*

Complementizer		Situation	
		Toy-task	Unstructured
'That'	To adults:	Fairly common[a]	Uncommon
	To two-year-olds:	Very uncommon	Fairly common
'Wh'	To adults:	Fairly common	Very common
	To two-year-olds:	Common	Fairly common

[a] Very common: 1 occurrence in every 10 or fewer utterances.
  Common: 1 occurrence in every 10–20 utterances.
  Fairly common: 1 occurrence in every 20–30 utterances.
  Uncommon: 1 occurrence in every 30–100 utterances.
  Very uncommon: 1 occurrence in every 100 or more utterances.

effect on the four-year-olds' tendency to use 'wh' predicate complements with two-year-olds. In both settings they appear fairly commonly in talk to two-year-olds. But the change in setting does alter the four-year-olds' tendency to use 'wh' construction with adults. In the toy-explanation setting, utterances containing such constructions occur fairly commonly, just as they do with two-year-olds. In the unstructured situation, utterances with 'wh' constructions occur even more frequently in talk addressed to adults. The variations in the four-year-olds' tendencies to use 'that' and 'wh' constructions with two-year-olds and adults in the two different conversational settings is summarized in Table 7.1.[2]

If we choose to describe the speech adjustments of four-year-olds in terms of specific syntactically-based rules, we must conclude that children of this age are inconsistent in their application of rules governing the use of these sorts of complex constructions. There are two reasons for rejecting this sort of 'inconsistency' explanation of variation. One is that children tend to apply their rules about language very generally, even to the point of overgeneralization (e.g. Brown & Bellugi, 1964). Why, then, should rules blocking certain syntactic constructions to particular listeners be applied sporadically?

The second objection concerns the very nature of the rules governing listener-dependent adjustments. As mentioned above, it seems implausible that the regulation of speech to very young listeners should be carried out at the level of syntactic selection. It is intuitively more plausible to assume that a child would (and could) choose not to talk about certain things with certain listeners than to assume he would (or could) choose not to use certain syntactic constructions with certain listeners. Thus, the postulation of a listener-dependent rule regarding syntactic selection *per se* may be in error. For, it is meanings that are mapped onto syntactic devices; often a given surface structure can convey more than one sort of meaning, and selection for a particular listener may be made at the level of meaning rather than the level of syntax. It seems advisable, therefore, to ask: what were the meanings of those utterances that contained the syntactic constructions which occurred with seemingly arbitrary frequencies? In particular, what meanings did the children in the toy-task convey by their use of 'that' constructions to adults; were they meanings that the speakers knew to be inappropriate for two-year-olds? Did utterances containing 'that' constructions convey different meanings in the unstructured situation? Finally, what meanings were conveyed by utterances containing 'wh' constructions which, despite their length and syntactic complexity, were apparently considered appropriate for both sorts of listeners?

To answer these questions we carried out a *function-meaning-in-conversation* analysis of the utterances in question. A detailed description of this analysis can be found in Gelman & Shatz (1977). Briefly, the procedure for determing the *functional meaning* of an utterance containing a 'wh' or 'that' predicate complement was as follows. First, together we assigned a functional meaning to each target utterance by considering its meaning in context. The context used included the speech preceding the target utterance, the listener's response, the speaker's subsequent response to the listener's response, what the participants in the interaction were doing and what the topic of conversation was. How much we relied on these contextual features depended on the ambiguity of the target utterance when considered out of context. Having assigned a functional meaning to each utterance, we then organized these meanings into categories. Several months later, we once again assigned functional meanings to the same utterances. The second round assignments of functional meanings agreed with over 90% of our initial assignments.

When we combined all the 'that' and 'wh' predicate complement utterances together and examined them in terms of the functional roles they played in conversational interaction, we found they served three main purposes: modulation, talk about mental state and directing the interaction.

In the first category are the predicate complement utterances in which the certainty of the asserted proposition was modulated or 'hedged', as Lakoff (1972) calls it. In cases like (4) and (5)

(4) I'm sure this fits too.
(5) I think these are dogs and these are lambs.

the children were explicitly marking the degree of certainty with which they expected the truth of their statements to be accepted. Such modulations often occurred when the children were being questioned or when they were voicing some sort of opinion that was open to argument from a knowledgeable listener.

Second, the children used these constructions in talking about their own or others' mental states. Utterances like (6) and (7)

(6) Wonder who put that wooden thing?
(7) She knows how to lift that up.

illustrate the use of complementation in talk about mental state.

Finally, (8)–(11) are all instances of the four-year-old directing the interaction. There were deictic utterances like

(8) That's how he's sitting.

and there were announcements of intent to demonstrate a toy, as in

(9) I'll show you how to get gas.

There were calls to attend to something as in

(10) Ann, see what you do?

Finally, there were attempts to initiate topics or activities politely, as in

(11) I think we'll get washed.

These various realizations of the speaker's intent to direct his listener's attention to some event, object or activity in the real world, or to direct his behavior in some way, we call 'show and tell' speech.

What functions did predicate complement utterances serve in the speech directed to two-year-olds? Table 7.2 shows that in the toy-task situation, 95 % of the predicate complement constructions were used in 'show and tell' utterances; in the unstructured situation 82 % were so used. Modulation and comments about mental state rarely occurred in either situation. Thus, predicate complement utterances mainly served the simple 'show and tell' function.

This limitation on functional meanings directed to two-year-olds can be taken as evidence that the four-year-old speaker utilizes a system of conversational constraints in formulating messages.[3] A speaker who follows a system of, say, Gricean conversational rules (Grice, 1975) is primarily concerned with maintaining a cooperative

Table 7.2   *Percent of 'that' and 'wh' predicate complement constructions falling into each meaning-in-conversation category*

Category	Situation			
	Toy-task[a]		Unstructured[b]	
Directing the interaction	To adults:	25	To adults:	59
	To children:	95	To children:	82
Mental state	To adults:	28	To adults:	22
	To children:	5	To children:	14
Modulation	To adults:	31	To adults:	13
	To children:	0	To children:	4
Other[c]	To adults:	16	To adults:	6
	To children:	0	To children:	0

[a] Based on the 81 predicate complement constructions to adults and 21 to two-year-olds produced by 16 subjects.
[b] Based on the 32 predicate complement constructions to adults and 28 to two-year-olds produced by 5 subjects.
[c] A breakdown of this category can be found in Gelman & Shatz (1977).

interaction and does so by providing clear, relevant information adequate to the needs of his listener. Given the cognitive limitations of a two-year-old, abstract talk about mental state and qualifications about propositional certainty would be inappropriate. On the other hand, simple deictic utterances like 'Here is the shoe' and 'See the doggie' are common in speech to young children. Now we see that *complex* utterances like those containing predicate complements can serve the 'show and tell' function too. When a complex construction functions in a demonstrative or directive role, it can appear in speech to young children, provided it does not violate some other conversational constraint operating in the situation.

What might some of these other conversational constraints be? As an example, consider the differences in the way the children realized their intentions to direct the interaction with the two-year-olds in the two situations. In both the toy-task and unstructured situations, utterances like (8)–(10) appeared. 'Wh' complement constructions occurred in utterances that served to accompany or announce demonstrations and to direct the young listener's attention. But 'that' utterances like (11) appeared only in the unstructured situation. While (11) serves the same 'show and tell' function as (8)–(10), it incorporates a social element as well. It is a polite way of making a suggestion. The children were constrained to show some regard for politeness in one situation but not the other because situational differences produced *different* conversational priorities for the speaker.

We have already noted that maintaining a cooperative interchange is the speaker's primary goal in any conversational interaction. And Gricean maxims like Be relevant to your listener's needs, Say what you know to be true, Be polite and so on, provide guidelines for attaining that goal. But the priorities determining the application of these maxims require a consideration of context. A given maxim may be very important to successful interaction in one situation and less so in another; for, what is necessary to maintain the *cooperation* of one's listener varies with situation.

We can identify two aspects of the situations that we believe worked together to produce different conversational priorities: one is the degree to which information transmission was important, the other is the presence or absence of the two-year-old's mother. In the toy-task situation, the four-year-old was under an obligation to get the younger child to pay attention to the experimenter's toy. He had information he had been directed to convey and a poor listener to whom to convey it. But he did have some help. The two-year-old's mother was hovering nearby. And two-year-olds are notoriously anxious to stay near Mother. So, the four-year-old, confident that the adult would help maintain the two-year-old on the scene, could concentrate on his task: unadorned information transmission, showing and demonstrating the toy. But in the unstructured situation, the two-year-old's mother was no longer nearby, nor was the four-year-old under any obligation to prove his prowess as an instructor. He was still in a position to direct the interaction by making suggestions, but now he had to take account of the increased possibility that his young listener would be unwilling to follow his lead and would wander off into activity of his own. By qualifying his suggestions, he both recognized the weakened constraints on his listener to follow his lead *and* communicated the increased flexibility of his own position; for in this situation, he could drop his own suggestions without loss of face, if it became necessary to do so in order to maintain the interaction.

The different demands created by the two different situations forced a reordering of conversational priorities. Clear information transmission, so important in the toy-task situation, was secondary to maintaining an amiable interaction in the unstructured one. While 'that' and 'wh' predicate complement constructions served roughly the same function in child-directed speech, they were used selectively to emphasize situation-specific conversational and social considerations that were differentially relevant to successful interaction.

We have focussed on what four-year-olds said to two-year-olds in two different situations in order to illustrate the functional meaning of certain constructions in conversation and to show how the forms chosen to express functional meaning reflect the priorities given to conversational constraints in particular situations. The variations in the speech four-year-olds address to adults in the same situations can be similarly analyzed.

Table 7.1 shows that the rate of 'that' complementation to adults decreased from the toy-task situation to the unstructured one, while 'wh' complementation increased. These changes *also* can be explained in terms of the reordering of conversational priorities. In the toy-task situation, the adult was either the experimenter, or the speaker's mother in the presence of the experimenter, both of whom attended closely to the child. Clearly, talking about mental state was appropriate as was the hedging of statements to capable, attentive listeners. Table 7.2 shows that 31 % of the predicate complements occurred in statements of modulation, 28 % in comments on mental state, and only 25 % in interaction-directing statements. In the unstructured situation, the adult listeners were behaving like typical mothers, attending to household chores as well as to children. The speaker's primary concern had to be with attracting his or her mother to the interaction, rather than qualifying statements for an already attentive listener. Accordingly, we expected to find many more calls for attention and much less modulation in this situation as compared to the toy-task one. As can be seen in the right-hand column of Table 7.2, this is indeed what happened. Fifty-nine percent of the complement constructions serve to direct the interaction; only 13 % modulate the certainty of propositions. Since modulation typically involves 'that' complementation, and calls to attend utilize 'wh' complements, we can now understand why the frequencies of the two types of complementation changed with situation.[4]

It is also possible to explain the between-listener variation occurring in 'that' complementation in the toy-task study — fairly common use to adults, very uncommon to two-year-olds. Recall that the two functions served by 'that' complementation were modulation and polite directing of the interaction. In the toy-task situation, modulation was prevalent in speech to knowledgeable listeners, the adults, but virtually non-existent in speech to two-year-olds; and we have already seen that politeness, or flexibility, was not a prominent concern with the young listeners. 'That' constructions occurred with adults, therefore, but not with two-year-olds.

To summarize, the sorts of between- and within-listener variation in the use of predicate complementation that are illustrated in Table

7.1 can be explained in terms of the functional meanings these constructions carry in conversation, and the conversational constraints governing both the selection of these meanings and the specific forms appropriate to express them. The introduction of conversational constraints provides for an explanation of syntactic variation in cases where the hypothesis of syntactic simplification is insufficient to account for all the data.

Thus, it appears that speakers produce speech modifications for very young children not only because of their lack of linguistic ability but, at least as importantly, because of their general cognitive immaturity, which influences *what* is said to them as well as *how* things are said. Some things are just not said to young children even though they may be expressible in syntactically simple three-word sentences; for example, 'I know calculus'. We are not suggesting that the producers of speech simplifications make *no* use of notions of linguistic complexity or that cognitive simplifications, on the average, correlate merely coincidentally with linguistic simplifications. Rather, it seems likely that a speaker bases his modifications on a notion of *psychological* simplicity which involves cognitive, social and perceptual factors as well as syntactic ones. For example, the tendency to produce short utterances for very young listeners may be motivated as much by an attempt to deal with their short attention span as with their linguistic inadequacies. As we have seen, being polite or friendly is in some situations considered more important for maintaining interaction than is promoting the understanding of the propositional content of a message by using a short but possibly curt sentence. If extra-linguistic factors do play so central a role in the speech selection process, then we must question the position that speech simplification derives solely from some syntax-specific ability which has evolved in order to assure the new generation's acquisition of grammar.

Similarly, considering the task of the young listener, we must view with skepticism the idea that speech modifications to young children serve only, or even mainly, to teach the child the ideal grammar. In the first two years of life, a child makes enormous discoveries about the world around him. The primary function of the speech directed to him is to help him discover that world, and undoubtedly to help him to map language onto the invariances and relationships he discovers there. Moreover, the child learns all of this in a social environment, where sequencing, turn-taking and feedback are relevant at the earliest stages of language development (cf. Bruner, 1975; Shatz, 1975). Since attentional, social and cognitive considerations seem to figure so prominently in speech modifications, it is likely that the adjustments function to provide social and cognitive, as well as linguistic, information to the developing child. We know very little of the young child's ability to make grammatical inferences based on his knowledge in other domains. Yet it would be surprising if he did not bring to bear on the language acquisition task all the capacities he had acquired in the perceptual, social and cognitive spheres. By fostering growth in other areas, speech modifications may contribute to the acquisition of grammar indirectly as well as directly.

Of course, we do not yet understand how speech modifications affect these simultaneously developing systems or how these systems may interact to affect language growth. Analyses of the functional meanings of speech in conversation together with a more fully explicated system of conversational constraints are one way to explore some of the interrelationships. But one thing has already been made clear by this line of investigation: speech modifications are based on more than syntactic rules for grammatical simplification.

NOTES

1.   We thank Marjorie Horton for her assistance with data analysis. This research was supported by NIHCD grant No. 04598 to R. Gelman and an NIHCD traineeship to M. Shatz. Reprint requests can be sent to M. Shatz, CUNY Graduate Center, 33 W. 42nd St, New York, New York 10036 or R. Gelman, Psychology, 3813—15 Walnut St, Philadelphia, Pennsylvania 19174. An expansion of the argument first presented here can be found in Gelman & Shatz (1977).
2.   In Shatz & Gelman (1973) only utterances five words or more in length ('long utterances') were analyzed for complex syntactic features. The discussion here is limited to those long utterances containing 'wh' and 'that' predicate complement constructions. Rates of occurrence reported in Table 7.1 differ from those reported in Shatz & Gelman (1973) in that here the data from children speaking to siblings and to non-siblings are combined.
3.   See Garvey (1975, 1977) for additional evidence on preschoolers' conversational abilities.
4.   On the basis of MLU analyses, we argued earlier that the children treated adult listeners the same in both the toy-task and the unstructured situations (Shatz & Gelman, 1973). We now see that the functional meaning analyses reveal a difference that was masked by the grosser MLU analysis.

8 Talking to children: some notes on feedback

JEAN BERKO GLEASON

Department of Psychology, Boston University, Boston,
Massachusetts 02215, USA

Our ideas about language acquisition have undergone a number of
significant changes during the past four or five years, changes that
have yet to be reflected in the main body of linguistic theory. Linguistic theory has always accepted the postulate that in order to acquire language a child must be exposed to language, but has failed to
consider what the necessary aspects of that exposure must be. A
common view has been that the barest brush with actual spoken
language will suffice to set in motion a basically innate language-gen-
erating machine. Studying interchanges between young children and
their caretakers has led to some new insights about the acquisition
process: children do not acquire language all by themselves — they
are not simply miniature grammarians working on a corpus composed
of snatches and fragments of adult discourse. Nor is language acquisition verbal behavior alone. Except in the rarest of cases, the acquisition process requires more than one input channel — most typically,
in children who are neither blind nor deaf, an auditory and a visual
one. Sitting in peoples' homes listening to them say to their young
children things like 'Where's the ball? There's the ball. Give Mommy
the ball. That's right, give me the ball. Give it to me', hardly seems an
activity that might lead to changes in theoretical models of language
development, yet it has done just that. The parents' language contains strikingly predictable features. Just as there may be universals
in child language, it is also possible that there are universals in the
language directed *to* children: while the early utterances of children
the world over contain statements like 'That kitty', the language of
parents the world over appears to contain statements like 'See the

199

kitty'. The conclusion that these behaviors are related is ineluctable. We recognize now that language acquisition is an interactive process that requires not only a child with the appropriate neurological equipment in a state of readiness, but also an older person who engages in communicative interchanges with him, and some objects out there in the world as well. It is thus a dyadic, or even triadic, process. To understand how all this unfolds, it is necessary to study verbal and gestural behavior together, the reaction to speakers' language as well as the language of speakers. Parental labelling is an example of this: when looking at filmed or videotaped records, one common thing we have seen is the parent engaging in some sort of naming behavior while at the same time pointing at the object being named. Thus far we know very little about the evolution of the child's ability to look at the object that lies somewhere beyond the parent's finger. Young babies look into people's faces. At a later stage, they look at the finger of the person who is pointing. Finally, they learn to make the visual leap of looking beyond the finger to the object. Little is known about this clearly developmental progression, or what its exact relationship is to the attainment of referentiality.

Since it appears that adults engage in special behaviors when talking to children, one kind of question we can ask is: what is there in the child's behavior that elicits this special behavior in adults? For instance, as I noted above, babies look at people, and not where people point. Moreover, a study by Haaf & Bell (1967) has shown that four-month-old babies show particular interst in the human face, and will prefer to look at pictures of human faces when they are given a choice. The fact that babies tend to fix their gaze on adults' faces may have an effect on the adults' behavior, and may be related to the face-making behavior we so frequently see adults engage in when dealing with small babies. Further, it is possible that being stared at brings out in adults a tendency to make faces back, whether the starer is a baby or another adult.

Similarly, the language-learning child's responses, or lack of them, may have their impact on the form of the adults' language: why, for instance, do we find so many instances of repetition in mothers' language? Adult repetitions undoubtedly aid the child in learning language, but it would be a mistake to confound their function with their motivation. It is unlikely that parents repeat themselves because of their adherence to pedagogical principles. Rather, it is probable that the repetitions are triggered by some immediate behavior of the child. One obvious factor may be that the child has not yet learned to give the adult the appropriate feedback, the little nods, grunts and other signals that indicate that the message has been received and that it is all right to continue.

In order to gain some insight into the role of feedback in adult—child conversations, I visited an elementary school and a daycare center in Palo Alto, California, and I was also able to examine some videotaped interactions of six mothers and their 18-month-old sons. These mothers and their babies were in a laboratory—playschool situation at Boston University, and were engaged in some standard tasks; playing with toys and drawing with crayons. They were all part of an ongoing study of early social behavior. The children in California were four-year-olds, kindergarteners, first graders and fourth graders.

The daycare and grade school children made eye-contact with their teachers and provided feedback signals at important points in the conversation. They gave the impression of being very expressive, in fact, quite exaggerated in their expressions, but on closer inspection it turned out that the expressiveness was more a concomitant of their own utterances than a reaction to those of their teachers. For instance, it was not unusual for a child to shake his or her head from side to side while saying negative things like 'I don't like that', or to nod vigorously when saying positive things. The teachers, as well, tended to be very expressive when they talked and were clearly speaking a language that contained special modifications for children. These modifications did not, however, contain many exact repetitions, and tended to be more of the 'language of socialization' type that we have described elsewhere (Gleason, 1973). These children were providing enough feedback to allow the teachers to go on, even though that feedback may not have been as rich as the feedback typically supplied by adults.

By contrast, the mothers of the 18-month-olds repeated themselves very frequently, and it soon became clear that the repetitions themselves served several distinct functions. These children did not nod their heads when spoken to, and in fact produced none of the standard feedback signals. Their tendency was to respond with direct action if they were going to respond at all, rather than first signal their understanding and then act.

Not surprisingly, the most obvious type of repetition in the mothers' language did indeed occur when the child either failed to look up at the mother when she spoke, or failed to exhibit the expected behavior. Thus, non-responsiveness, whether physical or linguistic, leads to repetition. The same effect is felt in adult—adult conversations, except that adults are much freer to provide paraphrases or semantic repetitions when talking with one another. When speaking to babies, the prior restraints of the baby talk register limit the kinds of variation that are possible, thus leading to many exact repetitions.

A second kind of repetition occurs in the following example:

Child: (Points to book with crayon) Uh.
Mother: (Nods) Book. Book.
Child: (Grabs book)
Mother: See the book?

Here the child is clearly paying attention. The mother interprets his pointing and grunting as a request for a label, and she supplies it. This looks very much like a lexicon lesson and is the kind of example many researchers have cited when characterizing mothers' language as a teaching language. Unfortunately, we have no way of knowing what the child actually had in mind when he pointed and grunted. His acceptance of the label may indicate that his request has been satisfied. Or it may mean that he has been distracted from what he originally intended, or that he is good natured enough to accept a substitute. It is interesting to note that for this prelinguistic child the mother initially provides a one-word utterance, 'Book', whereas if he had said 'Book', she probably would have supplied the expanded form, 'That's a book'. Here, she expands her own utterance.

A third, and very important, kind of repetition occurred under circumstances where the child was neither unresponsive nor questioning in his behavior. These exchanges were marked by comprehension and compliance on the part of the child, and repetition on the part of the mother:

Mother: Get the ball.
Child: (Picks up ball and approaches mother)
Mother: That's right. Get the ball. Get it.

or

Child: (Puts crayons in box)
Mother: Do one at a time. Now put that one in.
Child: (Puts crayon in box)
Mother: That's right. Now put this one in. That's right. That's right. There you go.

Since these children understood and were doing what was asked of them, why did their mothers continue to repeat themselves? This kind of repetition serves another function. It is what Luria (1959) would call the 'directive function' of language. It guides and directs the behavior of the child from the outside, in much the same way that his own inner speech will guide and direct him in a few years' time. It is as if the adult is supplying for the child the parts of his language that he cannot yet supply, in this case, inner speech.

This filling of the child's role is also evident in other parental behaviors. Language acquisition is to a great extent the learning of how to make conversations. In fact, most of the data we have on early language acquisition are actually the child's half of conversations with adults. Only very recently have we begun to look at what the adults have been saying, and now perhaps it is time to consider how both halves of the conversation fit together, how child—adult discourse is maintained and sustained, and what pressures the life of the conversation itself brings to bear. Silence, for instance, signals the death of the conversation. When one partner fails to take his turn, or performs inadequately, the more competent partner may take that turn for him in order to keep the conversation alive. We have noticed, for example, that the parents of grade school children will frequently ask them questions and then provide the answers. Or if the child is not particularly adept at answering wh- questions, the parent may quickly append a yes—no question: 'How was the game? Did you have a good time?' This lightens the child's conversational load without impeding the flow of the conversation itself.

Similarly, at earlier stages, if children cannot maintain their end of conversations adults tend to talk for them. But this phenomenon is by no means limited to child—adult discourse. Adults whose utterances are ill-formed can also elicit this behavior in their hearers. When conversing with a friend with a speech impediment, for instance, the temptation to speak for him is very difficult to avoid, once you think you know what he wants to say. Or it sometimes happens that we see an aphasic patient who appears at the hospital with his wife. The interview goes smoothly because she answers all of the questions for him; she may actually have taken over much of his conversational role without even realizing how aphasic he has become. By the same token, when the baby says 'Wawa' and the mother says 'You want a drink of water' it may be that the pressures on her are similar to those produced by aphasic or impeded adult speech: in her expansion she is actually speaking *for* the baby.

This again is not surprising. The developmental history of conversation begins with prelinguistic infants and competent adults. In the beginning, all of the conversation is provided by adults, and only slowly do children assume their conversational roles. Until they do, the adults speak for them as well as for themselves. As children acquire language in the traditional sense, the grammar and the lexicon, they also acquire the signals that keep conversations flowing. At the same time, adult speech to children gradually changes to complement their emerging competence: as children grow older, the speech directed to them becomes more complex in every sense of the word. This fact is obvious, but the actual mechanics underlying the change in adult speech to children are not easily specified.

CONCLUSION

Many studies have now shown that mothers' speech contains special design features that appear to facilitate children's acquisition of language. A slower rate, many repetitions, simple well-formed sentences and topics limited to the here-and-now are only some of those special features. Moreover, it is not just mothers who modify their speech to children in this way: non-mothers, fathers, and older children also produce these typical modifications. In fact, there is no reason not to suppose that basically everyone who talks to children takes into account their special linguistic and cognitive state, at least to some extent. Now that we know that speakers modify their speech when addressing children, it is appropriate to ask both why and how they do so. Why, for instance, does a four-year-old speak more simply to a two-year-old than to other four-year-olds? And how does a parent decide, if decide is the right word, that it is time to start using dependent clauses?

One possibility, as I have suggested, is that children themselves help shape the language behavior of those who speak to them by the kind of feedback they produce. This was evident in some of the mothers' repetitions in our observations, and can be seen in other situations, where the feedback need not be totally linguistic or paralinguistic. At the most global level, a speaker who attempts to address a child in language that is either too complex or on a topic that is inappropriate may be deserted or ignored. Preschool children simply leave if the utterances directed to them are at the wrong level. Hence, conversations with young children have to be on topics suitable to them and couched in simple form, if they are to exist at all.

Immediate feedback from children in the form of eye-contact, blinking, nodding and other small responses undoubtedly aids adults in tailoring their speech to children. At the same time, much more than this kind of simple interaction is involved in talking to children. The mother who decides that her prelinguistic infant is asking for the name of an object has made a cognitive decision based on her estimate of the child's wishes, needs and state of linguistic and cognitive development. The same sorts of judgments must enter into most linguistic interchanges with children: adults appear, to varying degrees, to be 'tuned in' to children and to be sensitive to even small changes in children's capacities as they develop, a sensitivity that is reflected in the adults' speech. This is all the more remarkable since it may be totally unconscious on the part of the adult. Small things, like the presence or absence of feedback signals in linguistic interchanges, can provide some clues to the process, but at the present time we do not really know how it is that adults become attuned to children, and this question must remain for future research.

I am thankful to Edward (Ned) Mueller of Boston University for allowing me to view his videotapes; to Sandra Weintraub, who also saw them and provided valuable observations on them, and to Charles DeStefano for a number of very insightful comments.

Section II

Baby-talk registers and cross-cultural perspectives

9 Baby talk as a simplified register

CHARLES A. FERGUSON

Department of Linguistics, Stanford University, Stanford, California 94305, USA

In all speech communities there are probably special ways of talking to young children which differ more or less systematically from the more 'normal' form of the language used in ordinary conversation among adults. This special 'register' of the language felt to be appropriate for use with young children is often called 'baby talk' (hereafter BT); it is one of a set of such registers which are used in addressing people such as foreigners, retarded, or hard of hearing who are felt not to be able, for one reason or another, to understand normal language in the usual way. Since these registers, in at least some respects, seem to be simplified versions of the normal language they have been called 'simplified registers' (Ferguson, 1975), and linguists have attempted to analyze their structure, not only to provide characterizations of such marginal or deviant phenomena but also to clarify the notions of simplification in language and to gain a better understanding of the use of language. The purpose of the present paper is to summarize the findings of linguists as to the structure and use of BT in different languages, regarded from this point of view.[1]

In 1921 Antoine Meillet, the great French linguist, in one of his characteristic brief notes in the *Bulletin* of the Linguistic Society of Paris, reported observations on the way a French mother modified her pronunciation of the initial consonant of *genoux* (knees) when addressing her baby, and he pointed to the modification of speech for addressing children as a promising field of linguistic research. The first modern linguist to investigate the problem in some depth, however, was probably the famous Danish linguist, Otto Jespersen, who discussed it in 1923 in his book, *Language*, which gave more

209

attention to the speech *of* children and *to* children than any general work in linguistics since that time. The phenomena of BT had been noticed by scholars long before that and references go back at least as far as the Roman grammarian Varro in the first century B.C. (Heraeus, 1904). A number of American anthropologists studying American Indian languages noted BT items in their fieldwork and mentioned them in their papers and short notes, the most important being a brief account of Nootka baby talk by the great student of language Edward Sapir (1929). The American linguist Allen Walker Read presented a paper on the topic in December 1946 at a meeting of the Modern Language Association (Read, 1946), and, later, in response to requests gave versions of that paper as addresses on at least six different occasions between 1956 and 1962. Unfortunately his paper and his large collection of material were never published. He was particularly interested in tracing opinions about the use of BT, and cited authors from the seventeenth century to the twentieth. He was also interested in the contexts, other than addressing children, in which BT was used and his analysis noted all the principal contexts mentioned by later linguists.

The detailed description of BT in modern linguistic literature began with four articles, each written essentially in independence of the others, which appeared between 1948 and 1956 (Casagrande, 1948; Voegelin & Robinett, 1954; Austerlitz, 1956; Ferguson, 1956), analyzing the baby talk registers of Comanche, Hidatsa, Gilyak and Syrian Arabic. Ferguson (1964) made use of these four papers and other articles, and recent papers generally refer back to this group of studies. (See Table 9.1 for available BT studies.)

SIMPLIFIED REGISTERS

One of the central facts about human language is the way it varies in structure depending on the use to which it is put. Every speech community and every individual user of language exhibits this kind of variation in language behavior. It is not only the semantic content which varies according to the use but also phonological and syntactic patterns, choice of vocabulary and forms of discourse. In some societies this variation can be illustrated dramatically by turning the dial of a radio to find a particular program. It often takes less than a sentence of speech to decide whether we are hearing a news broadcast, commercial message, 'soap opera', campaign speech, or sermon. In other societies a tape recording might just as readily be identified

Table 9.1 *Major sources of baby talk data*

Language	Reference	Dialect	Natural observation	Elicited	No. of informants	Own experience	Published sources	Comment
Arabic	Ferguson, 1956	Syria, Palestine, Lebanon	–	+	2 Families + 3 Additional Informants	–	+	Other dialect references in footnotes.
Berber	Bynon, 1968	Central Morocco	–	+	1 Principal Informant	–	+	Material tape recorded; Other dialects included; Extensive use, published sources.
Cocopa	Crawford, 1970		+	+	1 Family	–	–	Notes on other Amerindian languages.
Comanche	Casagrande, 1948		–	+	8 Informants	–	–	From memory; Comanche no longer spoken by children; notes on other Amerindian languages.
English	Read, 1946 Ferguson, 1964	Great Britain; USA USA	– +	– +	6 Informants	– +	+ –	Including published sources, eighteenth century on; casual elicitation, friends, colleagues.
Gilyak	Austerlitz, 1956	SE Sakhalin	–	+	1 Informant	–	–	Mother reporting her own use.
Greek	Drachman, 1973	Athens, Cypriot Acarnanian	?	+	Several; no. not indicated	+	–	Including detailed comparison, pet names; BT material collected, Athens. Elicitation, Linguistic Institute, 1953; some material taped.
Hidatsa	Voegelin & Robinett, 1954		–	+	1 Informant	–	–	
Japanese	Fischer, 1970 Chew, 1969	Fukuoka Tokyo	– +	+ –	35 Informants 6 Families	– +	– –	Interviews, mothers, schoolchildren, 1961–62; observed usage, own children, compared others.
Kannada	Bhat, 1967	Southern Havyaka	+	–		+	–	
Latvian	Rūķe-Draviņa, 1961		+	+	Not indicated	+	+	
Maltese	Cassar-Pullicino, 1957		–	–		+	+	External use, published sources, eighteenth century on; including analysis of pet names.
Marathi	Kelkar, 1964	Standard	+	–		+	–	
Romanian	Avram, 1967		–	+	Not indicated	+	+	Data represented only *'partie de ceux que nous avons recueillis'*.
Spanish	Ferguson, 1964	Mexico, Chile	–	+	2	–	–	

as adolescent instruction, recitation of a myth, joking between uncle and nephew, or spirit possession.

Since most of this variation is conventional, systematic and culturally shared, it lies in the province of the linguist to analyze it and search for universal tendencies and explanatory principles. The notion of 'register' serves as a basic organizing concept in this kind of analysis (Reid, 1956; Ellis & Ure, 1969). On the one hand, register variation is distinct from regional and social dialect variation and, on the other hand, it is distinct from idiosyncratic and stylistic variation. A register in a given language and given speech community is defined by the uses for which it is appropriate and by a set of structural features which differentiate it from the other registers in the total repertory of the community.

As with dialect variation, the determination of register boundaries and significant discontinuities is to a certain extent arbitrary, since in some instances the variation may be continuous and in other instances there may be overlapping of two or more quite different registers. The 'naturalness' of register analysis is apparent in the extent to which clusters of structural features consistently delineate identifiable uses, and the analyst must be prepared to find different boundaries as well as different kinds of criterial features in different speech communities. Some of the most promising findings of register analysis at this stage come from comparing the structural features of similar registers in different languages, as in the comparison of the language of municipal traffic codes in Great Britain and the Soviet Union (*Report of the contemporary Russian Language Analysis Project*, 1972).

Each speech community seems to have one or more registers appropriate for use with people who for one reason or another are not likely to understand normal adult speech in the usual way. Several reduced or 'simplified' registers of this kind have been studied, e.g. the 'foreigner talk' addressed to foreigners who do not know one's language (Ferguson, 1975, Hatch, Shapira & Gough, 1975, English; Clyne, 1968, German), a 'language of socialization' addressed to four- to eight-year-olds (Gleason, 1973, English), a foreign language instruction register (Henzl, 1974, Czech), and BT.

The processes which derive simplified registers from adult speech (AS) are not always simplifying in nature. Some processes are clarifying in that they modify in the direction of greater redundancy, often by adding material to the model. Sentences may be pronounced more slowly and articulated more carefully; vowels normally reduced or elided may be supplied; words, phrases or whole sentences may be repeated; ambiguous words or near homophones may be replaced by synonyms; everything may be uttered more loudly; ambiguous constructions may be paraphrased. Such clarifying processes are part of the competence of all users of language and occur outside simplified registers. Details vary across languages and indeed across registers in the same language. For the linguist they are of special interest in the clues they offer for basic 'underlying' forms and they raise the old issue of 'clarity norm' versus 'frequency norm' (cf. Hockett, 1955: 220—1). The 'clarified' pronunciation of people addressing young children and its role in child language development are discussed in Leopold 1939—49, I:9 under the concept 'presentation' (cf. also Braine, 1974: 288—91).

Some processes apparent in simplified registers are neither simplifying nor clarifying but seem to be 'expressive', i.e. add affect to the utterances, as in the high frequency of diminutive and hypocoristic formations in Baltic and Slavic BT registers. These diminutives are typically more complex than the corresponding non-diminutives and usually do not clarify the utterance in any obvious way. Other pro- cesses are adaptive to the target group or the situation in ways which seem not to be simplifying or clarifying. For example, in speaking to deaf people the voice may be lowered almost to inaudibility to normal hearers, and the motions of the lips may be exaggerated beyond their clarifying effect for normal hearers. Some processes may represent the use of attention-getting devices or attempts at getting feedback from the addressee on his level of understanding, as in the use of rising intonations and tags such as *see? savvy? OK?* in various simplified registers. All these kinds of processes and doubtless others (e.g. sound symbolism, archaizing, euphemism) also seem to mark a particular register as being in use and have a special salience corresponding to dialect markers and recognized stylistic features.

In some instances particular features and hence processes may seem to have only this identifying function; this is especially obvious in cases of lexical replacement as in *understand → savvy* in English foreigner talk or *rabbit → bunny* in English BT.[2]

STRUCTURE OF BABY TALK

The structure of the BT register in a particular language could be shown by a formal 'grammar' of the register which makes explicit the processes relating the grammar of the AS to all possible BT utterances. BT grammars of this kind for different languages could be compared, and cross-language generalizations could be discovered and presented. Since we have neither the grammars nor an adequate theoretical framework in which to write them and compare them, we must settle for a general characterization based on existing descriptions. We can, however, organize the presentation according to types of linguistic processes, beginning with those which seem to simplify the AS.

Since a simplified register is largely a reduced and otherwise modified version of normal adult speech, a promising way of describing it is to specify the relations between adult speech, viewed as the source or norm, and the register, viewed as a derivative or deviation. Such specification can be done by identifying processes of the form $X \rightarrow Y$ (X becomes Y) or $X \rightarrow Y/Z$ (X becomes Y under conditions Z) in which the input is some part of the AS structure and the output is the corresponding part of the structure of the simplified register. Examples of such processes are

(1) Japanese: AS [s] → BT [tʃ]

as in the honorific suffix *-san* of adult speech and the corresponding suffix *-chan* of BT (Chew, 1969; Fischer, 1970); or

(2) English: AS COPULA → BT ∅ /N Adj.

as in the word *is* in the sentence *the baby is hungry* of adult speech having no corresponding equivalent in a BT sentence *baby hungry* (Ferguson, 1971). Process statements of this kind ('rewrite rules') are a widely-used analytic device in contemporaneous linguistics and are particularly appropriate where two related structures are to be systematically matched in a descriptive account.

Two dangers must be recognized in the use of synchronic process statements in linguistic analysis. The first is the temptation to interpret a process as a chronological sequence in which X occurs in real time before Y. Linguistic analysis is often concerned with such diachronic processes, as when a linguistic change between an earlier period and a later period in the history of a language is being analyzed. Diachronic processes will be rigorously identified as such in this paper and in formal notation the traditional inequality sign will be used ($X > Y, X > Y/Z$) instead of the arrow. Thus

(3) Latin BT *papa* ~ *pappa* 'food' > Spanish BT *papa* 'food'

asserts a diachronic process: the earlier Latin form 'became' the

Spanish form, a short-hand way of expressing the linguistic continuity of these elements in the language behavior of particular speech
communities over a period of centuries.

Similarly

(4) Japanese BT *nenne-da-nenne* > *nenne sinasai* 'go to sleep'

asserts the linguistic development from the earliest stage of baby talk
used by the mother to a later stage when the child is a little older.

The other danger in using process statements is the possibility of
interpreting a particular linguistic process as an actual process in the
mental activity of a language user. For example, the relation between
English AS *stomach* and BT *tummy* could be represented by the processes of initial cluster reduction, final consonant deletion, and replacement of the final vowel by the diminutive suffix *-y*.[3]

(5*a*) AS #CCV → BT #CV
(5*b*) AS VC#   → BT V#
(5*c*) AS CV#   → BT C-*y*#

While such process statements obviously represent plausible mental
processes, it is perfectly possible that a particular user of the
language, child or adult, might learn and use both forms independently and never 'notice' the systematic relation between them. Additional behavioral evidence, such as the creation of a new baby talk
form manifesting the processes (e.g. *stopper* → *toppy* or *spinach* →
pinny) is required before claims could be made about their 'psychological reality'.[4]

By expressing these cautions about the interpretation of linguistic
process statements, I do not mean that process statements are empty
formalism or are purely linguistic rules without psychological or
social implications. On the contrary, linguistic rules of this kind provide highly useful clues to understanding the psychological and social
processes of language behavior, but they must not be interpreted
automatically in such terms. To continue the *stomach/tummy*
example, the processes of cluster reduction, final consonant weakening and the addition of hypocoristic suffixes are well attested processes in child language development and the derivation of BT registers[5] in many languages, and it seems very likely (*a*) that the first
creation of *tummy* was the result of such processes and (*b*) that the
presence of the *stomach/tummy* pair in the repertory of users of
English contributes to the phonological organization which forms
part of their processing of language (cf. Ferguson & Farwell, 1975).

SIMPLIFYING PROCESSES

The BT register as defined here consists only of language material identifiable as primarily appropriate for speech to young children. The actual speech addressed to young children may, of course, include other material. BT lexical items may, for example, be embedded in AS, or otherwise normal AS may be spoken with BT intonation or other prosodic features. BT in this narrow sense is clearly very restricted in scope and structure compared to normal AS. It has fewer types of sounds and permissible sound sequences, a very small lexicon and only a rudimentary grammar, even though it is to some extent open in that a new BT word may be created or a word from AS may be modified and newly used as BT. Accordingly, insofar as BT may be regarded as derived from AS by linguistic processes, many of these processes are simplifying or reducing in nature.

The simplifying processes used in BT are not universal in the sense that they all occur in all languages. They differ from one speech community to another depending on differences in the language structure of the matrix language and on the actual BT conventions developed over time in the community. Some kinds of simplifying processes, phonological, grammatical and lexical, are, however, quite widespread and may be found in the BT registers of unrelated and geographically distant languages.

Among the most widespread phonological simplifying processes in BT are the reduction of the structure of words to a few limited favorite shapes ('canonical forms'); the substitution of easier, simpler, less marked sounds for more difficult, complex, marked ones; and various assimilatory processes such as types of consonant or vowel harmony. These processes may overlap or interact as, for example, when a favorite canonical form includes features of consonant or vowel harmony.

Canonical forms differ from one language to another. In Berber BT the favorite form is a reduplicated CVCV of which either the second consonant or both consonants may be geminated (e.g. *bubu* 'lump of sugar', *dud:u* 'butter', *p:ap:a* 'bread'); in Syrian Arabic the favorite structure is CVC where the final consonant is geminate (e.g. *baħ:* 'all gone', *tif:* '(go) bye-bye'); in Japanese it is (C)VCCV where the medial consonantism is either a long voiceless consonant or a nasal plus a consonant (e.g. *batʃ:i* 'dirty', *eŋko* 'sit down'). The general tendency across all languages seems to be toward a reduplicated CVCV with possible lengthening of the medial consonant (e.g. Arabic *ku:ku* 'birdie', Japanese *pop:o* 'birdie'), but the AS structure of each language apparently modifies this tendency; consonant gemination is a pervasive morphological feature of Berber, Arabic has many closed syllables, and the only syllable-final consonants in Japanese are nasals and voiceless obstruents, the latter only before identical consonants.

Sounds of the AS which require more delicate adjustments in articulation (e.g. fricatives) or are marked by having special added features (e.g. glottalization) are of low frequency in BT, reflecting either an avoidance of these sounds in the selection and creation of words or a process of substitution which replaces them by simpler sounds in BT. Kannada BT, for example, has no nasal vowels, retroflex consonants, sibilants, or liquids, all of which are in the phonology of the AS, and the length distinction in vowels is neutralized in BT words. Other examples are the nearly total absence of emphatics and labialized velars in Arabic and Berber BT and the widespread simplification of clusters. The general tendency across all languages is for labial and apical stops and nasals to predominate and for liquids (*l* and *r* sounds) to be replaced or omitted. The *r*-sounds are particularly interesting because of the different substitution patterns across languages. In some languages the BT retains the apical place of articulation and reduces the *r* to a stop, in others the BT retains the liquid sonorant quality but reduces the trill or frication of *r* to a lateral continuant *l*; in others even the liquid quality is lost so that the *r* appears as a semi-vowel *y* or *w* or is omitted entirely. For example,

$r \to t, d$	Gilyak	AS /raf/ → BT /daf/ 'rice'
	Comanche	AS /ʔaraʔ/ → BT /ʔata:ʔ/ 'mother's brother'
	Hidatsa	As /miréh/ → BT /mi:dé:h/ 'door'
$r \to l$	Berber	AS /s-ɣuri/ → BT /ɣuli/ 'to me'
	Cocopa	AS /rápm/ → BT /in-lápm/ 'hurt'
$r \to j, w, \wp$	Japanese	AS /kire/ → BT /kiekie/ 'clean'
	English	AS *rabbit* → BT *wabbit*

The treatment of *r* is a good illustration of simplifying processes in BT. The universal tendency seems to be to reduce the consonantality of *r* from trill to continuant to lateral to palatal semi-vowel to zero, and examples along this scale can be found in many languages. Marathi apparently offers the whole sequence of possibilities except total deletion (as in English *little* → *'ittle*), but the details vary greatly and the tendency may be outweighed by other factors such as the phonological alternation *r* ~ *d* in Gilyak AS or the labialized quality of English *r*. Avoidance of *r* in suppletive BT words seems almost complete except when the trill itself constitutes an onomatopoeia or a game (Arabic or Marathi *kurr*).

Assimilatory processes commonly found in BT include nasal

harmony, by which several nasal consonants in the BT word reflect a single nasal somewhere in the AS source word, and consonant—vowel adaptation, by which front vowels (e, i) co-occur with apical consonants and rounded back vowels (o, u) with labial and velar consonants. For example,

nasal harmony	Japanese	AS /damé/ 'bad' → BT /me:me/
	Marathi	*l* → *n* when a nasal (*m* ~ ŋ) occurs in the word
	Gilyak	AS /damk/ 'hand' → BT /ŋama/
C/V adaptation	Japanese	*dede* 'go out', *bubu* 'hot water, tea'
		ni:ni 'cook', *pop:o* 'bird'

The assimilations may work in either direction:

1st syllable dominant	Japanese	AS *kutsu* 'shoe' → *kuk:u*
	Latvian	AS *nazis* 'knife' → *nan:is*
	Comanche	AS *t ɨkap* 'meat, fowl' → *tata:*
2nd syllable dominant	Japanese	AS *mu ʃi* 'bug' → *tʃitʃi*
	Latvian	AS *sap-* 'hurt' → *papa*

In spite of the widespread examples of these assimilatory processes they never seem to be carried out consistently even in a single language (cf. e.g. Japanese *tonton* 'stamp'; *ke:ke* 'fur'; *nonno* 'ride'). In fact the assimilatory processes give their impression of prevalence largely because of the strong BT tendency toward reduplication in words not derivable from AS (e.g. Berber BT *p:ap:a* 'bread'; *ʃiʃ:i* 'meat'; *huhu* 'sleepy-byes') and in words derived from monosyllabic words in AS (e.g. Japanese BT *há:ha* 'footsie' ← AS *há* 'foot'; Comanche BT *papá: ʔ* 'water' ← AS *pá:*).

Common simplifying processes in BT grammar include the reduction of inflections, the use of an all-purpose auxiliary 'make' with BT nouns and interjection-like words in place of inflected verbs, and the replacement of second person pronouns by other forms of address. Most of the descriptions of BT focus on phonology and lexicon and less information is available on grammatical simplification. Reduction of inflectional affixes is attested, however, for Arabic, Berber, English, Gilyak, Japanese, Kannada, Marathi and Romanian. In Gilyak and Marathi, overgeneralization of regular affixes is mentioned; the use of the definite article even when other inflectional affizes are lost is noted for Arabic and Romanian; and Berber BT seems to use the diminutive suffix as an imperative marker. In all studies of BT in which syntactic features are mentioned, the point is made that BT words may be used as sentence-words with a wide range of grammatic—semantic function or may be embedded in AS sentences in the position of nouns, adjectives, or interjections.

The BT lexicon generally has few words derived from AS verbs and reduced or non-existent verbal inflections. The use of a colorless auxiliary such as 'make', 'go', 'give' with BT words to make action words is described for five languages of our sample: English (e.g. *go sleepy-byes, make peepee*), Japanese (*X suru* 'do'), Kannada (*X ma:du* 'do'), Marathi (*X kar* 'do'), and Romanian (*face* 'do' *da* 'give'), and examples can be cited for other languages, such as French *faire* 'do' (e.g. *faire dodo* 'sleep') and Sahaptin *koʃa* 'do' (e.g. *mǿmak koʃa* 'sleep', Weeks, 1973). This would seem to be a way to limit the verb inflection to one stem and thus avoid the complication of conjugation with each verb. It is worth noting that three of the languages which have this construction in their BT, Japanese, Kannada and Marathi, are languages with verb-final word order which have compound verbs of this kind in their normal AS. Their compound verbs make use of a number of auxiliaries (do, go, come, give, take, rise, fall, say, etc.) with varying meanings, and the use of a single predominant auxiliary in BT constitutes a reduction in this grammatical subsystem. It would probably be a safe prediction that other verbfinal languages with compound verbs, such as Turkish or Amharic, would also have the 'do' construction in their BT register.

. One of the most interesting processes simplifying AS to BT is the avoidance of first and second person pronouns. Wills (this volume) deals with this question in detail for both AS and BT in English; here only a few observations can be made. Unfortunately, most studies of BT do not discuss pronoun avoidance, but the use of third person nouns is well attested for English, Japanese, Marathi and Romanian. All four make use of constructions such as *Baby is finished? Mommy is coming*, in which a personal name, kin term, epithet, or indefinite is used to refer to the speaker or the addressee instead of 'I' or 'you'. Probably all four also use this construction in AS for special effects and in other special registers, as is shown by Wills for English. Japanese, however, has a BT usage which is not attested for any other language and certainly sounds rare or marginal for English. Chew (1969) and Fischer (1970) both report that Japanese parents often use AS first person pronouns in place of second person pronouns in addressing young children, the former basing his results on several years' observation in his own and other Tokyo families and the latter on extensive interviewing of mothers in Fukuoka. A boy child is called *boku*, which is the common adult male word for 'I' used, especially between adult males of similar age or status. Similarly a girl is addressed as *ataʃi*, a common adult female word for 'I'. Apparently this practice is continued (as well as third person reference constructions) until the child begins to refer to himself/herself with the pronoun whereupon the adults begin to use first and second person pronouns with their normal AS values. Perhaps this can be seen as a reduction of the complex pronominal system of AS Japanese with its great fluctuation depending on age, sex and status. If so, it would be worthwhile to investigate the BT practices in other languages of East and Southeast Asia, such as Vietnamese, which have similar systems.

The omission of the copula, predicted as a general feature of BT in Ferguson (1971), is attested explicitly only in the Romanian study among our major sources. The evidence is inconclusive since some languages of the sample normally have no copula expressed in AS (e.g. Arabic and Berber), Japanese BT omits the copula with adjective (no examples cited with noun complement), and most of the studies give only a very limited treatment of syntax. This feature still deserves further investigation.

Probably the most obvious reduction between AS and BT is in the lexicon. Presumably any lexical item of AS could be used in utterances which include BT and presumably any lexical item of AS could be modified by the phonological processes of BT derivation, but in fact the set of words — whether independent or AS-derived — normally used in BT utterances is very small, on the order of 100 or fewer. Kelkar (1964) makes the interesting assertion that BT is 'semantically as ambitious in its range as adult speech. . .only it is less successful'. This may be true in the same sense that any AS word is available for BT modification, but more important is his acknowledgement that in BT 'certain areas of experience naturally come in for greater attention'. Ferguson (1964) lists BT lexicon under four major headings: kin, body, qualities and animals and games. On the basis of subsequent BT studies, two categories, food and animals, should probably be taken out and treated separately because of their number of lexical items. (See especially Bynon, 1968 for discussion of these categories.) All deserve comment. 'Kin' includes kinship terms, personal names, nicknames and epithets. The particular kin terms current in the BT of a community will tend to vary according to its social organization but terms for baby, parents and grandparents, at least, seem to be universal. Often, cover terms for several kin relationships are used in BT which will be sorted out in AS; a good example is Japanese BT *dʒiidʒi* which is used for 'grandfather', 'uncle' and 'old man', which are in AS *odʒiisama, odʒisama* and *dʒidʒii*. (Note that BT versions of the first two exist using *-tʃama* for the *-sama* honorific suffix; see below.) 'Body' includes names of body parts and bodily functions; the two must be kept together since often the same lexical item is used not only for the part of the body but also for the activity associated with it, e.g. Japanese BT *anjo* 'footie' as in *anjo suru* 'do footie' = 'walk'. Here may be included also the words for clothing and footwear.

Although there may be a general word for 'food', the BT register of some communities includes a variety of special BT words for particular foods, which will depend on the eating habits of the society. Berber and Kannada will serve as examples:

Berber

BT	AS	Gloss
p:ap:a	aɣrum	bread
t̥:ut̥:u	aħtuʃ	kind of bread cooled in hot ashes
ʃiʃ:i	askum	meat
yuɣu	ayu	milk
dud:u	udi	butter
mama		
b:wa (with labial trill)	aman	water
m:aħ:a	ataj	tea
bubu	aħbub	lump of sugar, grain of roasted corn
ħbubu		
b:ʕu	tibʕuʃin	dates

Berber

BT	AS	Gloss
ħmam:u	tiʒlit	egg
baḏar	tabaḏart	kind of omelet
t̥:at̥ʕa		
sisu, susu	sksu	couscous
ħriri	aħrir	gruel, soup

Kannada

BT	AS	Gloss
baʤ:i	maʤ:ige	buttermilk
bo:tʃu	mosaru	curds
dʒa:ji	ha:lu	milk
na:ni	do:se	cake
pa:tʃa	pa:jasa	pudding
haŋ:i	haŋ:u	fruit

A BT lexicon for animals seems universal. Although the exact range of animals named differs from one speech community to another, it is not limited either by familiarity with domestic animals or the existence of pets. Clearly the animal vocabulary reflects the salience, in the child's life, of animate, moving beings with faces, legs and fur or feathers, and the consequent important role of this semantic field for language development.

The category 'Qualities' refers to adjectival predicates used of objects or events in the environment which in the adult's opinion are interesting or dangerous for the child. In some instances the BT word refers both to the object and to the attribute which is being asserted (e.g. fire = hot = burn). The basic list of predicates of this kind used in addressing small children is probably almost universal, but in some instances normal AS words are used, in others BT words, independent or modified AS, are used. In some cases the BT word is related to an AS interjection of similar meaning, as in English BT *ow* for a hurt or something painful, cf. AS interjections *ow*, ouch!

The final lexical category comprises a set of terms designating infants' games involving simple physical actions or special sounds or both. All speech communities seem to have a repertory of such games which are played with very young children before they can produce any recognizable speech, and which may be continued with somewhat older children. It is likely that these may play a helpful role in the development of the child's ability to recognize the specific, essentially arbitrary connection between vocal signal and referent. Typical games include actions such as clapping hands, raising hands over head, clenching fists, hiding face, making noise in the ear and carrying piggyback. It is likely that these game cues constitute one of the sources of action predicates in the child's language development, and the handful of more generalized verbal predicates 'go up' or 'fall down' which may not be tied to a game could also be included in this category.

Other BT words are found which do not fall neatly into the categories set up here, an interesting example being the 'bogeyman'. Nine of the major sources examined here (Arabic, Berber, Comanche, English, Gilyak, Greek, Maltese, Marathi, Spanish) explicitly mention a mythical monster who is used to frighten children, and such an item may have simply gone unmentioned in the others (cf. Chamberlain (1890), Sapir (1929) and Sabar (1974) for a bogeyman in Algonkin, Nootka, and Neo-Aramaic, respectively).

CLARIFYING PROCESSES

All speech communities presumably have clarifying processes which are used by speakers to give extra clarity to their utterances when needed. For example, when the addressee has not understood an utterance directed to him and asks for a repetition the speaker may reply in a slower, more carefully enunciated style, fill in ellipses of his original utterance, or reword the utterances in a less ambiguous way. Some of these clarifying processes are also used in BT, and a BT register may employ special clarifying processes of its own. Unfortunately linguists have done very little systematic study of clarifying processes in general, and even published BT studies offer little information. Accordingly, the comments here are tentative.

The most obvious clarifying process in BT is repetition. Words, phrases and whole sentences are repeated in addressing the young child, in a way and to an extent not done in normal AS. This process is so 'natural' and universal (?) that speakers are only barely aware of using it. Adult informants from whom BT is being elicited by the linguist do not report repetitions, and adults asked by the psycholinguist in an experimental situation to speak as though they were speaking to young children do not do much repetition. However, observation of BT in natural settings and in experimental situations with children present shows extensive use of repetition, and this repetition is a very noticeable feature of BT when recordings are played out of context for adult reaction. In the psycholinguistic literature on speech to young children, all experimenters seem to have noted repetition; for a review of this see Snow (this volume). The intra-word reduplication described above may also be related to the repetition process and thus represent both simplifying and clarifying processes.

A second clarifying process characteristic of BT is the exaggeration of intonation contours, chiefly by extending the pitch range of the intervals. Pike and others (Pike & Lowe, 1969; Pike, 1973) have noted this process in English and now Garnica (1974, this volume) gives solid experimental data for it in English BT. It has been noted also in Marathi and Japanese BT, and it is probably quite widespread but not reported or included with the raising of pitch (see below).

The set of phonological processes which result in lento speech constitute the most generally acknowledged clarifying processes in ordinary AS phonology, and they are also described as characteristic of BT registers. One of the best descriptions is in Voegelin & Robinett (1954) where the authors noted that the informant's BT pronunciations were very similar to the clarified forms she used in dictating Hidatsa to members of the Field Methods seminar. It has repeatedly been observed that lento forms tend to be closer to the 'underlying' forms posited to account for morphophonemic alternations (e.g. Kazazis, 1969); as Voegelin & Robinett put it, the 'mother language' form often 'coincides with or resembles the morphophonemic formulae which we are tentatively setting up' (*op. cit.*, 70). These lento processes in various languages include supplying elided vowels or consonants, separating fused vowels, increasing the number and level of stresses, inserting additional junctures (= use of non-medial allophones in medial position).

Some phonological clarifying processes in BT seem to represent segmental strengthening which goes beyond the morphophonemic alterations of normal AS. These strengthening processes typically increase the perceptual salience of particular consonants or vowels either by lengthening, gemination or by quality changes (e.g. fricative → stop or affricate). In some instances there are even additional segments, such as *h* or *ʔ* added after a final vowel. For example,

	AS		BT
Berber	tiyyni	'crushed dates'	(n)ninni
	atay	'tea'	ttattay
	afa	'fire'	fuffu
Comanche	ʔïnï·	'insect'	ʔïnï·
	káhhI	'house, tipi'	kanï·ʔ
	wáʔo·	'cat'	waʔó·ʔ
Japanese	(o-)saru(-san)	'monkey'	otʃarutʃan
	ha	'leaf'	happa
	(o-)heso	'navel'	opetʃo

In Berber 'there is a considerable increase in gemination accompanied by some apparent weakening of its contrastive value (in initial position)' (Bynon, 1968: 121–2). In Comanche BT words derived from adult vocabulary are put into 'the baby word phonetic pattern of two syllables with the second vowel accented, long and usually ending in a glottal stop. . .Presumably it is in this phonetic form that words are first presented to the child. This seems consistent with our practice of carefully enunciating words when teaching them to a child' (Casagrande, 1948: 13). In Japanese BT /h/ is sometimes strengthened to /p/, medial consonants are geminated, and *s* → *tʃ*. The *h* → *p* process reverses diachronic weakening, since modern Japanese *h* generally goes back to earlier **p*, and it is conceivable that the *p* in BT words may in some instances continue the earlier sound unaffected by the sound change.

EXPRESSIVE AND IDENTIFYING PROCESSES

The most prominent expressive feature of BT is probably the hypocoristic affix. In BT registers morphological devices, most commonly suffixes, which are used in AS to form diminutives or hypocoristics, are used more frequently and in different ways. An excellent example is the increased use of diminutive suffixes in Latvian BT. The language has a rich selection of diminutives in AS but these are even more used in BT (Rūķe-Draviņa, 1959, 25–35). Often one particular device is used chiefly or exclusively in BT and thus serves to identify the register. The English suffix -*y*/-*ie* is an example of this, but perhaps even better examples are Gilyak -*k*/-*q*, Berber -*ʃ*/-*ʃtt*, and

Japanese *-ko*. These suffixes are added to AS words or may replace part of the AS word, and they are used almost exclusively in BT, although the Gilyak suffix may sometimes be used in language play apart from BT. Some BT words without AS counterparts may have the suffix, and in some instances a BT word may occur either with or without it. For example,

	AS		BT
Gilyak	gi	'shoe'	gik
	als	'berry'	alq
	daf	'house'	dafk
	(ŋawř)	'abdomen'	gomk
	(leqrnt)	'toy'	bapa, bapk
Berber	ixxa	'nasty, dirty'	xxiʃtt
	ʒn	'sleep'	ħu, ħuʃ, ħuʃtt
	iff	'breast'	bbu, bbu
	(fʃi timitt)	'(give me a) kiss'	bbaħħaʃtt, mmaħħaʃtt
Japanese	daku	'hug'	dakko
	neru	'sleep'	ńefiko (suru)
	ńn	sound of making effort	úfiko (suru)

Other examples include the Quileute BT suffix *-ck*, which is one of a set of affixes characterizing different kinds of abnormal speech (Frachtenberg, 1918); Syrian Arabic *-o*, which is also used to make nicknames and kinterms of address in AS, Latvian *-in-* used only in BT verbs; and Comanche *n-* also diminutive in AS.

The addition of a derivational affix produces a longer form which a simplifying process may reshorten. In Romanian this process has been noted for a number of words, e.g. *unchi* (uɲtʃ) 'uncle' + *-utul* diminutive suffix → *unchiutul* → *chiutul* (tʃutsu) (Avram, 1956: 139). Gilyak has five BT words which lack the -k/-q suffix which the corresponding AS words have and Austerlitz (1956: 271−2) argues that the AS words are originally BT in origin while the new BT words are shortenings.

It is conceivable and open to empirical investigation that the characteristic BT suffix may play a role in the development of the child's grammar, since it may be the first morphological element which the child finds segmentable and thus may begin the development of derivational and inflectional morphology. We could wish that Brown (1973) had included *-y/-ie* among the 14 grammatical morphemes he investigated.

The most prominent expressive feature of pronunciation in BT is probably the use of higher pitch in addressing children. This feature, which is distinct from the exaggeration of intonation contours mentioned above and which is very likely universal, is probably the principal component of the phenomenon of *Ammenton* 'nursery tone' mentioned by many observers. Its ultimate origin is presumably in the adaptation being made to the child's own higher fundamental frequency resulting from the smaller vocal tract and other differences in the shape of the cavities, size of vocal cords, etc. Garnica (1974) now provides experimental data for this phenomenon on the part of American mothers. This prominent prosodic characteristic may well play an important role in identifying speech addressed to the young child, thus signalling to the child that he should attend to it and signalling to older children and adults present that it is not directed to them.

The displacement of word accent to a position different to AS is characteristic of some BT registers, and is often hard to attribute to simplification or clarification. Examples of displaced accent in BT include Japanese (BT initial accent except in reduplicated adjectives) and Comanche (BT final accent, cf. Clarifying processes, above). Of special interest is the pattern of contrast between CVCV and CVCV́ BT words in Spanish and Romanian, which has no obvious lexical source in AS, e.g. Romanian *pápa* 'food' versus *papá* 'bye-bye'; *nána* 'older sister, aunt' versus *naná* 'watch out, no no'; Spanish *pipi* 'bird' versus *pipí* 'peepee'. This could be regarded as a device for helping the child to acquire the distinctive use of stress for AS.

A striking feature of BT phonology is the presence of sounds or phonetic modifications not found in the corresponding AS. This phenomenon can hardly be viewed as simplifying or clarifying, but makes sense in terms of sound symbolism, limitation of child speech, or simply register identification. The commonest modifications seem to be 'softening' or palatalization of consonants and the corresponding 'sharpening' of vowels, and labialization of consonants and vowels. For example, labialization and palatalization are both reported for Latvian and Marathi baby talk, labialization is attested for English (Joos, 1948: 108, fn.) and palatalization for the Western Desert Language of Australia (Miller, n.d.). Retroflexion as a BT feature is reported for the San Felipe dialects of Otomi (Bartholomew, 1960: 319).

Examples of specific BT sounds are especially common in American Indian languages: *v* in Cocopa (Crawford, 1970), *l* in Nootka (Sapir, 1929), labials *p b m* in Iroquois (Chamberlain, 1890), *x* and long *m*: in Comanche (Casagrande, 1948), but they are also well attested in other languages: *p* in Berber and Arabic (Bynon, 1968: 116 and 141),

long *m*: and ʔ in Gilyak (Austerlitz, 1956: 268 and 277), final *-m* in
Japanese (Chew, 1969: 10). It is worth noting that almost all these
examples are labials. The special role of labial sounds is shown also
in the frequency of emphatic /ḅ/ and /ṃ/ in Arabic BT words (including BT *ḅāba* and *māṃa* used also as affective terms in AS) in
comparison with the complete absence of non-labial emphatics, thus
reversing the frequencies of AS. Berber and Latvian BT include a
labial trill not part of the regular AS.

Typically, these specific BT sounds are anchored to particular lexical items, and adult speakers find them difficult or impossible to pronounce otherwise. BT registers also tend to have exclamatory segments consisting of a prolonged fricative or sonorant which does
not occur as a syllabic in AS; this reflects (and encourages?) the
child's creation of such items in his own early language development.
For example, *ʃ:* 'urinate' in Japanese and Marathi.

VARIATION

BT registers, like any other variety of human speech, show internal
variability in the sense that some elements and structural relations
may vary under partially or completely non-linguistic conditions.
The dimension of regional and social dialect variation in BT has been
explored relatively little and that little has not been systematic, i.e.
incorporated into final linguistic statements of co-occurrence or variance. Treatments of regional variation vary from an impressionistic
observation (Kelkar, 1964) that there is no dialect variation in the
Marathi BT register — an improbable assessment for a speech community of millions of people — to an attempt (Bynon, 1968) to
assemble exhaustively all the information about BT published for
any variety of Berber. Explicit treatment of regional variation also
appears in Ferguson (1956) (Arabic) and Rūķe-Draviṇa (1961) (Latvian) but nowhere is there an attempt to characterize the variation
either in traditional dialectological terms (isoglosses, focus areas, relic
areas), or by means of Labovian variable rules, or in any other variation framework. Social variation has been studied in English and
Dutch BT from a different perspective, cf. Drach, Kobashigawa,
Pfuderer & Slobin (1969) and Snow *et al.* (1976).

The most interesting dimension of variation from the viewpoint
adopted here of linguistic processes relating AS and BT is that of
degree of 'babyishness'. Several authors have pointed out that utterances addressed to children as well as specific BT forms within them

fluctuate within the same language in the degree to which they diverge from AS. Kelkar (1964) was apparently the first to formalize this phenomenon by writing rules with successive outputs of increasing degree of babyishness. Avram (1967) discussed the same phenomenon by means of an extended example, giving different forms of telling a baby to go to sleep:

AS	BT 1	BT 2	BT 3
dormi (copile)	copilul face nani	copilul nani	pilul nani
	or	or	
	face nani copilul	nani copilul	

The first degree of babyishness replaces the AS word for 'sleep' with a BT equivalent 'make sleepy-byes' and uses 'the-baby' as a third person subject instead of the optional vocative. The second degree omits the 'make' and the third degree drops the initial syllable of 'baby'. Drachman (1973) formalizes the notion of degrees of babyishness by positing 'stages' of successive operation of rules but prescinds from any judgment of whether the forms classified in the various stages are rated by members of the community in appropriate degrees of babyishness or whether they have developed historically in the order of his rule application. Clearly this whole area deserves investigation of the kind becoming increasingly common in studies of pidginization and decreolization (cf. DeCamp, 1971; Bickerton, 1973; Cedergren & Sankoff, 1974); it should also be tied in to the kinds of experimental investigation which test BT modifications to children of different ages.

The one linguistic description which reports a systematic relationship between the degree of babyishness in the BT register and the state of the child's language development is the study of Japanese BT by Chew (1969). The author had the opportunity to observe the use of Japanese with the same children over a two-year period and he posits five 'styles' from the earliest (or most 'babyish') BT to normal AS. Although Chew allows for overlapping and inconsistency in detail, he claims a succession of styles as follows: Style 1 consists of one-word BT utterances with optional repetition and the insertion of *ko* or *da*, together with certain features of intonation and tempo; only a few lexical items are used. Style 2 extends the lexicon and makes use of a number of processes modifying AS items. Style 3 has utterances of more than two lexical items, but without inflectional and connective particles. Style 4 has many of these particles and multiclause sentences. Style 5 is approximately AS. Chew does not discuss the conditions for shifting to successive styles, but Fisher (1970), in discussing this phenomenon of the Japanese, notes how complex the issue is, involving both the adult's estimate of the child's language development and the child's own perception of his readiness to shift.

This is one of the most promising areas of research in child language development: to describe the nature and scope of variation in degree of BT divergence from AS, and the relation between this variation on the one hand and the attitudes of the speech community and the actual progress of language development on the other.

USE OF BABY TALK

The primary use of the BT register is to speak to young children, but it may have a variety of secondary, 'displaced' uses (Ferguson, 1975: 2) which evoke one aspect or another of the adult—child communication. Unfortunately, the uses of BT have rarely been described in any detail, and the published studies which give data on lexicon, etymologies and striking features of structure give only very fragmentary information about use. This lack of information reflects both the linguistic bias of the investigators of BT and the method of elicitation employed as a short cut to observation in natural settings. Even the primary use is rarely specified in terms of who uses BT, the ages of the children addressed and other basic information. Here we can only report what the published studies provide.

A number of studies report on the ages of the children with whom BT is used. They tend to agree on use from about one to about age three or four while allowing for its use with older children under special conditions. Gilyak speakers are reported to use BT until weaning, which is usually at age three but may be anytime from two to eight. The Comanche speech community is said to use BT when the baby is old enough to understand speech (about one year of age) up to the time he has mastered the fundamentals of the language; if a child uses BT forms as late as age five he is ridiculed. Cocopa BT use is the most interesting: it is used for boys up to the age of six or seven years, girls up to 10 and even in early and mid-teens when the mother wants to show affection, and at least one informant reports that BT may be addressed to an unmarried female of any age as a reminder of her status. In Japanese, use is reported to begin before the child speaks at all and the upper limit seems to be kindergarten or nursery school age.

In several studies investigators record reasons given by the informants for the primary use of BT, usually 'to teach the child to speak' (e.g. in Berber and Comanche) but sometimes in other terms. Fischer reports 'the key words are easier to pronounce for the child, and the child cannot understand the adult words as well', 'the adults in the family used these words because they were cute', and one mother 'wanted to use the same words as the children used' (Fischer, 1970: 109).

The interesting and important questions about the use of BT register with children require research techniques of anthropological observation and psycholinguistic experiment: use by older children and adult non-mothers, differential use to different ages, sexes, and social groups; who initiates the shift to AS and how, and all the rest. Fischer (1970) and Chew (1969) combine to give us more information about BT use in Japanese than any other language, but it is still fragmentary and unsystematic.

Secondary uses are even less well reported. Bynon (1968) asserts that there are *no* secondary uses in Berber, explicitly noting that the BT register could not be used to animals or between lovers. Yet it is hard to believe that there is no extension at all to situations which call for some aspect of the values of BT, since registers tend to be extended by analogy, metaphor, and 'semantic' extension in the same way other units and levels of language are extended. Use of BT to animals is well documented for English and reported for Marathi but goes unmentioned in most BT studies. Read (1946) gives a number of examples including Shaw's *Androcles and the Lion* and modern newspaper stories; one American linguist of my acquaintance claimed never to use BT at all, only to realize she spoke almost constant BT to her cat. Since it seems safe to assume that the speaker is not attempting either to make his speech easier to understand or to teach the animal to talk, the use of BT to animals must be expressing affection or reinforcing the speaker's own feeling of taking care of the animal.

Another extension of BT which expresses its nurturant, caretaking message is its use with hospital patients, elderly people and other adults being tended by nurses, doctors, attendants, technicians, or family. In this situation the full range of BT features is not used, and it would be of interest to determine which features are found most appropriate for this use. The avoidance of first and second person singular pronouns, which is common in this use of BT, can hardly be explained as a means of facilitating the eventual mastery of the pronoun system, which seems a reasonable motivation in the use of BT with young children. It may possibly be seen as a way of mitigating the directness of commands and questions between caretaker and person-cared-for, but it is likely that the BT register is in some sense being extended as a unit, since a significant number of other features in the cluster of features constituting the BT register appear also in this use.

The use of BT between intimate friends and lovers, which is also well attested for English, Spanish, Latvian, Marathi and other languages, may similarly express a re-creation of the nurturant—nurtured roles, but it may also simply express affection between the users. Read (1946) and Kelkar (1964) both cite the classic example of Jonathan Swift's *Journal to Stella* but many other examples can be given, and this use is a familiar phenomenon and seems to be quite widespread in spite of often being discounted or ridiculed. In this use many of the phonological features of BT are more frequent than in the caretaker use. Once again it seems that the use of the register is extended as such, but that certain features are selected as more appropriate for the particular use.

The BT register often serves the purpose of coaxing or persuading in adult—child, caretaking and intimate uses, and in all three situations the coaxing may go in either direction, i.e. adult-to-child or child-to-adult etc. A further extension of BT is to attempt to persuade or cajole the addressee not in the categories of the uses already identified. This 'wheedle' use, as Read calls it, can even be extended to objects or to unknown addressees. Read offers, among other examples, Alexander Woolcott's amusing habit of using BT in addressing his dice at backgammon, this from a person who repeatedly ridiculed in print the use of BT in other settings. Another example of extension is its use in certain forms of advertising (cf. Read (1946) for discussion).

Finally, some secondary uses of the BT register seem to have little or no trace of the affective, nurturant, or coaxing aspects of the primary use, but seem to serve only to signal the childhood status of participants in the communication situation. In a number of languages the BT register is used to report child speech, much as foreigner talk is used to report the speech of foreigners (Ferguson, 1975); an excellent example is provided by Norwegian as discussed in Haugen (1942), where a novelist may use BT register to represent the speech of children even though the children being portrayed would not talk that way, given their age and situation. A use which signals childhood status with pejorative flavor is what might be called the 'mocking' use, as seen in sarcastic and satirical language. Read offers one example in which it is senility or need for caretaking which is being suggested by the use of BT, i.e. the American presidential campaign of 1840 in which Harrison's political opponents represented his friends as speaking baby talk to him.

Further examples of the status-attribution use can be found in the use of BT features in nursery rhymes, songs, riddles; adult literature about children; and in conventionalized adult word-play. Sabar (1974) gives examples of BT register in Neo-Aramaic nursery rhymes, Rūķe-Draviņa (this volume) discusses the use of BT terms in Latvian pediatric publications, and Austerlitz (1956) mentions word-play phenomena.

Closely related to questions of the use of BT is the set of attitudes toward BT held by members of the speech community. Several authors have mentioned the issue of attitudes (cf. especially Ferguson, 1964: 112) and it is clear that communities may differ greatly in their overt approval or disapproval of BT and the occasions for which it is appropriate, but there has been no systematic investigation along the lines of recent studies of language attitudes (cf. Agheysi & Fishman, 1970; Shuy & Fasold, 1973).

BABY TALK AND LANGUAGE ACQUISITION

The universal presence of BT in speech communities requires explanation. What functions does BT fill which have assured its survival everywhere as a component of language structure and language use? It is possible to speculate on answers to this question, given the facts as summarized in this paper.

First, there are direct functions of *communication* and *self-expression*. The structure of BT is, like that of any other simplified register, in large part a response to the need for improved communication when one of the participants has only a limited ability to use language normally. By neglecting some of the complications of normal speech and modifying it in other ways which clarify it and adjust it to the child's ability, BT is easier to understand. This claim needs experimental validation in order to determine the extent to which various features of BT increase intelligibility under what conditions, but it certainly seems likely that the overall effect of the use of BT is to increase the attention holding and intelligibility of the adult's speech to the child even if some of its features may have no such effect or even a negative effect. Also, the use of BT facilitates the adult's expression of his emotions toward the child and the situation, giving him a special means to show affection, irritation, protectiveness, amusement and so on, which goes beyond normal AS. In this use BT is similar to such other expressive devices as compliments, insults, interjections, nicknames and so on. The importance of this expressive dimension for the speaker of BT should not be overlooked; its strength can be seen when a parent talks BT to a sleeping child or in some of the displaced uses listed on p. 230–31.

Second, there are *language-teaching* functions. If one were to design a plan of language exposure to accelerate mother tongue acquisition, it would very probably be along the lines of BT. One would indicate by special signs when speech was being addressed to the infant, and the talk itself would be primarily in situations and on matters of immediate concern for child and parent. One would make certain simplifications and gradually restore the complexity as the child's language progressed. It might even be a part of the plan to have a separate lexicon which could function outside of the regular grammatical structure in semantically more transparent and flexible ways; such an extra lexicon could then gradually be abandoned as the grammatical structure itself is acquired or might even be retained for some special expressive use. Of course, this is purely speculative until there is experimental evidence that learning is actually assisted or accelerated by the use of BT. Given the wide variation in the details of the structure and use of BT from one community to another and from one family to another, it seems highly unlikely that it is a crucial element in the acquisition process. If the effects of BT as a teaching device were decisive, this would certainly have been noticed long ago in many societies, and in particular by child development researchers. But in the absence of detailed experimental evidence one can still join Snow's (1972: 561) observation that the speech addressed to young children 'in many ways seems quite well designed as a set of "language lessons"'.

Even if one did not accept the value of BT in acquiring the language as a whole, it cannot be denied that its use with young children has the effect of teaching this register for use in other situations in adult life. To take an extreme example, the exaggerated use of diminutives in Latvian BT undoubtedly succeeds in ingraining the forms and functions of diminutive expressions for affective and topical use in AS.

Third, there are non-linguistic functions of *socialization*. BT offers a means of identifying the social roles which the child must learn as requiring differential behavior in his society. All BT registers have words for male and female adult caretaker and baby which are 'taught' very early. The use of BT intonation, lento articulation and such features, in itself delineates roles: typically caretakers use them to the child, not to one another; older children use them to younger children, not to still older children; female caretakers use them more often than male caretakers and so on. Age, sex and kin roles are thus signaled insistently by BT. The most striking example in our data is the differential use of male–female pronouns in Japanese BT register.

The lexicon of BT by its 'Qualities' category begins the assignment of the society's values. From its earliest exposure to speech the child has objects and events around it called good, bad, dirty, dangerous, hot, cold, painful, sweet and the like. The teaching of values which Gleason (1973) notes as so important in the 'language of socialization' which she observes in use with four- to eight-year-olds, has begun long before in the earliest use of BT. A convincing example is the acquisition of the word *pretty* by children learning English. This word, pronounced in exaggerated BT style, is so often and so emphatically used in talking to infants that it is frequently among the first words acquired, the most famous instance being Hildegard Leopold. It was her first word and was pronounced with great phonetic precision (for discussion, see Leopold 1939–49 1: 24, 119–20; 11: 265).

In addition to these three basic functions which BT seems to fill in all speech communities, additional uses may be made of the register in particular communities, as with any cultural resource in a society's inventory. We may note the widespread, but not universal uses of reporting child speech and addressing animals (cf. Use of baby talk, above). A function which has been noted by several observers is the provision of childish euphemisms for taboo words. For example, when a child learns the name for a body part or physiological activity he may use it in public conversation at inappropriate times causing embarrassment to adults, but if what he uses is a baby talk term instead of the normal adult name the occurrence may be only annoying or 'cute'. A related function, noted already in nineteenth-century linguistic studies, is to serve as a source for affective or euphemistic vocabulary in the adult language, as when *atta* becomes the Gothic word for 'father' or *tummy* the English word for 'stomach'.

The data available from BT studies, together with some cautious speculation, suggests that baby talk registers are universal because they have been effective in meeting universal needs in communication and self-expression, acquisition of language and the general processes of socialization. Before their exact role in language acquisition can be determined, more experimental work of the kind summarized by

Snow (this volume) and more cross-cultural studies of language socialization of the kind discussed by Blount (this volume) are needed. For
the incorporation of BT phenomena into linguistic theory the most
promising lines are the variation models (cf. Bailey & Shuy, 1973)
and register analysis (cf. Ellis & Ure, 1969; *Report of the contemporary Russian Language Analysis Project*, 1972: 47–76); both of these
require much more extensive and exacting data collection than has
yet been the case in studies of BT registers.

NOTES

1. Note that in this paper no attention is given to questions of the origin and
diffusion of BT features which are of considerable importance for understanding
processes of language change, but are less relevant for the purposes of the paper.
See, however, comments on these questions in Ferguson, 1964: 104, 111–2;
Bynon, 1968: 136–48; Crawford, 1970: 12, 13.
2. Absolute, pure examples are difficult to find since almost always some element of simplification, clarification, or other kind of process can be claimed.
Thus *bunny* avoids the difficult sound *r* and drops the troublesome final consonant, but since something more directly related to *rabbit* such as *wabby* or *babby*
would be possible, it seems reasonable to see this item as primarily register-identi-
fying, whatever its historical origin may have been.
3. The rules are given here in simplified form. In writing a formal 'grammar' of
English BT, more specific rules of cluster reduction and final weakening would
be given, comparable to similar rules in child language development and language
change (cf. Ingram, 1974), and explicit treatment of rule ordering would be
necessary.
4. The etymologizing of a BT form by showing its derivation from an AS
model by linguistic processes is fraught with the same difficulties as any etymologizing, whether of word histories or nonce formation (cf. Malkiel, 1962). For
example, the final *y* of *tummy* replacing *-ach* may not involve final consonant
loss at all but may be the reduction to monosyllabic stems usual with nicknames
in *-y/-ie*, e.g. *Stephen* → (*Steve* →) *Stevie*.
5. The simplifying processes of language development and BT are often identical, but important differences also exist. For example, of the three types of cluster reduction in child language development discussed in Ingram (1974) two,
sC → C and CL → C, are found in English BT but the third, NC → C (when C is
voiceless), is not attested in BT.

10 Modifications of speech addressed to young children in Latvian

VELTA RŪĶE-DRAVIŅA

Department of Slavic and Baltic languages, University of Stockholm, Fack, 104 05 Stockholm 50, Sweden.

My article on Latvian baby talk *Ns. lastenhoitajain kielestä* ('On so-called nursery language') was published in 1961 in Finnish, with a short summary in German (Rūķe-Draviņa 1961; see also Rūķe-Draviņa, 1976). The aim of the present study is to concentrate on new material and on controversial questions still found in professional literature on this subject. The analysis is based mostly on Latvian linguistic data and cultural traditions: Latvian is my mother tongue and I have studied the use of Latvian baby talk in my own family as well as in the homes of other Latvian-speaking children; many examples are taken from two longitudinal studies of the language development of my own children (0;6—4;6 and 0;6—6;0), and from tape recordings which were taken during a period of two years (1972—74) when three Latvian-speaking children in Stockholm were tape recorded in their homes in conversation with adults — parents and researchers (Rūķe-Draviņa, 1973).

Additional data and comments come from Lithuanian, Swedish and other European languages in the North-European countries. About 30 Swedish-speaking three- and four-year-old children were tested during their visit to the dentist in connection with the official Swedish dental control in Eksjö, Southern Sweden (Rūķe-Draviņa, 1972). The aim was to examine their ability to recognize and to name things in three pictures which were shown to them. However, as the mother (or father) stayed with the child and often helped, when necessary, with a question or an answer here and there, these dialogues also illustrate the mother's way of explaining the action represented in the picture. For example, various pet names such as

kisse 'pussy', *kissemisse* 'pussycat', *mjau!* 'meow!' — as designations
for the cat — appeared in the answers of the children as well as in the
speech of their mothers. The above materials were supplemented by
data from interviews with Latvian-, Lithuanian-, Polish- and Russian-
speaking parents. In order to get illustrations for the use of baby talk
words in Latvian poetry, excerpts were made from several anthol-
ogies of poems for young children.

The usage of the term for the phenomenon in question still varies:
'baby talk', 'parental speech' and 'nursery language' are the most
popular terms in English. 'Baby talk' (BT) signifies here any particular form of a language which is regarded as being primarily appropriate for talking to very young children and which is used by adults
and other children when addressing an infant.

In Latvian, BT is not an instinctive creation of young children but
a conventionalized part of the language, transmitted by the same
means of language transmission as other speech elements, e.g. abusive
words or slang utterances used by teenagers or soldiers. Naturally
these nursery language elements are employed by the infant itself
when attempting communication with adults and other children.
Thus, when analysing the fundamental stock of words used actively
by Latvian children in the first stages of their speech development,
we find that a high percentage of these words are so-called nursery
forms, onomatopoetic forms, interjections etc. In some respects, an
individual 'cooperation' can be noticed in some families between the
adult-used BT forms and the forms reproduced by the young child.

In Latvian, BT utterances are generally addressed to an infant up
to the age of about three years, although it seems to me that now-
adays parents stop using these forms earlier than was the case about
50 years ago. No striking difference can be noted with respect to
boys and girls as concerns the usage of BT. Latvian BT forms can
sometimes be employed between adults, e.g. lovers, in order to get
attention or to be treated in some way as a baby. They are also common in contacts with (young) domestic animals. According to the
attitude of the ancient Latvians, domestic animals were to be treated
in the same way as small children who have not yet mastered the
adults' speech.

Latvian BT vocabulary is widely used in Latvian folklore
(especially in lullabies and folksongs for small children) as well as in
individual written poetry, and it is found in Latvian novels and
stories when infants and small children are depicted. See Appendix
II, Folksongs and Children's Poems.

CHARACTERISTIC FEATURES OF LATVIAN BABY TALK

INTONATIONAL AND PARALINGUISTIC PHENOMENA

(*a*) higher overall pitch ('Ammenton')
(*b*) tendency to labialization (e.g. *mana mazā meitiņa* → *mǻna mǻzā möitiņa!* 'my dear daughter')
(*c*) occasionally somewhat slower and more careful pronunciation.

PHONOLOGY

(*a*) All phonemes of the standard Latvian language are represented: *a, ā, e, ē, ę, ę̄, i, ī, u, ū, o, b, c, č, h, d, dz, dž, f, g, ǧ, k, ķ, l, ļ, m, n, ņ, p, r, ŗ, s, š, t, v, z, ž.*

(*b*) A bilabial vibrant, absent in standard forms, appears in several baby talk words, spelled here *ptr*, e.g. *ptrūta* 'cow', *ptrū-iņš* 'horse'.

(*c*) The frequency of affricates and sibilants (*c, č, dž, š, ž*) is much higher than in standard Latvian.

(*d*) Palatalized consonants have a higher incidence in nursery words than in words of the standard adult language.

(*e*) Diphthongs and consonantal clusters seldom occur.

(*f*) The distribution of some phonemes (e.g. *ę*) does not correspond to that of standard adult words (cf. *męmmę* — with open *ę* at the end of the word; *pę̄ki-pę̄ki* — with an open *-ę̄-* in spite of *-i* in the following syllable; *gugiņa* — with *g*, instead of *dz*, before *-i-*), i.e. the rules of the vocal assimilation and consonant palatalization are not always followed in BT words, in the same way as they are ignored in interjections and onomatopoetic words.

(*g*) In some nursery words there is a simplification of consonant clusters (*nīpis* 'nose' instead of *snīpis*), omission of the tremulant *r* (as in *bāļa* = *brālis* 'brother') or a replacement of affricates by apicals (e.g. *tite* for *cice* 'teat').

MORPHOLOGY

(*a*) At least one diminutive/hypocoristic suffix frequently occurs. In order to express the personal feelings of the speaker towards the addressee or the subject matter to which they refer, almost all words (nouns, adjectives, even verbs) appear in diminutive form (e.g. *maziņš mīliņš bērniņš nāciņās šurp!* = *mazs mīļš bērns nāks šurp!* 'the little dear child will come here'). A characteristic feature is the parallel use of hypocoristic forms, e.g. when addressing the mother, the father and the infant.

(*b*) Occasional irregular types of diminutive suffixes differing from those normally used in the same local dialect appear (e.g. *uodzīte* from *uoga* 'berry' instead of *uodziņa*).

(*c*) Masculine gender can replace the feminine in some hypocoristic forms (e.g. *ruocīš* from *ruoka* 'hand' in the Stende dialect, north-western Latvia, not *ruociņ*, as usual).

VOCABULARY

BT vocabulary is characterized by the following structural and semantic features:

Structural features

(*a*) The majority of BT stems are constructed from open syllables (e.g. *mā-ma, tē-te, ti-ba, ci-ba, cu-be, ka-ne, kā-ne, gu-ga, gu-ža* etc.) but closed syllables are also represented (e.g. *ņam-ma, nin-ne, min-cis, pun-cis, min-ka*). The pronunciation in such words as *čuča, tita, tite, koša, kuka* etc. varies depending on dialect (*ču-ča* or *čuč-ča*).

(*b*) Reduplication of identical or non-identical syllables and of words occurs (e.g. *tete, kaka, papa, pepe; caca, cice, tita, tite, kuka; čuku čuku, urru urru, tiki tiki*).

(*c*) Many baby talk words are disyllabic, and there is no tendency to avoid long forms, since the accumulation of hypocoristic suffixes expands some words into four- and five-syllabic forms, cf. *māma*, diminutive *māmuliņa* 'mummy'.

Semantic features

The best represented semantic groups in Latvian BT are the terms for

(*a*) parts of body:
feet: *peciņas, capatas, cipatas, cebītes, čabiņas, čapas, čāpas, tožas*
hands: *ķepiņas*
nose: *dedžiņš* or *dēdžus, snīpis, nīpis, šņīpītis*
mouth: *muža, mužiņa*
head: *buoze*
stomach: *puncis, pencuks, pendēris, pumpiņa, bumbuls, būča, būčiņš, būčelis*

backside: *dupa, dupsis, dipsis, dupucis, pača, pačka, cūce*
sex organs:
  vagina: *čoža, čožiņa, cīcis, pākstiņa*
  penis: *pincis, pinkulītis, skuostiņa, krāniņš*
mother's breast: *cicis, cice, ciča, tizis, tita, tite*
  (*b*) bodily functions:
to eat: *ammāt, ņammāt, ņęmmāt*
to drink: *ninnāt, nēņāt*
to bathe: *pičāt*
to take a bath: *pičāties, piču paču iet, pičiņās iet, pļunku pļunku*
to sleep: *čučēt, čučāt, čučiņāt, iet uz čuču muižu, braukt uz miega*
    muižu
to kiss: *bučuot, duot buču/bučiņu, duot mužu/mužiņu*
to walk: *čapāt, čāpāt*
to fall: *blauks!*
to want: *bidzēt* (present tense *bigu*)
it hurts: *pāp, (ir) biba/bibis/bibītis*
  (*c*) food and drink:
food: *amma, ņamma, ņęmma*
drink: *nenne, ninnis, niņņa, nēnes*
bread: *kuka*
milk: *picītis*
meat: *pępa, pepe, papa, pāpiņa, čīča*
porridge: *bendzīte, biezīte*
potato: *kapulis, cācis, čācis*
carrot: *būciņš, kaniņi*
pea: *ninnis, čīča, čīči*
anything sweet: *uku,* (inspiratory-) *ć-ć-ć!*
  (*d*) domestic animals:
horse: *ī-ha-ha, koša, košiņa, kuze, kuža, kuziņa, tprū-iņš*
foal: *ciga, čiga, cigiņš, čigiņš, cigus, čigus, suka*
cow: *mū, mū-iņa, mūmiņa, mūjęns, tprūta, tprūte, tprūtiņa*
dog: *vau vau, vauviņš, vavucītis, una, amis, amītis*
puppy: *kuča, čučiņš, čūčiņš, vavucītis*
cat: *incis, mincis, pincis, minka, ņurītis, kicītis, kaksis, ņau ņau*
hen: *ciba, cibe, cibīte, tiba, tita, tite, cibiņa, čibiņa, tibiņa*
chicken: *cibis, cibulis, cibulītis*
rooster: *kikarigū! ķikariga,* (in Stende dialect) *makks*
goose: *kane, kāna, kāne*
duck: *pęki pęki*
sheep: *bęja, bice, bidze, bidža, badze, męja*
lamb: *bicis*

ram: *bika*
pig: *uša, ušis, rukse, ruksītis*
dove, pigeon: *dūdiņa*
(bird: *čivi čivi*)
  (*e*) immediate environment, things around the child:
cradle, crib: *aces, aijas, nūnas, pūbas, pūbiņas*
to rock, to swing to sleep: *aijāt, pūpuot, pūbuot, lullināt*
nipple: *pupiņš, knupītis, lučuks*
toys, playthings: *caces, paijas*
doll: *nūnis, nūne, lelle, lulla, lullis*
train: *čuku čuku* (*bānītis*), *tuku tuku* (*bānītis*)
(baby) carriage: *urru urru*
watch, clock: *tik tak, tiki tiki*
bell: *bim bam*
fire: *udža, udže, udžiņa, udžiņš*
knife: *nannis*
goblin: *bībis*
  (*f*) kin terms:
mummy: *māma, mamma, mẹmma, memme, māmiņa, māmuļa,
  memmīte,* etc.
daddy: *tētis, tēte, tete, tātis, papa, paps, papus, tētiņš, papucis,
  papiņš*
nurse: *ẹmma, ẹmba*
baby: *maziņais, bēbis, bēbītis,* and numerous pet names
  (*g*) basic qualities:
good/fine: *pai*
bad/dirty: *pẹ̄, vẹ̄*
  (*h*) expressions of encouragement or discouragement to perform
specific actions:
(stand) up!: *opā! upā!*
don't touch!: *ai ai!*

A full list of BT words is given in Appendix I, together with the
corresponding source words in adult speech.
    In addition to the above mentioned semantic groups, individual
simplification in the use of vocabulary is often observed in Latvian
families, e.g. a tendency to avoid adult 'international terms' and
'foreign words' and to replace them with descriptive native words (as
'disaster car' (*nelaimes auto*) in place of 'ambulance'; 'big school'
(*liela skuola*) instead of 'university').
    In regard to the use of personal and possessive pronouns, it is
mostly the shift in reference which makes these pronouns difficult for

small children to master. In Latvian, as in most other European languages, one must choose between two pronouns (Latvian *tu* and *Jūs*) when addressing a person, and the choice is made according to various criteria: family relationship, the degree of intimacy, the relationship of age, status, etc. Besides, according to Latvian traditions, the Christian name (with or without hypocoristic suffixes) is normally used when the husband is talking to his wife, and vice versa; and when parents are talking to their children, but not vice versa — 'mummy/mother' and 'daddy/father' are then the usual addresses.

In Latvian families the adults usually assume the *position of the infant* when naming the members of the family. Thus, the mother can call her own mother 'granny', and the grandmother, her daughter 'mummy'. Sometimes two hypocoristic forms of 'mummy' have been specialized so that one of them is used to address the mother, the other one the grandmother.

(*e*) Greater use of short sentences of a simple structure is prevalent, especially when trying to explain something or to convince someone of something: *Anniņa ir maza. Anniņa ir nuogurusi. Anniņa ies gulēt. Rīt Anniņa varēs atkal ruotaļāties.* 'Anne is little. Anne is tired. Anne will go to sleep. Tomorrow Anne can play again'.

The form of the child's Christian name is usually adapted to his age: a boy, Peter by name, is not called so as an infant or as a pre-school child, the forms of address being, for example, *Pēčiņš* (an infant) → *Pēčus* (a teenager) → *Pēteris* (an adult). Similar examples illustrating this naming tradition can also be found in Latvian literature (*Andžiņš* → *Andžus* → *Andrejs*; *Ilžele* → *Ilze*).

Latvian BT vocabulary has a core of words which are known to every competent native speaker, e.g. *ņammāt* 'to eat', *ņamma* 'food', *ninne* 'drink', *čurāt* or *cizāt* 'wee wee', *mūjiņa* 'cow', and a peripheral sphere including words used only in a single Latvian dialect or known only within one or two families.

PHRASEOLOGY AND SYNTAX

(*a*) Some idiomatic phrases are used only in BT, e.g. *iet uz čuču muižu* or *iet uz miega muižu* (literally 'to go to the Sleepy Manor' = 'to go sleep'), *miega Miķelis nāk* (literally 'Michael Sleep is coming' = 'you are sleepy').

(*b*) Many nursery words, when used in a sentence, may function indiscriminately as a noun, an adjective, a verb or an imperative or interjection:

tas ir pę̄ puika 'he is a *bad* boy'
nekāp iekšā, tur ir pę̄ 'don't step in! that's *dirt*!'
paskaties, kur ir ņau ņau 'look where the *pussy-cat* is'
pincītis ņau ņau 'pussy-cat *mews!*

In another group of BT words the flexion is in full correspondence with the rules of Latvian standard adult language. These words are declined/conjugated regularly, e.g. kur *pincītis?* 'where is the stomach?', kas bę̄rnam *pincītī?* 'what do you have in your stomach?'

(*c*) There is a greater use of nouns than of personal and possessive pronouns, since third person constructions replace first and second person ones, e.g. *memmīte gaida!* 'mummy is waiting' = 'I am waiting', *Anniņa jau dabūja!* 'Ann did get (it) already' = 'you got it already'.

(*d*) The first person plural form is used for the second person singular, e.g. *mums nāk miegs* 'we are sleepy' instead of *tev nāk miegs* 'you are sleepy', *vai mēs gribam ēst?* 'do we want to eat?' instead of *vai tu gribi ēst?* 'do you want to eat?'

ORIGIN OF BABY TALK VOCABULARY

Some of the nursery forms seem to come from their standard equivalents through phonetic changes which are to be expected in the pronunciation of young children, e.g. *ninnis* (cf. *zirnis* 'pea'), *nannis* (cf. *nazis* 'knife'), *una* (cf. *suns* 'dog'), *nīpis* (cf. *snīpis* 'nose'), *kapulis* (cf. *kartupelis* 'potato'), *kaniņi* (cf. *burkāniņi* 'carrots'), *būciņš* (cf. *burkāniņš* 'carrot'), *ipa* (cf. *istaba* 'room'), *pāp* (cf. *sāp* 'it hurts'), *pept* (cf. *cept* 'to bake, to fry'), *bigu* (cf. *gribu* 'I want'), *bāļa* (cf. *brālis* 'brother').

In several cases, the names of the parts of body which in the standard language are used only in respect of animals, have been transferred into the human sphere, e.g. *ķepiņas* 'small hands of the infant', cf. *ķepa* 'paw'; *peciņas* 'the child's feet', cf. *pękas* 'paw'. This tendency has also been observed in the slang vocabulary used by teenagers.

Many onomatopoetic words imitating the cries of domestic animals are used as names for the corresponding animals, especially when expanded by some diminutive/hypocoristic suffix, e.g. *mū* (the mooing of a cow) — *mūjiņa* or *mūmiņa* 'cow', *ņau ņau* (the mewing of a cat) — *ņauiņš* 'cat', *vau vau* (the barking of a dog) — *vauviņš*, *vavucītis* 'dog'. Calls employed as commands to domestic animals are also used as a basis for animal names in BT, e.g. *koš koš* (a call to a horse or foal) — *košiņš* or *koša* 'horse, foal'.

Other groups of onomatopoetic words and interjections also function as BT words.

Some BT words are of unknown origin or are loans from the BT vocabulary of a foreign language. According to the traditional etymology, there are several BT words of Finnish and German origin in Latvian, e.g. *kane, kāne* 'goose' (Finnish), *papa* 'daddy' and other kin terms (from German).

BABY TALK AND LANGUAGE DEVELOPMENT

Latvian BT vocabulary plays a special role in the linguistic development of the child since a high percentage of the fundamental stock of words actively used by children in the first stages of their speech development consists of these nursery forms. Adult—child conversations followed by direct observation and tape recording show that (many) babies, during some intermittent periods of their development, repeat many of the words with which adults address them, cf.

(language input) nursery forms as used by the adults:	(language output) the same words as pronounced by the young child:
0;8 *aijā žūžū, lāca bērnis, aijā žūžū*	*aija jā aijā aijajā*
1;2 *kā ūdens burbuļuo? bur-bur-bur-bur*	*bu-bu-bu-bu*
1;5 *plunku plunku*	*pu-pu*
1;7 *uzraksti kaut kuo skribi-skribi*	*bi-bi-bi-bi*

The children easily copy also the movements and gestures of adults. Some illustrative examples:

(*a*) Father is walking about the room reading a newspaper. Child (1;2) follows behind with an opened book in his hands, occasionally glancing into it.

(*b*) Child (1;2) who still does not say 'yes' and 'no', uses (instead of these verbal expressions) head movements taught to him by the father, i.e. a nod (wanting something and confirming it) or shaking head (rejecting something).

A word can be learned together with an accompanying gesture, e.g. a child (1;8) started to use the BT word *pai* 'fine' patting herself or some other (loved) person's hair, head, hands, thus copying the word and gestures of adults.

Latvian adults often correct children in their incorrect use of lexical elements (terminology) and of morphological forms (an incorrect
choice of an affix, case ending or gender form) as well as their defec-
tive pronunciation.

(a) Mother: *kas zivīm ir?* 'what does a fish have?'
     Child (2;6): *asajas* (= *asaras*) 'tears'
     Mother: *nē, asaras ne, bet asakas!* 'no, not *tears*, but *fishbones*'
     Child: *asakas!* 'fishbones'
     Mother: hmm (= *jā*) 'yes'.
(b) Child (2;6): *tikai pilsētuos var raudāt* 'you can cry only in *cities*'
     (uses the word 'city' in masculine instead of feminine).
     Father (repeats first, with a questioning intonation, the incorrect
     form, then uses, with emphasis on the correct ending, the femi-
     nine form): *pilsētuos? kāpēc pilsētās var raudāt; vai Ananēs
     nevar raudāt? kāpēc nē? kuo?* 'in cities? why only in cities,
     can't you cry in (our country home) *Arnanäs?* why not?
     what?'.
(c) (correction of a syntactic construction):
     Child (about three years): *viņš nāk miegs* 'he is getting sleepy'
     (*viņš* 'he' is used in the nominative form instead of the correct
     dative form *viņam* in the debitive construction in Latvian).
     Interviewer: *O jā, viņam nāk miegs. Viņš aiztaisījis actiņas un guļ.*
     'o yes, he is getting sleepy. He has closed his eyes and is sleep-
     ing'.

As a rule, in Latvian families the young child is not corrected when
it uses BT words instead of the adult equivalents. As exceptions to
this rule there are some young Latvian-speaking families in Sweden
and America, in which the parents try to avoid nursery forms
altogether.

As seen in the above examples, a very common means of correction is the transformation of the child's utterance into a well-formed
standard sentence. The degree of difference between the child's utterances and the corresponding utterances repeated correctly by the
adult diminishes when the child grows older and its speech develops.

These corrections serve several purposes:

(a) to check whether the adult has understood what the child has
wanted to say, cf. a dialogue between the mother and her child (1;3):

Child: *pu-pu*
Mother: *vai Dainis grib pḷunku pḷunku?* 'does Dainis want to *splish
    splash?*

Child: nods happily, pointing to bathroom;

(*b*) to employ an effective tutorial technique by giving a standard model which the child can imitate. The imitation can occur immediately as in the following example:

Interviewer: *jā, es tev duošu! lūdzu!* 'yes, I will give it to you, please (take it)!' (passes a plaything to the child)
Child (approximately 3 years old) repeats: *lūdzu!* 'please'
Interviewer: *nē, tu saki 'paldies'* 'no, *you* must say "*thank you*"!'
Child repeats: *paldies!* 'thank you!'

Sometimes it takes a day or a somewhat longer interval before the correction made by the adult is imitated by the child, cf.

Girl (2;6) narrates that she herself, without mother's help, had opened a box): *varēja [vajēja] attaisīt vaļā. Zīlīte varēja!* 'could open it, Zīlīte (= girl's name) *could!*' i.e. 'I could open it!'.
After a short pause she adds: *varēju [vajēju]* 'I could!'

In the repeated statement the girl corrected the verb form from third person to first person singular ending, as it is used in the adult language. During the foregoing weeks, her parents had several times corrected her utterances in this respect.

In adult speech there is sufficient parallel use of standard forms and BT forms to make it possible often for the child to 'translate' words and phrases from one code to another, i.e. from standard language into BT correspondences. Hearing the adult use a normal language word, e.g. *ūdens* 'water', *gulēt* 'to sleep', *sāpēs* 'it will hurt', it can immediately replace it with a corresponding synonym from its baby talk vocabulary — *ninne* 'any kind of drink', *aiju žūžu* 'to sleep', *ai jai ai ai!* 'it hurts'.

Several tape recorded adult and child dialogues with such transfers serve as examples of the above:

(*a*) A dialogue between a mother and a girl of about two and between this girl and her eight-year-old brother:

Mother: *pasauc Daini pusdienās!* 'call Dainis *to dinner!*'
Child (runs to the brother into the other room): *Daini, ņammu ņammu! [ņeņe ņam ņammi!]* 'Dainis, *eat!*'

When the addressee does not immediately obey her, the girl grabs the brother's legs and coaxes: *opā! ņammu ņammu!* '*hoppa!* (= get up!) *eat!*' In the dialogue given here the normal adult form is *pusdienas* 'dinner' but *ņammu ņammu* 'to eat' is its BT equivalent.

(b) Child (1;10) narrates to the mother: *Dainis tuku-tuku* [*ŋɛŋŋɛ tu tukī*] 'Dainis (has gone) *by train*'.

Mother corrects: *nē, Dainis aizgāja kājām uz skuolu* 'no, Dainis has *walked* to school'.

Child understands the adult language form and translates it into its baby talk vocabulary: *tapu tapu* [*t'ap t'apī*] 'walking'.

(c) Mother is warning the child: *neej pie plīts! uguns iekuodīs!* 'don't go near the stove! *the fire will bite you!*'

(In the mother's talk the expression 'the fire will bite you' is used instead of the more neutral adult phrase 'will burn you').

Child understands and repeats the sense by a nursery form: *aijai ai ai!* '*ow ow!*'

At this age (1;3) the child understood the warnings used by the parents (*neej pie uguns!* 'don't go near the fire!' *uguns iekuodīs!* 'the fire will bite you!', *Dainim būs aijai ai ai!* 'it will hurt Dainis', *ass!* 'sharp!', *kuož!* 'bites!', *karsts!* 'hot!') as designations for something of which one must beware, be on guard against.

COMPARATIVE DATA AND COMMENTS

The comparison of the BT vocabulary used in Latvian-, Lithuanian-, Polish- and Russian-speaking families shows that:

(a) The total sum of the BT words used in one family usually does not go beyond 30. In addition to these traditional terms, several individual spontaneous new formations appear.

(b) There are some similar structural elements in the nursery words in all the above mentioned languages, e.g. reduplication of syllables with or without modifications of the vowel.

But there is also a marked difference between the languages in regard to the phonetic inventory and the semantic relations in BT words. Thus, a quite different formal structure of the word can be connected with the same meaning in several languages, e.g.

'(to) sleep':	Latvian *aiju žūžu* or *čučēt*, Lithuanian *čiučia liulia* Polish *luli luli*, Russian *baju baju*
'goose':	Latvian *guža* or *kane*, *kāne* or *kana*, Lithuanian *girgargar* Polish *gę gę*, Russian *ga ga ga*
'to take a bath':	Latvian *piču paču* or *pļunku pļunku*, Lithuanian *pliušku* Polish *badi badi*, Russian *bul' bul'*
'pig':	Latvian *ɾuk ɾuk* or *rukse*, Lithuanian *kriu kriu* or *ciukė* Polish *nöf nöf*, Russian *chŕ u chŕ u*
'food':	Latvian *ŋamma* or *ŋɛmma*, Lithuanian *niam niam* Polish *papu papu*, Russian *ŋam ŋam* or *am am*

On the other hand, the very same form can have quite different meanings in different languages and dialects, e.g. *papa* [pa-pa] means 'daddy' in Russian, [papa] 'meat' in Latvian but 'food' [papu papu] in Polish BT.

(*c*) The difference in the nursery vocabulary between Latvian and Lithuanian (related Baltic languages) seems to be more significant than the difference between the corresponding adult terms in these Baltic languages, cf.

Lithuanian (standard): *višta* 'hen'
Lithuanian (BT): *putė* or *kar kar*

Latvian (standard): *vista* 'hen'
Latvian (BT): *ciba* or *guga* or *tita* or *tiba*

and

Lithuanian (standard): *ugnis* 'fire'
Lithuanian (BT): *žižė*

Latvian (standard): *uguns* 'fire'
Latvian (BT): *udža* or *udže*

APPENDIX I: GLOSSARY OF LATVIAN BABY TALK VOCABULARY

The glossary of BT vocabulary given below is mostly based on the Latvian—German Dictionary of Mīlebachs-Enzelīns (four volumes) and Supplements (two volumes) in which the words appropriate for talking to young children are marked by 'in der Kindersprache'. Following the BT form the English equivalent is given and then the corresponding word in the standard language. In some cases (marked by '?') no direct correspondence can be mentioned, or the adult form sounds very rude, vulgar.

Contrary to the usual spelling, *uo* as a symbol for the diphthong, and *ę, ȩ̄* (for open *e, ē*) are used.

aces 'cradle' — *šūpulis*
aijas 'cradle' — *šūpulis*
aijāt 'to rock' — *šūpuot*
aijā, aijajā! (interjection)
aijā žūžū! (interjection)
'to make the baby sleep'
am am! 'bow-bow' — *riet* ('to bark')
amis, amītis 'dog' — *suns*
amma 'food' — *ēdiens*
ammāt 'to eat' — *ēst*
atā! 'bye-bye' — *ardievu, sveiki* 'good-bye'
bendzīte 'porridge' — *biezputra*
bę̄, bę̄ja 'sheep' — *aita*
bēt 'to bleat' — *blēt*
biba, bibis, bibītis 'slight wound, scratch' — *pušums*
bice, bidze, bidža 'sheep' — *aita*
bicis 'lamb' — *ję̄rs*

bidzēt 'to want' — *gribēt*
pres. *bigu*   pres. *gribu*
biezīte 'porridge' — *biezputra*
bika 'ram' — *auns*
būciņš 'carrot' — *burkāns*
buča, bučiņa 'kiss' — *skūpsts*
bučuot, duot bučiņu 'to kiss' — *skūpstīt*
būča, būčiņš, būčelis 'stomach' — *vę̄dęrs*
bumbuls 'stomach' — *vę̄dęrs*
buoze 'head' — *galva*
cabītis, pet name for child
caces 'playthings' — *ruotaļlietas*
capatas, cipatas, cebītes 'feet' — *kājas*
cipata capata, cipatuot 'to walk' — *iet*
cācis 'potato' — *kartupelis*
ciba, cibe, cube 'hen' — *vista*
cibis, pet name for child

cib cib!, cibu cibu! words to call hens
  and chickens
cibulis 'chicken' — cālis
cicis, cice, cíca 'teat' — krūts ('mother's
  breast')
cīcis 'vagina' — ?
ciga, cigiņš, cigus 'foal' — kumeļš
cizāt (verb) 'wee-wee' — ?
cizis (noun) 'wee-wee' — ?
cūce 'backside' — dibęns
cūce, cūcis 'dog' — suns
čabiņas, čapas, čāpas 'feet' — kājas
čapāt, čāpāt 'to walk' — staigāt
čācis 'potato — kartupelis
čiga, čigiņš, čigęns 'foal' — kumeļš
čīca 'meat' — gaļa
čīcas, čīci 'peas — zirņi
čivi čivi 'bird' — putns
čoža, čožiņa 'vagina' — ?
čuča 'sleep' — guļa
čučēt, čučiņāt, iet uz čuču muižu 'to
  sleep' — gulēt
čučiņš, čūčiņš 'young dog' — suns
čuku čuku 'train' — vilciens
čurāt, čurēt, čurināties 'wee-wee' — ?
dędžiņš, dędžus 'nose' — dęguns
dipsis, dupsis, dupa, dupucis 'backside'
  — dibęns
doņņa 'stomach' — vędęrs
dūdiņa 'dove, pigeon' — dūja
ērmanītis 'sleep' — miegs
guga, gugiņa 'hen' — vista
guz(n)iņa 'stomach' — vędęrs
guža 'goose' — zuoss
iepa 'vesicle' — pūtīte
ī-ha-ha 'horse' — zirgs
incis 'cat' —kaķis
ipa, ipača 'room' — istaba
kakas 'excrements' — ?
kakāt ' to do number two' — ?
kakināt 'to let a child "do number
  two"' — ?
kaksis 'cat' — kaķis
kane, kāna, kāne 'goose' — zuoss
kaniņi 'carrot' — burkāni
kapulis 'potato' — kartupelis
kicītis 'cat' — kaķis
kikeriga!, kikerigū! 'rooster' — gailis
koša, košiņa, košiņš 'horse' — zirgs
krāniņš 'penis' — ?

kuča 'dog, puppy' — suns
kuka 'bread' —maize
kuze, kuziņa, kuža 'horse' — zirgs
ķepiņas 'hands' — ruokas
lulla, lullis 'doll' — lelle
lullu!, luļļu!, lulluo! (interjection when
  rocking to sleep)
lullināt 'to rock' — šūpuot
luļķis 'teat' — krūts
mačus, maķis 'sleep' — miegs
mamma, māma, męmma, memme
  'mummy' — māte
mēja 'sheep' — aita
Miķelītis 'sleep' — miegs
mincis, minka 'cat' — kaķis
muža, mužiņa 'mouth' — mute
mū, mūiņa, mūjęns, mūmiņa 'cow' —
  guovs
nannis 'knife' — nazis
nenne, nēnes, ninna, niņņa 'drink' —
  dzēriens
ninnāt, nēņāt 'to drink' — dzert
ninnis 'pea' — zirnis
nīpis, snīpis 'nose' — dęguns
nūnas 'cradle' — šūpulis
nūne, nūnis 'doll' — lelle
*ņam ņam!, ņammu ņammu!, ņammāt,
  ņęmmāt* 'to eat' — ēst
ņamma, ņęmma 'food' — ēdiens
ņurītis 'cat' — kaķis
pača, pačka, pāča 'backside' — dibęns
pača, pačka 'birch besom for a stem
  bath' — pirtssluota
pača, pačka 'bath-room, bath-house' —
  pirts, vannas istaba
pačāt 'to steam and to flap with birch
  branches' — pērt
pačiņas 'bath' — pirts, pelde
pai 'good, fine' — labs, mīļš
paijas 'playthings' — ruotaļlietas
paijāt 'to stroke' — glāstīt
papa 'meat' — gaļa
papa, papas, papus, papucis, papiņš
  'daddy' — tēvs
pākstiņa 'vagina' — ?
pāp 'it hurts' — sāp
pāpiņa 'meat' — gaļa
pāpiņa 'a child who cannot stand pain'
  — ?
pępa, pepe 'meat' — gaļa

pept 'to bake, to fry' — cept
pāpulis 'potato' — kartupelis
peciņas 'feet' — kājas pēdas
pelce 'urine' — ?
pelcēt 'to urinate' — ?
pencuks, penderis 'stomach' — vēdērs
pę̄ 'bad, dirty' — netīrs, nejauks
picītis 'milk' — piens
piča 'sauna' — pirts
pičāties, piču paču, pičiņās iet 'to take
   a bath' — mazgāties
pincis 'cat' — kaķis
pinkulītis 'penis' — ?
piža 'anus, vent' — tūplis
piža 'urine' — ?
pižāt 'to urinate' — ?
pļunku pļunku 'to bathe' — mazgāties
pujāt 'to do number two' — ?
sapujāt 'to soil' — saķēzīt
pujas 'excrements' — ?
puliņa 'hen' — vista
pumpiņa 'stomach' — vēdērs
puncis 'stomach' — vēdērs
puža 'backside' — dibēns
pūbas, pūpas, pūbiņas 'cradle' — šūpulis
pūbuot, pūpāt, pūpuot 'to rock' —
   šūpuot
rukse, ruksītis, ŗuk ŗuk! 'little pig' —
   cūka
sīmanis 'sleep' — miegs
skuostiņa 'penis' — ?
suka 'foal' — kumeļš
šņīpītis 'nose' — dēguns
tātis, tēte, tētis, tete, tetis 'daddy' —
   tēvs
tiba 'hen' — vista
tik tak, tiki tiki 'clock, watch' —
   pulkstenis
tita, tite 'hen' — vista
tita, tite, tizis 'teat' — krūts
tožas 'feet' — kājas
tprūta, tprūte, tprūtiņa 'cow' — guovs
tprūiņš 'horse' — zirgs
tuku tuku 'train' — vilciens
tutū! 'all gone' — nav (vairs)
udža, udže, udžiņa udžiņš, udžis 'fire'
   — uguns
uļļa 'baby blanket' — lakatiņš
una 'dog' — suns
upā! 'up' — augšā

urru urru 'to drive, to go by bus or
   train' — braukt
uša 'pig' — cūka
vau vau!, vaut 'to bark' — riet
vauviņš, vavucītis 'dog, puppy' — suns
vę̄ 'bad, dirty' — netīrs, nejauks

APPENDIX II: FOLKSONGS AND CHILDREN'S POEMS

The folksongs given below are cited
from Kr Baron & H. Wissendorff,
Latwju Dainas, 6 volumes in 8 parts,
Mitau and St Petersburg 1894—1915,
abbreviated BW.
   The children's poems given below
are poems for small children or about
children written by individual authors,
among them well-known Latvian
writers such as V. Plūdonis, J. Poruks
and K. Skalbe. They are cited from the
following two collections:
   L. Kronberga, *Runča vezums*;
Dzejoļu antoloģija bērniem.
Copenhagen, 1953, abbreviated to
'Runca vezums'
   H. Dorbe, Br. Saulītis, V. Valeinis,
Saules gadi. Riga, 1965, abbreviated
to 'Saules gadi'.
   The BT vocabulary items in the
folksongs and poems are underlined
here for identification.

FOLKSONGS

Čuči, guli, mazbērnin,
Es tecēšu puķu raut;
Es aijinas izpuškošu. (BW 2106,2)
Aijā, bērniņ, pūpās,
Kas tev rītā šūpos? (BW 2049)
Jau tas miega Ērmanūt(i)s
Ap Ancīti diņģējās. (BW 2066)
Incīt, pincīt, atvelc miedziņu.
                              (BW 2065)
Vistiņa, gāgiņa, palīdzi dziedāt.
                              (BW 2476)
Būs bērniem čīčas, pupas,

Būs apaļi rācentiņi. (BW 2281)
Arsim čičiņas, arsim pupiņas. (BW 2281, var.)
Atej, tēta, kliņģeriem,
Memma siltiem pīrāgiem. (BW 2914).

CHILDREN'S POEMS

VILIS PLŪDONIS
   (zemenītes) *Prāvākās kārbiņā,*
               Sīkākās guziņā,
               Bālās lai paliekas,
               Kamēr ietekas. ('Saules gadi' 191)
pičiņu pačiņu austiņām:
modriņi, modriņi sadzirdēt tām. ('Saules gadi' 192)
Nāc, kaķīti, nāc, incīti! ('Saules gadi' 193)
Dzer pie upes āzis vecs,
Buku-bē! buku-bē! ('Saules gadi' 194)
Actiņas, rau, veras ciet |...|
   Varim čučēt jāiet ir. ('Saules gadi' 195)
JĀNIS PORUKS
    Ej peles ķert, minka! lec laktā, tita!
    Jau pulkstens vakaram astoņus sita!
    Un Edis lai žigli nu laukā skrej:
    Tāds una, kas kož, lai nu tumsā rej!
    Ar Lulliņu kopā es gultiņā čučku;
    Vēl mīļajai māmiņai vienu bučku,
    Tad tā kā dūmi nāk reibinošs miedziņš,
    Un sapnītī lido balts balts sniedziņš.
    Pa sniegu brien una, minka un tita,
    Kā pasakā Lulla tiek pavadīta. ('Runča vezums' 65)
KĀRLIS SKALBE
    Ģiģis brauc uz miega muižu.

       Miglas muiža - miega muiža ...
       Brien pa smilti kumeliņš.
       Egles aijā, bērzi aijā,
       Aijā ceļa braucējiņš! ('Runča vezums' 32)
LIJA KRONBERGA
    Lien šurp labāk! Vakaru aijāsim,
    Pamīšus viens otru paijāsim. |...|
    Un tad? Tad pēc pudeles klaigāsim
    Un uz miega muižu staigāsim. ('Runča vezums' 22)
ANDREJS BALODIS
    par lapsu un drošo tibi ('Saules gadi' 252)
   Atdod manu dēlu, manu Kikerigu! ('Saules gadi' 253)
JŪLIJS VANAGS
    Steidzas tā uz putnu kūti
    — Ti – – ti!
    — Gā – – gā!

– Ku – kur – gu!
Cāļi
Gaiļi
Raibā Tīta
Zosutēviņš,
Tītarpaps. . . ('Saules gadi' 422).

11 The derivational processes relating Berber nursery words to their counterparts in normal inter-adult speech

JAMES BYNON

*Department of Africa, School of Oriental and African Studies,
University of London, London WC1E 7HP, England*

Most societies have, as a normal part of their language, a register
reserved primarily for addressing very young children; such registers
are commonly referred to as baby talk (BT) or nursery language. The
existence of a special set of speech forms for talking to young children is so widespread a phenomenon that we may in fact reasonably
suspect it to be a linguistic universal, at least in so far as traditional
societies are concerned. In such societies the BT register often shows
a greater degree of structuring and a more extensive development,
notably as regards the special lexicon employed, than anything we
are used to in present-day Western society so that they constitute a
particularly favorable field in which to study the phenomenon.

Although so far students of BT have usually been linguists or philo-
logists whose prime concern has been with the detailed description
of their particular language and not with problems of first language
acquisition as such, I believe that both the linguist and the developmental psychologist stand to gain by attempting to communicate
across the boundaries of their respective disciplines, the linguist after
all wants to know, or at least *should* want to know why his BT words
have the forms they do and are used in the way in which they are,
and the student of first language acquisition should also feel it
necessary to ask him(or her)self why BT registers exist over such a
wide area of the globe and why it is that, in societies which are quite
unconnected historically, these registers have so many features in
common.

One such feature is the widely-held belief that the function of BT
is to help children to learn to speak, that it is in fact a teaching aid.

Naturally I am not seeking to imply that the traditional tenets of pre-
literate society are superior to information acquired through the
application of modern methods of scientific investigation, but science
would, I think, be unwise to discard as irrelevant or without significance any feature which is either a universal or a near universal of
language.

In a previous article (Bynon, 1968) I described and partially analyzed a corpus of about 100 BT words from one such traditional society, a Berber tribe of central Morocco. In that article I showed that,
while some 20 % or less of the words were suppletive, the remainder
could be derived from words of normal inter-adult speech having
identical or similar meanings. The derivational processes involved
normally entailed deletion, that is to say the loss of part or parts of
the word, often followed by partial or total reduplication of what
was left so as to produce forms complying with, or at least more
closely approaching, the canonical types of the Berber BT word —
that is to say words of pattern C(:)V or CVC(:)V. Other characteristic features included the modification or replacement of individual
segments, the gemination of consonants short in the inter-adult
counterpart and the addition of one or more hypocoristic suffixes. I
did not, however, make any attempt at relating all the BT forms in a
systematic way to their counterparts in normal inter-adult speech.

Charles Ferguson (this volume) has suggested that a promising way
of describing BT would be to specify the relations between adult
speech, viewed as the source or norm, and BT, viewed as the derivative or deviation, in terms of rewrite rules. That approximately is
what I have attempted to do here, although the extent to which the
operation is successful varies somewhat according to which words one
is prepared to admit into one's corpus as genuine examples of BT and
which category of derivational process is involved. One of the difficulties of working from a corpus obtained indirectly through informants is that these have a tendency (and this too appears to be quasi-
universal) to confuse forms used by adults for addressing young children with forms used by the children themselves, so that any collection of BT words obtained in this way is likely to include examples
of what might perhaps more appropriately be classed under the heading of infant speech, or at least of the adult stereotyped concept of
how infants mispronounce words.

The material analyzed comprises all those BT words of the original
corpus for which a likely source in normal inter-adult speech could
be identified, to which have been added 20 close kinship terms and
hypocoristic forms of personal names of the type that we would call

'first' or 'given' names. These are categories that I quite wrongly omitted from my 1968 description, for it is precisely the names of the members of the family that it is claimed the child learns first.[1] All the data are given in the Appendix, where the normal adult source words, the BT words, and the derivational processes which account for the formal relationship between the two, are laid out in the form of a table. The words have been grouped into semantic fields; although this is sometimes rather arbitrary it does often reveal a close relationship between word structure, semantic category and derivational process. I have set up five categories of derivational process, which I have labelled *mutation, deletion, gemination* (which could equally well be called consonant tensing or lengthening), *reduplication* (stretched, in order to avoid the multiplication of categories, to include the repetition of a single vowel) and *suffixation*.

MUTATION

This is the most complex of the categories of derivational process and apparently the least susceptible to reduction to rule. Individual cases are sometimes open to more than one possible interpretation, and children's mispronunciations, or what are locally believed to be such, clearly play an important role. Mutation may affect both vowels and consonants.

(*a*) Vowels. There are four cases of assimilation across an intervening consonant: No. 45 *udi* → **udu*,[2] No. 71 *yxxa* → **yxxi*,[3] No. 72 *ixxann* → **ixxinn*, No. 75 *uggadn* → **uggudn*. In another four cases, all verb stems used as imperatives, a *schwa* has been replaced by a full vowel (No. 64 *bədd* → *bidd*, No. 67 *qqən* → *qqin*, No. 68 *ffər* → *ffur*) or the vowel quality has been altered (No. 66 *babb* → *bibb*).

(*b*) Consonants. Regressive assimilation across an intervening vowel is clearly the explanation in the cases of No. 40 *ayyul* → **aɣlul* and No. 79 *idušan* → **išušan*. For the first of these there is independent evidence of the reality of the postulated intermediate stage, since *aɣlul* exists in the dialect as a stereotyped infantile mispronunciation of *ayyul* (alongside *tazwawt* for *tazyawt* 'basket' and *aɣmum* for *aɣɣum* 'bread'). Whether such claimed children's mispronunciations are in fact the product of accurate observation is irrelevant in the present circumstances; what matters is that an adult member of the speech community *believes* that this is how small children mispronounce normal words of the language. There are three instances of cluster reduction as the result of assimilation, either progressive or regressive, to a neighboring consonant: No. 70 *yɔla* → *yɔɔa*, No. 77 *aɔndir* → **aɔnnir*, No. 81 *tayŋʒawt* → *tayʒʒawt*. Of the apparently unconditioned mutations, two are cases of the replacement of a consonant by a vowel to produce an open syllable (No. 46 *sksu* → *sisu*, No. 65 *ɣʷʒ:lm* → *ɣʷʒ li*) and the remaining five have the appearance of stemming from children's mispronunciations, either actual or assumed (No. 55 *ɬɬaʒin* → **ɬɬavin*, No. 62 *s-yuɽ-i* → **s-yul-i*, No. 78 *agʷunun* → **ahunun*, No. 85 *islli* → *itlli*, No. 86 *aʒɖiɖ* → *ahɖiɖ*).

From the above it can be seen that mutation, whilst undoubtedly characteristic of the BT register, cannot be classed amongst its most frequent derivational processes (21 instances in a total of 86 BT words examined). Furthermore, several of the words in which it occurs commence with a vowel or terminate with a consonant, features which are atypical of the register as a whole and which suggest that they are probably not among the most central members of the system.

DELETION

This is by far the most important process, occurring in some three-quarters of all derivations (65 out of a total of 86), and is in fact the only one used in two major classes of BT word, kinship terms and hypocoristic forms of personal names. The only classes where deletion does not feature are those names of domestic animals which are derived from their command calls (Nos. 21 to 32) and the five verb stems used as imperatives (Nos. 64 to 68), to which must be added three cases in which the pattern is already CV (Nos. 1 and 2) or CVCV (No. 46) and three rather atypical examples of the 'childish mutation' type (Nos. 70, 85 and 86).

The deleted segments may be either initial, final or both initial and final (there are only two instances of internal deletion, Nos. 69 and 80, both resulting in cluster reduction) and it is convenient to refer to the product of this reducing process as the 'base' of the BT word. But although deletion itself appears as a rather heterogeneous process, its *results* are very much more uniform, the base most commonly having the form of a single open syllable of C(:)V or CCV pattern (44 examples) or, more rarely, of a sequence of two open syllables (9 examples).

While the general tendency is clearly towards an open syllabic pattern, there are 14 cases in which the result is a single closed syllable and four in which it is bisyllabic with final closed syllable. In the case of No. 13 the final *d* has probably been retained in order to avoid homonymic clash with No. 20; in the cases of Nos. 33 to 36 and No. 38, all names of domestic animals derived from the ideophones representing their cries, the term 'deletion' is not so strictly applicable since the cries could perhaps equally well have been cited in their unreduplicated forms; and in Nos. 53 and 54 retention of the final consonant is optional. There still remain, however, a small group of monosyllabic (Nos. 57, 58, 75, 80, 84) and bisyllabic (Nos. 52, 60, 79, 81) forms which terminate in a consonant so that reduction to an open syllable pattern is not the inevitable end product of deletion.

GEMINATION

Only eight examples figure in the gemination column, from which it might be assumed that this is a process of relatively low importance in the formation of BT words. Such a conclusion would, however, be incorrect for, as I have shown in my 1968 study, the ratio of geminated to non-geminated consonants in Berber BT words is more than double that found in the equivalent forms of normal inter-adult speech. The apparent discrepancy is due to the fact that in our presentation we have treated deletion as leaving geminated consonants intact in the base whenever they appear as geminates both in the inter-adult model and in the final BT form. Had we adopted the alternative solution of reducing the base to its absolute minimal phonemic skeleton and then reintroducing gemination at the present stage (an analysis which we rejected as unnecessarily complicated) the picture would have been very different (54 examples of gemination instead of 8). For the frequency of geminates is raised not only by the additional cases of gemination shown in the column but more importantly by the fact that many more non-geminated consonants are eliminated during the process of deletion than geminated ones; these latter are in fact almost invariably retained (the only exceptions are No. 34 and, optionally, No. 33), a fact which is at least in part due to the structure of the Berber word.[4]

In seven out of the eight cases of added gemination it is a step in the process leading to the canonical pattern CVC:V (the only exception to this is No. 47).

REDUPLICATION

Although not present in the BT forms of the kinship terms and of the personal names, reduplication is nonetheless of fundamental importance and one of the characteristic features of the register; the great majority of words in the remaining categories are in fact bisyllabic and reduplication is the commonest means of achieving this pattern.

There are essentially three types of reduplication: either the entire base may be repeated (total reduplication) or only a part of it and in this latter event the reduced segment may either precede the base (regressive partial reduplication) or follow it (progressive partial reduplication). We have seen that the base may consist of a closed or an open syllable and this has an important bearing on the selection of the rules governing its reduplication:

(*a*) when the base is a closed syllable the reduplication is always regressive and partial, the final consonant being deleted in the repeat segment (No. 53 *tta.ttay*, No. 54 *tta.ttaʒ*, No. 57 *ḍa.ḍaɣ*, No. 75 *ggu.ggud*, No. 84 *da.ddar* or *dda.ddar*);

(*b*) when the base is an open syllable of simple CV pattern reduplication is always total (No. 24 *zi.zi*, No. 41 *ɣu.ɣu*, No. 42 *ma.ma*, No. 43 *su.su*, No. 50 *bu.bu*, No. 56 *mi.mi*).

When the base is an open syllable with geminate initial consonant, C:V, then reduplication is always total if this geminate consists of a tense plosive for which there is no corresponding member in the phonemic system distinguished from it only by the feature [− tense] (No. 51 *ṭṭu.ṭṭu*, No. 82 *qqa.qqa*).[5]

In the remaining cases reduplication may be total (No. 21 *rra.rra*, No. 23 *šša.šša*, No. 49 *rri.rri*), optionally total or regressive partial by reduction of the geminate (No. 44 *nni.nni* or *ni.nni*, No. 45 *ddu.ddu* or *du.ddu*, Nos. 53 and 54 *tta.tta* or *ta.tta*, No. 59 *ddi.ddi* or *di.ddi*) or only regressive partial (No. 72 *xi.xxi*, No. 83 *fu.ffu*), the general tendency clearly being towards a pattern CVC:V.

When the base is an open syllable with an initial cluster there is a single example of total reduplication (No. 22 *šta.šta*) but in all other cases the cluster is reduced in the repeat segment by deletion of one or other of the consonants. If the reduced segment is suffixed (progressive partial reduplication) then it is the first consonant of the cluster which is deleted (No. 24 *ʦzi.zi*, No. 40 *ɣlu.lu*, No. 49 *ʦri.ri*, No. 50 *ʦbu.bu*, No. 51 *ʦṭṭu.ṭṭu*), if it is prefixed (regressive partial reduplication) there is one case in which it is the first consonant which is deleted (No. 76 *ba.ɛba*) and one in which it is the second (No. 48 *ṭṭa.ṭṭɛa*).

From the above it can be seen that the majority of partial redupli-cations are regressive (13, against 5 progressive).

Nine names of domestic animals may also be dealt with as cases of reduplication; in them the final BT form is achieved through the ad-dition to the base, which always consists of a single closed syllable of pattern CVC, C:VC, CVC: or C:CVC, of a vowel. In seven of these words the vowel that is added is the same as that of the base (No. 25 *ɽaw.a*, No. 26 *ttɛay.a*, No. 27 *ttɽay.a*, No. 33 *buɛ.u* or *bbuɛ.u*, No. 34 *baɛ.a*, No. 35 *mmuh.u*, No. 37 *ɛiww.i*) and one is tempted to see here a special case of partial reduplication; but in the two remaining examples the vowel is different and in these it looks as if it may have been treated rather as a suffix (No. 35 *mmuh.a*, perhaps by analogy with *ɽaw.a*, etc.; No. 38 *habb.u*, in which such human personal names as *ɛddu*, *ɽddu*, *hnnu*, *yɽɽu* could have played the role of model?). At any rate, whether one classes it as a case of reduplication or of suffixation, the process is limited to this one category of word and its result is to produce the canonical BT pattern of a sequence of two open syllables.

SUFFIXATION

There are two hypocoristic suffixes, *š* and *tt*, which may occur singly or in combination, in the latter event always in that order. Although where they do occur their presence is probably always optional (with the possible exception of No. 71), it is equally clear that they are not simply added at random; the rules governing their incidence cannot however be formulated on the basis of our present data.

While there can be no doubt regarding their hypocoristic function and their rightful place as true elements of the BT register (they are also found suffixed to a number of the suppletive forms), there are only eight examples of their use in our corpus and they clearly do not play a very productive part in the formation of the BT lexicon.

CONCLUSIONS

What inferences can be drawn from the above attempt to analyze the structural relationship between inter-adult speech forms and their BT counterparts? And in particular what support does it lend to the widely-held belief in traditional society that the function of BT is that of helping children to learn to speak?

At least a proportion of the *mutations* have the appearance of be-ing imitations of childrens' mispronunciations and might therefore be interpreted as the result of an effort to meet the child halfway by accommodating to its own natural speech habits. In other cases mutation appears as an assimilatory process resulting in a reordering of phonemes or in cluster reduction, both features that have been reported from children's speech.

Owing to its uni-directional nature *deletion* must be an innovatory and not a relational mechanism, for no rules will allow the recovery of the adult form from the BT form once it has taken place. The primary function of deletion is therefore clearly the creation of a limited set of simple minimally contrastive lexical bases consisting for the most part of open monosyllables (but which also includes a small number of closed monosyllables and bisyllabic forms). There is, however, sometimes a choice regarding the sequences to be deleted or retained which at the moment appears arbitrary and here again a comparison with the habits of children in their reductive treatment of adult forms might be revealing.

Gemination and *reduplication*, on the other hand, are processes of expansion which do not normally result in an increase of semantic distinctiveness, although this may on rare occasions be the case (cf. for instance, No. 12 *ddu* and No. 45 *dduddu*, No. 19 *ṭṭu* and No. 51 *ṭṭuṭṭu*, No. 20 *εi* and the suppletive *εεi* 'excrement'). In the vast majority of instances, however, the semantic content is limited to the base and gemination might be supposed to have as its function an increase of clarity, reduplication a reinforcement of the message. It would, however, be of interest to see to what extent these two features are also reflected in the children's natural speech habits.

While all the processes discussed so far could be described as simplifying processes, the third means by which the base is expanded, namely *suffixation*, does not appear either to reflect anything in the child's own speech habits, to bring added clarity, or to reinforce the message. Nor, in view of its optional nature, is it likely that it could have any oppositional value within the code. But to simply describe it as a marker of the register does not seem very meaningful either, since the register is already very well characterized by the previously described features. Perhaps the clue to its function may be found in the fact that, as a suffix attached to the hypocoristic forms of personal names, it is the only BT feature carried over on any scale into normal inter-adult speech; here it would appear to function as a bearer of attitudinal information, expressing the feelings of affection of the speaker towards the addressee, and it would seem reasonable to assume that it probably fulfils a similar function in BT.

If we turn finally to the *semantic* aspects of Berber nursery language here too we seem to find support for the claim that its function, or its intended function, is that of a teaching aid. We have seen that deletion operates inwards from the two ends of the word. One result of this is the loss of all exponents of grammatical category so that the BT word is marked neither for gender nor for number nor for the opposition definite/indefinite; grammatical meaning is, in fact, totally eliminated. Where lexical meaning is concerned, the restricted number of items involved and the distribution of these in discrete semantic fields (usually areas of special interest or natural attraction to the child) where a set of clearcut semantic units is matched to an equally simple set of formal ones, produces a miniaturized model of language particularly well suited to the requirements of teaching — for, after all, the acquisition of language is essentially learning to make semantic and formal oppositions and to associate particular forms with particular meanings.

If then, we are to accept that the intended function of BT is to help the child to learn to speak, we should clearly be asking ourselves whether or not it is effective in this aim — does it in fact work? Only properly conducted experiments accompanied by all the necessary controls could provide a useful answer, but it is perhaps worth remembering that a somewhat similar teaching system, also adapted to the child's requirements and intended as an intermediate stage to be eliminated after it has fulfilled its purpose, is being used today in our schools, presumably with at least some measure of success. I refer to the Initial Teaching Alphabet which is used to help children to acquire another language skill, namely the ability to read.

NOTES

1.   Naturally not all the hypocoristic forms of personal names here listed would be employed by any particular child but only those applicable within its own family.
2.   Fictitious forms set up as intermediate steps in the derivational process are starred in the text.
3.   The morpheme y- is realized phonemically as /i/ in absolute initial position before a consonant.
4.   Gemination is a common feature of the *stem* in Berber morphology and in the derivation of BT words deletion operates mainly on the peripheral morphemes in which gemination is much less frequent.
5.   The non-geminate counterparts of the voiceless plosives /ṭṭ/ and /qq/ in the dialect are the voiced plosive /ḍ/ and the voiced fricative /ɣ/, respectively.

APPENDIX

The source word in adult speech is given in the left-hand column, the nursery word in the far right-hand column, and the derivational processes are shown in the middle columns. Segments enclosed by round brackets are optional

Adult speech	Mutation	Deletion	Gemination	Reduplication	Hypocoristic suffix	Baby talk
Kinship						
1 *bba* 'father'	—	—	—	—	—	*bba*
2 *mma* 'mother'	—	—	—	—	—	*mma*
3 *nanna* 'grandmother'	—	*nna*	—	—	—	*nna*
4 *dadda* 'grandfather'	—	*dda*	—	—	—	*dda*
5 *ɛmmi* 'uncle'	—	*mmi*	—	—	—	*mmi*
6 *ɛtti* 'aunt'	—	*tti*	—	—	—	*tti*
Personal names						
7 *xlla*	—	*lla*	—	—	—	*lla*
8 *ʊsayn*	—	*sa*	—	—	—	*sa*
9 *zayd*	—	*za*	—	—	—	*za*
10 *ɛli*	—	*li*	—	—	—	*li*
11 *bassu*	—	*ba*	—	—	—	*ba*
12 *ʈddu*	—	*ddu*	—	—	—	*ddu*
13 *sɛid*	—	*ɛid*	—	—	—	*ɛid*
14 *muʕa*	—	*mu*	—	—	—	*mu*
15 *ʃqqiʕyya*	—	*qqi*	—	—	—	*qqi*
16 *hnnu*	—	*nnu*	—	—	—	*nnu*
17 *faqma*	—	*fa*	—	—	—	*fa*

Adult speech	Mutation	Deletion	Gemination	Reduplication	Hypocoristic suffix	Baby talk
18 rabʕa	—	ra	—	—	—	ra
19 ylṭu	—	l ṭ!u	—	—	—	l ṭ u
20 ʕɛisa	—	ɛ i	—	—	—	ɛ i
Domestic animals						
21 rra! 'advance!'	—	—	—	rra.rra	—	rrarra 'donkey'
22 šta! 'stop!'	—	—	—	šta.šta	—	štašta 'mule'
23 ṡṡa! 'stop!'	—	—	—	ṡṡa.ṡṡa	—	ṡṡaṡṡa 'mule'
24 hzi! 'come!' (kid)	—	(h)zi	—	(h)zi.zi	—	zizi, hzizi 'goat'
25 ʕaw! 'advance!'	—	—	—	ʕaw.a	—	ʕawa 'cow'
26 ttɛay! 'come!'	—	—	—	ttɛay.a	—	ttɛaya 'horse'
27 ttʕay! 'come!'	—	—	—	ttʕay.a	—	ttʕaya 'mule'
28 sibsi! 'come!'	—	—	—	—	—	sibsi 'cat'
29 kkullu! 'come!'	—	—	—	—	—	kkullu 'hen'
30 ppθya! 'come!'	—	—	—	—	—	ppθya 'cow'
31 ppθza! 'come!' (calf)	—	—	—	—	—	ppθza 'cow'
32 kkssi! 'come!'	—	—	—	—	—	kkssi 'dog'
33 bbuɛ bbuɛɛ '(cry of camel)'	—	(b)buɛ	—	(b)buɛ.u	—	buɛu, bbuɛu 'camel'

Adult speech	Mutation	Deletion	Gemination	Reduplication	Hypocoristic suffix	Baby talk
34 *baɛbaɛɛ* 'maa'	—	*baɛ*	—	*baɛ.a*	—	*baɛa* 'sheep'
35 *mmuhmmuh* 'moo'	—	*mmuh*	—	*mmuh.u, mmuh.a*	—	*mmuhu, mmuha* 'cow'
36 *ɛawwɛaww* 'miaow'	—	*ɛaww*	—	—	—	*ɛaww* (?) 'cat'
37 *smɛiww* 'to miaow'	—	*ɛiww*	—	*ɛiww.i*	—	*ɛiwwi* 'cat'
38 *habhab* 'bow-wow'	—	*hab*	*habb*	*habb.u*	—	*habbu* 'dog'
39 *afullus* 'hen'	—	*fullu*	—	—	—	*fullu*
40 *ayyul* 'donkey'	*aylul*	*ɣlu*	—	*ɣlu.lu*	—	*ɣlulu*
Foodstuffs						
41 *ayu* 'milk'	—	*ɣu*	—	*ɣu.ɣu*	—	*ɣuɣu*
42 *aman* 'water'	—	*ma*	—	*ma.ma*	—	*mama*
43 *sksu* 'couscous'	—	*su*	—	*su.su*	—	*susu*
44 *tiyyni* 'dates'	—	*ni*	*nni*	*(n)ni.nni*	—	*ninni, nninni*
45 *udi* 'butter'	*udu*	*du*	*ddu*	*(d)du.ddu*	—	*dudu, dduddu*
46 *sksu* 'couscous'	*sisu*	—	—	—	—	*sisu*
47 *tibɛusin* 'dates'	—	*bɛu*	*bbɛu*	—	—	*bbɛu*

Adult speech	Mutation	Deletion	Gemination	Reduplication	Hypocoristic suffix	Baby talk
48 ʈɭɛam 'couscous'	—	ʈɭɛa	—	ʈɭa.ʈɭɛa	—	ʈɭaʈɭɛa
49 atʃrir 'gruel'	—	(τ)ri	—	(τ)ri.ri	—	riri, τriri
50 atʃbub 'sugar lump'	—	(τ)bu	—	(τ)bu.bu	—	bubu, τbubu
51 atʃtluʃ 'sort of bread'	—	(τ)ttu	—	(τ)ttu.ttu	—	tʃutʃu, τttuttu
52 tabaɖaʃ 'omelette'	—	baɖaʃ	—	—	—	baɖaʃ
53 atay 'tea'	—	ta(y)	tta(y)	(t)ta.tta(y)	—	tatta, ttatta, ttattay
54 ataʒ 'tea'	—	ta(ʒ)	tta(ʒ)	tta.tta(ʒ)	—	tatta, ttattaʒ
55 ʈɭaʒin 'stew'	ʈɭavin	ʈɭavi	—	—	—	ʈɭavi
Bodily parts, activities, sensations, etc.						
56 imi 'mouth'	—	mi	—	(mi).mi	(tt)	mimi, mitt, mimitt
57 aɖaʃ 'foot'	—	ɖaʃ	—	ɖa.ɖaʃ	—	ɖaɖaʃ
58 afus 'hand'	—	fus	—	—	(tt)	fus, fustt
59 adəddi 'sore place'	—	ddi	—	(d)di.ddi	—	diddi, ddiddi
60 amzzuɣ 'ear'	—	mzzuɣ	—	—	—	mzzuɣ

Adult speech	Mutation	Deletion	Gemination	Reduplication	Hypocoristic suffix	Baby talk
61 *a-ddu-d* 'walk!' (lit.: come here)	—	*addu*	—	*(d)d.addu*	*(š)*	*ddaddu, dadău, dadduš, ddadduš*
62 *a-ddu-d* *s-ɣuɟ-i* 'come to me!'	*a-ddu-d* *s-ɣul-i*	*a-ddu* *ɣul-i*	—	—	—	*a-ddu* *ɣul-i*
63 *aʦbu* 'front of dress'	—	*ʦbu*	—	—	*(š(ʦʦ))*	*ʦbu, ʦbuš, ʦbušʦʦ* 'hide in my clothes'
64 *bədd* 'stand up!'	*bidd*	—	—	—	—	*bidd*
65 *ɣʷʒdm* 'sit down!'	*ɣʷʒdi*	—	—	—	*(ʦʦ)*	*ɣʷʒdi, ɣʷʒditt*
66 *babb* 'come on my back!'	*bibb*	—	—	—	—	*bibb*
67 *qqən* 'tie!'	*qqin*	—	—	—	—	*qqin*
68 *ffər* 'hide!'	*ffur*	—	—	—	—	*ffur*
69 *ɣsmar* 'it's all gone'	—	*yma*	—	—	—	*yma*
70 *yʦla* 'it's nice'	*yʦʦa*	—	—	—	—	*yʦʦa*
71 *yxxa* 'it's nasty'	*yxxxi*	*xx(i)*	—	—	*(štt)*	*xxištt, xx*
72 *ixxann* 'excrement'	*ixxinn*	*xxi*	—	*(xi).xxi*	—	*xxi, xixxi*

Adult speech	Mutation	Deletion	Gemination	Reduplication	Hypocoristic suffix	Baby talk
73 *abaxxu* 'creepy-crawly'	—	(b)xxu	—	—	(š)	xxu, bxxuš
74 *bxxu* 'bogey-man'	—	xxu	—	—	—	xxu
75 *uggadn* 'urine'	uggudn	ggud	—	ggu.ggud	—	gguggud
Clothing, familiar environmental objects, etc.						
76 *tiɛbanin* 'clothes'	—	ɛba	—	ba.ɛba	—	baɛba
77 *aʕndir* 'cloak (mother's)'	aʕnnir	(a)ʕnni	—	—	—	ʕnni, aʕnni
78 *agʷunun* 'hood'	ahunun	gʷunu / hunu	gʷunnu / hunnu	—	—	gʷunnu / hunnu
79 *idusan* 'shoes'	išusan	šusan	—	—	—	šusan
80 *amɛɽaɖ* 'stick'	—	(a)mɛaɖ	—	—	—	mɛaɖ, amɛaɖ
81 *tayñʒawt* 'spoon'	tayʒʒawt	(ta)yʒʒawt	—	—	—	yʒʒawt, tayʒʒawt
82 *aqqayn* 'beads'	—	qqa	—	qqa.qqa	—	qqaqqa
83 *asafu* (?) 'firebrand'	—	fu	ffu	fu.ffu	—	fuffu 'fire'
84 *taddart* 'house'	—	ddar	—	(d)da.ddar	—	daddar, ddaddar
85 *islli* 'stone'	itlli	—	—	—	—	itlli
86 *aʒḍiḍ* 'wild bird'	ahḍiḍ	—	—	—	—	ahḍiḍ

12 Participant deixis in English and baby talk

DOROTHY DAVIS WILLS

Department of Anthropology, University of Texas, Austin, Texas 78712, USA

Baby talk (BT) is a kind of speech possessing characteristics inspired by the peculiar interactional status of a child and the special relationship obtaining between parent and child. One such characteristic in English BT seems to be a system of terms of reference which, among other things, uses third person forms for Sender and Receiver, replaces a singular Sender and a singular Receiver with a plural Sender form, and deletes independent pronouns from the surface structure in declarative sentences. These usages result in a semantic system whose properties and effects are very different from those of conventional pronouns in discourse between adults. However, unconventional pronouns occur even in adult–adult interaction. How, then, is one to describe the English participant deictic system so as to account for expressions which deviate from the basic formal pronoun paradigm and its supposedly inviolate dimensions of person, number, case, gender and humanness?

The structure of the domain of participant indicators (most often pronouns) and other deictic and indexical expressions must be different from that of other semantic domains, by virtue of its sensitivity to extra-linguistic (socio-cultural and interactional) factors. Syntactic, semantic and interactional rules all govern the choice of terms of reference. Given the small number of pronouns, names and noun-phrases available to English-speakers for identification of participants, referents must be made clear by manipulation of covert dimensions rather than by selection of separate terms from a longer list. Parent–child interaction is an excellent theater for the study of this problem because the number of possible factors which permit unambiguous manipulation is smaller and the factors themselves are relatively stable, though the system as a whole appears to be complex.

The problem of people using special pronouns when talking to their small children and in some other situations is directly related to several issues in linguistics, sociolinguistics, and language acquisition, such as

(1) What other components besides ability to produce grammatical utterances must be included in the description of a speaker's communicative competence?

(2) What kinds of semantic and pragmatic information are attached to underlying forms, or alternatively at what point are they assigned in the derivation?

(3) What kinds of structural and functional differences are there between different kinds of semantic domains (e.g. deictic as opposed to non-deictic)?

(4) What is the nature of rules for use?

(5) What, if any, aspects of the structure and content of linguistic input to a young child are relevant to his acquisition of language and communicative behavior?

Adequate answers to such questions await extensive cross-cultural data. The numerous studies of pronominal systems from a componential point of view are not usage-oriented, for the most part (cf. Harris, 1948; Wonderly, 1952; Thomas, 1955; Austerlitz, 1959; McKaughan, 1959; Conant, 1961; Krupa & Altman, 1961; Conklin, 1962; Berlin, 1963; Buchler, 1966; Buchler & Freeze, 1966; Boxwell, 1967; Trager, 1967; Ingram, 1970 1971a; Fought, unpublished; Hymes, 1973; Suseendirarajah, 1973). Fought and Ingram have made a substantial contribution to the understanding of participant deictic systems, but do not discuss ways in which the system may be manipulated in actual discourse. Many studies of pronominals and terms of reference and address have been concerned with the semantic organization of performance but not with whole semantic or deictic systems (cf. Evans-Pritchard, 1948; Garvin & Riesenberg, 1952; Chao, 1956; Befu & Norbeck, 1958; Brown & Gilman, 1960; Jakobson, 1960b; Brown & Ford, 1961; Milner, 1961; Slobin, 1963; Fischer, 1964; Foster, 1964; Friedrich, 1964, 1966, 1972; Lawton, 1964; Goodenough, 1965; Frantz, 1966; Howell, 1967; Jacobsen, 1967; Lambert, 1967; Wijeyawardene, 1968; Pike & Lowe, 1969; Lind, 1971; Pike, 1973). Together, these studies do suggest that the boundaries of the system of participant indicators are not coterminous with the basic componential boundaries of the pronominal system. The bulk of conversational usages of pronominals can be understood with a certain degree of precision through their components, but speakers can achieve greater (or less) exactness by ignoring or combining certain elements; it is not the statistical frequency of unusual usages which is of interest or importance but their place within the system as a whole. BT pronouns are not mentioned in any of this literature.

The studies dealing more directly with language acquisition, and with parent—child interaction, have in general ignored BT or treated it as a peripheral phenomenon. Even the studies which have dealt specifically with BT and linguistic socialization, such as those reviewed by Ferguson (this volume) and Snow (this volume), have only occasionally contained references to the use of pronouns (e.g. parents' referring to themselves by kin term has been noted). No one has attempted to collect, describe, or explain all the various usages which occur.

The analysis of BT pronouns presented here cannot be conclusive until there is further information on the usages of participant indicators in other areas of discourse. Conversely, some abnormal pronouns in adult—adult speech cannot be explained without reference to the BT pronoun system. Thus, though the main interest of the paper is BT pronouns, examples of adult—adult usages will also be considered. The focus of the study is the process by which people can employ limited linguistic resources under certain circumstances to indicate not only roles in conversation but also alternative role possibilities, intentions of and relationships between participants in the service of maintaining certain overriding interactional frames and promoting activities, such as teaching, joking, arguing.

CONVENTIONAL PRONOUN USAGE

Most BT pronouns are conventional pronouns used grammatically but deviantly in regard to participant role, number, or gender. BT pronouns are related in a complex way to the basic componential analysis of English pronouns, as presented in Table 12.1 (cf. Hymes, 1973). These markings are adequate for the operation of agreement and other syntactic functions (except gender agreement). The presence of + and − notations for the same feature for two of these forms (*you* and *we*) indicates their indefinite nature with regard to the problem of inclusion—exclusion, of R in the case of *we*, and of 3P in both cases. The possibility of −R and +M co-occurring

Table 12.1 *Componential analysis of pronouns*

	Receiver	Sender	Minimal membership
I	−	+	+
			+
you	+	−	−
3P	−	−	+
	+		+
we	−	+	−
they	−	−	−

3P = *he, she* or *it*

(making *we* a singular pronoun) might be excluded, as Hymes suggests, by introducing a further category of membership range within plural pronouns (Hymes, 1973: 107). Otherwise we have to allow for a singular *we* which, though it does occur, is not conventionally recognized as being part of the meaning of the pronoun generally identified as first person plural. Inclusive and exclusive pronouns have not always been familiar to English-speaking linguists (Haas, 1969), but English-speakers do in fact indicate a variety of situations and relations, including inclusion and exclusion, using the five basic forms.

The conventions presented in Table 12.1 undoubtedly account for the great majority of instances of pronoun use in adult—adult speech. Nonetheless, deviations from these conventions occur in contexts of joking, sarcasm, mockery, cajolery, intimacy and extreme formality during adult—adult interaction. For example, though *I* normally refers to the Sender, it can also be used to refer to the Receiver in mocking him, e.g.

Speaker A has fixed something with celery in it, knowing Speaker B
    does not like celery:
A: 'But I don't like celery.'
B: You mean you think I should eat it anyway.

This is a case of role substitution, i.e. the Sender speaking for the Receiver. Similarly, *we* can be used to refer to a singular Sender, e.g. the familiar editorial and royal *we*, or to Receivers excluding the Sender, e.g. the *us* in

Let's quiet down so I can start the meeting.

Furthermore, pronouns are deleted or replaced by nouns or names in adult—adult speech, e.g.:

Wish you were here.
Does Charlie want more coffee? (to Charlie)
The President is not a criminal. (spoken by the president)

The fact that people use a small number of pronouns to refer to a large number of possible participants or a large number of pronouns to indicate one participant, and still manage to communicate effectively, may at first seem unremarkable. However, this is not merely a case of polysemy and of synonymity gone wild. *We* is not equivalent to *you* in meaning even if both have the same referent. *We* has a finite set of semantic elements which can function in a variety of ways in an infinite set of environments to produce diverse semantic and pragmatic effects (meanings). This is true of adult—adult interaction, but is even more noticeably the case in adult—child interaction. The non-standard pronoun usages noted above, plus several others, all occur frequently as a part of BT. A detailed analysis of some of the problematic usages of pronouns in BT should throw light on the rules by which choices within these person paradigms are made.

BABY TALK PRONOUNS

BT terms of reference are somewhat more accessible to analysis than non-standard adult—adult usages, because BT can more easily be identified in terms of context, message, key and participants than non-standard adult—adult registers. There is thus less ambiguity when BT is being produced than when an appropriate adult—adult context for non-standard pronoun usage is occurring. BT has been said to be simpler than other talk. Perhaps it is this linguistic simplicity, in combination with the simplicity of situation and interaction which typifies BT, which make possible a complex semantic system like BT terms of reference.

The BT pronoun system (or any pronoun system) is not precisely definable in terms of either form or function alone, since a collection of forms would exclude some items which are pragmatically clearly relevant (like epithets or reference to self in the third person using nouns), and a collection of functions would tend to obliterate the significance of having a 'basic' formal paradigm at all. One of the most significant differences between BT and adult talk is in the number of ways of expressing different participant categories. In adult talk, there are more ways to express the category Sender than any other. In BT, the Receiver category is far more elaborated than in adult talk, even more so than the Sender category, which is as multi-faceted in BT as in adult talk. This makes sense in terms of the propositions that BT is radically different from adult talk and that the child is the center of attention in the American family. For the ordinarily most intricately organized and sensitive category Sender to be surpassed in intricacy and sensitivity by the normally unelaborated category Receiver, is a remarkable departure which forces a pragmatic interpretation of the subordination of Sender to Receiver in adult—child interaction.

The principal and most obvious departure of BT pronominals from those we are accustomed to hearing used in speech between adults is in the apparent intermixture of pronouns denoting Sender and Receiver. Of the basic pronouns, only *they* is used consistently in its adult—adult sense. Some variations on the sense of these pronouns which occur in adult talk are very infrequent in speech addressed to children, for example, the impersonal *you*. This is not to say that people do not use 'normal' pronouns when talking to young children: they do so well over 90 % of the time. But the fact is that the variations produce a system which, as a whole, is strikingly different from adult talk.

BT pronouns differ from adult talk pronouns in both nature and frequency of occurrence. That is, there are BT pronouns which are both different in kind from other pronouns and which are understood as BT in whatever situations they appear (such as Receiver alone being expressed as *we*), and there are BT pronoun usages which occur in adult—adult speech as well but are much more frequent in BT (such as Sender or Receiver being expressed in the third person).

METHODOLOGY

The BT terms of reference presented here were found in speech addressed to five children, four girls and a boy, by their parents. Tape-recordings of parent—child interaction were made by the parents on a weekly basis in their homes during the course of normal activities. At the start of the project, the children's ages were 9, 11, 12, 14 and 15 months. Tapes for each child analyzed spanned 18, 9, 13, 11 and 20 weeks, respectively. None of the children had siblings. One was learning French as well as English (a few French examples will be provided). The families were of comparable ages, socio-economic levels and educational backgrounds. Breakdowns of the individual BT style of each family are to be found in the Appendix.

Unusual pronominal usages were isolated from the transcripts of the recordings and checked with the intuitions of other native English-speakers. They were written down within a minimal context of dialogue, and the following features were noted in addition to the actual form, its referent and the identity of the Sender (parent) and Receiver (child): other participants, the situation, the setting, the key (tone and apparent function of the utterance) and any other BT characteristics of the utterance. (The latter are described in terms of 26 phonological, paralinguistic and grammatical features which typify English BT, according to findings of the project.)

CATEGORIES OF BABY TALK REFERENCE TERMS

Eleven categories of BT terms of reference arose during preliminary analysis of the data. They will be presented along with examples by participant category (Sender, Receiver, or Other) according to the frequency of use within each (commonest first). Each pronoun category is identified by the person or role being indicated and the kind of pronoun expressing it. The roles or persons being indicated included: Sender (S), the speaker in all these BT cases; Receiver (R); anyone or anything other than the Sender or Receiver, including both participant non-speakers and non-receivers and non-speaking, non-receiving objects and people in the environment of the speech act (A = Alia). Other symbols used include: 3P for any third person pronoun; $\emptyset$ meaning no surface pronominal manifestation; $\rightarrow$ meaning 'is designated by'; M for mother; F for father; C for child.

The collection of the data may have been biased in some way by the necessary subjectivity involved in the process of selection, but it is hoped that this possible bias is counteracted by the sheer number of pronouns contained in the data, and by having occasionally checked with other people's information and intuitions. The examples given are as representative as possible. Remarks about adult—adult usages are added when appropriate.

1 S → 3P

   (*a*) M: Where are mommy's eyes?
   (*b*) M: Maman hasn't finished breakfast, bébé.
   (*c*) M: Oh, you gonna pound mama on the top of the head?
   (*d*) F: You gonna read daddy's book?

 The use of kin terms in place of *I* and its variants is by far the most common member of this category. Occasionally 3P pronouns occur, and the kin term may be realized either by 3P or by first person (1P) pronouns. The possibility of either kind of pronominalization supports the contention that the nature of this reference is out of the ordinary.

(e) M: Mommy's got holes in her shoes.
(f) M: Elle est là, maman. Elle est là, maman.
(g) M: (sneeze) Oh, she sneezed.
(h) M: You come to mean old mama, she'll put it on ya.
(i) F: This my shoes? See daddy's shoes?
(j) M: Cherches-moi; où est maman?
(k) F: Bring it to dad, I'll try to open it.
(l) F: Bring it to dad and we'll put it on for ya.

As is evident in the examples, these forms occur in all syntactic positions. They occur in both monologues and exchanges, and of course in role substitution. Furthermore, they are used to convey all kinds of messages: instruction, correction, command, and with a variety of tones: playful, affectionate, conversational, stern. They can appear in the absence of any other BT features. Third person self-reference in the framework of BT has the same characteristics as the more 'normal' usage of *I*, except that it is somewhat less frequent.

S → 3P appears in adult talk under special circumstances such as formal presentations or when the speaker wishes to disassociate himself either seriously or in jest as an individual ego from a given situation.

(m) Teacher: You're not supposed to make fun of the teacher.
(n) The author wishes to thank his wife.
(o) One feels odd at office parties.

These adult talk examples seem to be dissimilar in purpose, if not structure, from the BT examples, except insofar as the identity of the speaker as a particular person is obscured by its immersion in a larger category of persons (teachers, authors, people, mothers). One obvious reason for this operation in BT is the structural nature of the parent—child relationship. Referring to one-self by one's kin term stresses this relationship, and undoubtedly also helps to teach the child the proper kin term.

2 S → *WE (LET'S)*

(*a*) M: Let's get you some mittens, huh?

(*b*) F: Okay, we'll turn that up a little bit and see if that comes in better.

(*c*) F: Here, let's put a sock in the dump truck and then we can push it around.

(*d*) M: Okay, look, we're putting your barrette in your hair.

The BT pronoun *we* is the most ambiguous of all with regard to its exact referent. There are many cases in which the referent is clearly R (discussed below), but it is extremely difficult to tell the difference between its use as S and its use as S and R together. This is actually the source of its importance. Without a film of the proceedings, it is impossible to be positive of the identity of the actor (or actors) referred to by *we*, but for the cases 2(*a*)–(*d*) it does seem to be the parent alone who is doing the action for the child. The action taking place is thus not appropriately described with the 1P plural subject pronoun. This use makes the child a participant in events which are not of his creation and are generally out of his control. S → *we* not only erases the individuality of the speaker–actor as does S → 3P, but also it overrides the structural distinction as well. Parent and child are a unit, even though the real action is done only by the parent.

In addition to its usual sense of 1P plural inclusive and exclusive, *we* in adult talk can also mean 1P singular when used by royalty, in formal situations (especially writing), or by politicians wishing to convince their audience they are speaking for someone in addition to themselves (*we* seems to have the greatest imprecision of referent of all English pronouns, and therefore is the most frequently exploited for strategic ends). S → *we* also appears in informal, highly formulaic utterances.

(*e*) We'll see ya later.

(*f*) Let's see that one again.

(*g*) Here we go. (Followed by a report delivered in class by one person.)

The BT uses of *we* to express S are similar to these in their informal, conversational tone and lack of vital message. They occur in monologues and exchanges, most commonly in playing situations. Sometimes imperatives are stated or instructions given indirectly using this form.

(*h*) M: We'll put some music on, wait, wait, wait.

(j) F: Let's have it, let's have it.

The appearance of S → *we* is always accompanied by certain kinds of activity. It is much more restricted in applicability, and hence less frequent, than S → 3P.

3 S → ∅

(a) F: Shouldn't teach you those things.
(b) M: Gonna get you.
(c) F: Puttin a dress on you.

This category is most commonly observed in the context of 'gotcha' games (e.g., 'gonna getcha', 'gotcha belly'). This suggests that there may be a standard formula for the playing of this game which includes de-individualizing the parent (or 'getter'). There are no examples for two of the children, and the ones for the remaining three are not plentiful, but on the basis of what evidence exists a few tentative conclusions can be drawn. First of all, this usage is most often associated with play situations and with playful or conversational tones, and may be ritualized in some environments.

In adult talk, people can also drop their *I*'s in informal situations and semi-formulaic utterances.

(d) [*I*] doubt it.
(e) See ya later.
(f) Sure hate to see you go.

It may be that the S → ∅ category in BT is structurally and functionally no different from that in adult–adult talk. Probably the greater frequency of the appropriate situations and keys in parent–child interaction produces the increased frequency of the category. The de-emphasis of speaker (parent) resulting from this usage makes sense in terms of the activities and the nature of the interaction which it accompanies (ritual play, parental monologue, desultory play, daily activities like getting dressed). Pronoun-dropping also occurs in the BT categories of R and A (see below). The connection between subject-pronoun dropping in BT and that in adult talk, i.e. whether it is a BT usage applied derivatively in particular adult–adult interactions or whether it is merely one special mechanism available for certain kinds of interactions with either adults or babies, cannot be determined.

4 R → 3P

(a) M: Did Adam eat it? It's in Adam's tummy.
(b) M: Joelle, bien sur elle est là. Voilà, voilà Joelle.
(c) M: Oh, that's a mad baby.
(d) M: Oh, look at Jeanne-Marie with her slippers on.
(e) M: Where's Rebecca's baby?

It is not generally acceptable to talk about people in their presence without addressing them, except to make a joke or intentionally treat someone as inferior or unimportant. It is, however, acceptable to do this with small children (especially those whose speech is as immature as that of the five children under study). Even at this stage of development, though, most children seem to recognize and respond to their own names, so they probably do know when they are being talked about much of the time. This was a major problem in isolating instances when 3P pronouns and objective nouns and verbs are used to address—refer to the Receiver. Except in interactions between a parent and a child when it is certain that no one else is present, it is thus difficult to know who is the intended Receiver of a given objective remark about the child.

The solution to this problem lies in one very interesting aspect of adult—child interaction in which more than one adult is participating. This is that children are potential Receivers of almost any conversation, since they are not expected to be aware of the rules of turn-taking and roles of address—answer—observe which characterize adult interaction. This situation was illuminated by the occurrence of BT features in speech addressed by one parent to the other, in the child's presence, even in a context of adult talk. This does not necessarily mean that anything said in BT is *ipso facto* being said to a baby, or that anything said in a child's presence is directed to him, but in the case of parents talking about their child, the child may be a Receiver at the same time as a subject of discussion (3P). The language meant especially for him is strikingly different from talk on television or between his parents and their friends when he is not being talked about, to which he pays little attention. Verification for a constant confusion of referent and receiver status of the child is further established by comparing known cases of R → 3P (when there is no other possible Receiver than the child) with known cases of talking about the child in his presence using BT. They are alike. In fact, with regard to 3P reference to a child, it is impossible to tell who is addressed or who is present on purely linguistic evidence.

Third person can replace *you* in speech addressed to a child in all

syntactic positions, for all communicative purposes (except imperatives, strictly defined), and in all interactional settings. However,
R → 3P occurs more frequently in some contexts than others, the
most common form being as a possessive (as in 4(a) and 4(e)). It also
often appears as a kind of narrative device for remarking on ongoing
activity by the child. It is not used in any instances with a stern, corrective or admonitory tone. Playful, affectionate and conversational
tones predominate, with attention-getting and instructive tones falling somewhere in the middle of the frequency range. R → 3P appears
in both monologues and exchanges.

Epithets are quite similar to these 3P usages, sometimes impossible
to distinguish even on the grounds of their linguistic content. These
too are ordinarily positive in tone and message (or merely conversational).

(f) M: That's a good little girl.
(g) M: Oh, what a sweet baby.

Because of this likeness, epithets (as long as they don't contain *you*
as they would if spoken to an adult) are counted as a subdivision of
R → 3P, as BT, in short. Epithets of this kind (without *you*), as well
as, of course, ordinary epithets (which are also used in BT profusely),
occur in adult talk as insults, jokes and endearments when directly
spoken to the referent, and as insults, jokes and nasty remarks when
they are addressed to someone else in the referent's presence. R → 3P
and epithets together (not even counting those 3P references to the
child which are not addressed to him or said in BT) constitute a high
percentage of the references to himself the child is exposed to, and as
much as 30 % of all BT pronouns.

The exclusion and objectification accomplished by usage of 3P are
ordinarily a threat to people. Why then, are they allowed in BT? BT
itself makes children special and privileged beings, and BT pronouns
(for example, the category at issue here) do more to confuse the
roles and identities of parents and child than they do to distinguish
them. Exclusion by means of 3P reference is an empty threat here.
As far as objectification is concerned, this is not necessarily undesir-
able, since the independence on the part of the child which is emphasized by this usage is essential to his maturation. Also, R → 3P may
help the child to learn his name (since this is the most numerous
member of the category), or learn that he has a name.

5 R → ∅ (AND R → *YOU* IN IMPERATIVE)

This category was rather difficult to define. In normal speech, people drop clause-initial subject pronouns, so the BT quality of *you*-dropping as well as *I*-dropping may derive from a higher frequency as opposed to a different structure or function. However, on the basis of subjective reactions by several people, some of these usages are farther from the standard than others, i.e. they are closer to BT. Pronoun-dropping in yes—no questions, for example, is a generally acceptable practice for adult talk, but BT *you*-dropping occurs in ordinary declarative sentences and a certain kind of command.

(*a*) M: Sings in the shower.

Note that in this case it is not *you* but *he* which is dropped. This is one of the few examples of the operation of two BT 'rules' on a single form (*you* → *he* → ∅).

(*b*) F: Dumped it all out.
(*c*) F: Gettin long hippie hairs.
(*d*) M: Knows its nose.
(*e*) F: No, can't do it.
(*f*) F: Got that duck on ya now.

R → ∅ is frequently used as a kind of narrative accompaniment to the child's play, and spoken in playful, conversational or affectionate tones. It was also used when the child had accidentally hurt himself or spilled something. In these situations it seemed to have the effect of minimizing the potential seriousness of the occurrence for the child, since in the recorded instances the children in question did not respond with tears as might have been expected. One parent in fact dropped *you* in attempts to comfort the child after she had already started crying.

Example 5(*e*) is interesting in that it is like an ordinary imperative (in which the pronoun would typically be eliminated from the surface structure as an independent morpheme) but the usual manifestation would be 'You can't do it'. There are probably some selectional restrictions involving negative commands with the verb *can* and some others which are responsible for the appearance of *you* in the adult talk version. A comparable example is:

(*g*) F: Shouldn't talk with your mouth full.

Other imperatives appear in BT with *you* added (observed in the data of two children):

(*h*) F: You stay there a minute.
(*i*) F: You go get a sponge.

These imperatives are said in a friendly, playful way (though with instructional, correctional overtones), like the examples of *you*-dropping for declarative sentences. The situational evidence and the responses of the children in these cases suggest that introduction of the independent pronoun is an emphatic device which operates less frequently than pronoun-deletion. There were no other examples of $\emptyset \rightarrow you$ in this data. This is probably because in the standard model of English there are few cases, other than imperatives, in which it is customary to drop the pronoun, but also because, in dealing with the spoken model of English, the prediction of whether a speaker will use *you* or drop it (especially in questions) is extremely problematic.

(*j*) Wanna go outside?
(*k*) Ya wanna go outside?

In order to determine whether or not a given *you* spoken by a parent to a child was an emphatic usage, the observer would have to know whether he intended to drop it or not in the first place.

6 R → *WE (LET'S)*

(*a*) M: Let's be gentle with the pages, alright?
(*b*) F: We sure are tired, aren't we?
(*c*) F: Let's give up choo-choo in here.
(*d*) M: Put some socks on, our piggies are so cold.
(*e*) F: We don't want to put anymore mud on the floor.

These examples are the only clear cases for this category. As in S → *we*, however, there is a borderline area in which it is not clear who is being referred to, the child alone or the child and the speaker (without being able to see what is actually occurring).

(*f*) We see? We see. (said while reading a book)

There is also the problem that a prohibition placed on the child often applies to the parent as well, so he is in effect speaking for himself as well as to the child.

(*g*) M: No, we're not goin' outside.

After eliminating instances in which the *we* might be a conventional 1P plural, we are left with child-references intended to include the parent in spirit and a fairly orderly collection of 1P plural imperatives which are used to direct non-serious activity (non-serious being anything which does not single out the child for punishment). This combination of plural subject uttered in a conversational, playful or cajoling tone of voice makes the command form and the situation as a whole matter-of-fact. That is, the child, though he still gets ordered around much more often than any adult, is not always ordered in a customary ordering fashion.

At this point the role category facet of the analysis breaks down somewhat because there are so few examples for any category, especially for Sender, in the remaining BT pronouns. Thus the following examples of BT pronouns are presented in terms of the particular pronouns which are being manipulated and their BT manifestation, rather than the general participant category and its surface representations. The situation is further complicated by the fact that the following 'categories' are smaller in number than the foregoing and seem to have less internal consistency (with respect to uniformity of rule-application and variety and disparity of adult talk pronouns affected).

7 *IT* → $\emptyset$ (AND ARTICLE → $\emptyset$)

(*a*) M: Orange is all gone.
(*b*) M: Fell down. (a hat)
(*c*) F: Works better with the spoon out of your mouth.
(*d*) F: Wants to be fed.
(*e*) M: Dog's got your purse.
(*f*) F: Too big, won't fit.

The fact that nullification operates on both 3P pronouns and articles is good evidence for the theory that pronouns and modifiers, like articles and demonstratives, have the same representation in the underlying structure of sentences. Nullification in the 3P category is much less common than in either S or R categories, but it has the same characteristics of occasion and method of application (during play, language practice or mundane activities in a playful or conversational tone). Its value as a narrative device is underlined by its frequent use by the parent while looking at a book with the child. 3P → $\emptyset$ appears primarily in subject position in the sentence, as do S and R → $\emptyset$.

8 PERSONAL PRONOUN → IMPERSONAL (ARTICLE, QUANTIFIER, ETC.)

(*a*) M: Toes in the nose? Toes in the — oh!
(*b*) M: Où est le papa?
(*c*) Parent: What is that in the mirror, Miranda? (meaning the child)
(*d*) M: You wrinkle that nose, can't you?
(*e*) M: Now, one more arm in this sleeve. One more in that sleeve.

This category could be considered a subset of R → 3P which re-places possessive pronouns with *the, those, that, some*, etc. and *who* with *what* and inserts gratuitous articles, demonstratives and quanti-fiers, except for two clear examples and one questionable one in which the referent of the pronoun which is substituted for by a non-personal pronoun is not the child, but the speaker or a third person (as in 8(*b*)). There are other cases (for example, 8(*a*)) in which the referent could be either S or R. In these pronouns, as in BT *we* and to a lesser extent ∅, it is the action rather than the pronoun which identifies the referent.

The most typical representative of this category is the replacement of R possessive (*your*) with a non-possessive 3P pronoun or article, as in 8(*a*) and 8(*d*). This is definitely a playful form in the fullest sense of the word. Parents often use it in language practice sessions as a variant of the standard format or in situations like getting dressed. R possessive → non-possessive often occurs in a semi-formulaic context: 'Gimme that [or those] [*body part*]' during the process of getting dressed. The tones of voice associated with it are playful, lively con-versational, attention-getting and speech-eliciting. The messages con-veyed are not restricted only to play by any means, but can be in-formative and corrective observations which are delivered playfully. Depersonalization of this kind usually appears in adult talk in a jok-ing or love-making frame.

9 IMPERSONAL → PERSONAL

(*a*) M: Who is it. . .
   C: Hmaikú
   M: Microphone?
(*b*) F: He goes in there. (a block)
(*c*) M: Kitty, did you have a good dinner?
(*d*) F: Okay, plant, you just stay right there.
(*e*) M: No, it's a pig. That's close, though. Who is this? (an animal)

The interchangeability of *who* and *what*, *he* or *she* and *it*, and 3P and *you* (addressing things or beings not generally considered to be endowed with participant potential) produces the familiar BT (and poetic) phenomenon of personification. These forms are strictly reserved for non-serious situations (e.g. language practice, play, chatting) and are always said in a playful, animated manner. They occur primarily in exchanges.

10 ROLE SUBSTITUTION

(*a*) M: Hey, let's put Snoopy on the slide. . . 'I wanna go sliding'.
(*b*) M: All gone, mommy.
(*c*) F: Daddy, give me back my toys.
(*d*) F: Of course not, I'm too grumpy.
(*e*) M: He's hiding behind my daddy's chair.

Role substitution is invariably playfully done, though it often occurs in non-play situations, e.g. when the child is tired, unhappy, rebellious or scared, as well as during real play.

There are not very many examples of role substitution, and none for one of the children, but intuition and general observation indicate that it is a fairly common and widespread phenomenon which occurs not only in interaction with babies but also with animals and other personified beings and things. Personification seems to be related to role substitution in that in the former, the Sender (parent) personifies a thing by a pronoun and, in the latter, he personifies it himself using normal Sender pronouns. Role substitution is treated here primarily because it is an extension of personification (which clearly does involve unusual pronominal usages) in which ordinary pronoun usage but abnormal Sender category membership occurs. Role substitution may occur in BT because children fit into an ambiguous participant category, particularly if they do not talk very well. The majority of cases of role substitution observed occurred on behalf of the child. Role substitution pronouns may not present a problem, since they are Sender pronouns appropriate for use by the Sender. The parents who engaged in role substitution, however, seemed to try very hard to indicate that they were producing special utterances, i.e. by using several other BT features.

11 UNGRAMMATICAL CASE FORMS

Your → you

    (*a*) M: Wanna brush you hair?
    (*b*) F: Let's get you little pillow.
    (*c*) M: Oh, I hurt you mouth, huh?

Nominative → objective

    (*d*) F: Me [need?] a drink.
    (*e*) M: Yeah, her tired, dad. (the child)

These are a few examples of BT pronouns which seem to strike people as ungrammatical, as opposed to categories 1–10 which, though unlike adult talk usages, are not felt to be incorrect or unacceptable. Ungrammatical usages are extemely rare, as indicated in the Appendix. The existing cases are very playful in tone and applied to playful situations or those the parent may wish to make playful (as in 11(*c*)). It may be that this playfulness is simply extended to the grammar and that these are BT pronouns in a different sense from the others (they are not the result of rule-applications and do not derive from a systematic communicative class of behavior, i.e. the pronoun-participant system). Probably the selection of the ungrammatical form takes place at a level near awareness.

THE STRUCTURE OF BABY TALK PRONOUNS

The BT pronoun usages observed can be described (and ultimately explained) in relation to the basic English pronoun paradigm. The structure and rules for use of BT terms of reference are not independent of the structure and rules for use of adult talk pronouns, but are derived therefrom by manipulation of the possibilities inherent in English pronouns. Extra-linguistic factors may necessitate the use of non-standard pronouns. The most important of these extra-linguistic factors determining the BT pronoun system are, of course, the peculiar interactional status of a young child and the unique relationship between parent and child.

The structure of the pronominal system can be approached in terms of sets of contrasts at different levels of perception, as represented in Fig. 12.1.

In English adult–adult talk pronouns, the overt distinctions made

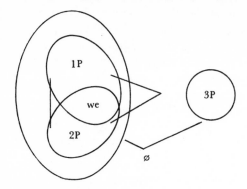

Fig. 12.1. Form and person contrasts.

are in participant categories (S = 1P, R = 2P, 3P = 3P), which are kept strictly separate for most purposes. Within participant categories, there are contrasts of number for two (1P and 3P) and gender for one (3P singular). The number contrast, for example, is exploited by the Sender (*I* → *we*) under certain circumstances and in certain ways to emphasize a departure from the norm (be it formal versus informal or impersonal versus personal), or to convince the Receiver that there is a departure taking place. The meaning of a pronoun is its relationship with other pronouns as categories. The concept of levels of contrast explains how different referents can be glossed identically, why there are parts of speech, and why *I* and *you* are in opposition from one perspective and not from another.

In BT, contrasts are exploited within the pronouns for each participant category, between participant categories and between surface realization of pronouns and their absence in the surface structure. These multiple contrasts implemented regularly provide a higher-level contrast between BT as a whole and adult talk as a whole.

Frequency of BT terms of reference indicates that the most important contrast is between S/R and 3P, the second between pronoun and no pronoun, and the third between *I/you* and *we*.

No notion of binary oppositions is being offered here, nor of any hierarchy based on such oppositions. Each member of the English pronoun paradigm potentially contrasts with all the others in different contexts and from different analytical vantage points. A contrast in itself is neither the definition, the motive nor the natural unit of the pronoun system but merely one of the processes through which usages assume structured meanings, i.e. meanings which are reliable and simple enough to be manipulated (or to serve in the manipulation of something else).

Broadly speaking, the outstanding functional contrast between adult talk and BT pronouns seems to be in specificity. Ordinary pronouns are used to increase precision in identification of both interactional roles ('persons') and individual identities of actors, *I* being the most precise of all and *you* the next most precise. BT pronouns seem to work the other way around, obscuring either the identity or the role of the person referred to, or both. This contrast is accomplished in the domain of pronouns through four operations, which make semantic sense of 10 of the 11 analytical categories of pronoun usage in BT.

FOUR DEICTIC CLASSES OF BABY TALK TERMS OF REFERENCE

The four operations which explain BT pronouns, objectification, humanization, disassociation and unification, are presented in Table 12.2.

Table 12.2   *Four pronominal proceesses*

Role	Usual pronoun	Objectification /humanization	Disassociation	Unification
S(1P)	*I*	3P	$\emptyset$	*we*
R(2P)	*you*	3P	$\emptyset$	*we*
3P	3P	1P, 2P, human 3P	$\emptyset$	

'Objectification' comprises S → 3P and R → 3P as well as personal → impersonal pronoun. The first two of these categories together constitute most of BT pronoun use. This is logical since most of the talk going on between two people (especially if one of them is a child) relies on the use of *I* and *you*, these being not only the most vital to immediate interactions but also (because of their immediacy) the most easily altered without ambiguity. Manipulating an anaphoric pronoun (3P) automatically implies greater abstraction. Thus there are relatively few examples of 'humanization' (3P → 1P, 2P) (not to be confused with its special case 'personification' in which *what* → *who*, *it* → *he, she*, and *it* → *you*). Humanization thus includes personification (3P non-human → 3P human, 3P → 2P) and role substitution (in which a class of non-speakers comprising 3P and the child → *I*). Role substitution presents some problems in that its pragmatic effect could be much more logically called objectification, the child having been grouped in the 3P category.

Objectification ignores the referent's role *vis-à-vis* the interaction, often by stressing his role *vis-à-vis* the relationship. It does not single the child out in quite the same way *you* does, since it places him in the much larger 3P category (including people referred to by their names). The use of the child's name may be the only practical purpose of this process, but eventually a child has to learn that he has three labels which go with different roles (*I*, *you*, and name or 3P pronoun). Perhaps by confusing these roles in our speech we help each other learn them! Role substitution seems to be a kind of objectification, in that it makes the child a third person (something that must be spoken for), but then it humanizes him again into an *I*.

'Disassociation' deletes nominative 1P, 2P and 3P pronouns from the surface structure of BT sentences. Both identity and role are de-emphasized as a result, though this de-emphasis is mitigated by the number of the verb in occasional (3P and copula) cases. Precision and separation are thereby decreased, but this does not impair understanding since the referent is invariably obvious.

S and R $\rightarrow$ *we* is a process of 'unification' in that it blurs the distinction between singular and plural (self and self as part of a group) and obscures any role separation of S and R (giving them the same surface realization). The situation, message and key which permit the emergence of pronominal and personal unification are the most restricted of the four. This is to be expected since *we* is not only used in unification but also in various 'strategies' in adult talk (most non-simple or non-literal uses of *we* outside BT confuse S and 3P, never S and R). Only under very particular circumstances is it desirable to mingle the identities and roles of Sender and Receiver.

Data for some usages are too sparse to be related to a particular BT operation. It has been suggested that ungrammaticality and emphasis are a single-point contrast in the linguistic system. Such cases as R $\rightarrow$ *you* in the imperative (as opposed to R $\rightarrow \emptyset$ in non-imperative, discussed under disassociation) can simply be described as emphatic because they represent the logical contrast to disassociation.

THE MEANING OF BABY TALK PRONOUNS

There are no data available concerning either the long-range effect of BT pronouns on the child's acquisition of language, or on the pronominal usages of young children. Studies of child language including the acquisition of pronominals do not refer to BT as a possible source of either correct or incorrect forms (cf. Cooley, 1908;

Grégoire, 1911; Smith, 1926; Markey, 1928; Davis, 1930; Bain, 1936; Goodenough, 1938; Leopold, 1939—49; Young, 1942*a, b*; Ames, 1952; Templin, 1957; Fraser, Bellugi & Brown, 1963; Menyuk, 1964; Brent & Katz, 1967; Gruber, 1967; Chomsky, 1969; Huxley, 1970; Webster, 1972; Webster & Ingram, 1972; Nelson, 1973).

A complete portrayal of the BT system embodied in the four central pronominal processes is highly relevant to the study of meaning, the common ground of semantics and pragmatics. An understanding of BT pronoun usages must be based both on the stated properties of individual pronouns or pronouns as a class and on the way these properties are incorporated into interactional roles (and rules for roles). Pronouns have an ascribed denotation which is embellished in a variety of ways but which does have a stable range of connotation established in relation to the roles they are associated with. This means that there are restrictions on the transformations of a proper pronoun into BT — there are ungrammatical utterances, even in BT. Furthermore, the meaning of a sentence changes if the pronoun is changed, even though the referent can remain the same.

Repetition, a commonly noted feature of BT discourse, serves to foreground certain linguistic structures and mechanisms for the child. Play is foregrounding in a wider sense. Play between parents and children is structured by the parents differently from the way other kinds of play are structured, so different aspects of reality are brought to the foreground. Furthermore, parent—child play often involves role-playing. Play and foregrounding seem to be the most logical motivation for the production of BT pronouns (among other things) and the only broad conceptual framework which accounts for their internal order from the linguistic to the interactional perquisites. The idea that BT pronouns are qualitatively different from adult talk pronouns is seen in this light as an illusion based on an epiphenomenon; BT pronouns are an image of adult talk pronouns reflected in the different poses and problems of parent—child interaction. The issue, then, of whether BT pronouns are a secondary system derived from adult talk is seen as irrelevant and misleading. Neither system is more fundamental than the other.

This perhaps oversimplified concept of BT pronoun use is given some credence by both the ease with which adults (and probably children over a certain age) talk BT and the diversity or frequency (and styles) in which they do it. Something about BT pronouns must be 'built in' to the pronoun system and people's heads, but not something specific or deterministic enough to prevent a great deal of variation in form of delivery and range of application. It is unnecessary to postulate an innate BT device as long as the principles which order BT pronouns have 'meaning' (i.e. are part of a semantic-pragmatic system, which may itself have some innate properties). Stated slightly differently, there is a basic 'semantic' beneath the usage of pronouns in discourse which, in combination with a number of social, interactional and contextual factors (like play and repetition), gives rise to the diversity of expressions to which it is put. That a linguistic form can be used to indicate praise at one time and disapproval at another does not imply that it can mean anything at all or that it has many unrelated meanings, but that there is some linguistic and/or non-linguistic commonality of all the usages. Studying the features which control non-standard use of pronouns in BT may cast some light on the meaning of both standard and of non-standard pronoun usages in other interaction situations.

This study was carried out as part of the Austin Project on Speech Input in Language Acquisition in Spanish and English Speech Communities, directed by Ben G. Blount, Office of Education Grant OEG-0-72-3945.

APPENDIX

Miranda (aged 9 months)

Eighteen weeks of tapes over a six-month period
99 total pages of transcription
approximately 20 pronouns/page = 1980+ pronouns

Both parents have instantly recognizable BT registers including many phonological and grammatical deviations from the norm, made-up words and noises. For this reason, it is surprising that they use as few BT terms of reference as they do. Epithets, R → 3P and Ø were problematical, so it is possible that not all actual examples were recorded. The parents talk about the child in front of her very frequently (in fact, both parents are present in most of the tapes, which is not true of any other family; it may be that less total speech recorded is actually for the benefit of the child, so that there are fewer BT pronouns).

BT terms of reference constitute at least 4 % of the total pronouns Miranda hears.

Jeanne-Marie (aged 11 months)

Nine weeks of tapes over a three-month period
155 total pages of transcription

approximately 20 pronouns/page = 3100+ pronouns

Both parents are extremely 'good' (and prolific) baby talkers. They use an enormous amount of epithets, from which only the unusual ones were selected for analysis. At the beginning of the taping, the child was very immature as an interactor, so that a lot of monologue was required on the part of the parents. The father was much better at this than the mother, and managed to maintain his BT during monologue consistently, which other parents seem not to be able to do. His tireless efforts at eliciting response from the child seem to be paying off.

BT terms of reference constitute over 10 % of the total pronouns Jeanne-Marie hears.

Joelle (aged 12 months)

Thirteen weeks of tapes over a four-month period
176 pages of transcription
approximately 15 pronouns/page = 2640+ pronouns

Joelle's parents in general do not talk very much BT. Both seem to monologue most of the time, since the child is not a skilled interactor and frequently says nothing despite all efforts to get her to interact. Almost every tape has a lengthy sound practice session.

BT terms of reference constitute between 3 and 4 % of the total pronouns Joelle hears.

Rebecca (aged 14 months)

Eleven weeks of tapes over a three-month period
41 total pages of transcription
approximately 15 pronouns/page = 615+ pronouns (These are mostly not personal pronouns, but *who, what, that*, etc.)

The major method of interaction used by Rebecca's parents with her is oriented around reading, looking at pictures, and language practice, and consists of a standard exchange format from which they do not deviate and which is usually unrelated to any situation requiring personal pronoun use or reference to participant categories. Even the 3P category, which is predominant in these tapes, presents little internal variation. Both parents have pronounced paralinguistic BT features, and a limited (almost pivot) BT grammar. The child is an excellent interactor (in the pattern established by her parents), has a large vocabulary (not larger than Adam's), and was using a pivot construction at age 12 months (which she had not expanded by the end of taping).

BT terms of reference constitute far less than 1% of the total pronouns Rebecca hears.

Adam (aged 15 months)

Twenty weeks of tapes over a six-month period
300 total pages of transcription
approximately 10 pronouns/page = 3000+ pronouns

Adam's parents use the fewest number of pronouns/page of transcription of any of the parents, though the ones they use are highly flexible and varied. Not all epithets or role substitutions were recorded, only the ones which were obviously BT. The same was true for Ø in all categories, since the mother (who did most of the recording sessions) uses a lot of elliptical sentences (a general characteristic of BT, anyway). Both parents do consistently use BT to Adam, but the general conduct of their conversations with him is much closer to adult talk than for any of the other families. He is treated more as a full participant: more 'normal' speech is addressed to him, comparatively speaking, and he is talked about less in his presence than the other children.

BT pronouns constitute about 6 % of the total terms of reference Adam hears.

Table A12.1   *Frequencies of the baby talk pronoun usages for five children*

	Miranda	Jeanne-Marie	Joelle	Rebecca	Adam
S → 3P	13	91	22	0	36
S → *we*	10	15	12	0	11
S → Ø	4	9	4	0	0
R → 3P	25	32	13	1	81
R → Ø	15	32	9	1	13
R → *we*	7	10	8	0	11
Ø → *you*	0	4	4	0	0
Article → Ø	1	0	2	0	3
Personal → impersonal	1	29	4	0	5
A → Ø	0	8	2	0	1
Impersonal → personal	1	3	0	3	1
Epithets	4	6	2	0	3
Role substitutions	1	21	3	1	4
I → *me*, ungrammatical	1	0	0	0	0
Your → *you*	0	2	2	0	2
She → *her*	0	1	0	0	0

S = Sender; R = Receiver; A = others; 3P = any third person pronoun; Ø = no surface pronominal manifestation.

13 Ethnography and caretaker-child interaction[1]

BEN G. BLOUNT

Department of Anthropology, University of Texas, Austin, Texas 78712, USA

BACKGROUND: SOCIALIZATION RESEARCH

Systematic research on socialization from a cross-cultural perspective has only a limited history as compared to studies of child development in the Western world. Only with the emergence of culture and personality studies in anthropology during the 1920s and 1930s was there a concerted effort to study child-rearing among non-Western societies. An early study in that tradition was Margaret Mead's famous *Coming of age in Samoa* (1928), followed in the next few decades by works such as Mead's account of the Manus of the Admiralty Islands (1930), Wayne Dennis' study, *The Hopi child* (1940), John Whiting's description of the Kwoma (1941), and Cora DuBois' work, *People of Alor* (1944). The most thorough investigations of socialization, cross-culturally, have been produced in the well-known studies of six cultures by John and Beatrice Whiting and associates (Whiting, 1963; Minturn & Lambert, 1964; Whiting *et al.*, 1966).

Cross-cultural studies in socialization, and the Whitings' work in particular, have produced valuable comparative information on child-rearing, particularly in terms of personality development as a function of differences in social organization and subsistence patterns. The research interests, however, did not include the topic of language either as a product of socialization or an as integral part of the socialization process. Yet language is fundamental to ego-development and personality formation, and it also affords a convenient source for the investigation and measurement of personality. Dell Hymes was the

297

first anthropologist to call attention to the importance of language in personality development and to note the general lack of studies on language socialization (Hymes, 1961). Stressing the fact that even basic social and cultural information about child language socialization was yet to be collected, Hymes proposed the ethnography of speaking as a useful perspective for research on child language and socialization.

Hymes pointed out that for children to become participating members of their society, they must learn not only the correct structure of their language but how to use the structure appropriately to communicate. Acquisition of communicative skills is essentially a social phenomenon, necessarily involving social interaction. An ethnography of speaking approach to child language emphasizes the study of interaction, as can be seen in the types of information that Hymes designated as preliminary to such an approach: (1) who the caretakers of children are during the early language acquisition years; (2) what the characteristics of caretaker—child interaction are with regard to questions such as frequency of interaction, contexts of usage, sanctions, appropriate topics and styles; and (3) the changes that occur as children advance in their acquisition of language and communicative competence (Hymes, 1962).

At present we are far from having adequate sources of cross-cultural data of the types Hymes proposed, but accounts of parental language usage, of caretaker—child interaction and of language socialization practices are beginning to appear. This paper will review recent studies, principally from the perspective of caretaker speech, its linguistic and interactional characteristics, and its relationships to language acquisition. Recommendations will be made for research procedures and topics that are especially relevant for and susceptible to ethnographic descriptions of caretaker—child interaction. Those topics are also viewed as fundamental to a model of language socialization and would be included in the construction of such a model.

INTERACTION AND LANGUAGE SOCIALIZATION

Several studies of language socialization were produced by the project on children's communicative competence at the University of California, Berkeley (cf. Slobin, 1967). Jan Brukman, summarizing the experiences of fieldworkers in Kenya, India and Samoa, noted that two earlier assumptions of the group proved to be naive (Brukman, 1973: 45—47). Firstly, the notion that a child's mother would be the major, almost exclusive, source of language input for a child simply was not the case for the societies under study; Luo, Koya and Samoan. Primary socialization of children in those societies was spread among a circle of individuals, kin and non-kin and older siblings or cousins were given much of the responsibility for care of the younger children. Secondly, the expectation that caretakers would be responsive to language mistakes by children was not met. Caretakers seemed to pay almost no attention to correctness of linguistic structure in the children's utterances. What they did pay attention to, and frequently gave explicit instructions for, was the social appropriateness of children's speech. Children's caretakers provide them with information, examples, guidance and practice relating to interaction. Acquisition of interactional skills is thus relatively more accessible as a research objective than the acquisition of linguistic structure, the latter being more abstract and less culturally sensitive.

Brukman notes that anthropological interests have tended, as one would expect, toward the cultural organization of interaction and interactive environments. Claudia Mitchell-Kernan and Keith Kernan, for instance, analyzed children's insults in two speech communities, Samoa and a Black urban community in the United States, showing how the insults reveal cultural values on the one hand and processes of enculturation on the other (Mitchell-Kernan & Kernan, 1975). Children learn that some behavior or facets of behavior are unacceptable and that disapproval of them may be registered in the form of insults. Children learn formulas for using insults, but they do not always have adequate control of the content and consequently overgeneralize the range of insults. The Kernans report the interesting and amusing case of a Samoan child using the formula 'you sleep with so-and-so' to produce the intended but ineffectual insult 'Your father sleeps with your mother' (Mitchell-Kernan & Kernan, 1975: 313). Overgeneralization and reaction to it constitute a process through which refinements are made and through which cultural values and interactional skills are acquired. It is a familiar phenomenon in child language where, for example, regular past tense markers may be extended to irregular verbs to produce items such as 'goed', 'wented' and 'sleeped'. Overgeneralization is also a common feature in language change in the form of hypercorrection, and in all of these instances, the appropriate forms must be learned through contextual support.

Brukman (1973) used a similar perspective to the Kernans to raise questions about joking behavior by Koya children of South India. He found that the children first learned the rules that constitute the interaction necessary for the game of joking behavior, and then they become socialized to the finer requirements of the game. They learn from experience to joke with other individuals in socially appropriate ways, i.e. according to content, rules and interactional form, and the bases are cultural in nature.

A distinction can be made between the linguistic phenomena that a child must learn, that is, the knowledge required to produce correct linguistic structures, and the constitutive phenomena of social interaction, but an important question to raise is the relatedness of the two types of knowledge. In what ways and to what extent is interaction necessary for the acquisition of linguistic knowledge and, given a particular level of linguistic competence by children, how do they employ that knowledge to enlarge their interactional skills? In depth studies of individual cases are of course needed before definitive answers can be given for those questions, but for research in language socialization, both linguistic and interactional perspectives need to be employed. In child language studies, there has been a tendency to attribute little or no importance to interaction as contributing to the acquisition of language. The reasons are straightforward. Children are not taught language structure in any direct, observable way and, as we have seen, their mistakes are usually not even corrected, at least not in terms of phonology or gammar. Thus it seems that interaction does not serve to instill linguistic knowledge in any direct sense, and the argument has been made that an interactional perspective is not central and perhaps not even necessary for the study of language acquisition. That viewpoint, however, is too narrow and restrictive. Although a theory of language acquisition certainly must include statements about children's strategies, hypotheses and techniques in acquiring their languages, contextual considerations must also be included, since strategies, hypotheses, etc. are formulated and applied in relation to meaning, not in an abstract philosophical sense, but in immediate, practical contexts of interaction.

The medium through which context is structured, through which children can assess the adequacy of their speech and remedy inadequacies by altering linguistically and/or interactionally their performances then, is interaction. A child obviously learns in other situations and contexts, but it is in interaction that he/she is presented with primary data and that immediate processing occurs. The primary data undoubtedly serve as corrective feedback, but their relationship to a child's acquisition of language is much more intimate. The discoveries of the important distinctions in language structure, however they are made in terms of strategies and hypotheses, must be related to the structure of the input the children receive, although, again, not necessarily (and in fact probably infrequently) in a direct, one-to-one way. At any given stage of development, the relationship between primary data and acquisition would be complex. However, to consider the primary data as the linguistic structure of adult language, unrelated to use, function, and especially without reduction and structural simplification, would make the relationship much more complicated than is necessary.

DIMENSIONS OF MODIFICATION IN CARETAKER SPEECH

When adults and older children speak to young children, especially to infants, they use styles of speech that are adapted for caretaker—child interaction. Even casual observation of caretakers speaking to children shows altered, adjusted speech, including such features as variations in rate of speech, short, simple sentences, modified intonation and occasionally special baby talk (BT) words. Systematic observations reveal more detail of caretaker—child speech. One approach has been to describe the modifications in linguistic terms, comparing BT features with standard adult terms and forms. Several studies in this tradition were produced early by anthropologists, for example, descriptions of BT structure among the Nootka (Sapir, 1929), Comanche (Casagrande, 1948) and Huasteco (Larson, 1949). In 1964 Charles Ferguson summarized the description of BT in six societies, noting such factors as the use of simple, basic consonants, a small selection of vowels, special affixes (usually the diminutive) and the absence of inflectional affixes (Ferguson, 1964: 109–110). Using a larger sample of languages, Ferguson (this volume) has demonstrated that processes of modification, such as simplification, reduction and redundancy, are common to various speech communities and that some linguistic features tend to occur regularly across societies.

BT is a speech register that contains conventionalized aspects of language, and linguistic descriptions of those are very useful. For language socialization, however, caretaker speech must be viewed in broader contexts to include instances of usage that do not contain BT features but that reflect modifications along other dimensions. For example, Phillips (1970) found in a study of speech by mothers to their children that utterances to 28-month-old children contained more morphemes on the average than utterances to 18-month-old children. In a pilot study of Black English, adult—adult speech, compared with adult–child speech, contained on the average more morphemes, showed greater lexical variability, contained more syntactic complexity and was spoken at a faster rate (Drach, 1969: 9). Comparing the derivational complexity of sentences addressed to young children, Carol Pfuderer showed that sentences became more complex syntactically as children advanced in their language acquisition. Additional semantic information is included in parental speech as children progress, semantic information as carried by category symbols (e.g. PP, Adj) (Pfuderer, 1969: 18).

In a study of speech to two-and-a-half-year-old Luo and Somoan children, types of wh- questions were related to the mean length of utterance (MLU) of the children. The more advanced the children, the greater the use of semantically more complex wh- forms, such that advanced children were asked 'why' questions, requiring some notion of causality, whereas 'what' questions, involving simple naming, were more characteristic of speech to less advanced children (Blount, 1972a). To take still another example, Dorothy Wills (this volume) has shown that parental speech to young children makes use of personal pronouns in markedly different ways from the use of these pronouns in adult–adult speech. American English-speaking parents use, however, not merely a reduced, simplified version of the English pronominal set in talking to children. Rather, they use pronouns interactionally to reduce rather than to increase their deictic specificity and thereby reduce the amount of information necessary for efficient encoding, decoding and interaction. For example, 'we' rather than 'I' is often used as a means of neutralizing role separation of adult–child in an activity.

Older children also modify their speech when talking to younger children. In a preliminary study with English-speaking American children, Jean Berko Gleason (1973) noted that four-year-olds did not use BT features in talking to two-year-olds, but eight-year-olds used a BT style in addressing four-year-olds, and their speech was characterized by short, repetitive sentences, sing-song style and special intonation. Marilyn Shatz and Rochel Gelman found that four-year-olds were able to adjust their speech when talking to two-year-olds, using shorter, simpler utterances and greater frequency of attentional utterances, such as 'hey!', 'see!' (Shatz & Gelman, 1973). These studies raise a number of interesting questions. When do children learn to modify their speech for young children? Are there developmental phases for the acquisition of BT, such that features appear in some orderly progression? Are there cross-cultural differences? This last question seems especially relevant because older children are the primary socializers of younger children in many non-Western societies. If there are different rates of BT acquisition, e.g. if the modified speech of six-year-olds is different from that of adults, what are the consequences for interaction and acquisition of language by younger children?

At present not enough information is available to draw specific conclusions concerning effects of differential modification of input on language acquisition. Nor are their effects on interaction well documented. A probable function of modificational features is to mark speech styles associated with social categories of individual — peer group, infants, young children, adults. Gleason notes, for example, that four-year-olds use different speech styles for interaction with their mothers, peers and non-familial adults, and that eight-year-olds have the same styles but with politeness routines for interaction with adults and BT styles for younger children (Gleason, 1973: 167).

SPEECH STYLES AND SOCIAL POSITIONS

The association of appropriately marked speech styles with social categories of individuals can be seen in the behavior of Luo children. Although a Luo infant's mother is his primary caretaker for the first few months of life, older siblings quickly assume responsibility, and by the time a child is 10—12 months of age, his mother has yielded much of her responsibility to a nursemaid, a young girl or boy 5—12 years of age. At 18—20 months, a child spends most of his time in the company and care of other children, and a consequence is a sharp separation of children's activities from those of adults. The segregation is particularly strong between children and adult males and becomes acute when visitors are present in a Luo home. When Luo children are approximately three years old, the social exclusion becomes marked and reinforced with language behavior. The children learn to use deferential, respectful speech, signalled by lowered volume and brief, clear remarks. Acquisition of that style coincides with changes in the social status of the children, brought about not by the reduction of social distance but by providing contexts in which the formality could be underscored. For example, a young Luo boy, when he becomes approximately three years old, will no longer be allowed to eat his meals with his mother and younger children but will be required to eat with his older brothers and his father. In that context, deferential speech is required and reinforced.

Young Luo boys are very aware of the importance of using the deferential style, having been cautioned by older children and their parents about the necessity of showing respect. Furthermore, the practice of using deferential speech to elders is not a brief, passing phase of Luo socialization. The evening meal is the setting in which the authority of elder over younger is constantly acted out and given symbolic sanction. A fully adult young man must show his father and father's brothers exactly the same verbally marked respect as a young boy of three or four years of age is expected to use, and a father uses the context to apply sanctions, no matter what ages his sons are. Young men of 20–25 years of age often complain of the impossibility of defending themselves verbally against their father's admonitions, accusations, criticisms and so forth.

Social allocations of roles and social positions to children in various stages of development represent another dimension along which caretaker speech may vary. Depending on social positions allocated to children, speech addressed to them may take particular forms, and variation among societies is likely to be the rule. For instance, Japan and the United States are both 'child-centered' in the sense that considerable overt attention is devoted not just to child-rearing but to considerations of child-rearing. However, Fischer (1970), in a comparison of linguistic socialization in the two societies, noted a fundamental difference in attitude toward the social position of children. In contrast with Americans, the Japanese place more emphasis on the adult–child distinction within the family. More precisely, the social position of a child as *child* is more strictly maintained, and there is an indulgence of dependency rather than the push for precocity common among American families. The types of communicative behavior observed were consistent with the Japanese family pattern. In comparison with their American counterparts, Japanese mothers tend to use more non-verbal communication, to be more favorably disposed toward use of BT, and to be more tolerant in assigning meaning to deviant utterances of the children.

A comparison of Luo and Samoan with Black English in the United States revealed differences similar to Fischer's findings regarding social positions allocated to children. Luo and Samoan children received almost no input from their parents that could be interpreted to indicate that the children were regarded as conversational partners. They were addressed with large percentages of commands and questions, but almost none of the questions were yes–no, i.e. designed to elicit preferential responses from the children. However, in Black English there were many more yes–no questions, and children were consulted more in terms of what they wanted, and generally treated so as to indicate that they were, for practical purposes, interactional equals (Blount, 1972*a*).

Cultural definitions of social positions that children occupy are a major component in the language socialization process. They serve to regulate what is expected of children and what the forms and functions of interaction should be. They help to establish conditions that promote acquisition by adjusting or altering the communication pressures that are applied to children. In discussing the reasons why children advance in their language acquisition, Roger Brown suggests that the tendency to study Western children in their homes, where accommodation to communication is maximized, has impeded our understanding of sources of change. He identifies the extension of a child's activities beyond the home as a likely source for pressures bringing about change (Brown, 1973: 245). Pressures for a child to communicate clearly and in new ways undoubtedly accrue from expansion of his/her activities into contexts where old patterns of behavior are not always reliable, but similar pressures can come from within the family itself. Re-definitions of children's status and re-evaluation of their communicative potential can lead to different expectations and altered interactional and verbal patterns. Children four years of age in American society are less likely to be regarded as infants than children who are two years old, and they are neither allowed the same behavioral privileges nor treated by their parents in the same ways as two-year-olds.

ASSESSMENT CATEGORIES

The fact that adults and children alter their speech to young children, and that their adjustments vary according to the children's development, indicates that assessments are made of children's interactional capacities. Caretaker assessment probably proceeds in part on readings of children's linguistic capacity — the wh- questions serve as an example — but the information on this point is sketchy. It would be very useful to have precise measurements of caretaker speech as a mirror of varying linguistic competence by children. Assessment, though, surely involves more than linguistic components. It would in fact be surprising if caretakers relied primarily on linguistic features in their assessments of children's speech, since they exhibit no strong interest in linguistic technicalities.

Although caretakers probably attend to the structure of children's utterances in relatively gross linguistic ways, what they primarily attend to is the ability of children to communicate. Parents are aware that children can understand more than they can say — folk-models include the principle 'comprehension precedes production' — and what parents do is construct contexts and interaction that allow children to communicate in accordance with what they can understand and what they can say. In other words, assessment of a child's communicative ability on the basis of linguistic productions alone would contradict what parents already know — communicative capacity surpasses the capacity to produce particular linguistic structures.[2] Linguistic skills are assessed as only one facet, and probably a minor one, of a broader communicative competence.

In a perceptive article, Gordon Wells (1974) identified attributions of children's utterances that are related to inter-personal functions. These attributions — evaluation and possession — reflect a joint activity of the children and their parents in which the latter give linguistic expression to meanings that the children are capable of attending. Numerous semantic and interactional dimensions other than evaluation and possession can serve for assessment of children's developing competence. Such dimensions reflect underlying cultural categories, referred to here as assessment categories. Caretakers, as cultural agents, assess overall communicative competence in relation to culturally defined categories which are based on stages of overall development. Categories are less specific than social positions in that they do not have associated roles, and they are based on developmental factors rather than achieved or ascribed roles. Also, categories are societally specific. Thus the number, organization and behavioral expectations will vary from society to society, and a central task of ethnographic research on language socialization is the identification of the assessment categories.

One source of evidence for the categories is terminology. Societies often have different terms for the various categories that are employed in socialization. In American society, terms commonly used are infant, baby, toddler, child, preschooler, and in Black culture, lap baby (a child who still has the privilege of sitting in his/her mother's lap). The relevance of these categories can be seen clearly in their use as social control devices, as for example, when a child is admonished for behaving like an infant or a baby. Each of these categories has associated expectations for parental behavior and language. To take just one example, in a study of caretaker speech in Austin, Texas, two parents used greater ranges in pitch and volume, more frequent falsetto and more nonsense items in their speech to their 3-month-old infant than to their 16-month-old toddler (Blount, n.d.).

Another source for the discovery of assessment categories is the cultural recognition of and response to developmental milestones. It has long been noted that at the age of approximately nine months, children exhibit an increased ability to fixate aurally and visually on their environment. This feature has been detected in markedly different societies, including the !Kung Bushmen, where the increased attention-span was concomitant with a fear response to strangers (Konner, 1972), and among the Luo, where a clear application of an assessment category was noted (Blount, 1971).

The regular appearance of 'first words' at 12—14 months represents another juncture at which category differentiation may apply. Again, the Luo serve as a clear example. At that point of development, the number and frequency of BT features in parental speech decrease considerably. The distribution of the use of BT is altered; it becomes reserved as a code appropriate for expressing affection and is employed when a child is unhappy or a parent is attempting to influence or placate him (Blount, 1972a). Another biological milestone, for which almost no behavioral data are available but which should be promising for ethnographic research, is the slimming process which children undergo at approximately five years of age. Children at that age begin to lose fatty tissue, especially the buccal pads, which alters their physical appearance considerably. Konner (1972) noted that among Bushmen children the change is accompanied by major shifts in status and responsibility, and a similar phenomenon is found among the Luo. A Luo child at approximately five years is expected to assume far more responsibility in the upkeep of the homestead than the younger children, and in fact the younger children become charges to the older ones. The use of BT to younger children then becomes a regular occurrence in the speech of older children.

Some discontinuities in children's early socialization result from application of assessment categories that are defined less on developmental milestones than on specifically social factors. In Bushman and Luo societies, children at approximately 18 months of age become members of a peer group, numbering from three or four to as many as thirteen or fourteen children. Prior to that age, a child spends the majority of his time with his mother or nursemaid. After entering the peer group, however, most of his time is spent in the company of other children, including sharing sleeping quarters with them. This new routine alters the communication demands placed on children. They are subjected to verbal input that contains fewer BT features and that demands more reciprocity than previous speech with their parents or nursemaids. Within a few months, a peer-group style of speech becomes part of the repertoire of a child, contrasting with the earlier instructional, interactional style and in time with the new, more formal style for use with adults, as already described.

SUMMARY

Although our knowledge of the organization and use of caretaker—child speech has advanced considerably in the past few years, much remains to be done. There are few longitudinal studies of sufficient linguistic and interactional detail to allow comparison across speech communities, and relatively little is known about cultural differences in the organization, incidence and frequency of caretaker—child speech. Ethnographic studies of caretaker—child speech are required to provide much-needed information on those points. Information on factors responsible for the special qualities of caretaker speech would be especially valuable in evaluating the effects of that speech on the communicative competence of children.

Caretaker involvement in interaction reflects the cultural bases of communication since interaction is the process through which the underlying organization is manifested in behavior and thus made available for study. The expectations, norms and consequences regulating interaction can be documented, and these in turn can be seen to operate in terms of social positions and assessment categories. The discontinuities inherent in category assessment are responsible for new communication pressures on children. New social demands must be met and new requirements for speech acceptable for meeting those demands must be learned. New interactional skills are fostered, and language acquisition is facilitated. All of those factors are necessary for a model of language socialization.

NOTES

1.   An ealier version of this paper was presented at the Conference on Language Input and Acquisition, Boston, 1974. The paper has benefited from comments by Willett Kempton, Dorothy Wills and especially Elise Padgug.
2.   I am indebted to Elise Padgug for this observation.

14 Aspects of social environment and first language acquisition in rural Africa[1]

SARA HARKNESS

Department of Psychology, Harvard University, 33 Kirkland Street, Cambridge, Massachusetts 02138, USA

The question of teaching in relation to learning in the process of child language acquisition has been with us ever since Brown and his associates raised the issue of 'training variables' (Brown, 1970). Subsequent studies have established several recurring features in the way American mothers modify their speech to very young children (Broen, 1972; Baldwin & Baldwin, 1973; Nelson, 1973; Remick, 1976). The question raised by Brown's research, of whether such modification promotes child language development, still remains largely unanswered, however. Other related questions have just begun to be explored: are the characteristics of American mothers' speech to young children typical of other cultural groups (Harkness, 1975; Slobin, 1969)? what is the role of siblings and others in the socialization of child language (Gleason, 1973; Shatz & Gelman, 1973)?

Over the past three years, I have been studying the roles of both mothers and children in first language socialization of rural African children. The study has been carried out in Kokwet, a Kipsigis community in the western highlands of Kenya. The community of Kokwet consists of 54 homesteads of about 7 ha each, arranged along a ridge of land about 5 km long. The land is divided into grazing pasture for cows and goats, and agricultural plots where maize, millet, pyrethum and small amounts of green vegetables are grown. Each household has several small mud houses which are clustered together at a central or commanding position on the homestead, overlooking the fields during the earlier part of the year, hidden by the tall maize as harvest time approaches. Kokwet is a new community, one of many formed by the Kenya Government at Independence in 1963 to re-settle citizens on land formerly occupied by European farmers. This gives it several unusual features in relation to other Kipsigis communities: relative uniformity of land holdings, a predominantly young to middle-aged population and relative modernity in agricultural practices as required by the Kenyan Ministry of Lands and Settlements. At the same time, Kokwet is far from Westernized in many respects. Many adults in the community have had no education, and none has had more than primary school. Until the advent of free primary education in 1974, only half the children in Kokwet began attending school by age ten. Adolescents of both sexes still almost unanimously opt to undergo the circumcision rites which mark the passage to adulthood. Despite half a century of Christian missionary activity in the area, most families have made at most a minimal conversion.

The subjects for my study were 20 children between ages two and three and a half, virtually the whole population of that age group in Kokwet. Each child was tape-recorded for about two hours at home using a small transmitter which the child wore under his shirt. Ten brief 'spot observations' were carried out on each subject, to form a composite picture of how and with whom the children spent their days. Each child was also observed intensively for three 20-minute periods, during which the observer used a checklist of individual and social behaviors which was filled out every 30 seconds. The mothers of all the subjects were interviewed about their beliefs and practices related to language learning. Census information and a modernization survey completed the data.

For the present sketch of social environment, language teaching and language learning in Kokwet, I will start with an overview of different factors which appear to be interrelated. These factors can be seen as a chain of antecedent and consequent variables, leading from demographic measures to a measure of child language development.

The Kokwet children spent virtually all their time on their own homesteads. A little more than half their time, on the average, was spent in the immediate vicinity of their houses, while the remainder was divided between the grazing fields, where they helped older children keep an eye on the cows and goats, or in the family gardens where they watched people ploughing, planting, weeding, or harvesting. The children were almost always with other people — an average of three others over all the spot observations. Other small children (generally siblings) were the most frequent companions, being present about three-quarters of the time. The subjects' mothers were present about half the time, as were older children; other women (second wives, grown-up sisters, grandmothers or neighbors) and fathers were present in about one-quarter of the observations.

Although the subjects were in the presence of both adults and children for extensive periods of the day, proportions of actual interaction varied markedly, as data from the intensive observations indicate. The intensive observations were carried out at times of day when both adults and children were likely to be present. Nevertheless, the proportions of interaction time with adults during these observations vary from 0% to 100%.

One important determinant of the amount of attention a young child in Kokwet receives from adults appears to be birth order. As the Whitings (1975) have noted, the youngest child of the family in communities similar to Kokwet is apt to be the focus of family recreation: he is played with, talked to, cuddled, carried and requested to perform for others. Eight of the twenty subjects were either only children or last-borns. These children were more likely to be observed relating to adults than were children who had a younger sibling ($r = 0.56, p < 0.05$).

Obviously, young children interact differently with other children from the way they do with adults. The present data suggest that talking is a greater component of interaction between young children and adults than among young children alone. Of the time the subjects spent relating to adults, a higher proportion was spent talking than was the case when they were relating to other children (t-test, $p < 0.05$). Consequently, there was a significant positive relationship between the amount of time spent relating to adults in the intensive observations and the total amount of time the subject talked ($r = 0.47, p < 0.05$).

Does practice make perfect? In this case it evidently helped. A measure of Mean Length of Utterance (MLU), controlled for age through regression analysis, was obtained for each child and correlated with the amount of time he spent talking during the intensive observations. There was a strong positive relationship between the two measures ($r = 0.70, p < 0.01$). In other words, children who spent more time talking were linguistically more advanced in relation to their age than their less talkative companions.

According to this analysis, adults in Kokwet are more effective language socializers than children are, in that adults seem to encourage more practise which is in turn associated with faster progress. But what of the quality of adult speech to very young children as compared with the speech they hear from other children? An analysis of speech by mothers and children (aged four to eight years) to some of the Kokwet subjects[2] allows us to assess similarities and differences between these two classes of speakers, and also makes possible a comparison with American studies of speech modification to young children.

Table 14.1   *Comparison of frequencies of variables in mothers' and children's speech to subjects* $(N = 8)$

Speech variables	Mothers' means	Children's means	t	p value of difference
Mean length of utterance	2.84	2.27	5.19	0.01
Complexity	113	94	2.92	0.03
Repetitions	17%	23%	− 1.61	n.s.
Expansions and echoes	3%	1%	1.56	n.s.
Language practice	10%	8%	0.51	n.s.
Continuous dialogue	68%	47%	2.10	0.10
Questions	29%	21%	2.57	0.05
Imperatives	44%	37%	0.89	n.s.
Statements	20%	38%	− 3.25	0.02

In Table 14.1, the speech of mothers and children to the subjects is compared.

MLU, here measured in words, has become a standard measure of child language development as well as of speech modification to young children (Brown, 1970; Snow, 1972). Complexity of speech has been measured through a variety of indices (Baldwin & Baldwin, 1973; Phillips, 1973). For the present study, a complexity score was derived from the number of verbs in each utterance. Proportions of utterances containing no verb, one verb, two verbs and three or more verbs were calculated, weighted accordingly, and summed to produce a total complexity score. Repetition of utterances in close sequence has been a frequently noted feature of mothers' speech to young children in America (Kobashigawa, 1969; Broen, 1972; Snow, 1972). Repetitions as defined here include repetitions of phrases or whole utterances, but not paraphrasing. Probably the most well-known feature of mothers' speech to young children is the expansion, first described by Brown and his associates (Brown, 1970). The mothers in their longitudinal study produced expanded and corrected versions of their children's short utterances in response to as much as 30% of the children's speech. Occurrence of expansions was tabulated for the Kokwet mothers and children, together with a similar phenomenon: the 'echo', a repetition or slight variation of the child's utterance, but without the extension of length which defines the expansion. Because of their extremely low frequency, expansions and echoes were analyzed as a single category. Language practice is a general category including all utterances whose primary intent was judged to be the elicitation of speech: for example, asking questions to which the speaker knew the answer, or commanding the child to say something. Continuous dialogue is a measure of continuity in conversation. An utterance was considered to be part of a continuous dialogue if it occurred in a sequence of at least three utterances, uninterrupted by long pauses or by a third speaker, in which the topic did not change. The occurrence of different sentence types in speech to young children has been analyzed in relation to social and didactic functions (Blount, 1972*b*; Remick, 1976). Proportions of questions, imperatives and statements in mothers' and children's speech to the Kokwet subjects were calculated.

As can be seen in Table 14.1, the Kokwet mothers and children did not differ significantly from each other in use of repetitions, expansions and echoes, and language practice speech. In the speech of both mothers and children, proportions of expansions and echoes were highly correlated with amounts of language practice ($r = 0.72, p < 0.01$ for mothers; $r = 0.66, p < 0.05$ for children). It appears that the use of expansions and echoes is one of several features of a style which seemed to be consciously aimed at eliciting speech. Other features of this style which, however, were not used exclusively in this context, were questions ('What's that?' 'Where's Daddy?') and repetitions. Utterances were apt to follow closely upon one another, and consequently topic and vocabulary were maintained over several utterances. When all these features were present, the speech elicitation style resembled a language drill.

Mothers' and children's speech differed in MLU and complexity, with the mothers providing a significantly more complex language environment, characterized by longer utterances, than did the children. Differences between mothers and children in rates of continuous dialogue and proportions of sentence types indicate characteristic modes of talking for the two groups. Mothers' speech was characterized by more continuous dialogue and a higher frequency of questions in comparison with children's speech. The children, on the other hand, used significantly more statements than the mothers did. This contrast agrees with a subjective impression gained from the transcriptions: the mothers relied more on questions for communication, whereas the children's communication was more often in the form of a dialogue based on statements. Mothers' questions could serve the purpose of language elicitation or they could be used, often rhetorically, in connection with children's tasks ('Is this all the water that's been added to the vegetables?' 'Have you only brought a little firewood?'). Children's statements were used in a characteristic 'commentary style', in which members of a play group described aspects of the passing scene ('Here comes Mother'; 'The truck passing over the bridge went "crunch"'; 'Mine is red'). The fact that these comments were apt to be interspersed with silences or with singing, humming, or talking to oneself probably contributed to the lower rate of continuous dialogue between children in comparison with that between mothers and children.

It has been suggested (Snow, 1972; Moerk, 1974; Remick, 1976) that some aspects of speech modification described here should be helpful in the child's acquisition of language, although an experimental manipulation of expansions did not produce positive results (Cazden, 1965). Relationships between mothers' and children's speech variables and the Kokwet subjects' MLU[3] do not prove the usefulness of these variables, but they do indicate that most of them are relevant to a study of child language socialization and development. Table 14.2 shows that mothers and children adjusted the length and (in the case of mothers) complexity of their speech as a

Table 14.2 *Correlations between mothers' and children's speech variables and subjects' MLU and adjusted MLU*

Speech variables	Mothers (N = 13)		Children (N = 12)	
	MLU	Adjusted MLU	MLU	Adjusted MLU
MLU	0.80***	0.71***	0.65**	0.63**
Complexity	0.88***	0.76***	0.23	0.38
Repetitions	0.09	0.14	− 0.79***	− 0.61**
Expansions and echoes	− 0.62**	− 0.56**	− 0.51*	− 0.41
Language practice	− 0.68***	− 0.63**	− 0.60**	− 0.62**
Continuous dialogue	− 0.02	0.21	− 0.29	− 0.27
Questions	0.32	0.51*	0.08	0.15
Imperatives	− 0.16	− 0.32	− 0.55	− 0.67**
Statements	− 0.17	− 0.30	0.73**	0.66**

*$p < 0.10$ **$p < 0.05$ ***$p < 0.01$

function of the subjects' MLU. Both groups used significantly more expansions and echoes, and more language practice speech, with the linguistically less advanced subjects, and children also repeated themselves more to these subjects. Patterns of correlation between sentence types and MLU measures show interesting differences between mothers and children: use of questions by mothers is positively correlated with subjects' adjusted MLU, whereas in children's speech the significant positive correlation is with use of statements. Since the mothers' and children's speech modes were distinguished by relatively greater use of each of these sentence types, it appears that there may be different optimum styles of communication for young children with different classes of speakers. For mothers, this optimum style may involve a higher proportion of questions which the young child learns to answer; for other children, the optimum may be a dialogue in which observations are shared in a sociable peer relationship. Only the use of imperatives seems to have an intrinsically negative effect regardless of speaker, although this effect reaches significance only in the case of children.

We may now return to our original questions with some tentative answers. First, it seems evident that mothers and children in cultures far removed from our own modify their speech to children learning to talk in some of the same ways Americans do. At the same time, it seems probable that mothers and children each provide somewhat different kinds of language environments to the young child. The present analysis suggests that mothers and children can each have a favorable impact on the young child's language development through their own particular styles of verbal interaction. Contact between adults and young children seems to lead to faster language learning through a higher rate of verbal interaction; but we cannot yet conclude that the language environment provided by adults is qualitatively superior in all respects to that provided by other, slightly older children. Finally, this analysis suggests that the ethnographic study of speech may help to answer some questions raised by psycholinguistic studies. The 'training variables' which Brown and his associates identified in American mothers' speech occur in speech directed to young children in Kokwet, and they are part of a style which seems consciously aimed at encouraging language practice. From this vantage point, it does not seem surprising that the experimental separation of expansions in Cazden's (1965) study failed to produce postive results. Training variables may be most accurately seen as interdependent components of a language teaching system rather than as teaching devices in and of themselves.

NOTES

1.   This research was supported by grants from the Carnegie Corporation of New York to the Child Development Research Unit and its successor, the Bureau of Educational Research, University of Nairobi, Kenya.
2.   Eight of the twenty subjects received enough utterances from both mothers and children for analysis. The minimum corpus necessary for analysis was empirically determined to be 30 utterances.
3.   Correlations are reported for both absolute MLU and adjusted MLU. The two measures are highly correlated $(r = 0.91)$ since variation within the sample was only weakly predicted by age $(r = 0.39)$.

Section III

15 A sociologist's point of view

ALLEN D. GRIMSHAW

*Sociology Department, Indiana University, Bloomington,
Indiana 47401, USA*

The papers published in this volume present a considerable range and
quantity of empirical data on how mothers and other 'caretakers' talk
to small children and on that special variety of that talk which is
known as 'baby talk' (BT). While all the papers have implications for
a theory or theories of early acquisition, no author has attempted to
develop a theoretical statement on early acquisition and few of the
papers explicitly deal with questions concerning how the data they
present can be used to confirm or disconfirm either current developmental theories, e.g. Brown (1973) and Halliday (1975), or social
contextual models, e.g. Halliday, McIntosh & Strevens (1964) and
Hymes (1972). Nor, moreover, is there much attention to theories of
socialization for aspects of behavior other than speech. Indeed, I was
the only sociologist present and attended as an observer from the
Committee on Sociolinguistics rather than as a contributor with research credentials.

   I asked myself why no other sociologists were at the meeting, and
concluded that few sociologist would have had much to contribute.
Among early sociologists, Charles H. Cooley looked at and listened
to his children; some contemporary sociologists have looked at young
school children (e.g. Aaron V. Cicourel and his associates, 1974), but
only Denzin (1975a, b), Lindesmith, Strauss & Denzin (1975), Bernstein and his associates (Bernstein, 1971, 1973; see also, especially,
Cook-Gumperz, 1973), and very recently, Corsaro (1975, 1976; see
also Corsaro & Cook-Gumperz, unpublished 1975)[1a] have done work
which fits easily into the theme of this volume. It is not immediately
clear why sociologists have not attended to questions of input to small

children; it seems to me to be an obvious area for studies of socialization, norm learning and the like. I suspect it reflects a generalized unenlightened lack of interest in topics having to do with language in social contexts.

My own immediate interest in the topic of the conference stemmed from two sources: (1) while only semi-literate on the topic of early acquisition, I had been very impressed with the great magnitude of the acquisition accomplishment (I am tempted to say 'miracle') and the implications of that accomplishment for theories of innateness, stimulus—response and other theories of social learning. The emphasis on inputs, and therefore, on the social contextualization of acquisition, made the conference far more attractive to me (as a sociologist) than one which might have emphasized psycholinguistic developmental stages; and (2) while I am not working on infant acquisition I have been interested in continuing language socialization with particular reference to adolescence (Grimshaw & Holden, 1976). Continuing language socialization in adolescence is a curiously neglected research arena (I have been told that some linguists believe that the language acquisition device (LAD) self-destructs at puberty; sociologists can tell us little more than that adolescence is traumatic for young persons in our society and that children everywhere disengage themselves from their early socializers during the period). Studies of adolescence, however, could provide us with rich data about the learning of appropriateness rules and behavioral strategies as well as about new dialect learning with concomitant questions of 'prestige', peer — or other — reference groups, interference and so on (Payne, n.d.). A look at inputs in early acquisition seemed likely to provide clues about social *processes* which would have implications for continuing acquisition.

The immediate interest just outlined is located in a larger context of questions about how changes in the language production of individuals are somehow aggregated into patterns of language change. The latter interest, in turn, is related to a curiosity about how social change occurs. It is, thus, for selfish reasons that I am interested in a continuing search for ways of improving the character of the ongoing exchange between sociological and linguistic data and theories.

My comments in the following pages will reflect the particularities of my interest in the papers and discussions at the conference; I will discuss what I perceive to be the implications of findings on early acquisition for continuing language socialization and the implications of materials presented in papers and discussions for better understanding of sociological questions. Finally, I will say something about methodological issues raised by some of the papers.

The LAD does *not* self-destruct and there is evidence that language learning and acquisition is a continuing process throughout most of our lives. It is certainly obvious to any academic that people in the academy do not talk at age 25 the way they did at 15. There are doubtless other occupations where the risks of jargonization, the diseases of logorrhea and the hazards of multiple embedding are less endemic; nonetheless, relearning and new learning are probably ubiquitous at least in complex modern societies. Moreover, it is also clear, if we reflect on it, that the new learning is not just a matter of lexical accretion or, for example, the appearance during adolescence of more complex grammatical structures. We know that there is second and higher order code learning; we are sometimes less attentive to the facts of continuing phonological change (which Ferguson claims goes on throughout life) and, more particularly of interest for my purposes, continuing learning of both appropriateness rules and of strategies for getting things socially accomplished with talk. There are, for example, kinds of talk associated with the management of bereavement (what I have called 'doing' condolences) or with the termination of social relationships (breaking up with sweethearts or firing employees) which can't be done very effectively by small children but which seem to be in the repertoires of some, though not all, adults. These things seem to be learned in the adolescent years. Stafford (unpublished)[1a] has identified certain techniques that much older people use to assure continuity in social relationships (eliciting promises for return visits at specific times) which don't appear to be necessary for people with wider access to social relationships; these social modes of talk are also, somehow, acquired. In addition to the specific learning of such modes of talk, we are throughout our lives involved in language related activities of monitoring the speech of others, and through that monitoring also involved as 'caretakers' for the speech activities of relevant social others.

The question of relevant social others is an important one for studies of early acquisition. It is true that adolescents use other adolescents as models and that they are subjected to continuous monitoring from their age peers; this does not imply that only parents (generally mothers in the studies reported in the pages above) and teachers are the sources of relevant inputs and monitors of infant and early child speech. A few of the papers in this volume note the importance of other (usually older) children as models and monitors. It seems reasonable to expect that older children start to function as models as soon as a child begins to move into the adult system (Phase III in Halliday's (1975) exposition of the process), which happens long before a child enters preschool or school in our society. Inputs and monitoring from older children may begin even earlier in societies or sectors of societies where early socialization is less bound by constraints of single family residence as well as for children living in nuclear families when older siblings are present. Cross-cultural evidence presented by several of the authors in this volume indicates that older children frequently function as models and monitors in other societies; it is probably the case in our own society for nonsuburban children. It would be interesting to see whether there is some point in the development of a child when she or he comes to be seen as a relevant social other (and not 'just a baby', an object) by other children, and therefore as warranting monitoring, correction and instruction.

If we are to talk about relevant social others, *viz.* those who can be models and can act as monitors, there are also considerations of what part of the speech production of these relevant others is relevant input for the language learner. Snow (this volume) has characterized relevant input as that which is controlled semantically but not syntactically by the learner; Halliday (1975) makes a similar emphasis on semantic priority. This is a highly productive notion, but we should also consider the notion of social readiness for certain kinds of language learning; there may be stages in development with concomitant social expectations about behaviors appropriate to ages and other statuses (to say nothing about maturational readiness). Indeed, the notion of such readiness may have a more profound implication, *viz.* as Gelman stated (in discussion), that two-year-olds hold the floor no matter how their interlocutors may try to change the topic and that small children control both topics and topic changes. This is another way of putting the observation that only that input which is matched to structures the child does control semantically is relevant — but emphasizes the complementary nature of verbal interaction even at very early ages. It similarly may validate Gleason's observation (in discussion) that mothers speak for two until the child is able to hold up its end of a conversational exchange, Sachs' observation that mothers patter to *themselves* while servicing infants who don't speak at all (Halliday's observations suggesting that even very small infants have communicative systems, however, make this at least problematic), and Shatz's observation (also in discussion) that such language for the self (produced by the mother) may be that which drops out of the mother's repertoire as soon as the infant begins to talk. Sachs agreed with the point (made in discussion by Henrietta Cedergren) that rather than a genetic basis for speech modifications, adults may be conditioned by certain physiological limitations of the infant's productive capacity (the observation was made relative to pitch; it might equally be said of cognitive development). All of these factors underline the importance of an interactive perspective and the need for attention to the productive and interpretative capacities of all participants in speech events. It seems to me that there are instructive parallels to exchanges between adolescents and adults and to those interactions between monolinguals controlling different codes which result in the continuing reinvention of pidgins.

Most people who talk to infants and small children, whether adults themselves or simply older children, adjust their talk to what they perceive to be the interpretative capacities of their little interlocutors. (There are, of course, instances in which adults use 'adult' speech to even very small children. These are usually marked and are probably meant as much for entertainment of other auditors as for communication with the child.) This is nothing peculiar to such exchanges; anybody who has a repertoire with more than one code and/or style and/or register adjusts to perceived capacities of interlocutors (for discussion of this phenomenon see, e.g. Grimshaw, 1966, 1973). Less clear, however, are the determinants of such adjustment. One such determinant will be the speaker's perception of the interpretative capacities of the hearer. One reason for simplification, e.g. in BT or foreigner talk (Ferguson 1964, 1971) is simply an attempt to maximize communicative effectiveness (the fact that this may not be the outcome is beside the point).

I would like to argue that another criterion for adjustment of code selection is the intended functional load of the communication. Is it possible that some kinds of things can't be done with BT? Are special modes of talk like BT viable vehicles for variant functional loads, e.g. *can strong negative affect be carried in BT*?[16] One attack on this question might be to look at variables which constrain strategy selection in attempts at verbal manipulation within the adult system, e.g. the choice of order, or persuade, or cajole. It has been suggested (Grimshaw & Bird, 1973) that status relationships between interactants (e.g. of superordination—subordination), costs and saliency of goal to participants and affect between participants constrain such selections. We are not prepared to state that there are rules for selection, but there are certainly appropriateness conditions.

The same would seem to hold for use of BT. During the course of discussion at the conference somebody (I believe it was Wills) made the claim than nobody would say in BT, 'Is Mommy mad?' Probably not, as such an unmarked production would be a reportable event (in the sense of Labov, 1968). I am even more sure that no mother would say, 'Is baby mad?' as an unmarked BT utterance (although it might be used, quite typically, as a *marked* taunt by an adult to a pouting four- or five-year-old). I suspect that the relationship between those who engage in BT exchanges must be one in which the interactants like one another *unless* the BT is used in a marked fashion to insult one's interlocutor or a third party. (I don't believe the same condition necessarily holds for foreigner talk.) My untested intuition is that if the affectual conditions are wrong, children (and sweethearts) will reject BT inputs. Here again, then, there are questions regarding appropriateness conditions. We are a long way from being able to state what these conditions are in terms of measures of the variables of status, affect and cost. But surely we can use some device such as the heuristic suggested by Hymes' (1972) 'SPEAKING' or an alternative specification of who uses what codes in speaking to whom, when, and under what constraints, to begin more fully to characterize what it is that is being developmentally and socially accomplished. If, as Cedergren implied in her comments in discussion, BT is really just a variable within a non-special code, then we ought to think about what things people try to accomplish in their talk with infants and how those intended accomplishments are influential in determining selection or non-selection of that variable.

Whether BT is simply a variable, or whether it is a register or even a distinctive code, there are additional questions about how it is learned and how its learners also learn when it can be properly used. With regard to the learning of BT, we might ask about people who learn BT not in their own childhood but at later ages (a parallel to the learning of sign by previously unexposed adolescents, a question which has intrigued Bellugi), or who attempt to transfer BT skills across languages. Are problems of interference, for example, compounded by the fact that BT varies from standards in every language with regard to pitch, intonation and lexicon? (Again, a similar question might be asked about sign learning.) It has been noted that foreigner talk employs many of the devices used in BT; what might be the difficulties in trying to use foreigner talk to babies?

Additional questions can be raised about the learning, by children themselves, of appropriateness conditions for use of BT and other available modes of speech. Considerable attention was given, in both papers and discussion, to variables of pitch, intonation, phonology, lexical inventions and so on, in BT. No one, as far as I can remember, attended to questions of how little ones learn appropriateness constraints. How do they learn, for example, that BT can be used as an insult, first to other children and, in adulthood, to both peers and children?[2] How do they learn that it can effectively be used, *some of the time*, in apologies, or in wheedling and coaxing. (But only some of the time. Mommies do get in certain moods which children learn to recognize, where the use of BT to them will call forth negative reactions.) For at least some acquisition of appropriateness constraints, we can observe explicit sanctions being applied by adults. Children soon learn not to ask questions about certain social and physical stigmata, for instance, that questions such as, 'Mommy, why does that man walk funny?' or, (to elderly spinsters), 'Why aren't you married?' are likely to be followed by another, *viz.* 'Mommy, why did you pinch me?' We can also hear older children explicitly instructing their younger friends 'how to get around' their mothers. I have heard 'Tell her she's real pretty, and then ask her', 'Wait until she's busy, and then ask her' and, 'Well, if she won't do it any other way just nag her', all suggested as specific strategies during a tactical briefing session. At this point, however, all we can do is cite anecdotes; we have no systematic information on either the distribution or the relative effectiveness of, *inter alia*, trial-and-error, explicit instruction, sanction manipulation, or simply modelling learning.

The questions I've raised here are not exhaustive, and probably seem more important to me, as a sociologist, than they do to many students actually studying early acquisition. I don't believe they can, in the long run, be ignored, though in many instances they will need reformulation. In the discussion following my comments at the conference, for example, there were two partial reformulations which seem to me to lead in interesting directions.

First, Wills observed that she interpreted my comments as implying that individuals *learn* how to produce BT, *learn* how to terminate relationships, and so on. She stated that she preferred a perspective of 'learning how to learn,' *viz.* that attention should be directed to the acquisition of generalized linguistic and social competences rather than to a perspective which suggests that we develop repertoires of codes and social skills that we gradually augment as we grow older. She claimed, moreover, that in cases where people don't learn how to do these things — or do them badly — that this is a consequence of some failure on their part to gather information from interaction (*viz.* they don't pick up the right cues) rather than underexposure to codes or skills at optimal points in their developmental histories. The notion of a generalized social competence in the same sense as generalized linguistic competence is a reasonable one; I think that Halliday (1975) has argued such a perspective quite persuasively in his *Learning How to Mean*. At the same time, I think that it can be argued that people do go through various stages in terms of learning particular aspects of what turn out to be performance rules; I think that Brown (1973) and Carol Chomsky (1969) have argued for such a developmental perspective quite persuasively in their work on early language learning and continuing acquisition, respectively. It is probably true that the only way we can learn appropriateness rules is by processing social information available to us in the same way that we get linguistic information to process and thereby learn language. Proficiency in social skills, however, does vary with age, possibly more so than is the case with linguistic skills (this is an interesting empirical and theoretical question which again no one seems to have addressed). While there is doubtless some new information available to us as we grow older, and while there may be new varieties of feedback as social expectations for behavior change (*viz.* there come points at which we are expected to 'know better'), there seem to me to be fairly noticeable changes in skills of social interaction despite the absence of increments of new social information of comparable magnitude. We don't understand how this comes to be.

Second, Gleason's recasting of the 'affect' question may provide us with a clue as to where to look for a partial answer. She observed that she was hesitant to label the 'doing' of condolences or the terminating of social relationships social or linguistic 'skills', arguing that what makes it difficult to do these things is the high affectual content involved in such acts. If this is so, she suggested, perhaps it is simply the case that as we get older we can better deal with certain affective situations. The speculation that people are better able to handle affective situations as they grow older is an interesting one; but this may simply move the problem back one lamination. How would it be that such increased ability to deal with affect increased with age? Is it simply a matter of maturation or is some variety of social learning involved? If the latter, how is it learned? If the former, how are we to explain the fact that some people are never able to perform some of these acts effectively, an interpretation which seems to be compatible with the flourishing sympathy card industry? Then, if it is maturational, is there some genetic defect which incapacitates some people from managing heavy affect? This would be a discovery of some magnitude. The fact of the matter is that some societal members do learn to manage complicated social relations of considerable threat and affect, and most of them learn changing rules in the course of growing up, e.g. changing expectations for personal responsibility within educational institutions. Throughout high school, youngsters have to ask for permission to go to the bathroom — in high school in the US, I'm told, written passes are required. In college it would be a reportable event that such permission was sought. I've been unable to find anyone who can recall ever being told of this change in rules. There are, however, other rules which remain unchanged, for example, there is never any question even in the most advanced graduate seminar about who is in charge. I suspect that there are sanctions associated with the use of BT once one is in school, and that learning not to use BT in school has some carryover into other settings (to say nothing about the sanctions which would be invoked by schoolmates). Similar kinds of things happen with all varieties of speech behavior and other social behaviors. The question remains — how are appropriateness constraints learned?

An additional topic which is of considerable interest to a sociologist is that of how children learn to sort out roles, role relationships and their own identities. Halliday (1975) has some very detailed observations of the development of the use of language for 'interactional' and 'personal' functions in very early language and presents considerable data to show that what might be termed as pronominal confusion is, rather, a systematic and 'logical' usage. Corsaro (1976) has richly-detailed videotaped material on role-playing with children in preschool. Wills (this volume) notes that some BT inputs may be gratuitous, or even injurious to children through creating role confusion (but also notes that normal pronominal usages may be more likely to be used on 'serious' occasions, for which she may not have data, because she suspects that self-recording may have been terminated by parents during family crises). Ervin-Tripp (in discussion at the conference), provided an illustration of one child saying to another, 'You can't say "honey," I'm the mother!' It is clear that peers as well as adults participate in the teaching of role structures. Holzman suggested (in discussion) that when children indicate an understanding of who's who, mothers stop calling themselves 'Mommy', i.e. that children themselves provide the cues which relevant others use in assessing what kinds of inputs to make. There is a rich amount of anecdotal material and some fairly systematic data on the learning of roles and role relationships, but here, as in the case of appropriateness constraints, critical questions have yet to be asked, let alone answered.

In my view, both the papers and the discussion at the conference were replete with interesting data, provocative observations and insights, interesting questions and fragments of proto-theoretical statements. It did not appear to me that the status of research on what might be called the acquisition of sociolinguistic rules has reached the point which I understand to have been reached in studies of the acquisition of syntax (I simply don't know what has been accomplished in the study of acquisition of the phonological component). In my comments above I have attempted to provide some illustrative examples of the kinds of questions which occurred to a sociologist presented with an unorganized cornucopia of facts and ideas. In my discussion I have attended principally to unanswered and unasked questions which seem to me to have theoretical implications for sociology, sociolinguistics and, perhaps, linguistics. I have not attended to problems of data collection and other 'methodological' issues. In the remainder of my discussion I'd like to remark briefly on those issues.

I have become increasingly interested in the study of language in use in a period in which there have been critically important (some would say revolutionary) changes in linguistics.[3] While the controversies over theories of language structure have probably been most visible to non-linguists, I strongly suspect that changes in notions of what constitutes good data may turn out to be more fundamental in their long range impact on linguistics; this will certainly be true for what some have called the 'hyphenated' fields such as sociolinguistics. If Chomsky has been a major figure in the controversy over transformational grammar and spin-off disputes over generative versus interpretive semantics, Labov has certainly been the major figure in the methodological 'shift' in modes of collection and analysis of linguistic data within autonomous linguistics. As recently as the early sixties most linguists still worked with single informants or their own intuitions (Labov's 1971 and 1972 'bush' and 'closet'). The data elicited in dialect surveys hardly reflected 'language in use'. Only pioneers like Labov, Gumperz and Ferguson were attending to such issues as careful versus casual speech and to the fact that all speech occurs in social situations.[4] Labov was, if not the first, one of the earliest users of probability sampling among linguists; he also developed elicitation techniques and measurement modes which have subsequently been widely adopted. Finally, as well as I can determine, Labov's emphasis on variable rules has had an important influence on the increasing use of 'errors' as important data rather than as idiosyncratic exceptions and performance lapses.

The influence of this new methodological perspective and the utility of many specific technical innovations is much in evidence in several of the papers in this volume and related considerations were often invoked in discussions. At the same time, however, I must report an uncomfortable suspicion that some scholars with linguistic backgrounds, or with training in non-social science fields, have sometimes adopted technical innovations without having first grounded themselves in the epistemological bases for the change in methodological perspective. Thus, I sometimes had the feeling that reported research results reflected adoption of new instrumentation (e.g. better recording equipment), new data collection techniques (e.g. enrollment of societal or group members as data-collecting collaborators), and analytic techniques (e.g. tests of statistical significance) either without awareness of some of the implications of such adoptions or, if aware of those implications, the researchers in question have essentially ignored them. I will not detail specific instances; I will hope that the researchers whose work is reported here, and others, will themselves attend more closely to these issues.

I would, however, like to comment on two issues which seem to me to be basic to the soundness of all research in this, or any other, area. First, the importance of controls is a fundamental tenet in experimental design, and research design generally (for an excellent introduction to the niceties of design, see Stouffer, 1950). How can one know that stimulus x changed characteristic y in group z unless there is another group n, with the same characteristics as group z, which did not experience x and in which y did not occur? For purposes of this discussion the analogous question is, 'How do we know adults talk differently to babies or small children unless we have control instances of adult–adult speech in similar contexts and on similar topics?' Blount's interesting paper (this volume), in which he discussed some of the issues implied in the paragraph immediately above, generated a discussion of the issue of such controls.

Blount reported that two features of adult–child speech in Luo are exaggerated intonation and repetition (actually, expansion, not necessarily exact repetition). Garnica asked how exaggerated intonation was assessed; Blount responded that it was intonation different from that addressed to adults, and defined an utterance as one round of an interactional turn-taking sequence and repetition as an expansion. Brukman then asked whether a comparable list for adult–adult speech was available. Blount responded that he had taped interviews with parents, which showed a low proportion of such expansions, but that he had no corpus of adult–adult casual speech which would permit the relevant comparison to be made. Newport then asked what kind of adult—adult speech would be needed. Would it, for example, need to be similar in content? Holzman then observed that a satisfactory answer to the questions being raised would necessitate data collection on adult—adult interaction comparable to adult—child interaction except that an adult was being addressed — *with coding being done blind*. Ervin-Tripp added that adults in families studied should serve as the reference point for contrasts, *viz.* that not just any adults would do.

What I interpreted the various participants in the discussion as saying was something like, 'Our intuitions are that it probably *is* true that adults use exaggerated intonation and more expansions when they speak to children — but we can't know unless we introduce controls for similarly spontaneous adult—adult speech, simultaneously attending to topic, social relationships and other aspects of social context'. No participant disagreed in principle with this position, but work in the area of early acquisition will not be fully persuasive until ways are found to overcome the problems of matching adult-addressed and child-addressed interactions and more investigators have succeeded in using appropriate controls.

My second point has to do with the incorporation of what we can learn from deviant productions *and* deviant interpretations into our understanding of the acquisition process — and of language in use more generally. It may very well be that the talk which is used in talking to children and which children themselves use, is not a different code but simply a variant of standard speech. If this is so, there are nonetheless productions which are violations of semi-categorical rules and therefore (in the Labovian sense) 'reportable'. It may be, as Brown suggested in discussion at the conference, that there are simply 'errors', but that important cues to the understanding of the acquisition process can be gained from examining deviant production to see where errors can be expected, whether they cluster and whether all children make the same errors. The more fundamental question, it seems to me, has to do with the determination of which are genuinely linguistically principled errors and which are simply performance lapses (in some Chomskian sense). Attention to deviant performance will help in elucidating not only developmental stages in acquisition, and possibly, questions of how prior mislearning can carry over 'interference' effects into later learning, but also will provide insights into the questions addressed in this volume, *viz.* those concerning the impact of social relationships with models and input givers on the development of language skills of new learners.

A second dimension of error, and one seldom attended to, has to

do with mistakes in interpretation. It seems generally to be agreed
that children have more passive than productive competence. But it
would also seem to be clear that children must sometimes misappre-
hend speech directed to them, even when that speech is simplified
(see Jefferson, 1972 for a discussion of misapprehension sequences).
Some such misapprehension presumably results simply from conditions of linguistic readiness; children will not understand some
utterances simply because they have not reached a sufficiently
mature stage in language development. I suspect, however, that social
contexts also have an effect on interpretative success or failure. Consider, for example, the following instance from an adolescent—adult
exchange.

  A fifteen-year-old male, shirtless, is sitting with his mother and
  younger brother at the breakfast table on a cool, Sunday, winter
  morning. His mother is opening a bottle of vitamin pills. His father,
  also shirtless, enters the room and puts his arm around the young
  man's shoulders. The adolescent says something; the father steps
  quickly back and says, 'I'm sorry.' What did the young man say?
  The ensuing discussion among the four persons involved revealed
  four different interpretations:
    (1) self-report: 'Give me one.' (a reference to the vitamins)
    (2) mother: 'Keep me warm.' (a reference to coolness and bare
    skin)
    (3) father: 'Leave me alone!' (an invocation of social coolness)
    (4) younger brother: 'Wha?'
Similar misinterpretations abound (a fragment overheard out of
context at the conference was heard as 'gays coupling'; a 'Wha?' response brought the correct interpretation, 'gaze-coupling') with clear
implications for acquisition. Sources of such misunderstanding can be
recovered in speech exchanges among fully competent speakers and
'remedial work' (Goffman, 1971) can be done. My point is that similar, socially-based errors must occur in adult—child speech — with
little possibility of remedial work and *unknown* consequences for the
acquisition process.

  One other comment on deviation. Ervin-Tripp (this volume) discusses the question of co-occurrence restriction in BT, e.g. whether
shift in pitch is necessarily accompanied by lexical specialization. It
seems to me that this, and similar questions for other kinds of production for children, could be an important consideration in determining the sort of corpus that is available to children learning
language; to the best of my knowledge there have been no studies
either of such co-occurrence restrictions or of the distributional

aspects of code-switching. If this is true, it raises again the question of controls and of possible problems of making statements about inputs without having data on exchanges involving other than 'caretakers' and those cared for.

I have, in my comments, focussed on questions having to do with social aspects of language acquisition, on continuities in that acquisition, and on what I consider to be some methodological problems of work thus far reported. It will be obvious, I hope, that I found the conference stimulating and the papers suggestive. I hope it will also be obvious that I think that sociologists are neglecting an important resource by neglecting work on acquisition — of small children as well as all of us who continue to learn through our lifetimes. Similarly, it should be clear that I believe that the work being done can be improved by closer attention to epistemological questions concerning the methods used. What will not be obvious to readers, I'm afraid, is that there were many other things discussed in papers and in conversations at the meeting which I found exciting and interesting, and which seemed to me to raise exciting and interesting linguistic, sociological, and sociolinguistic issues. While it may not seem to be the case, I have exercised some self-discipline in limiting my commentary. For example, I have said nothing about what to me are highly interesting questions hinted at in commentary on kinesic and paralinguistic (e.g. whispering) dimensions of early inputs and production. I look forward to learning more about these topics and about language socialization generally.

Notes

1a.   Carsaro, W. & Cook-Gumperz, J. (1975). Social-ecological constraints on children's communicative strategies. Unpublished paper.
    Stafford, P. (1974). Symbolic interactionism and aging. Unpublished paper, Indiana University.
1b.   I would like to raise some of the same questions about sign. Bellugi has remarked, in discussion elsewhere, that sign can be used to say the 'same' thing in poetic and non-poetic manners, and has given a rather convincing demonstration. I wonder whether one can 'plonk' or scold, etc. I suppose one can. Can one, for example 'plonk' (*vide* Potter, 1959, pp. 43—46 *et passim*) in BT? Can one scold, chide, or reprimand, or, beyond this, make a distinction between a gentle reproach and a strong reprimand?
2.   Corsaro (personal communication) notes that BT can be used not only as an insult but as a way of deliberately upsetting adults. He writes, 'Fours and fives will often slip into "talking" like babies. Such behavior persists even though there is a tendency for adults to continually disapprove — "If you talk like a baby I'll

treat you like one''. It seems to me that fours and fives do this to purposely upset adults. In this sense it is a way of using BT from a young child's perspective'.

3. Not all agree, of course. See Makkai & Makkai, 1975.

4. This is one of the several reasons why I consider myself particularly fortunate that it was Gumperz, Hymes, and Labov who served as my mentors and guides into the tangled thickets of the study of language in use. If I haven't learned, it certainly is not their fault.

16 A psychologist's point of view

SUSAN ERVIN-TRIPP

University of California, Berkeley, California 94720, USA

Baby talk (BT) can be examined from a variety of independent perspectives, each of which raises complex questions meriting research:

(*a*) BT can be viewed as the *input* or linguistic stimulus to an infant acquiring language. In this sense it has been described not only
in terms of features (more questions) but in terms of process (more
expansions). The focus in such studies is on the causal variables in
individual differences in rates of linguistic development.

(*b*) BT can be viewed as a *register* within the repertoire of those
men, women and children who speak to children.[1] The analysis of
this register raises all the issues of the social alternation of features,
co-occurrence rules and social meaning to listener of features that
we find in other studies of register, style and code-shifting. To the
extent that a child shifts register in addressing younger children, a
BT register may develop as part of the child's repertoire, and its
eventual similarity to the register of the adults in the milieu can be
studied too.

(*c*) BT can be viewed as *accommodative* language, in that some
features are changed as a result of expectations and feedback regarding the listener's comprehension.

Input research

It may be necessary to sort out the effective variables since linguistic
features often are incidental correlates of larger differences in child-
rearing milieu. For example, it is common to find a relation between
language-development measures and frequency of imperatives. But a

high frequency of imperatives is likely to be related to many other differences in milieu, including affective milieu, the functions to which language is put in the interaction between adult and child, and the linguistic strategies used for the realization of speech acts. It could be that function, not form, is the critical variable. I suspect that only controlled experimental input will sort out these factors.

In addition to the issue of which variables matter, we can expect that there may be critical periods for some treatments to have effects. The evidence from Popova's[2] work is very suggestive. We also know now that we can track much more finely grained stages of acquisition of forms. For example, it has been shown that children who produce a syntactic frame may not yet fully control all alternative component types well — they may use only pronouns and no nouns as objects, for instance, and at that period they may be particularly ready to imitate the structures at the front edge of developing skills (Bloom, Hood & Lightbown, 1974; Bloom, Lightbown & Hood, 1975). So the two directions I would like to see intervention studies go in would be towards better control over the critical level of structure through experimental studies, and more sensitive measures of the relation between stage of knowledge of a particular feature and the intervention effectiveness.

Register

There have now been numerous studies of gross differences in age of addressee and frequencies of particular linguistic features. But little systematic work has been done on the social distribution of these features, either in terms of social properties of the addressee and context which has to do with rules for social alternations, as in address studies, or in terms of meaning. When the addressee is not known, does higher pitch suggest speech to a child or to a larger class such as child, animal, or lover? When the addressee is known to the judge, is higher pitch heard as signalling affection or condescension? Is the difference a function of content as in the case of pronoun switching in Russian where deviation from the expected form is interpretable from other cues (Friedrich, 1972)?

An example of the utility of knowing more about the distribution of BT features is the use of 'we' in directives, as in these: 'We're going to take our naps now' or 'Let's all clean up' or 'We don't throw paint, do we?' which are heard as typical of nursery school teacher register.

In a study of directives in adults (Ervin-Tripp, 1976) it was found that when the expected person to carry out the act was the addressee, 'we' directives were always downward in rank or age. In a pilot study children heard 'we' from a child to an adult as funny. The particular property all such directives shared was that the act was explicit but the agent was deflected by a passive or by the plural: 'We have to do that analysis over'. 'We have to give him 4 cc. at midnight and 4 a.m.' The nursery school teacher's style then can be seen as a particular example of downward talk. What remains mysterious is why the agent deflection occurs. Various kinds of 'politeness features' occur in adult speech to children but their distribution is not well studied.

In addition to the social distribution features, we can look at the variation, analogous to code-switching, between particular role pairs. For instance, does pitch rise or palatalization features increase in comforting an injured child, in switching to persuasion?

Finally, we know very little about the relation between BT features. Some of them may be closely tied; for example, higher pitch and increase of pitch range, and use of sing-song intonational patterns could form an implicational scale or gradient series such that all speakers using sing-song raise their fundamental frequency, to children, but the reverse is not true. I expect some features will be relatively independent of each other. For example, BT suffixes and prosodic features may have a higher relation than some of the forms of simplification of semantics, or discourse-maintenance devices such as repetitions, which may be based less on affect. Only some features may have social meanings to hearers.

Children as young as two use prosodic shifts in speaking to puppets and infants. We do not know if the BT features young children use sometimes are maintained consistently, or whether failure to use them is heard as inappropriate, or whether there are shifts in and out of the use of these features which have functional correlates. The same issues that we need to investigate in adult registers can be pursued with children.

Accommodation

Speakers have wide experience in adapting their speech to channel problems such as noisy settings, deafness, ignorance of the topic, lack of knowledge of the language. Shouting, speaking extra clearly, repeating, simplifying vocabulary are examples of solutions. We don't know all the cues which bring out stereotyped simplified speech: articulatory problems in the hearer, physical disabilities — especially extreme cases in hospitals, old age. Infancy is only one of them.

If simplifications depend on accommodation, we might expect differences as a result of failure to understand or failure to respond. Such changes could be monitored through the course of an interchange as a function of specific kinds of hearer reactions. But a critical element is what the participants view as the function of the interchange. In a large proportion of conversations — certainly most of those between children — the exchange of information about the world is not the goal. Even the tapes we have of adults talking with children often have a tacit purpose of getting the child to talk, keeping their attention — and questioning is an obvious strategy for this. Earlier, when the adult often cannot understand the child's intent, repetition by the adult — like repetition by the child — can maintain the interaction. So in monitoring the features which appear to be simplifications in the face of communicative breakdown, one would certainly want to control purpose carefully.

In examining adult speech to second-language learners, Evelyn Hatch noticed many instances in which the adult seemed to imitate the learner (Hatch, Shapira & Gough, 1975). This is a kind of emulation implying identification, empathy, just as some 'chameleon' speakers adopt dialect features from their conversational partners. But using the partner's system is also a useful move when the hearer can't speak your own language. We might then look for an increase in emulation in cases where some communication problems arise. The problem, of course, is that the speaker may emulate his own stereotype of the hearer's speech. We see this when adults use syntax to children which is simpler than the syntax of the child.

Individual adults speaking to children bring to the task various accommodative skills arising from prior personal experience with channel problems. But if we look at actual processes of change at points where remedies are tried, we can see some of the learning occurring, and find out the levels of the language system at which speakers are able to make accommodation. We don't know whether adjustment of semantic difficulty, choice of speech acts, finding simpler or more frequent vocabulary are the only levels or whether direct operations on syntax also occur.

This conference was sponsored by the Social Science Research Council's Committee on Sociolinguistics. I hope that the study of BT can become an arena for the expansion of the new methods being developed for the collection and analysis of natural conversations and dialectal variation. It is particularly promising as a domain for examining universals since many of the features of BT may arise because of common aspects in the communication of older caretakers with babies rather than from arbitrary conventions. In this respect BT has a particular attraction beyond that of other social registers.

NOTES

1.   BT, while ambiguous with respect to describing a speaker or listener, at least has the merit of identifying the social category involved; 'motherese' leaves fathers and siblings out, not to speak of nursery school teachers, nurses and visiting linguists.

2.   Popova found that the Russian gender agreement could be taught relatively quickly to children with free variation between masculine and feminine forms but was very difficult to teach if forms of one gender were dominant. (Popova, M. I., 1973. Grammatical elements of language in the speech of pre-preschool children. In C. A. Ferguson & D. I. Slobin (eds.), *Studies of child language development*. New York: Holt, Rinehart and Winston.)

References

Agheyishi, R. & Fishman, J.A. (1970). Language attitude studies: a brief survey of methodological approaches. *Anthropological Linguistics* 12, 137—57.

Ames, L.D. (1952). The sense of self of nursery school children as manifested by their verbal behavior. *Journal of Genetic Phychology* 81, 193—232.

* Andersen, E.S. & Johnson, C.E. (1973). Modifications in the speech of an eight-year-old to younger children. *Stanford Occasional Papers in Linguistics* no. 3, 149—60.

Anglin, J.M. (1976). *Words, object, and conceptual development.* New York: Norton. (In press.)

Austerlitz, R. (1956). Gilyak nursery words. *Word* 12, 260—79.

Austerlitz, R. (1959). Semantic components of pronoun systems: Gilyak. *Word* 15, 102—9.

Avram, A. (1967). De la langue qu'on parle aux enfants roumains. *To Honor Roman Jakobson*, vol. 1. The Hague: Mouton.

Bailey, C.-J.N. & Shuy, R.W. (eds.) (1973). *New ways of analyzing variation in English.* Washington, D.C.: Georgetown University Press.

Bain, R. (1936). The self- and other-words of a child. *American Journal of Sociology* 41, 767—75.

Bakker-Rennes, H. & Hoefnagel-Höhle, M. (1974). Situatie verschillen in taalgebruik (Situation differences in language use). Master's thesis, University of Amsterdam.

Baldwin, A.L. & Baldwin, C.P. (1973). The study of mother—child interaction. *American Scientist* 61, 714—21.

Bartholomew, D. (1960). Some revisions of Proto-Otomi consonants. *International Journal of American Linguistics* 26, 317—29.

Befu, H. & Norbeck, E. (1958). Japanese usages of terms of relationship. *Southwestern Journal of Anthropology* 14, 66—86.

Berlin, B. (1963). A possible paradigmatic structure for Tzeltal pronominals. *Anthropological Linguistics* 5(2), 1—5.

Berlin, B. & Kay, P. (1969). *Basic color terms: their universality and evolution.* Berkeley: University of California Press.

Bernstein, B. (1971). *Class, codes and control, I: theoretical studies towards a sociology of language.* London: Routledge & Kegan Paul.

Bernstein, B. (1973). (ed.) *Class, codes and control, II: Applied studies towards*

* An asterisk indicates that papers are reviewed in the annotated bibliography.

341

a sociology of language. London: Routledge & Kegan Paul.

Bever, T.G. (1970). The cognitive basis for linguistic structures. In J. R. Hayes (ed.), *Cognition and the development of language*. New York: Wiley & Sons.

Bever, T.G., Fodor, J.A. & Weksel, W. (1965). Theoretical notes on the acquisition of syntax: a critique of 'contextual generalization'. *Psychological Review* 72, 467—482.

Bhat, D.N. (1967). Lexical suppletion in baby talk. *Anthropological Linguistics* 9 (5), 33—6.

Bickerton, D. (1973). The nature of a creole continuum. *Language* 49, 640—69.

Bingham, N.E. (1971). Maternal speech to pre-linguistic infants: differences related to maternal judgments of infant language competence. Unpublished paper, Cornell University. Mimeo.

Bloom, L. (1970). *Language development: form and function in emerging grammars*. Cambridge, Massachusetts: MIT Press.

Bloom, L. (1971). Why not pivot grammar? *Journal of Speech and Hearing Disorders* 36, 40—50.

Bloom, L. (1973). *One word at a time*. The Hague: Mouton.

Bloom, L., Hood, L. & Lightbown, P. (1974). Imitation in language development: if, when and why. *Cognitive Psychology* 6, 380—420.

Bloom, L., Lightbown, P. & Hood, L. (1975). Structure and variation in child language. *Monographs of the Society for Research in Child Development* no. 160, 40, no. 2.

Blount, B.G. (1971). Socialization and the pre-linguistic system of Luo children. *Southwestern Journal of Anthropology* 27, 41—50.

Blount, B.G. (1972*a*). Aspects of socialization among the Luo of Kenya. *Language in Society* 1, 255—48.

*Blount, B.G. (1972*b*). Parental speech and language acquisition: some Luo and Samoan examples. *Anthropological Linguistics* 14, 119—30.

Blount, B.G. (n.d.). Aspects of parental speech: English and Spanish. Unpublished manuscript, University of Texas. Mimeo.

Bolinger, D. (1964). Intonation as a universal. In L. Hunt (ed.), *Proceedings of the 9th International Congress of Linguistics, Cambridge, Massachusetts 1962*. The Hague: Mouton.

Bowerman, M. (1973). *Early syntactic development: a cross-linguistic study with special reference to Finnish*. London: Cambridge University Press.

Boxwell, M. (1967). Weri pronoun system. *Linguistics* 29, 34—43.

Braine, M.D.S. (1974). On what might constitute learnable phonology. *Language* 50, 270—99.

Brent, S.B. & Katz, E. (1967). A study of language deviations and cognitive processes. *Progress Report* no. 3, OEO-Job Corps Project 1209, Wayne State University.

*Broen, P.A. (1972). The verbal environment of the language-learning child. *Monograph of American Speech and Hearing Association* no. 17, December.

Brown, R. (1958). How shall a thing be called? *Psychological Review* 65, 14—21.

Brown, R. (1970). *Psycholinguistics*. New York: Free Press.

Brown, R. (1973). *A first language: the early stages*. London: George Allen & Unwin.

Brown, R. (1976). Reference: in memorial tribute to Eric Lenneberg. *Cognition*. (In press.)

Brown, R. (in preparation). *The new paradigm of reference.*

Brown, R. & Bellugi, U. (1964). Three processes in the child's acquisition of syntax. *Harvard Educational Review* 34, 133—51.

Brown, R., Cazden, C. & Bellugi, U. (1968). The child's grammar from I to III. In J.P. Hill (ed.), *Minnesota Symposium on Child Development*, vol. 2. Minneapolis: University of Minnesota Press.

Brown, R. & Ford, M. (1961). Address in American English. *Journal of Abnormal and Social Psychology* 62, 375—85.

Brown, R. & Gilman, A. (1960). The pronouns of power and solidarity. In T. Sebeok (ed.), *Style in Language.* Cambridge, Massachusetts: MIT Press.

Brown, R. & Hanlon, C. (1970). Derivational complexity and order of acquisition in child speech. In J.R. Hayes (ed.), *Cognition and the development of language.* New York: Wiley & Sons.

Brukman, J. (1973). Language and socialization: child culture and the ethnographer's task. In S.T. Kimball & J.H. Burnett (eds.), *Learning and culture: proceedings of the American Ethnological Society.* Seattle: University of Washington Press.

Bruner, J.S. (1974/75). From communication to language: a psychological perspective. *Cognition* 3, 255—87.

Bruner, J.S. (1975). The ontogenesis of speech acts. *Journal of Child Language* 2, 1—21.

Buchler, I.R. (1966). The analysis of pronominal systems: Nahuatl and Spanish. *Anthropological Linguistics* 9, 37—44.

Buchler, I.R. & Freeze, R. (1966). The distinctive features of pronominal systems. *Anthropological Linguistics* 8, 78—105.

*Bynon, J. (1968). Berber nursery language. *Transactions of the Philological Society* 1968, 107—61.

Casagrande, J.B. (1948). Comanche baby language. *International Journal of American Linguistics* 14, 11—14.

Cassar-Pullicino, J. (1957). Nursery vocabulary of the Maltese Archipelago. *Orbis* 6, 192—8.

Cazden, C. (1965). Environmental assistance to the child's acquisition of grammar. Doctoral dissertation, Harvard University.

Cazden, C. (1972). *Child language and education.* New York: Holt, Rinehart & Winston.

Cedergren, H.J. & Sankoff, D. (1974). Variable rules: performance as a statistical reflection of competence. *Language* 50, 111—55.

Chamberlain, A.F. (1890). Notes on Indian child-language. *American Anthropologist* 3, 237—41.

Chao, Y.R. (1956). Chinese terms of address. *Language* 32, 217—41.

*Cherry, L. & Lewis, M. (1976). Mothers and two-year-olds: a study of sex-differentiated verbal interactions. In N. Waterson & C. Snow (eds.), *The development of communication: social and pragmatic factors in language acquisition.* Wiley & Sons. (In press.)

Chew, J.J. Jr (1969). The structure of Japanese baby talk. *Journal-Newsletter of the Association of Japanese* 6, 4—17.

Chomsky, C. (1969). *The acquisition of syntax in children from five to ten.* Cambridge, Massachusetts: MIT Press.

Chomsky, N.A. (1965). *Aspects of the theory of syntax.* Cambridge, Massachusetts: MIT Press.

Chomsky, N.A. (1967). The formal nature of language. Appendix A to E.H. Lenneberg, *Biological foundations of language*. New York: Wiley & Sons.

Cicourel, A. Jennings, K., Jennings, S. Leiter, K. Mackay, T., Mehan, H. & Roth, D. (1974). *Language use and school performance*. New York: Academic Press.

Clark, E.V. (1973). What's in a word? In T. E. Moore (ed.), *Cognitive development and the acquisition of language*. New York: Academic Press.

Clark, E.V. (1974). Some aspects of the conceptual basis for first language acquisition. In R.L. Schiefelbusch & L.L. Lloyd (eds.), *Language perspectives – acquisition, retardation and intervention*. Baltimore: University Park Press.

Clarke-Stewart, K.A. (1973). Interactions between mothers and their young children: characteristics and consequences. *Monographs of the Society for Research in Child Development* no. 153 38, nos. 6–7.

Clyne, M. (1968). Zum Pidgin-Deutsch der Gastarbeiter. *Zeitschrift für Mundartforschung* 34, 130–9.

Collis, G. (1975). The integration of gaze and vocal behavior in the mother–infant dyad. Paper presented at Third International Child Language Symposium, London, September 3–5.

Conant, F.P. (1961). Jarawa kin systems of reference and address: a componential comparison. *Anthropological Linguistics* 3 (2), 19–33.

Condon, W.S. and Sanders, L.W. (1974). Synchrony demonstrated between movements of the neonate and adult speech. *Child Development* 45, 456–62.

Conklin, H.C. (1962). Lexicographical treatment of folk taxonomies. *International Journal of American Linguistics* 28 (2 part 4), 119–41.

Cook-Gumperz, J. (1973). *Social control and socialization: a study of class difference in the language of maternal control*. London: Routledge & Kegan Paul.

Cooley, C.H. (1908). A study of the early use of self-words by a child. *Psychological Review* 15, 339–57.

Corsaro, W. (1975). Sociolinguistic patterns in adult–child interaction. Paper presented at 70th Annual Meeting of the American Sociological Association, San Francisco.

Corsaro, W. (1976). The clarification request as a feature of adult interactive styles with young children. *Language in Society*. (In press.)

*Crawford, J.M. (1970). Cocopa baby talk. *International Journal of American Linguistics* 36, 9–13.

Cross, T.G. (1975). Some relationships between motherese and linguistic level in accelerated children. *Papers and Reports on Child Language Development* no. 10, Stanford University, Stanford, California.

*Cross, T.G. (1976). Motherese: its association with rate of syntactic acquisition in young children. In N. Waterson & C. Snow (eds.), *The development of communication: social and pragmatic factors in language acquisition*. Wiley & Sons. (In press.)

Davis, E.A. (1930). Developmental changes in the distribution of parts of speech. *Child Development* 9.

DeCamp, D. (1971). Toward a generative analysis of a post-creole speech continuum. In D. Hymes (ed.), *Pidginization and creolization of languages*. London: Cambridge University Press.

Delack, J.B. (1974). Prosodic analysis of infant vocalizations and the ontogenesis of sound-meaning correlations. *Papers and Reports on Child Language Development*, no. 8, Stanford University, Stanford, California.

Dennis, W. (1940). *The Hopi Child*. New York: Appleton—Century.

Denzin, N.K. (1975a). The acquisition of language in early childhood. Paper presented to 70th Annual Meeting of the American Sociological Association, San Francisco.

Denzin, N.K. (1975b). Play, games and interaction: the contexts of early child socialisation. *Sociological Quarterly* 16, 458—78.

Dil, A. (1975). Bengali baby talk. In W. von Raffler-Engel (ed.), *Child Language — 1975 Word* 27.

Dore, J. (1973). The development of speech acts. Doctoral dissertation, City University of New York.

*Drach, K. (1969). The language of the parent: a pilot study. *Working Paper* 14, Language-Behavior Research Laboratory, University of California, Berkeley.

Drach, K., Kobashigawa, B., Pfuderer, C. & Slobin, D. (1969). The structure of linguistic input to children. *Working Paper* 14, Language-Behavior Research Laboratory, University of California, Berkeley.

Drachman, G. (1973). Baby talk in Greek. *Working Papers in Linguistics* 15, Ohio State University.

DuBois, C. (1944). *The people of Alor*. Minneapolis: University of Minnesota Press.

Edwards, D. (1973). Sensori-motor intelligence and semantic relations in early child grammar. *Cognition* 2, 395—434.

Eimas, P.D., Cooper, W.E. & Corbit, J.D. (1973). Some properties of linguistic feature detectors. *Perception and Psychophysics* 13, 247—52.

Eimas, P.D. and Corbit, J.D. (1973). Selective adaptation of linguistic feature detectors. *Cognitive Psychology* 4, 99—109.

Eimas, P.D., Siqueland, E.R., Jusczyk, P. & Vigorito, J. (1971). Speech perception in infants. *Science* 171, 303—6.

Ellis, J. and Ure, J. (1969). Language variety: register. In *Encyclopedia of Linguistics, Information and Control*. London: Pergamon Press.

Ervin-Tripp, S. M. (1971). An overview of theories of grammatical development. In D. I. Slobin (ed.), *The Ontogenesis of Grammar*. New York: Academic Press.

Ervin-Tripp, S. M. (1973). Some strategies for the first two years. In T. E. Moore (ed.), *Cognitive Development and the Acquisition of Language*. New York: Academic Press.

Ervin-Tripp, S.M. (1976). Is Sybil there? The structure of some American English directives. *Language in Society* 5, 25—66.

Evans-Pritchard, E.E. (1948). Nuer modes of address. *Uganda Journal* 12, 166—71.

Fairbanks, G. (1940). Voice and articulation drillbook. New York: Harper.

*Farwell, C. (1973). The language spoken to children. *Papers and Reports on Child Language Development* no. 5, 31—62 Stanford University, Stanford, California.

Feldman, C. (1971). The effects of various types of adult responses in the syntactic acquisition of two to three year-olds. Unpublished paper, University of Chicago. Mimeo.

346   References

Feldman, H., Goldin-Meadow, S. & Gleitman, L.R. (1976). On describing a self-generated sign system: a study of deaf children of hearing parents. In A. Locke (ed.), *Action, Gesture, and Symbol: the Emergence of Language*. London: Academic Press. (In press.)

Ferguson, C.A. (1956). Arabic baby talk. In M. Halle (ed.), *For Roman Jakobson*. The Hague: Mouton.

*Ferguson, C.A. (1964). Baby talk in six languages. *American Anthropologist* 66 (6 part 2), 103–14.

Ferguson, C.A. (1971). Absence of copula and the notion of simplicity. In D. Hymes (ed.), *Pidginization and creolization of language*. London: Cambridge University Press.

Ferguson, C.A. (1975). Towards a characterization of English foreigner talk. *Anthropological Linguistics* 17, 1–14.

Ferguson, C.A. & Farwell, C.B. (1975). Words and sounds in early language acquisition. *Language* 51, 419–39.

Fillmore, C.J. (1968). The case for case. In E. Bach & R. Harms (eds.), *Universals in linguistic theory*. New York: Holt, Rinehart & Winston.

Fischer, J.L. (1964). Words for self and others in some Japanese families. *American Anthropologist* 66, (6 part 2), 115–26.

*Fischer, J.L. (1970). Linguistic socialization: Japan and the United States. In R. Hill & R. König (eds.), *Families in East and West*. The Hague: Mouton.

Fodor, J.A. (1966). How to learn to talk: some simple ways. In F. Smith & G.A. Miller (eds.), *The Genesis of Language*. Cambridge, Massachusetts: MIT Press.

Fodor, J.A., Bever, T.G. & Garrett, M. (1974). *The Psychology of Language: an introduction to psycholinguistics and generative grammar*. New York: McGraw–Hill.

Foster, G.M. (1964). Speech forms and perception of social distance in a Spanish-speaking Mexican village. *Southwestern Journal of Anthropology* 20, 107–22.

Frachtenberg, L.J. (1918). Abnormal types of speech in Quileute. *International Journal of American Linguistics* 5, 295–9.

Fraiberg, S. (1974). Blind infants and their mothers: an examination of the sign system. In M. Lewis & L.A. Rosenblum (eds.), *The effect of the infant on its caregiver*. New York: Wiley & Sons.

Frantz, D.G. (1966). Person indexing in Blackfoot. *International Journal of American Linguistics* 32, 50–8.

Fraser, C., Bellugi, U. & Brown, R. (1963). Control of grammar in imitation, comprehension, and production. *Journal of Verbal Learning and Verbal Behavior* 2, 121–35.

*Friedlander, B. (1968). The effect of speaker identity, voice inflection, vocabulary, and message on infants' selection of vocal reinforcement. *Journal of Experimental Child Psychology* 6, 443–59.

Friedrich, P. (1964). Semantic structure and social structure: An instance from Russian. In W.H. Goodenough (ed.), *Explorations in Cultural Anthropology*. New York: McGraw–Hill.

Friedrich, P. (1966). Structural implications of Russian pronominal usage. In W. Bright (ed.), *Sociolinguistics*. The Hague: Mouton.

Friedrich, P. (1972). Social context and semantic features: The Russian pronominal usage. In J. Gumperz & D. Hymes (eds.), *Directions in Sociolinguistics*. New York: Holt.

*Garnica, O. (1974). Some characteristics of prosodic input to young children. Doctoral dissertation, Stanford University.

Garvey, C. (1975). Requests and responses in children's speech. *Journal of Child Language* 2, 41–60.

Garvey, C. (1977). Contingent queries. In M. Lewis & L. Rosenblum (eds.), *Interaction, conversation and the development of language*. New York: Wiley & Sons.

Garvin, P.L. & Riesenberg, S. (1952). Respect behavior on Ponape: an ethno-linguistic study. *American Anthropologist* 54, 201–220.

Gelman, R. & Shatz, M. (1977). Appropriate speech adjustments: the operation of conversational constraints on talk to two-year-olds. In M. Lewis & L. Rosenblum (eds.), *Interaction, conversation and the development of language*. New York: Wiley & Sons.

*Gleason, J. Berko (1973). Code switching in children's language. In T.E. Moore (ed.), *Cognitive Development and the Acquisition of Language*. New York: Academic Press.

Gleason, J. Berko (1975). Fathers and other strangers: men's speech to young children. Paper presented at Twenty-sixth Georgetown Round Table. Georgetown University, Washington, D.C.

Goffman, E. (1971). *Relations in public*. New York: Harper & Row.

Goldin-Meadow, S. (1975). The representation of semantic relations in a manual language created by deaf children of hearing parents: a language you can't dismiss out of hand. Doctoral dissertation, University of Pennsylvania.

Goodenough, F.L. (1938). The use of pronouns by young children: a note on the development of self-awareness. *Journal of Genetic Psychology* 52, 333–46.

Goodenough, W.H. (1965). Personal names and modes of address in two oceanic societies. In M.E. Spiro (ed.), *Context and meaning in cultural anthropology*. New York: Free Press.

Górnowicz, H. (1967). Obserwacje nad rozwojem mowy dziecka. *Gdanskie Zeszyty Humanistyczne X. Ser. Fil.* 3, 31–44.

Grégoire, A. (1911). Essai sur les transformations d'un prenom d'enfant. Brussels/Paris.

Grewel, F. (1959). How do children acquire the use of language? *Phonetica* 3, 193–202.

Grice, H.P. (1975). Logic and conversation. In P. Cole & J. Morgan (eds.), *Syntax and semantics* – vol. III. New York: Academic Press.

Grimshaw, A.D. (1966). Directions for research in sociolinguistics: suggestions of a non-linguist sociologist. *Sociological Inquiry* 36(2), 319–32.

Grimshaw, A.D. (1973). Review article of J.J. Gumperz, *Language in social groups* (ed. by Anwar S. Dil), in *Language Sciences* 27, October: 29–37.

Grimshaw, A.D. & Bird, C.S. (1973). Verbal manipulations: II. Paper presented to the Linguistic Society of America in San Diego, December.

Grimshaw, A.D. & Holden, L. (1976). Post childhood modifications and social competence. *Items* 30, 33–42.

Gruber, J. (1967). Topicalization in child language. *Foundations of Language* 3, 37–65.

Haaf, R.A. & Bell, R.Q. (1967). A facial dimension in visual discrimination by human infants. *Child Development* 38, 893–9.

Haas, M.R. (1969). 'Exclusive' and 'inclusive': a look at early usage. *International Journal of American Linguistics* 35, 1–6.

Halliday, M.A.K. (1975). *Learning how to mean: explorations in the development of language.* London: Edward Arnold.

Halliday, M.A.K., McIntosh, A. & Strevens, P. (eds.) (1964). *The linguistic sciences and language teaching.* London: Edward Arnold.

Harkness, S. (1975). Cultural variation in mothers' language. In W. von Raffler-Engel (ed.), *Child language – 1975. Word* 27, 495–8.

Harris, Z.S. (1948). Componential analysis of a Hebrew paradigm. *Language* 24, 87–91.

Hatch, E., Shapira, R. & Gough, J. (1975). 'Foreigner talk' discourse. Unpublished paper, University of California Los Angeles. (Copies available from authors).

Haugen, E. (1942). Norwegian word studies, vol. I, part III, pp. vi–x. U.S. Library of Congress.

Heider, E.R. (1972). Universals in color naming and memory. *Journal of Experimental Psychology* 93, 10–20.

Heider, E.R. & Olivier, D.C. (1972). The structure of the color space in naming and memory for two languages. *Cognitive Psychology* 3, 337–54.

Henry, F. (1948). Discrimination of the duration of a sound. *Journal of Experimental Psychology* 38, 734–43.

Henzl, V. (1974). Linguistic register of foreign language instruction. *Language Learning* 23, 207–22.

Heraeus, W. (1904). Die Sprache der römischen Kinderstube. *Archiv für Lateinische Lexikographie* 13, 149–72. Reprinted in J.B. Hoffman (ed.), *Klein Schriften von Wilhelm Heraeus.* Heidelberg.

Hess, R.D. & Shipman, V.C. (1965). Early experience and the socialization of cognitive modes in children. *Child Development* 36, 869–86.

Hockett, C.F. (1955). A manual of phonology. *International Journal of American Linguistics* 21 (4 Part 1), Baltimore: Waverly Press.

Holzman, M. (1972). The use of interrogative forms in the verbal interaction of three mothers and their children. *Journal of Psycholinguistic Research* 1, 311–36.

*Holzman, M. (1974). The verbal environment provided by mothers for their very young children. *Merrill-Palmer Quarterly* 20, 31–42.

Horii, Y. (1972). Fundamental frequency measures estimated from analysis of one sentence voice samples. *Asha* 14, 466.

House, A.S. & Fairbanks, G. (1953). The influence of consonant environment upon the secondary acoustical characteristics of vowels. *Journal of the Acoustical Society of America* 12, 105–13.

Howell, R.W. (1967). Linguistic choice as an index to social change. Doctoral dissertation, University of California, Berkeley.

Huxley, R. (1970). The development of the correct use of subject personal pronouns in two children. In G.B. Flores d'Arcais & W. Levelt (eds.), *Advances in Psycholinguistics.* New York: American Elsevier.

Hymes, D. (1961). Linguistic aspects of cross-cultural personality study. In B. Kaplan (ed.), *Studying personality cross-culturally.* New York: Harper & Row.

Hymes, D. (1962). The ethnography of speaking. In T. Gladwin & W.C. Sturtevant (eds.), *Anthropology and human behavior.* Washington, D.C.: Anthropological Society of Washington.

Hymes, D.H. (1972). Models of the interaction of language and social life. In J.J. Gumperz & D. Hymes (eds.), *Directions in sociolinguistics.* New York: Holt, Rinehart & Winston.

Hymes, D. (1973), On personal pronouns: 'fourth' person and phonesthematic aspects. In M.E. Smith (ed.), *Studies in linguistics. In honor of George L. Trager*. The Hague: Mouton.

Ingram, D. (1970). The role of person deixis in underlying semantics. Doctoral dissertation, Stanford University.

Ingram, D. (1971*a*). Toward a theory of person deixis. *Papers in Linguistics* 4, 37–53.

Ingram, D. (1971*b*). Transitivity in child language. *Language* 47, 888–910.

Ingram, D. (1974). Fronting in child phonology. *Journal of Child Language* 1, 133–41.

Ivić, P. & Lehiste, I. (1969). Prilozi ispitivanju fonetske i fonoloske prirode akcenata u savremenom srpskohrvatskom jeziku IV. *Zbornik za filologiju: lingvstiku* 12, 115–65.

Jacobsen, W.H. (1967). Switch-reference in Hokan-Coahuiltecan. In D. Hymes & W.E. Brittle (eds.), *Studies in southwestern ethnolinguistics*. The Hague: Mouton.

Jaffe, J., Stern, N. & Perry, C. (1973). 'Conversational' coupling of gaze behavior in prelinguistic human development. *Journal of Psycholinguistic Research* 2, 321–30.

Jakobson, R. (1960*a*). Comments on Brown and Gilman. In T.A. Sebeok (ed.), *Style in language*. Cambridge, Massachusetts: MIT Press.

Jakobson, R. (1960*b*). Why 'mama' and 'papa'? In B. Kaplan (ed.), *Perspectives in psychological theory*. New York: International University Press.

Jefferson, G. (1972). Side sequences. In D. Sudnow (ed.), *Studies in social interaction*. New York: Free Press.

Jespersen, O. (1923). *Language*. New York: Holt.

Joos, M. (1948). *Acoustic phonetics*. Language monograph no. 23. Baltimore: Waverly Press.

Kaplan, E.L. (1969). The role of intonation in the acquisition of language. Doctoral dissertation, Cornell University.

Kazazis, K. (1969). Distorted modern Greek phonology for foreigners. *Glossa* 3, 198–209.

Kearsley, R. (1973). The newborn's response to auditory stimulation: a demonstration of orienting and defensive behavior. *Child Development* 44, 582–90.

Kelkar, A. (1964). Marathi baby talk. *Word* 20, 40–54.

*Klein, R. (1974). Word order: Dutch children and their mothers. Publication 9, Institute for General Linguistics, University of Amsterdam.

*Kobashigawa, B. (1969). Repetitions in a mother's speech to her child. *Working Paper* 14, Language-Behavior Research Laboratory, University of California, Berkeley.

Konnor, M. (1972). Aspects of the developmental ethology of a foraging people. In N. Blurton Jones (ed.), *Ethological studies of child behaviour*. London: Cambridge University Press.

Krones, R. (n.d.). How to use the pitch extractor with the computer. Unpublished paper, University of California, Berkeley. Mimeo.

Krupa, V. & Altmann, G. (1961). Semantic analysis of the system of personal pronouns in Indonesian language. *Archiv Orientalni* 29, 620–25.

Labov, W. (1968). A proposed program for research and training in the study of language. (Copies available from author.)

Labov, W. (1970). The study of language in its social context. *Studium Generale* 23, 30–87.

Labov, W. (1971a). Methodology. In W.O. Dingwall (ed.), *A survey of linguistic science*. College Park: University of Maryland.

Labov, W. (1971b). On the adequacy of natural languages: I. the development of tense. Unpublished paper, University of Pennsylvania. Mimeo.

Labov, W. (1972). Some principles of linguistic methodology. *Language in Society* 1, 97–120.

Lakoff, G. (1972). Hedges: a study in meaning criteria and the logic of fuzzy concepts. *Papers from the Eighth Regional Meeting of the Chicago Linguistic Society*. Chicago: Linguistics Department, University of Chicago.

Lambert, W. (1967). The use of 'tu' and 'vous' as forms of address in French Canada: a pilot study. *Journal of Verbal Learning and Verbal Behavior* 6, 614–7.

Larsen, K. (1949). Huasteco baby talk. *El Mexico Antigua* 7, 295–8.

Lawton, D. (1964). Social class differences in group discussions. *Language and Speech* 7, 183–204.

Lee, L.L. (1974). *Developmental sentence analysis: a grammatical assessment procedure for speech and language clinicians*. Evanston, Illinois: Northwestern University Press.

Lehiste, I. (1970). *Suprasegmentals*. Boston: MIT Press.

Lehiste, I. and Peterson, G.E. (1961). Some basic considerations in the analysis of intonation. *Journal of the Acoustical Society of America* 33, 419–25.

Leopold, W.F. (1939–49). *Speech development of a bilingual child*. 4 vols. Evanston, Illinois: Northwestern University Press.

Levelt, W.J.M. (1975). What became of LAD? *Peter de Ridder Publications in Cognition I*. Lisse, Netherlands: Peter de Ridder Press.

Lewis, M. (1936). *Infant speech: a study of the beginning of language*. New York: Harcourt–Brace.

*Lewis, M. & Freedle, R. (1973). Mother–infant dyad: the cradle of meaning. In P. Pliner, L. Krames & T. Alloway (eds.), *Communication and affect, language and thought*. New York: Academic Press.

Liberman, A.M., Cooper, F.S., Shankweiler, D.P. & Studdert-Kennedy, M. (1967). Perception of the speech code. *Psychological Review* 74, 431–61.

Lieberman, P. (1967). *Intonation, perception and language*. Cambridge, Massachusetts: MIT Press.

*Lieven, E. (1976). Conversations between mothers and young children: individual differences and their possible implications for the study of language learning. In N. Waterson & C. Snow (eds.), *The development of communication: social and pragmatic factors in language acquisition*. Wiley & Sons. (In press.)

Lind, G. (1971). A preliminary study of the pronouns of address in Swedish. *Stanford Occasional Papers in Linguistics* no. 1, Stanford University, Stanford, California.

Lindesmith, A.R., Strauss, A.L. & Denzin, N.K. (1975). *Social Psychology* (4th edition). New York: Dryden (Holt, Rinehart & Winston).

Linke, C.E. (1953). A study of pitch characteristics of female voices and their relationship to vocal effectiveness. Doctoral dissertation, University of Iowa.

Lord, C. (1975). Is talking to baby more than baby talk? Paper presented at Meeting of the Society for Research in Child Development, Denver, Colorado.

Luria, A.R. (1959). The directive function of speech in development and dissolution. I, II, *Word* 15, 341–52, 453–64.

Macnamara, J. (1972). Cognitive basis of language learning in infants. *Psychological Review* 79, 1–13.

Makkai, A. & Makkai, B. (eds.). (1975). *The first LACUS forum 1974*. Columbia, South Carolina: Hornbeam Press Incorporated

Malkiel, Y. (1962). Etymology and general linguistics. *Word* 18, 198–219.

Markey, J.F. (1928). *The symbolic process and its development in children: a study in social psychology*. New York: Harcourt–Brace.

McKaughan, H. (1959). Semantic components of pronoun systems: Maranao. *Word* 15, 101–02.

McNeill, D. (1966a). The creation of language by children. In J. Lyons & R.J. Wales (eds.), *Psycholinguistic Papers*. Edinburgh: Edinburgh University Press.

McNeill, D. (1966b). Developmental psycholinguistics. In F. Smith & G.A. Miller (eds.), *The genesis of language: A psycholinguistic approach*. Cambridge, Massachusetts: MIT Press.

McNeill, D. (1970). *The acquisition of language: the study of developmental psycholinguistics*. New York: Harper & Row.

Mead, M. (1928). *Coming of age in Samoa*. New York: William Morrow.

Mead, M. (1930). *Growing up in New Guinea*. New York: William Morrow.

Meillet, A. (1921). Quelques remarques sur des mots français. *Bulletin de la Société de Linguistique de Paris* 22, 166–8.

Menyuk, P. (1964). Alternation of rules in children's grammar. *Journal of Verbal Learning and Verbal Behaviour* 3, 480–8.

Menyuk, P. (1969). *Sentences children use*. Cambridge, Massachusetts: MIT Press.

Miller, W.R. (1970). A note on baby talk in the Western Desert Language of Australia. Unpublished mimeograph.

Milner, G.B. (1961). The Samoan vocabulary of respect. *Journal of the Royal Anthropological Institute of Great Britain and Ireland* 91, 296–317.

Minturn, L. & Lambert, W.W. (1964). *Mothers of six cultures*. New York: Wiley & Sons.

Mitchell-Kernan, C. & Kernan, K.T. (1975). Children's insults: America and Samoa. In M. Sanches & B. Blount (eds.), *Sociocultural dimensions of language use*. New York: Academic Press.

Moerk, E. (1972). Principles of interaction in language learning. *Merrill-Palmer Quarterly* 18, 229–57.

Moerk, E. (1974). Changes in verbal child–mother interactions with increasing language skills of the child. *Journal of Psycholinguistic Research* 3, 101–16.

Moffitt, A.R. (1971). Consonant cue perception by twenty- to twenty-four-week-old infants. *Child Development* 42, 717–31.

Morse, P.A. (1972). The discrimination of speech and non-speech stimuli in early infancy. *Journal of Experimental Child Psychology* 14, 477–92.

Mühlenbach, K., Endzelin, J., Hausenberg, E. *K. Mühlenbachs Lettisch–deutsches Wörterbuch. Redigiert, ergänzt und fortgesetzt von J. Endzelin*, 1–4, Riga 1923–1932, and J. Endzelin und E. Hausenberg, *Ergänzungen, und Berichtigungen zu K. Mühlenbachs Lettisch–deutschem Wörterbuch*, 1–2, Riga 1934–1946.

Nelson, K. (1973). Structure and strategy in learning to talk. *Monographs of the Society for Research in Child Development* no. 149 38, nos. 1 and 2.

Nelson, K.E. (1975). Facilitating children's syntax acquisition. Unpublished paper, New School for Social Research. Mimeo.

Nelson, K.E., Carskaddon, G. & Bonvillian, J. (1973). Syntax acquisition: impact of experimental variation in adult verbal interaction with the child. *Child Development* **44**, 497–504.

Newport, E. (1976). Motherese: the speech of mothers to young children. In N. Castellan, D. Pisoni & G. Potts (eds.), *Cognitive Theory:* vol. II. Hillsdale, New Jersey: Lawrence Erlbaum Associates.

Newport, E.L. & Ashbrook, E. (1976). The emergence of semantic relations in American Sign Language. University of California. Mimeo.

Newport, E., Gleitman, L. & Gleitman, H. (1975). A study of mothers' speech and child language acquisition. *Papers and Reports on Child Language Development* no. 10, Stanford University, Stanford, California.

Payne, A. (n.d.). The reorganization of linguistic rules: a preliminary report. *Pennsylvania Working Papers* **I** (6).

Peters, A.M. (1974). The beginnings of speech. *Papers and Reports on Child Language Development* no. 8, Stanford University, Stanford, California.

Peterson, G.E. & Barney, H.L. (1952). Control methods used in a study of vowels. *Journal of the Acoustical Society of America* **24**, 175–84.

*Pfuderer, C. (1969). Some suggestions for a syntactic characterization of baby-talk style. *Working Paper* **14**, Language-Behavior Research Laboratory, University of California, Berkeley.

Phillips, J. (1970). Formal characteristics of speech which mothers address to their young children. Doctoral dissertation, Johns Hopkins University.

*Phillips, J. (1973). Syntax and vocabulary of mothers' speech to young children: age and sex comparisons. *Child Development* **44**, 182–5.

Piaget, J. (1951). *Play, dreams and imitation in childhood*. New York: Norton.

Pierce, J.E. (1974). A study of 750 Portland, Oregon children during the first year. *Papers and Reports on Child Language Development* no. 8, Stanford University, Stanford, California.

Pike, K.L. (1973). Sociolinguistic evaluation of alternative mathematical models: English pronouns. *Language* **49**, 121–35.

Pike, K.L. & Lowe, I. (1969). Pronominal reference in English conversation and discourse – a group theoretical treatment. *Folia Linguistica* **3**, 68–106.

Port, D.K. & Preston, M.S. (1972). Early apical stop production: a voice onset time analysis. Status Report on Speech Research, SR-29/30, Haskins Laboratories, New Haven, Connecticut.

Posner, M.I. & Keele, S.W. (1968). On the genesis of abstract ideas. *Journal of Experimental Psychology* **77**, 353–63.

Potter, S. (1959). *Lifesmanship*. London: Rupert Hart-Davis.

von Raffler-Engel, W. (1973). The development from sound to phoneme in child language. In C.A. Ferguson & D. Slobin (eds.), *Studies of child language development*. New York: Holt, Rinehart & Winston.

Read, A.W. (1946). The social setting of hypocoristic English (so-called baby talk). Paper read at the annual meeting of the Modern Language Society. (Copies available from author.)

Reid, T.B.W. (1956). Linguistics, Structuralism and Philology. *Archivum Linguisticum* **8**, 28–37.

*Remick, H. (1971). The maternal environment of linguistic development. Doctoral dissertation, University of California, Davis.

Remick, H. (1976). Maternal speech to children during language acquisition. In W. von Raffler-Engel & Y. Lebrun (eds.), *Baby talk and infant speech*. Lisse, Netherlands: Swets & Zeitlinger.

Report of the contemporary Russian Language Analysis Project (1972). Colchester: University of Essex Language Centre.

Ringler, N., Kennell, K., Jarvella, R., Navojosky, B. & Klaus, M. (1975). Mother-to-child speech at 2 years — effects of early post-natal contact. *Journal of Pediatrics* 86, 141—4.

Rosch, E.H. (1973a). On the internal structure of perceptual and semantic categories. In T.E. Moore (ed.), *Cognitive Development and the Acquisition of Language*. New York: Wiley & Sons.

Rosch, E.H. (1973b). Natural categories. *Cognitive Psychology* 4, 328—50.

Rosch, E. & Mervis, C.B. (1976a). Children's sorting: a reinterpretation based on the nature of abstraction in natural categories. *Developmental Psychology*. (In press.)

Rosch, E. & Mervis, C.B. (1976b). Family resemblances: studies in the internal structure of categories. *Cognitive Psychology*. (In press.)

Rosch, E., Mervis, C.B., Gray, W., Johnson, D. & Boyes-Braem, P. (1976). Basic objects in natural categories. *Cognitive Psychology* 8, 382—439.

Ruhm, H.B., Mencke, E.O., Milburn, B., Cooper, Jr., W.A. & Rose, D.E. (1966). Differential sensitivity to duration of acoustic stimuli. *Journal of Speech and Hearing Research* 9, 371—84.

Rūķe-Draviņa, V. (1959). *Diminutive im Lettischen*. (*Acta Universitatis Stockholmiensis, Études de Philologie Slave* 8). London: H. Ohlssons Boktryckeri.

Rūķe-Draviņa, V. (1961). Ns. lastenhoitajain Kielestä ('On so-called nursery language'). *Virittäjä* 1, 85—91.

Rūķe-Draviņa, V. (1972). Individual and cultural variations in young children's ability to describe an event with the help of test-pictures. Paper presented at the 3rd International Congress of Applied Linguistics, Copenhagen.

Rūķe-Draviņa, V. (1973). The ability of Swedish—Latvian bilingual teenagers to describe events. Paper presented at the Symposium on Child Language, Belgrade.

Rūķe-Draviņa, V. (1976). Gibt es Universalien in der Ammensprache? *Salzburger Beiträge zur Linguistik* 2, 3—16.

Sabar, Y. (1974). Nursery rhymes and baby words in the Jewish Neo-Aramic dialect of Kaksh (Iraq). *Journal of the American Oriental Society* 94, 329—36.

*Sachs, J., Brown, Rt, & Salerno, R.A. (1976). Adults' speech to children. In W. von Raffler-Engel & Y. Lebrun (eds.), *Baby talk and infant speech*. Lisse, Netherlands: Swets & Zeitlinger.

*Sachs, J. & Devin, J. (1976). Young children's use of age-appropriate speech styles. *Journal of Child Language* 3, 81—98.

Sankoff, G. & Laberge, S. (1973). On the acquisition of language by native speakers. *Kivung* 6, 32—47.

Sapir, E. (1929). Nootka baby words. *International Journal of American Linguistics* 5, 118—9.

Schafer, P. (1922). Beobachtungen und Versuche an einem Kinde. *Zeitschrift Pädegogische Psychologie* 23, 269—89.

Searle, J.R. (1975). Indirect speech acts. In P. Cole & J. Morgan (eds.), *Syntax and semantics*, vol. III. New York: Academic Press.

Searle, J.R. (1969). *Speech acts: an essay in the philosophy of language.* New York: Cambridge University Press.

Sendak, M. (1967). *Higglety pigglety pop! or there must be more to life.* New York: Harper & Row.

Seuren, P.A.M. (1969). *Operators and nucleus.* London: Cambridge University Press.

Shatz, M. (1975). On understanding messages: a study in the comprehension of indirect directives. Doctoral dissertation, University of Pennsylvania.

*Shatz, M. & Gelman, R. (1973). The development of communication skills: modifications in the speech of young children as a function of listener. *Monographs of the Society for Research in Child Development* no. 152, 38, no. 5.

Shipley, E.S., Smith, C.S. & Gleitman, L.R. (1969). A study in the acquisition of language: free responses to commands. *Language* 45, 322–42.

Shuy, R.W. & Fasold, R.W. (eds.). (1973). *Language attitudes: current trends and prospects.* Washington, D.C.: Georgetown University Press.

Skinner, B.F. (1957). *Verbal Behavior.* New York: Appleton–Century–Crofts.

Slobin, D.I. (1963). Some aspects of the use of pronouns in Yiddish. *Word* 19, 193–202.

Slobin, D.I. (1967). *A field guide for the cross-cultural study of the acquisition of communicative competence.* Berkeley: ASUC Bookstore, University of California.

Slobin, D.I. (1968). Early grammatical development in several languages with special attention to soviet research. *Working Paper* 11, Language-Behavior Research Laboratory, University of California, Berkeley.

*Slobin, D.I. (1969). Questions of language development in cross-cultural perspective. *Working Paper* 14, Language-Behavior Research Laboratory, University of California, Berkeley.

Slobin, D.I. (1973a). Cognitive prerequisites for the development of grammar. In C.A. Ferguson & D.I. Slobin (eds.), *Studies of child language development.* New York: Holt, Rinehart & Winston.

Slobin, D.I. (1973b). Studies of imitation and comprehension. In C.A. Ferguson & D.I. Slobin (eds.), *Studies of child language development.* New York: Holt, Rinehart & Winston.

Slobin, D.I. (1975). The more it changes . . . : on understanding language by watching it move through time. *Papers and Reports on Child Language Development* no. 10, 1–30. Stanford University, Stanford, California.

Smith, M.E. (1926). An investigation of the development of the sentence and the extent of vocabularly in young children. *University of Iowa Studies in Child Welfare* 3, 5.

Snidecor, J.C. (1951). The pitch and duration characteristics of superior female speakers during oral reading. *Journal of Speech and Hearing Disorders* 16, 44–52.

*Snow, C.E. (1972). Mothers' speech to children learning language. *Child Development* 43, 549–65.

Snow, C.E. (1977). The development of conversation between mothers and babies. *Journal of Child Language.* (In press.)

Snow, C., Arlman-Rupp, A., Hassing, Y., Jobse, J., Joosten, J. & Vorster, J. (1976). Mothers' speech in three social classes. *Journal of Psycholinguistic Research* 5, 1–20.

Stern, D.N. (1971). A micro-analysis of mother—infant interaction. *Journal of the American Academy of Child Psychiatry* **10**, 501—17.

Stratton, P. & Connolly, K. (1973). Discrimination by newborns of the intensity, frequency and temporal characteristics of auditory stimuli. *British Journal of Psychology* **64**, 219—32.

Stott, L.H. (1935). Time-errors in the discrimination of short tonal durations. *Journal of Experimental Psychology* **18**, 741—66.

Stouffer, S. (1950). Some observations on study design. *American Journal of Sociology* **55**, 356—9.

Suseendirarajah, S. (1973). Pronouns in Batticoala Tamil. *Anthropological Linguistics* **15**(4), 172—83.

Templin, M.C. (1957). *Certain language skills in children: their development and interrelations*. Minneapolis: University of Minnesota Press.

Thomas, D. (1955). Three analyses of the Ilocano pronoun system. *Word* **11**, 204—08.

Tonkova-Yampol'skaya, R.V. (1968). Razvitiye rechevoy intonatsii u detey pervykh dvukh let zhinzni. *Voprosy psikhologii* **14**, 94—101. Translated from Russian in *Soviet Psychology* **7**, (1969) 48—54.

Trager, G.L. (1967). A componential morphemic analysis of English personal pronouns. *Language* **43**, 372—8.

Trehub, S. & Rabinovitch, M.S. (1972). Auditory—linguistic sensitivity in early infancy. *Developmental Psychology* **6**, 74—7.

Tulkin, S. & Kagan, J. (1972). Mother—child interaction in the first year of life. *Child Development* **43**, 31—42.

Van der Geest, T. (1974a). *Evaluation of theories on child grammar*. The Hague: Mouton.

Van der Geest, T. (1974b). Language acquisition as a hidden curriculum. *Communication and Cognition* **7**, 169—90.

Van der Geest, T. (1975a). Review of: C.A. Ferguson & D.I. Slobin (eds.), *Studies in child language development*. *Foundations of Language*. (In press.)

Van der Geest, T. (1975b). Revision of word order in child language. Unpublished paper, University of Amsterdam. Mimeo.

Van der Geest, T. (1975c). *Some aspects of communicative competence and their implications for language acquisition*. Assen/Amsterdam: Royal van Gorcum.

Van der Geest, T., Gerstel, R., Appel, R. & Tervoort, B. (1973). *The child's communicative competence*. The Hague: Mouton.

Van der Geest, T., Snow, C. & Drewes, A. (1973). Developmental aspects of mother—child conversation. Unpublished paper, University of Amsterdam. Mimeo.

Voegelin, C.F. & Robinett, F.M. (1954). 'Mother language' in Hidatsa. *International Journal of American Linguistics* **20**, 65—70.

Vorster, J. (1975). Mommy linguist: the case for motherese. *Lingua* **37**, 281—312.

Waterson, N. (1971). Child phonology: a prosodic view. *Journal of Linguistics* **7**, 179—211.

Webster, B. (1972). The comprehension and production of the anaphoric pronouns 'he, she, him, her' in normal and linguistically deviant children. Master's thesis, San Jose State University.

Webster, B. & Ingram, D. (1972). The comprehension and production of the anaphoric pronouns 'he, she, him, her' in normal and linguistically deviant children. *Papers and Reports on Child Language Development* no. 4. Stanford University, Stanford, California.

Webster, R.L., Steinhardt, M.H. & Senter, M.G. (1972). Changes in infants' vocalizations as a function of differential acoustic stimulation. *Developmental Psychology* 7, 39—43.

Weeks, T. (1971). Speech registers in young children. *Child Development* 42, 1119—31.

Weeks, T. (1973). A note on Sahaptin baby talk. *Papers and Reports on Child Language Development* 5, 65—7. Stanford University, Stanford, California.

Weir, R. (1962). *Language in the crib*. The Hague: Mouton.

Wells, G. (1974). Learning to code experience through language. *Journal of Child Language* 1, 243—69.

Whiting, B. (ed.) (1963). *Six cultures: studies of child rearing*. New York: Wiley & Sons.

Whiting, J.W.M. (1941). *Becoming a Kwoma*. New Haven: Yale University Press.

Whiting, J.W.M. *et al.* (1966). *Field guide for a study of socialization*. New York: Wiley & Sons.

Whiting, B.B. & Whiting, J.W.M. (1975). *Children of six cultures: a psychocultural analysis*. Cambridge, Massachusetts: Harvard University Press.

Wijeyewardene, G. (1968). Address, abuse and animal categories in northern Thailand. *Man* n.s. 3, 76—93.

Wonderly, W.L. (1952). Semantic components in Kechua person morphemes. *Language* 28. 366—76.

Young, F.M. (1942*a*). Certain social indices in the language of preschool subjects. *Journal of Genetic Psychology* 61, 109—23.

Young, F.M. (1942*b*). Development as indicated by a study of pronouns. *Journal of Genetic Psychology* 61, 125—34.

Bibliography

ELAINE S. ANDERSEN

Department of Linguistics, Stanford University

The annotations which follow cover a substantial proportion, though far from all, of the recent work on language input to children. The annotations are descriptive, rather than evaluative. They summarize the design of each study, the nature of the data, and provide some of the results and conclusions. In general, the studies treat four closely related questions: the nature of input language; the effect of the child's own language on the input he receives; the acquisition of 'mothers' speech' as a sociolinguistic skill; and the relation of such modified speech to the language acquisition process. Items numbered 3, 4, 5, 6, 7, 14, 16, 17, 19, 21, 23, 24, 26, 27, 31 and 33 deal mainly with the first question; 9 and 10 are reviews of a good part of this literature; and 2, 11, 12, 18 and 22 present cross-cultural data. Numbers 20 and 25 treat the second topic, while numbers 1, 15, 28 and 30 cover the work that has been done on the third. The remaining articles (i.e. 8, 13, 29, 32 and 34) represent preliminary approaches to the last and perhaps most important question: the significance of the specialized nature of input language for the process of acquiring a first language.

1. Andersen, E. & Johnston, C.E. (1973). Modifications in the speech of an eight-year-old to younger children. *Stanford Occasional Papers in Linguistics* no. 3, 149–60.

   This pilot study examines the speech of an eight-year-old to an adult, to a peer, and to children five, three and one and one-half years old, in three different linguistic environments: telling a story, explaining a task and free play. Speech samples were analyzed along several of the dimensions on which adults have been found to modify their speech to children, including rate and fluency, syntactic complexity, pitch and intonation. As in the adult studies, the subject's speech to younger children was found to be characterized by slower rate, greater fluency, less complex surface structure, higher pitch and exaggerated intonation contours. The data also suggest a distinct story-telling register.

2. Blount, B.G. (1972*b*). Parental speech and language acquisition: some Luo and Samoan examples. *Anthropological Linguistics* 14, 119–30.

   One of the few cross-cultural studies published, this analysis of adult—child dialogues in Samoan (mother and elder sister to one boy aged 2; 6) and in Luo (father and research assistant to one boy and one girl, both 2; 6) classifies input utterances by sentence type. Interrogatives are divided into 11 different subtypes (e.g. What [equational], What [verbal], Who, Where, Why) and declaratives are categorized as Active or Imitative. It is found that speech to children patterns similarly in these two quite different cultures: interrrogatives are the most frequent sentence type, followed by imperatives and declaratives. The suggestion is made that differences between this speech and adult conversation are a result of different social definitions and constraints: in adult—child interaction, a hierarchical relationship is established which gives the adult superordinate position and the role of conversation initiator. This may also explain differences in choice of interrogative type between this data and that in an American sample, where children seem to be allocated 'conversational peer status'. It is concluded that adults universally adjust their speech for children in relation to the child's social status and linguistic competence.

3. Broen, P. (1972). The verbal environment of the language-learning child. *Monograph of American Speech and Hearing Association* no. 17, December.

The subjects of this study were ten mothers, each of whom had one young language-learning child (between 18 and 26 months) and one older, linguistically more advanced child (over 45 months). Speech to these children during both free play and story-telling situations, as well as informal conversation with the experimenter, was analyzed and compared on several measures: rate of speech (words/minute), rate of disfluency, diversity of vocabulary (type—token ratio), percent of repetition, percent of overlap in sentences used by different mothers and pause placement. There were some differences associated with the speaking tasks, but in general, mothers' speech to the younger children was slower, more fluent, and contained less diverse vocabulary and more repetition; sentence boundaries were clearly marked by pauses (unlike adult—adult speech); and sentence type seemed to indicate two basic patterns (an imperative form and a naming frame). The monograph includes detailed appendices of individual subject data, coded protocols (with coding rules), sentence types used (actual sample sentences) and repetitions and sequential sentences from the data.

4. Bynon, J. (1968). Berber nursery language. *Transactions of the Philological Society* 107—61.

From a corpus of 100 lexical items collected by an adult male Berber informant, an analysis is made of the characteristic features of Berber nursery language, followed by a discussion of its function and origins. A comparison to standard language reveals: (1) a higher percentage of vowels and geminates, and a greater frequency of uvular and pharyngeal consonants (found also in other registers for their 'expressive value'); (2) two or three special suffixes which perform no essential grammatical role but probably carry attitudinal information; (3) a higher frequency of open syllables; (4) a strong tendency toward reduplication; (5) meanings clustered around a small number of semantic fields (e.g. foodstuffs, domestic animals, body parts). This language is used only by adults or older children in addressing young children to age three (and by the infant), for the purpose of 'teaching them how to talk'. The origin of a high proportion of these words appears to be the standard language, though the opposite process is also found, especially in kinship terminology.

5. Cherry, L. Sex differences in preschool teacher–child verbal interaction. Doctoral dissertation, Harvard University, 1974. Reported in: *Child Development*, 1975, 46, 532–5.

This dissertation on differential socialization of preschool girls and boys examines the spontaneous verbal interaction between four female preschool teachers and the children (aged 2; 9 to 4; 5) in their classes. The author tested the four following hypotheses, based on findings of other studies: (1) teachers would verbally interact more with boys than with girls; (2) teachers would be more likely to initiate a verbal interaction with a boy than with a girl; (3) there would be no difference in the syntactic complexity as measured by mean length of utterance of teachers' speech to girls and boys; (4) teachers would have different verbal interactional styles with girls and boys – including a greater proportion of attentional markers, directives, repetitions and verbal acknowledgments to boys, but more fluent speech to girls (i.e. longer and more reciprocal) and a higher proportion of teacher-initiated speech. The first three hypotheses were confirmed. The fourth was partially confirmed: teachers' speech to boys contained more attentional markers and directives; speech to girls contained more verbal acknowledgments. Results confirmed the fact that there are patterns of differential socialization for girls and boys through their verbal interaction with preschool teachers.

6. Cherry, L. & Lewis, M. (1976). Mothers and two-year-olds: a study of sex-differentiated verbal interactions. In N. Waterson & C. Snow (eds.), *The development of communication: social and pragmatic factors in language acquisition*. Wiley & Sons. (In press.)

Tape recordings were made of 12 upper middle class mothers interacting spontaneously with their two-year-old children (six male, six female) in a laboratory playroom. To examine whether there are differences in verbal interactional style related to sex of child, such as those found in earlier studies of mother–infant dyads (see 18, below) the investigators did a sex of child analysis on 12 verbal measures. Results showed (*a*) four significant differences and (*b*) several non-significant trends: (*a*) mothers of girls talked more (i.e. greater number of utterances), were more likely to ask questions and use other-repetition, and had greater MLUs; and (*b*) mothers of girls used more verbal acknowledgment and talked more as measured by number of turns, whereas mothers of boys used more directives; moreover girls talked more than boys as measured by number of both utterances and turns. These findings support those of studies with younger children. It is suggested that mothers of girls may be placing greater demands on their daughters to become involved in conversational exchanges, while mothers of boys may be encouraging their sons to act in a non-verbal fashion.

7. Crawford, J.M. (1970). Cocopa baby talk. *International Journal of American Linguistics* 36, 9–13.

The author presents a rather limited corpus of baby talk in Cocopa (a Yuman language spoken along the lower Colorado River in Arizona and Mexico), elicited from one female adult informant during one session. Based on this data, a comparison is made of the consonant inventories of baby speech and adult speech, revealing that the former is considerably reduced. The more specific nature of baby talk replacement is then

described, and instances of agreement between these replacements and re-
constructed consonants of Proto-Yuman are discussed. The suggestion is
made that baby speech may be more stable than adult speech.

8. Cross, T. (1976). Motherese: its association with the rate of syntactic acquisition in young children. In N. Waterson & C. Snow (eds.), *The development of communication: social and pragmatic factors in language acquisition.* Wiley & Sons. (In press.)

   This study was designed: (*a*) to test the prediction that degree of speech
   modification in a child's linguistic environment is associated with the pace
   of syntactic development; and (*b*) to specify which features of input serve
   a facilitative role in acquisition. Subjects (16 middle class mother—child
   dyads) were divided into two groups (mean age difference of 6.5 months)
   by putting the older child of pairs matched for MLU into a 'normally-
   developing' group, and the younger child into a language 'accelerated'
   group. From each mother's speech sample of 300 utterances (recorded
   during spontaneous, 'at home' mother—child conversations), percentages
   of 30 syntactic, semantic, discourse and fluency features were calculated
   and compared for the two groups. While no significant differences were
   found in measures of syntactic modification, the most significant group
   differences indicated that rapid acquisition was most closely related to the
   incidence of utterances in mothers' speech that were semantically similar
   to the semantic intention of the child's preceding utterance (s).

9. Dodd, D.H. & Glanzer, P.D. (1973). Environmental factors in early language
   acquisition. Unpublished paper, University of Utah. Mimeo.

   The authors critically review a wide range of literature relating to the
   effects of environmental factors in first language learning theory (emphasis
   on association principles); from linguistic theory (emphasis on innate capacities); and from cognitive theory (emphasis on the nature of input, the
   primacy of semantics and strategies of processing language data). A model
   similar to Farwell (1973) is proposed, with the child's innate facilities and
   varied aspects of his linguistic and non-linguistic environment all interacting in the process of acquisition. The need for further research into the
   nature of necessary or even helpful environmental factors is presented.

10. Farwell, C.B. (1973). The language spoken to children. *Papers and Reports
    on Child Language Development* no. 5, 31—62. Stanford University, Stan-
    ford, California.

    This thorough review of some of the most important work on language
    input to children deals with three very basic and interdependent issues: the
    author questions the general linguistic approach of the sixties on several
    theoretical points concerning language acquisition; she discusses the prob-
    lems involved in determining what might be the minimum input from
    which the child can learn language; and she summarizes the observations
    which have been made and the early studies carried out on the actual
    nature of language addressed to the child. Particular attention is given to
    work done by Ferguson (1964), to studies in the Berkeley Language Behav-
    ior Laboratory Working Paper (1969), and to the longitudinal investiga-
    tions of Brown and his colleagues at Harvard on the relations between
    parent and child speech. The author points out several interesting questions
    for future research.

11. Ferguson, C.A. (1964). Baby talk in six languages. *American Anthropologist*
    66 (6 part 2), 103—14.

This paper compares and contrasts general features of baby talk found in six linguistically and culturally different language communities: (Syrian) Arabic, Marathi, Comanchi, Gilyak, (American) English and Spanish. The author begins with the assumptions that baby talk is relatively stable and conventionalized, and is culturally transmitted (as opposed to universal and innate), most often being initiated by adults. He then divides the kinds of adjustments which take place in this subsystem of language into prosodic phenomena, phonological and grammatical modifications of normal language, and use of a special set of lexical items, focussing his discussion on specific examples of these last two characteristics. Also considered are the functions baby talk may serve, the variability which exists within and across cultures as to the exact form of baby talk and attitudes toward its use, and the special nature of its diffusion.

12. Fischer, J.L. (1970). Linguistic socialization: Japan and the United States. In R. Hill & R. König (eds), *Families in East and West*. The Hague: Mouton.

The notion of 'linguistic socialization', or learning the culture-appropriate use of language, as distinguished from simple language learning, is discussed. The author compares the aspects of linguistic socialization in the U.S. with those found in a study of Japanese middle class school children and offers an explanation for these differences in terms of cultural differences in family and social structure. Japanese mothers tend to talk less to their children (and children talk later), be more favorably disposed to use of baby talk (considering it easier for the child to pronounce and understand), and allow relatively longer use of baby talk (which may serve to signify the continuation of childhood status). Specific examples are longer delay in use of personal pronouns and the substitution of /č/ for /s/ in certain pronouns and terms of address. Cultural differences — which may account for contrasts — include hierarchical emphasis in Japan in contrast to egalitarian emphasis in the US (cf. Blount), and stress on cooperation as opposed to individualism.

13. Friedlander, B. (1968). The effect of speaker identity, voice inflection, vocabulary, and message redundancy on infants' selection of vocal reinforcement. *Journal of Experimental Child Psychology* 6, 443–59.

An experiment was designed to investigate the development of voice and listening discrimination in normal infants. Innovative methodology, using behavior analysis toys which offer selection between pairs of prerecorded voices and other audio reinforcements, made possible statistical analysis of selective listening of three infant boys (aged 11–15 months), during 300 separate play sessions in a naturalistic home setting. Findings included: (1) preference for mother's voice over simple musical feedback; (2) discriminative selection between stranger's and mother's voice; (3) shifting preferences related to variations of inflection, vocabulary, and speaker's identity, as well as to degree of feedback redundancy.

14. Garnica, O.K. (1974). Some characteristics of prosodic input to young children. Doctoral dissertation, Stanford University.

This study was designed to provide experimental evidence for distinguishing prosodic characteristics of speech to young children. Two groups of female speakers each performed several verbal tasks during two sessions. In one session speech was directed to another adult, and in the other to the speaker's own two-year-old or five-year-old child. Measurements of

fundamental frequency and duration were made on a subsample of sentences from each session. In comparison with the speech to the adult, speech
to the two-year-olds was characterized by higher average fundamental frequency, a greater frequency range, longer duration of content words, rising
pitch terminals in declarative and imperative sentences, and two primary
stresses in some sentences. Speech to the five-year-olds was characterized
by a greater frequency range and longer duration of some content words.
These characteristics of speech directed to the young child can be seen to
serve two functions: (1) a social function, to capture and retain the child's
attention to the adult's speech; (2) an analytic function, to aid the child in
its linguistic analysis by emphasizing key words and specifying the constituents of sentences.

15. Gleason, J. Berko (1973). Code switching in children's language. In T.E.
Moore (ed.), *Cognitive Development and the Acquisition of language*. New
York: Academic Press.

The author discusses observational findings of a study of natural conversations in five similarly constituted families with at least three children
each: a first- or second-grader (6—8 years old); a preschool child (4 or 5
years); and a child under age 3. Although the main purpose was to investigate the child's emerging control of different styles, language of adults to
children is also briefly described; in addition to the expected baby talk
style, a 'language of socialization' was found directed to four- to eight-
year-olds. Among children, stylistic variation was observed from the earliest
ages, the first being a distinction between speech to family, but silence to
strangers. Preschool children code-switched between mothers (whining),
peers (verbal play), and adult friends (discursive tales). By age 8, children
were seen to have learned formal adult speech, baby talk style and the
language of socialization.

16. Holzman, M. (1974). The verbal environment provided by mothers for their
very young children. *Merrill-Palmer Quarterly* 20, 31—42.

This paper compares aspects of the verbal environment which four
mothers provide for their children in middle and lower socio-economic
class homes, to ascertain the existence of certain class differences in
linguistic input which might be operational in causing 'intellectual' developmental differences. Two of the mothers are highly educated (middle class),
while two have no more than high school education (upper lower class);
the children are two boys and two girls ranging in age from 1; 3—2; 3. Data
are verbatim records of the verbal interaction of each mother—child pair,
with results based on two samples of 100 verbalizations from each mother
at the time when her child's MLU was two morphemes. The analysis
covers: (1) discourse structure of different elliptical forms and non-
elliptical sentences; (2) pragmatics (frequency of verbalizations with implicit directions for behavior as opposed to direct orders — the latter considered a possible cause of language deficit); (3) content areas taught by
mothers (e.g. names of objects, counting); (4) contexts provided for directions (e.g. moral or aesthetic valuations). Except for the presence of non-
standard utterances in the speech of lower class mothers, there are no findings of difference in verbal environment related to SES.

17. Jocic, Mirjana. (1976). Types of adaptations in adult speech when communicating with a child. In N. Waterson & C. Snow (eds.), *The development of
communication: social and pragmatic factors in language acquisition*.
Wiley & Sons. (In press.)

Data on syntactic and morpho-semantic adaptations in the child-directed speech of 10 Serbo-Croatian-speaking adults were gathered from diaries of four individual children (age 0; 6 to 4; 0) and three pairs of twins (age 1; 3 to 3; 0); the adult subjects were of high socio-cultural background and were all closely associated with the children with whom they interacted. Syntactic modifications (numerous examples given) included: use of nouns instead of personal pronouns, along with finite verbal forms; use of first person plural in place of first and second person singular (present tense); omission of the verb copula *jesam*; omission of the particles *li* and *da* and the interrogative expression *da li*; use of 'special' imperatives and questions; and changes in word-order. The morpho-semantic features noted were: a large number of diminutives, of hypocoristics and of modified lexemes of a 'universal kind' (i.e. 'baby talk'); and use of lexemes created by the individual child as part of the familiar code. The author suggests that the bases for these speech modifications lie in the emotional relationship between child and adult, their different cognitive and experimental capacities, and the need to communicate successfully — the stronger the emotional tie or the more the adult cares for the child, the more frequent are the observed types of grammatical adaptations.

18. Klein, R. (1974). Word order: Dutch children and their mothers. Publication 9, Institute for General Linguistics, University of Amsterdam.

The author examines the word order preferences (mainly in terms of grammatical categories) of two Dutch children and their mothers. Based on speech samples ranging from 44–294 selected utterances per subject — recorded during mother–child interactions when the children were aged 2; 0 and 2; 3 — this study reports that children's productions mirror the order preferences of their mothers and that the rank order of frequencies are the same for all four subjects. The findings are compared to those discussed by Brown (1973) for English and a number of other languages, and in particular to those reported by Park (1970) for German. A new interpretation of the non-Dutch data is offered, with the general conclusion that children never produce utterances with a word order that has not been provided for them with a certain minimum frequency in their mother's speech.

19. Language-Behavior Research Laboratory. The structure of linguistic input to children. University of California, Berkeley, 1969, *Working Paper* 14.

This volume is a collection of four pioneering articles in the area of language input to children:

1. Drach, K. 'The language of the parent: a pilot study.' The author compares the speech of an adult to her own child with her speech to other adults, finding the adult–child speech to be slower, shorter in utterance length, syntactically less complex, and less variable in lexical content.

2. Kobashigawa, B. 'Repetitions in a mother's speech to her child.' Working with the same speech sample as Drach, this paper describes the amount and the nature of repetitions in a mother's speech to her child. It was found that the repetitions constituted over 30% of all utterances, usually involved various alterations of their originals, and did not seem motivated by a need to communicate.

3. Pfuderer, C. 'Some suggestions for a syntactic characterization of baby-talk style.' This study indicates that a mother's speech to her child

becomes increasingly complex during the child's second and third year. It is suggested that simplification in baby talk is directly correlated to the language production or comprehension of the child.

4. Slobin, D. 'Questions of language development in cross-cultural perspective.' The language of Black Oakland school children to their peers is compared to the language of middle class parents to their children. Speech modifications are found to be quite similar.

20. Lewis, M. & Freedle, R. (1973). Mother—infant dyad: the cradle of meaning. In P. Pliner, L. Krames & T. Alloway (eds.), *Communication and Affect, Language and Thought*. New York: Academic Press.

The hypothesis is presented that the basis of language development can be found in aspects of the communication system operating between mother and infant at 12 weeks; each member of the dyad is seen as initiating interaction (both vocalizations and gestures) and affecting the other's behavior. Data was collected from two-hour (minimum) observations of more than 80 mother—infant pairs in a naturalistic setting. The infants were all three-month-old boys and girls from different socio-economic and racial groups. Results are interpreted as indicating that this early communication network is a non-random, sequential, and situationally determined system with considerable individual differences in infant vocalizations related to sex and socio-economic status at all levels of analysis. For instance, girls are vocally more responsive to maternal behavior, and higher SES infants appear to be more 'advanced' in their vocalizations. Pointing to follow-up testing of three infants at two years, it is suggested that these differences are relevant to subsequent formal linguistic skills.

21. Lieven, E.V.M. (1976). Conversations between mothers and young children: individual differences and their possible implications for the study of language learning. In N. Waterson & C. Snow (eds.), *The development of communication: social and pragmatic factors in language acquisition*. Wiley & Sons. (In press.)

This analysis of the conversational interaction of two mother—child pairs examines individual differences in: (1) the children's utterances; (2) the speech of the mothers to them; and (3) certain features of the linguistic interchanges between the dyads. Data covers a six-month period, beginning when one child (*K*.) was 1; 6, the other (*B*.) 1; 8. While the children were similar in terms of MLU, they appeared to use language for different ends: *K*. talked slowly and clearly about objects and events in her environment, with many utterances referring to 'locative action' or 'attribution'; *B*. spoke more to get her mother's attention, and used twice as much repetition, with relatively more utterances of 'notice', 'existence', and 'recurrence'. Analysis of their mothers' speech revealed many of the expected BT features, but also differences in overall responsiveness and in types of responses: *K*.'s mother responded more often and used a higher proportion of informational responses (e.g. extensions and expansions). Evidence from the investigator's speech to the two children supports the suggestion that effects of particular styles may be two-way — that a child's conversational skills may influence the quality of input he receives.

22. Oswalt, R.L. (1976). Babytalk and the genesis of some basic Pomo words. *International Journal of American Linguistics* 42, 1—13.

Using as informants the older members (i.e. grandparents and great grandparents) of several Kashaya, Southern and Central Pomo households, the author examines a small group of non-arbitrary baby talk terms concerned with four elementary infant needs: water, food, nursing, affection. For each area of meaning he traces a progression from pure icons or sound images, through forms exhibiting increasing adjustment to the phonological patterns of the adult languages, to independent words or verbal prefixes in the adult languages, and reconstructable for Proto-Pomo. For historical comparison, a partial appraisal of the similarities between these adult Pomo forms and sample forms in other languages of the Hokan Stock is presented.

23. Phillips, J.R. (1973). Syntax and vocabulary of mothers' speech to young children: age and sex comparisons. *Child Development* 44, 182—5.

This brief article reports the result of a study designed to compare the speech of adults to children of different ages and sex with that of adults to other adults. Subjects were 30 mother—son pairs and 27 mother—daughter pairs (with children aged 8, 18, and 28 months), each recorded interacting in a free play situation. Speech samples were compared to samples of casual conversation between the mothers and the experimenter, along 10 dimensions of syntax and vocabulary. Findings indicated that speech addressed to children is syntactically less complex and contains less varied and more concrete vocabulary, with some modifications a function of the age of the addressee (beginning at some point between 8 and 18 months) but no clear sex-based differences.

24. Remick, H.L.N. (1971). The maternal environment of linguistic development. Doctoral dissertation, University of California, Davis.

A detailed study of the speech of eight mothers to their daughters (A—C), aged 16 to 30 months, as compared to speech to the investigator (A—A), found A—C characterized by: (1) fewer words/minute; (2) lower type—token ratio; (3) fewer connectives, filler words and false starts; and (4) more well marked and grammatical utterances. Other measures showing developmental trends as well as differences between A—A and A—C included: (1) average fundamental frequency (the older the child, the lower the pitch) and range; (2) percent of questions requiring either (*a*) no answer (*b*) elicitation (*c*) clarification (*d*) yes—no answer or (*e*) explanation; (3) number of question pronouns used (first *what*, then *how* and *who* questions increased with age of addressee); and (4) percent of non-present tense verbs (very low for 20—24 months). Explanations increased in frequency in speech to the older children, as did incomplete answers to questions. Sentence subjects were often omitted in A—C, while negatives within clauses were frequent in A—A and most infrequent in the mid-range of the ages studied in A—C. The findings were discussed as evidence for complexity matching by mother and child, and as showing the possibility of two types of linguistic information in relation to a model of second language teaching. A detailed methodology is given.

25. Ringler, N. (1973). Mothers' language to their young children and to adults over time. Doctoral dissertation, Case Western Reserve University.

The subjects of this dissertation research were 10 lower class mothers, speakers of Black English, each of whom was recorded interacting with her child and with an adult interviewer in controlled interviews and in free play. Samples of each mother's speech to her child were collected at Times I (child aged 1; 0) and II (child aged 2;0). Child-directed speech was found to be slower and syntactically less complex, to contain more affirmatives and questions, and to have less varied, more concrete vocabulary, with more actor and locative nouns and more action verbs (no significant differences, however, in use of fragments, complete sentences, or pronouns). Findings indicate 'nursery' language changes after the child begins to talk — modifications from Time I to Time II included the following: an increase in amount and rate of speech and in complexity; a decrease in repetition; and greater use of function words, of nouns as objects and of abstract forms. The investigator suggests that the child's speech not only is influenced by but also may influence the speech of the mother.

(See also: Ringler, N. (1975). A longitudinal study of mothers' language. Paper presented at the Third International Child Language Symposium, London, September; and Ringler *et al.*, 1975. Mother-to-child speech at 2 years — effects of early postnatal contact. *Journal of Pediatrics* 86, 141—4.)

26. Rūķe-Draviņa, V. (1959). Diminutivgebrauch auf verschiedenen Gebieten der Sprache. 2. Ammensprache. *Diminutive im Lettischen* London: H. Ohlssons Boktryckeri.

This chapter of a dissertation describes the uses of diminutives in Latvian baby talk. Latvian is rich in diminutive formations, and diminutives are especially frequent in baby talk, sometimes as much as one word in three. Unlike adult speech, diminutives are made from various word classes, and a word may have two or three diminutive suffixes. Content areas include child names, body parts, animals, clothes and food. Diminutives in baby talk often do not refer to size but express affection or simply designate objects for the child as opposed to the adult, e.g. a child may sleep in a 'little-bed' which is actually the same size as the adult's. Diminutives of body part names are also used among adults as pet names. Baby talk has many lexical items not found in adult speech, mostly diminutive in form, at times simplified from the adult equivalent, and at other times of other origins. Diminutives are frequent in children's books and occur in technical books about children. The author notes the productivity of diminutives in child speech and parallels in other languages.

27. Sachs, J.S., Brown, R. & Salerno, R. (1976). Adults' speech to children. In W. von Raffler-Engel & Y. Lebrun (eds.), *Baby talk and infant speech*. Lisse, Netherlands: Swets & Zeitlinger.

The authors examined samples of continuous speech from each of five adults (three female, two male) who were videotaped telling a picture-based story, first to a 22-month-old girl and then to a female adult. The data was analyzed for rate of speech (number of words in first minute of speech sample), number of sentences, use of past tense (in two-minute sample), and type of sentence (interrogative/simple declarative/complex declarative). Comparison of adult—adult (A) and adult—child (B) speech revealed significant differences on each of these measures; B was slower, contained more sentences per time unit, a greater percentage of interrogatives, and a smaller percentage of complex sentences, but did not differ in use of past tense or simple declaratives. Subjectively, more repetition, higher pitch and more varied intonation contour were noted. The possible functions of this prosodic variation and its relation to use of interrogatives are briefly discussed. The suggestion is made that the ability of the child for language acquisition be viewed as part of the evolution of communication and enculturation typical of the human species.

28. Sachs, J. & Devin, J. (1976). Young children's knowledge of age-appropriate speech styles. *Journal of Child Language* 3, 81–98.

To further the investigation of children's knowledge of speech styles sensitive to the addressee (cf. Shatz & Gelman, 1973), and in particular to examine the importance of feedback in eliciting such styles, the speech of six children (aged two to five years) was recorded under several conditions: (1) talking *to* different listeners (adult, peer, baby, baby doll, peer doll); and (2) talking *as* different speakers (i.e. role-playing as a baby and as a peer doll). Analysis of this data showed that subjects' speech to a younger child or a doll was different from speech to a peer or an adult, with respect to such subtle attributes as types of questions, as well as to MLU, percent of sentence types, types of verb tenses, etc. Moreover, the results indicated that modifications of speech style to a younger listener are not dependent on cues in the immediate situation, but represent some more abstract knowledge of the appropriateness of speech to the listener. It is posited that this kind of ability may be an aspect of the child's 'specialization' for language acquisition.

29. Scollon, R. (1973). A real early stage: an unzippered condensation of a dissertation on child language. *Working Papers in Linguistics* 5 (6), Department of Linguistics, University of Hawaii.

In this preliminary report of a child's productive language development from age 1; 7 to 1; 10, the author presents a new approach to the description of the earliest stage of language. Instead of studying isolated sentences, the methodology of this approach insists upon careful examination of utterance context (i.e. discourse analysis) as a prerequisite for grammatical analysis. By developing a distinction between 'horizontal' and 'vertical' constructions, the investigator views the child as beginning to talk at an earlier age (eight months to one year) than usual. Vertical constructions differ from horizontal constructions (i.e. traditional linguistic constructions) in that they lack sentence intonation contour and contain pauses between elements; they are, however, composed of utterances with definite semantic connection appropriate to the context. It is proposed that these vertical constructions (which appear early and later lead into horizontal constructions) are learned through interaction with other [language-proficient] speakers, and that discourse structure is thus the core of sentence structure from the beginning of its development.

30. Shatz, M. & Gelman, R. (1973). The development of communication skills: modifications in the speech of young children as a function of listener. *Monographs of the Society for Research in Child Development* no. 152, 38, no. 5.

This monograph discusses the results and implications of three psychologically orientated studies designed to test whether four-year-olds possess the communicative skill necessary to adjust their speech to listeners of different ages (two-year-olds, peers, and adults). In Study A, 16 subjects, who had performed poorly on pretests of 'egocentrism', were recorded explaining a toy to a two-year-old and to an adult; in Study B, data was collected for five four-year-olds, each in spontaneous conversation with an adult and a two-year-old; and in Study C tapes of eight four-year-olds talking to peers were obtained and compared to conversations with their mothers. An analysis of the data from all three studies suggests that by age four, children (regardless of sibling status or sex) have the ability to adjust their speech as a function of the age and language ability of the addressee. Modifications included shorter, simpler, and more attentional utterances to younger children, and peers treated much like adults. The results are considered as support for an interactionist position on language acquisition.

31. Snow, C.E. (1972). Mothers' speech to children learning language. *Child Development* 43, 549–65.

In reaction to the assumption that language input to children is largely ungrammatical, this study discusses three laboratory experiments carried out by the author to investigate the actual syntactic nature of mothers' speech to children learning language, i.e. speech to 2-year olds was compared to speech to 10-year-olds. Experiments also tested the importance of the child's presence and reactions, the effect of task structure, and the significance of experience with children. The subjects were 42 middle class women (all college graduates) — 12 with children aged 9; 5 to 12; 4, 24 with children ranging in age from 2; 0 to 3; 4, and six who had no children. The results of these experiments revealed that the earlier assumption about language input was false: mothers' speech to young children was found to be simpler and more redundant than their normal speech. It was found that these differences were at least partially dependent on the reactions of the addressee, but that neither the difficulty of the task nor the experience of being a mother greatly affected modification of speech style.

32. Snow, C.E. (1972). Young children's responses to adult sentences of varying complexity. Paper presented at the Third International Congress of Applied Linguistics, Copenhagen, August.

Based on previous studies indicating that adults' speech modifications to children were directed by the child's responses, two experiments were undertaken to determine in what ways the child might do this. In the first experiment, a story session and an instruction task were used to obtain data on children's responses to simplified speech as compared to normal adult speech. During the story the children were scored on attentiveness, and in the instruction task they were scored on correct responses. For both situations, the subjects performed better under simplified speech conditions, suggesting that inattention and inappropriate responses from the child may be the motivation behind baby talk modifications. A second, longitudinal experiment (to cover about four months, starting at age 12–16 months) was designed to investigate exactly what variables determine the difficulty of a sentence for the child at different stages of language acquisition. The procedure was simply to address to the child questions, commands, and suggestions of varying degrees of linguistic complexity and then to observe his responses. The preliminary results and problems of a pilot study of two children are discussed. The author concludes that the process of language learning is not as difficult as linguists had previously assumed.

33. Traugott, E.C. (1972). On the notion 'restructuring' in historical syntax. Paper given at the Eleventh International Congress of Linguistics, Bologna, August–September.

This theoretical discussion of processes in syntactic change questions the notions of simplification and elaboration which have been prevalent in the literature on language input and language acquisition, as well as in historical linguistics and the study of pidgins and creoles. Critical of the generativist view that children simplify language by restructuring, while adults only innovate and elaborate, the author hypothesizes that simplification and elaboration are terms that apply to comparative linguistics and to meta-theory, with either simply a function of what one compares. The point is made that in acquiring greater proficiency in language, children construct and revise their grammars on the basis of their own systems, of universal principles, and of the output of other speakers, and therefore it is wrong to equate restructuring with simplification. It is also posited that the so-called 'simplification' which takes place in pidginization is a partial return to innate natural processes which speakers have as children and which probably are factors in determining the nature of baby talk and other varieties of modified speech.

34. Wertsch, J. (1974). Simply speaking. *Papers from the Tenth Regional Meeting, Chicago Linguistic Society* 732—41.

The author discusses the possibility that adults simplify their speech for young children, at least in part, in response to the child's lack of 'real world' experience and a cognitive limitation which restrict his ability to use contextual information in processing an utterance. Wertsch is concerned with what Grice (1968) has called the 'total signification of a remark'. This means the proper use of speaker coherence factors, both internal (interpreting an utterance on the basis of the text immediately surrounding it), and external (interpreting an utterance by using general expectations about the speaker). Adults cannot depend on young children to use speaker coherence factors properly because of the child listener's limited exposure to experiences which give rise to the shared information necessary for the interpretation of remarks and because of the child's purported egocentrism (Piaget, 1955). It is proposed that pronominal reference and conversational implicature are but two linguistic devices adults avoid in input language in response to this inability on the part of child listeners.